A Life of

Dance and

Dreams

GENE KELLY

A Life of Dance and Dreams

GENE KELLY

ALVIN

YUDKOFF

BACK STAGE BOOKS

An imprint of Watson-Guptill Publications / New York

First published in 1999 by Back Stage Books,
an imprint of Watson-Guptill Publications,
a division of VNU Business Media, Inc.
770 Broadway, New York, New York 10003
www.watsonguptill.com

Editor for Back Stage Books: Dale Ramsey
Book design: Derek Bacchus
Production Manager: Hector Campbell

Library of Congress Cataloging-in-Publication Data

Yudkoff, Alvin
Gene Kelly: a life of dance and dreams / Alvin Yudkoff
      p. cm.
   Includes index.
   ISBN (hardcover) 0-8230-8813-8
1. Kelly, Gene, 1912-   2. Motion picture actors and actresses--United
States--Biography   3. Dancers--United States--Biography. I. Title

PN2287 .K64 Y83 1999
791.43'028'092--dc21
[B]

99-051812
   CIP

ISBN (paperback) 0-8230-8819-7

Manufactured in the United States of America

First paperback printing, 2001
2 3 4 5 6/07 06 05 04

CONTENTS

ACKNOWLEDGMENTS

* * *

My research on the life of Gene Kelly was inevitably a lunging pursuit along two paths: a linking with those whose personal lives crossed his, to mutual pleasure or pain—fascinatingly, there was rarely a middle ground to a relationship with this man—and a paper trail of writings by and about the subject, in praise or in pique. All too often, then, in going both ways it became a matter of loving or loathing, whether in the testimony of those who knew him well, or embedded in Kelly memorabilia in the European and American archives where I spent many productive and absorbing hours.

Among the people who knew him in his lifetime and made significant contributions to this book in print or direct speech when contacted, I wish especially to single out Lois McClelland, Gene's personal secretary for over forty years since serving with him in the Navy during World War II; she maintained a diary invaluable in following the rapid-fire activities of her employer and friend, and I am grateful to her for sharing it with me. The many others, whom I list among my sources at the end of the book, lent me invaluable insights and memories—my deep thanks to all of them.

The library assemblages were indispensable to me, and so I thank the Gene Kelly Archives in the Boston University Department of Special Collections and Sean Noel, Director; in New York, the Lincoln Center of the Performing Arts and the Museum of Television and Radio; in Los Angeles, the Academy of Motion Picture Arts and Sciences Reference Libraries, where the advice of Ned Comstock was particularly helpful, the UCLA Special Collections and the Doheny Library, USC; in London, the British Film Institute; and an equally fervent *merci* to the Bibliothèque Nationale de France and the Bibliothèque des Arts du Spectacle, where they still pay respect to *An American in Paris* (and seemingly will do anything for visitors of that description).

Closer to home, I owe very special thanks to my agent, Linda Konner, always alert and forceful on my behalf; Dale Ramsey, a really sensitive and creative editor;

and Christina Young for her top-of-the-line word processing and research help via the Internet.

I owe the idea for this project to Ray Robinson, my long-time close friend and fellow *aficionado* of Kelly films, himself the author of a growing number of compelling biographies. My son Royce, always incisive and decisive about how to deal with problems, creative and otherwise, lived up to his billing, and his team at ABRY Partners was resourceful in securing film prints and videos no longer in distribution. I am surely indebted to my wife Lilli for her help as a translator, and for being a constant source of encouragement and fresh ideas. As Jerry Mulligan, that American in Paris, once put it: Who could ask for anything more?

ALVIN YUDKOFF

Water Mill, New York
September 1999

CBS Videotaping:
Beverly Hilton, May 7, 1985

* * *

Finally there is the cue, and with it the music and his voice, too, the loudspeakered reverb enhancing the urgency. Yet it is oddly tender, appealing, invitational to those waiting for him in the ballroom: "Got . . . ta dance. . . ."

Still unseen, he peers now at the gofer who will wave him down the aisle, feeling as always on these retrospective ceremonial occasions, obsessed as he is by sports icons, somewhat like the lithe, silver-haired DiMaggio, waiting to throw out another first ball at a season opener—or like his idol Harry Greb, lightweight champion of the world, in from training camp at Lake Conneaut, surrounded by his entourage for the lordly ascent to the ring, bathed by floodlights and wild adulation.

Down jerks the gofer's arm. At last he is on his way to the table of honor, the old bounce still there, the old jounce of the tune—still his tune—shortening his step in synch with the pelting lyrics. Wishing all the way he had used his reputed show-biz savvy to bring an umbrella, for chrissake, for a really boffo entrance. Why didn't he think of it?

. He knows what they're seeing, these movie moguls of a new generation, amid the crescendo of applause that Hollywood audiences always reserve for members of the club: just an old ex-hoofer. A smiling geezer, stutter-stepping up the aisle, his dancer's body long since upholstered by the billowing slipcovers of middle age (unlike the trim Joltin' Joe and his Spalding). With huge black-rimmed Mr. Magoo glasses and hair of frizzy gray (but everybody in this gossipy town knows he's worn a rug for years).

A pro to the core, though, he is exuberant and cocky, invincible and unstoppable—and don't they expect it? Hell, they all know his song as well as he does! Tonight, the American Film Institute, earnest and regal, is trying to make it up to him. So, on a CBS network broadcast, he will receive the AFI Life Achievement Award. Not exactly the Oscar he should have won, and he knows it. They know it, too.

And something else much more pertinent: that he will be the center of attention. Already the video cameras (now the medium of choice, ironically, for the Film Institute) are racking focus on him for the best reaction closeups, to be edited into the hour of TV to come, touching all bases of emotion—laughter, incredulity, absorption, wonder, and, of *course, tears (along with the umbrella he should have remembered Debbie Reynolds. He should have brought an onion from home).*

Like the champ he is, like DiMaggio, like Greb, he will give the performance every damn push and pull he can.

His way from the beginning.

PITTSBURGH, 1922

* * *

It was really asking for trouble.

The five of them would walk down Mellon Street in the East Liberty section, the two Kelly girls in spotless dresses, their three brothers enclosed in stiff Buster Brown suits and collars. They were not even going to Sunday Mass, which might have curbed the hostile instincts of the Polacks shooting craps on the sidewalk, a noisy knot of older toughs already bored with the game, now that one hustler had cornered all the coins. Instantly the Kellys knew what they faced: truants from the local "Protestant P.S."—it was their shorthand for the grimy, gray neighborhood public school. The Kellys attended St. Raphael's, the Catholic academy, at considerable financial sacrifice—a point made by their mother almost every day of the semester.

Nonchalantly, stretching up to his full height, jingling the pennies, nickels, and dimes in his pocket, the craps winner was the burliest of them, a head taller even than James Jr., Gene's older brother. Gene was the middle one, and behind him, advancing with quickening breath, came the youngest, Fred. The three boys formed a protective shield around their sisters. The Kellys would have to circle into the littered gutter, a move more symbolic than physical to Gene: the mark of a quitter. He measured the adversaries for the street fight to come: Hardened sons of immigrant steelworkers, restively and sullenly unemployed, still speaking in the hoarse accents of Middle Europe. The Kellys heard "sissies" and "fags" and worse taunts surrounded by curses.

Gene clenched his fists. This past summer at the lake, Harry Greb had taught him a thing or two. He was ready.

They formed a line facing the Kellys, and now, unbelievably, they were placing hands on hips and wiggling their asses, tongues extended for some reason. "Pussy . . . pussy. . . ." The drawn-out insult hissed like wet firewood about to inflame. Gene was only ten years old, but he guessed a crude and challenging evocation of femininity when faced with it.

Windows in the tenements along the sidewalks were jerked upwards. Heads poked out to watch. Spectators were ready. Everybody in the East Liberty section knew the Kellys were heading for the weekly dancing lesson.

In a sense, it was a public performance by the Kellys, a quintet of gussied-up children, eyes front. It always created a theatrical impact. Certainly it was not a scene one expected to see regularly in the thick of working-class Pittsburgh, the very heart of the hearth of the nation where the Allegheny joined the Monongahela

River. Where night and day tongues of flame rose from the largest blast furnaces in the world. The scorch and stink from the steel moving through the rolling mills and foundries hovered stubbornly over the slums where the workers and their families lived. The middle- and upper-class residential sections covered the far-off hills.

Fred Kelly still remembers vividly: "Jim, my oldest brother, was very tough, and he'd fight or Gene would start the fight and Jim would finish it. Sort of a daily routine. Fighting was the style in Pittsburgh in those days."

The exchange of blows, the shoving and kicking and tripping, spilled from sidewalk to street. Curses and insults, heavily profane and ethnic, went back and forth, reaching a crescendo when the Irish cops showed up, called by one of the Irish mothers watching from a window. This street battle was over quickly. But not always were the opponents dispatched so quickly. The fights had brooding psychological overtones. Gene Kelly later told his English biographer Clive Hirschhorn:

> Because I was so small, I felt I always had to prove myself and the best way was to do this with my fists. I wasn't going to be pushed around by anyone . . . especially not by the older guys. I was just as good as they were. I had this obsession to prove to them I was.

Not *quite* yet, and if the paddy wagon was late in coming and the Kellys could not hold their own, Gene and his brothers and sisters limped home, the boys bruised and bloodied, the girls fiery with indignation. Then, out of their apartment would charge their avenging mother, Harriet Kelly, to rout the Protestant bullies. They knew her temper, her take-no-prisoners mentality, and took flight.

By now the Kelly children were late for their dance classes. Their mother would insist they clean up and put on fresh clothes. The only way to be on time at the downtown studio was to forget the stop-and-go street car and go by taxi. Wincing at the expense, ignoring the children's willingness, almost eagerness, to skip the instruction for the day, Mrs. Kelly would call a cab.

It was a stubbornness entirely in character for the former Harriet Eckhart, a small but feisty matriarch worried about the downsized earning power of her husband, James Patrick Joseph Kelly. Born in Canada, a naturalized American citizen, his priorities jibed with his wife's, centering on the welfare of their five children. Periodically, when he took to the bottle, there would be blackouts and breakouts from his sense of paternal responsibilities. His wife and family adapted to these transgressions with patience and even humor.

All of them, especially Harriet Kelly, recognized that James Sr., as the family patriarch, was a worthy man of unimpeachable moral rectitude, a believer in hard work, hard drinking, and restorative attendance at Mass. An affable, extroverted salesman for the Columbia Phonograph Company, he was away on business trips a good deal of the time. The responsibility for raising the children was Harriet's.

If ever there was a person fit for the task of parenting, she was. To her, the Kellys were only temporarily deposited in a misbegotten Pittsburgh neighborhood. She had faith in herself, her children, her husband, and especially the Almighty.

She and James had met at an amateur concert in 1905, when she was singing with a chorale group. As the daughter of Billy Curran, a successful saloon keeper, Harriet was not one to be dismayed by his drinking habits. They were married a year later, despite a vestigial wariness on her part toward the Irish. Though her own father had emigrated from Londonderry, her mother's family, the Eckharts, had come from Alsace-Lorraine. She was proud of the maiden name and would always downplay the Irish provenance in her background. To her, being Irish was synonymous with being discriminated against. It was all about no loans at the bank, laboring at back-breaking manual tasks, shoulder-to-shoulder with the Polacks, Croats, and, mercy, even blacks, heaven help us! Baking in the sun on road crews in primitive work camps for weeks at a time. Being stripped of their miserable wages by rapacious company stores, with only home-brewed corn liquor to help forget the horrible conditions. It was a comfort to her that, in contrast with their neighbors, the Kelly family was at least "lace curtain Irish" and she saw no ironies in that description.

For above all, she was a forceful, positive person, with a long-term perspective always aimed at the future. Her red hair was always neat but rarely responsive to the fashion of the day. Her brown eyes reflected the play of her emotions and drives, flashing signals that never included fear or embarrassment. She took guff from nobody. There was absolutely nothing beyond her capacity, or her children's, especially regarding her youngest. Harriet's instincts told her Fred was "really the talent of the litter" who'd achieve success in the dream world of her choice—show business. The others had potential, of course, but she had different plans for them. It was Fred, it had to be Fred, who would be the George M. Cohan of his generation, leading them to affluence, finally leaving behind the stink of steel.

The third of the five children, Eugene Curran Kelly, was born on August 23, 1912. From an early age he was indoctrinated by both his parents, especially his mother, with the ethos of hard work. Out on the streets with his pals, Eugene quickly became Gene. He didn't particularly care for the abbreviation. He believed it to be a girl's name.

As early as 1913, Eugene Curran Kelly looked lively when made the center of attention. (Courtesy of Photofest)

Gene and his brothers and sisters knew it was a struggle for their parents to make ends meet, and they helped in any way they could as the years went by. They were constantly searching for after-school jobs and money-making ventures that could contribute to the family till. Idleness was considered by Harriet, quite simply, as the work of the Devil. With James away on his sales trips, she ruled the family with an icy determination to pursue any possible opportunity for her children, especially in the theatrical field.

Never once, unless his formidable temper got the best of him, would Gene speak to her disrespectfully. In conversation with others, he would always refer to Harriet Kelly, without any hesitation or a trace of irony, as "my sainted mother."

Gene sensed that his father did not measure up to his mother in many crucial ways, but he always relished time spent with him, often with a head-shaking smile of acceptance of the ways his father approached daily challenges. It was a mystery to Gene, always so handy and quick to master technical problems, why his father could not learn how to drive a car, surely a shortcoming for a traveling salesman and one that continued to make life difficult for the three sons. On Monday mornings James Sr. had to leave the house early, helped by the boys who carried his sample cases—packed with demo records and mimeographed manuals—all the way to the railroad station. During the next five days Gene's father had to contend with loading and off-loading the burdens of his trade throughout his sales territory. It was an exhausting routine, mitigated—the Kellys were aware—by the libations awaited at the end of the day at a town tavern or cheap boarding house. But the temptation of female companionship, yielded to by many of his competitors, was out of the question for James Kelly. He was resolutely straight-arrow. On Friday evenings, scrupulously on schedule, he would always step down from the arriving train, neat and sober, to be welcomed back by all five children and Harriet.

With a surge of energy he would then devote his weekend to family needs, church attendance, and one more activity that was to be integral to their lives, especially Gene's. That was sports. Unconcerned with the competition of the marketplace, not at all involved in the struggle to meet his sales quotas, he was somehow seized with a desire to win where athletics was concerned, a passionate participant and sports fan all his life. Despite being constantly pinched for money, James Sr. took his children, even the girls when they clamored to come, to baseball, football, basketball, and boxing events.

Hockey was a particular favorite, as befit his Canadian roots. Early on, he recognized his middle son's special talent on the ice. He made a point of purchasing for Gene, all of four years of age at the time, a pair of used ice skates with two blades instead of one, helping to instill in Gene a sense of balance that his son never lost.

By the time the boy was eight, he was without doubt the best skater in the neighborhood. He later precociously described himself as a "Mozart of the ice rink." In an autobiographical article for *Seventeen* magazine, Gene Kelly listed his athletic skills in that curious construct of self-deprecating humor upon a bedrock of absolute confidence that never left him. "I was very adept at playing baseball, had an excellent knack for street-fighting and an almost uncanny ability to break windows."

And to break limbs, joints, and bones—his own. As a child, indeed throughout his life, he was incredibly accident-prone. Even when not bloodied or injured, Gene's constant brushes with physical disaster brought the gray to Harriet Kelly's hair. Of course, in those ever-present street fights that littered the East Liberty section like garbage, he got as well as gave.

Though worried about by his mother as small and sickly, he was a tough Irish bantam of a fighter in the Pittsburgh tradition. When not throwing or receiving punches and bites and scratches, he relished the games he played with friends as the seasons changed—baseball, football, hockey—and the more crushing the body contact, the better. Gene was never one to flinch. He would never pull back.

One snowy day, when classes at St. Raphael's were over, he decided to ride the homemade sled shared by the Kelly children down a heavily trafficked street. He had barely started, manipulating the jerry-built steering attachment, and he did not see a truck bearing down on him. He was knocked over. The sled was a total wreck, but Gene was only bruised. Harriet made up for it; her son had missed the wheels by inches, and she slapped him hard in tribute to God's miracle. She decided then and there that any sort of professional sports career—his dream—was beyond his capacity. A more sedentary role, that of a lawyer, for example, was what she now had in mind for Gene.

Another time during his grade-school period the boy was not so fortunate, fortifying Harriet in her decision about Gene's future. Challenged to ride a tricycle without handlebars on Mellon Street, he tumbled over an exposed iron beam and landed on his head. A prong of the metal pierced his left cheek. The flow of blood from the deep gash was not easy to stop. The neighborhood family doctor stitched him up, leaving a small half-moon scar on his left cheek that, years later in Hollywood, would be clucked over by studio photographers on glamorous publicity shoots. Gene would always veto any airbrushing and insist the scar remain untouched and visible.

His brothers and sisters, luckier or less aggressive, made their way unscathed through the juvenile perils and even managed to avoid the usual childhood diseases. But not Gene. It was almost as if he had to taste all of them. The most worrisome by far was a serious bout of what was diagnosed as pneumonia. It may have been related to the mysterious but virulent worldwide influenza pandemic that killed more than 675,000 Americans in 1918. The Kellys prayed at home and in church, and Gene recovered completely.

James and Harriet Kelly cared. They saw to it that holidays were always a special treat, as were birthdays, which were always celebrated, whatever the calendar indicated, on a Sunday, when the father had not yet departed for the week's selling expedition. Other children were never invited to join in. Harriet believed the five Kellys were a self-contained, perfect group, needing no outside stimuli for projects and entertainment. "If you're bored, I'll find something for you to do!" was her mantra. St. Valentine's Day, the Fourth of July, and St. Patrick's Day, of course, when Harriet and the sisters would serve ice cream decorated with tiny shamrocks along with a towering, mouth-watering frosted cake, were celebrated in special style.

Each was a major Harriet Kelly Home Project. It seemed the Kelly parents were always home when everybody else's parents were away.

Harriet tried to avoid showing any favoritism. But her youngest, Fred, continued to be seen by her as the really gifted one, a natural for the theatrical career she had once craved for herself. It was clear where Fred's ambition was headed. On his own the boy would go to the library and withdraw books on magic and puppet shows. He set up and demonstrated Houdini-type escapes. Once he put on a special performance for the rest of the family. The closing act involved a stray mutt he had found and trained.

Dog acts were not Gene's style. He had very little to do with the performances of his younger brother. Fred was still very young when he realized that if his older brother did not lead the way, whatever the game, Gene would not put any energy into the effort. Harriet did not fail to notice his lack of cooperation. But she did not scold Gene. She was convinced his holdback of brotherly support was due to his health problems. Her answer was to put more greens on his supper plate and use the summer as therapy.

Concerned about Gene's lungs and passionate about the restorative value of the countryside, she insisted they could somehow afford an annual holiday, June through September. She first tracked down a cottage near Lake Erie. After a few seasons, always on the quest for improvement, she led her family to an even more secluded area and intimate body of water, Lake Conneaut, in western Pennsylvania. It also happened to be smack in the middle of James's sales territory, making some added impromptu visits possible.

Until 1924 the family would arrive from Pittsburgh by train and pile into a taxi for a short trip to the lakeside cottage that was to be theirs for almost three months. Convinced that very little meaningful work was done on the fringes of school vacations, Harriet would remove the children two weeks before the term ended and bring them back two weeks after the new term began.

The five children awoke early every morning to eat a full-scale breakfast prepared by their mother, who had awakened an hour before. Then they disappeared until suppertime. In contrast with her rigid home scheduling in Pittsburgh, Harriet set no fixed program for the day. It was take-your-pick from a brimming candy counter of fun and games: swimming, tennis, cycling, canoeing, horseback riding. At the outset of vacation, each of the children was credited by Harriet with a cash allowance for the summer. She served as the banker, of course, and doled out what was requested until there was nothing left in an account. It was her way of introducing the children to the value of money.

Gene was physically the most active and energetic of the group and ran out of money first. On the days it rained they were encouraged to read at home or to play games of their own invention. They were passionately competitive. That was the way Harriet wanted it: No child of hers would be corrupted by the sin of idleness.

There was always an aura of excitement when James Kelly arrived on weekends. Harriet would leave him to ride, swim, or fish with his children, or lead nature-study walks, or pick apples. In his own way his gift for parenting matched his wife's. Everything he did, he did with style, dressed with a neat formality on every occasion, not at all like Gene. The senior Kelly had a respect for elegance. He believed a man should be suitably attired at all times, even in his own house, in case anyone knocked on the door unexpectedly. But Gene was never to adopt the dress code of his father.

The highlight of the summer was when their father would take the boys to the nearby training grounds of prizefighters such as Harry Greb, the world lightweight champion. Greb generously gave a few boxing lessons to the Kellys. Feeling chesty and invincible, they would return to the cottage. The example of how Greb, a mere 140 pounds, could be such a formidable battler was very inspirational to Gene.

Harriet could not help noticing that when there was anything competitive in the range of summer activities that kept her children busy and cheery, it was Gene who would shine. But she most favored Fred's commitment to becoming a theater professional, believing that her own family line was the source of his zeal. It mirrored her own abilities, even though the flow of her own life had not allowed her to take advantage of what she had to bring to a stage career.

She used to confide to neighbors that she herself had been "on the stage" as a young girl—to what degree and in what particular way she never did clarify. Like a woman's age, Harriet's theater career, whatever it had been, was simply not considered a respectable subject to talk about. There was always some mystery about it. One biographer of Gene Kelly has stated that Harriet, after her marriage, continued her "theatrical career" with a local stage group. The San Francisco Museum of Art, in fitting out a Gene Kelly retrospective after he had attained stardom, had it that Harriet was an actress in her youth and her insistence that all her children attend dancing school stemmed from fond memories of footlights and applause.

The author of a monograph on Kelly, now in the Gene Kelly Archives at Boston University, has determined that Harriet's interest in show business commenced in a more roundabout way: She was one of several mothers who set up a cooperative dancing school for children as a neighborhood enterprise.

Fred Kelly speaks concisely about the Kelly start on the stage: "We all sang and danced right from the start. See, we came from a very musical family. Dad met my mother backstage in a show that she was in."

Whatever the actual circumstances, if Harriet had possessed the talent herself, despite her background as a carefully brought-up Catholic girl she would have tried to make her own way somewhere in show business. But she was, above all, a realist. So it is doubtful she herself ever truly pursued performing, amateur or professional, with any sense of career purpose. But as a manager she could be very effective. In a later generation, she would have been a remarkable success as a businesswoman.

Fred, doubtless, was headed for the heights, but the others, too, deserved the Harriet Kelly push, or such was her rationale. They all had a proficiency that was not commonplace. At least they were good enough—her practical side showing itself again—to support the family budget where their own educations were concerned.

Harriet also saw the need for another source of income in the event her husband lost his job. The possibility of unemployment was real and ominous. Free radio was cutting drastically into the phonograph business on which James Sr. depended for his livelihood. Still, the Kellys were determined to develop their children's potential to the fullest. If there were a sacrifice demanded of them, Harriet did not see it that way, and through her efforts all the children would get the appropriate training. They all took piano lessons and, once a certain level was achieved, each was expected to choose another instrument. Since they could now dance and sing with a verve and skill that attracted attention, Harriet formed them into a group called, not very inspirationally, the Five Kellys. They offered a program of current songs interspersed with solo and group tap routines. The quintet participated in amateur nights and won cash prizes, firming up Harriet's sense of being on the right road.

Still, she would not allow any lip-service to school homework requirements. If a child's marks slipped in an important examination, the group was quickly downsized to four or three Kellys until the missing performers regained their eligibility in Harriet's eyes.

Fred reported that Gene wasn't particularly happy with the performing scenario. "He never wanted to be a dancer. This was not his ambition in life. He wanted to be a ball player, he wanted to be a priest, he wanted to be a lawyer."

Which was, in the long run, just fine with Harriet Eckhart Kelly, especially the third option. Lawyer, Attorney-at-Law, Gentleman of the Bar—it had a magisterial ring that resonated in her. But it would not do for her precious middle son to become one of those starving, striving young "Irish mackerel snappers" renting desk space across the street from the county courthouse, middlemen in shiny Moe Levy suits, always sucking up to that Irish drunk of a County Clerk at City Hall, who doles out patronage jobs if you work like the devil come Election Day. No ambulance chasing for her straight-shooting Gene, no deadbeat defending, no serving of good, honest working people with eviction notices. Not her Gene! Honest, contentious Gene, never one to cut corners, a straight arrow like his father.

What better reward for Mr. and Mrs. James Kelly than to see their middle son reach the top? A position where he could do good for honest people. A secure post that was prestigious and even paid a decent dollar. Maybe the first Irish-Catholic judge to be appointed to the Supreme Court. It is a safe bet that, as she considered the odds, Harriet Kelly gave thought to how she could better her son's chances.

The ballroom walls are a riot of Day-Glo spotted with huge, white-matted blowups and main-title stills, a panorama of freeze-framed moments from his films. Directly ahead on the giant movie screen there is a fade into a montage with ear-rending quad sound, rapid cuts in a whirling succession of those same moments memorialized on the walls, one after another, him dancing and singing with Judy, then with Debbie, with Cyd, with Vera-Ellen, and Caron, too, a segue from one to the other, classic Hollywood overkill in Technicolor.

What the hell, though; he sits back, trying to relax. It's the standard opener for a star retrospective, practically an art form hereabouts. Movieland's version of the gold watch with the goodbye pat on the ass. Rule number one, even if it is a roast: Always open in gilded public rooms like the Hilton with the teary walk down Memory Lane—and what better way to say sayonara?

If he were in charge—it is his nature always to consider that question, even when not in charge—he has to admit he'd set up the evening the same way. Cutaways to billboard the show, him dancing and singing, a throwback to MGM big-time. In his prime. Looking young and trim. Taking on the main occupational disadvantage of every actor and actress in this room. The corny Dorian Gray factor. Whatever the hocus-pocus, the unrelenting lens reveals the ravages of age. Not for the first time does he think: In no other field is your past flung at you so mockingly, flaunting health and wealth and the good times when people turned to look. When the applause came down like, well, rain.

Better go easy on the rain metaphor. There will be a lot of it during the course of the evening.

PITTSBURGH, 1924

* * *

The growing popularity of radio was just beginning to cut into the sale of records and the rest of James Kelly's line. But his commissions from Columbia Phonograph still held up and, prodded by Harriet, the Kellys moved out of Mellon Street to a comparatively spacious three-story house on Kensington. It was a safer neighborhood, certainly more tolerant of children going and coming from dancing school.

James Sr. lost sleep over the brutal mortgage he took on, but Harriet focused on the large basement. Fred, her favorite, still the most talented of the brood in her eyes, would stage his shows for the new neighborhood. On Harriet's advice, admission was charged: three cents a ticket, unless accompanied by one of Fred's brothers or sisters. The Kelly boys and girls became the most popular kids on the block within a few weeks.

Gene's attitude from the start was that if you could not do something in a big way, better not to do it at all. Nevertheless, he would help out with the props, recognizing that it was Fred's show, pure and simple. He was proud of his tiny kid brother, who would stage ever more elaborate magic and puppet routines in the basement and backyard and continued his specialty of incorporating a trained dog into the act as the grand finale.

The takeover of the Kensington address added urgency and momentum to Harriet's efforts at putting the Five Kellys on the Pittsburgh theatrical map. She became even more aggressive at arranging bookings, now representing a "family show" along the lines of the famous Seven Little Foys, a group built around the talents of entertainer Eddie Foy. The absence of an adult star did not faze Harriet, who instinctively understood that the all-child participation was exactly what made the Kellys so different. As Fred Kelly recollects:

I was the baby, and we had to sing the song "K-E-L-L-..." and the only thing I had to say was "Y." I remember the orchestra cracked up, laughing even at rehearsals. They just stopped playing their instruments because my little voice screamed out. My big sister had the K, my brother James had the E, Gene had L, my other sister had the other L, and then I came in with the Y whenever I felt like it. I wasn't at all with the music. I just took a great big breath and yelled "Y!"

The pipsqueak never failed to bring down the house.

Aside from being a steel town and a breeding-ground for tough prizefighters, Pittsburgh deserved its reputation as a bustling center of show business. As America swung through the '20s there were at least two stock companies, two legitimate theaters offering more intellectual fare, three vaudeville houses, a clutch of nude and naughty burlesque joints, and a number of first-run movie palaces. Benefits to raise money for churches and charities were frequent; hospitals sparked fund-raising drives with gala banquets at downtown hotels for the wealthy, and a program of variety acts would support the speakers. Entertainment was always the drawing card.

Harriet was no snob when it came to booking her youngest son. Fred was barely seven when his mother escorted him to gigs all over the city, even honky-tonk places she never would have visited on her own. The boy would earn up to ten dollars per performance. Fred's new big finale no longer featured a dog from the neighborhood. Now it was an adagio dance with a six-year-old girl who would leap from the top of the piano into his arms, never failing to set off a cascade of applause.

The opportunity for augmenting her husband's income was there, and Harriet was determined to reap the harvest. But she was not satisfied that her children were receiving the best instruction. She saw to it that the money earned by them was not absorbed by the regular family budget but was re-invested in lessons at different dance and music schools around the city. And she had a broad vision of the cultural development of her children. She had no hesitation about declaring a holiday at St. Raphael's if a particularly gifted performer or worthy Broadway play was coming to Pittsburgh on tour. She hounded the children to visit the local library and reviewed their choices. She initiated discussions about literature at the dining-room table, where she herself would often recite epic verses, which she rendered with flair as she dished out the mashed potatoes.

It was all a gamble of energy and effort and expense, and Harriet Kelly was no believer in the luck of the Irish. Getting ahead demanded steadfastness in her view, hard work, focus. Luck was doled out by the Almighty in very small doses and couldn't necessarily be counted on more than once in a lifetime. She would never forget the circumstances leading to the breakthrough for the Five Kellys. When the famous Foys were billed, on their national tour, as the feature act of the season finale at the venerable Nixon Theatre, a sudden rainstorm following hurricane-level winds beat down on Pittsburgh, and all rail and road transportation into the city was cut off. It was impossible for the Foys to arrive on time and do the performance.

The manager of the Nixon made a flurry of panicky phone calls to dredge up some professional act as a substitute. Nobody was available. The rains did not let up; the roads were more like canals. Grimly, the manager made preparations for a ticket refund—when he remembered his delight at an unpretentious Foy-like family act during a fundraiser for the local Sisterhood of the Beth Shalom synagogue.

He placed a call immediately. "Rabbi, what's the name of those five kids you had on for your benefit—they danced, sang, did every darn thing and—"

"You mean those Irishers? The Kellys!" the Rabbi broke in pridefully.

Minutes later the manager reached Harriet and started to explain the situation. Again he was interrupted.

"When do you want my kids?" she said. "We can talk about money later."

Despite their lack of name recognition and major performance history, the manager would put them on. A local audience had heart. Never would a Pittsburgher walk out on hometown kids.

That night the manager stood tensely at the back of the Nixon for the performance. He could barely catch his breath. Then the Five Kellys bounded onto the stage. He had no cause for worry. The act quickly made the Foys forgettable.

All at once Harriet Kelly was a one-woman talent agency with one client: her children. Not just Fred anymore. She was beginning to see that her youngest did not have a monopoly on the God-given Kelly talent. Watching the Five Kellys from backstage, she had been astonished at Gene's progress as a dancer. When he moved downstage into the limelight, the force and excitement of his solo performance drew the loudest applause for anybody on the bill. Moreover, Gene seemed to be more interested in theater now (not making her deliriously happy, for she still had law school mapped out), and most of her bookings would make certain of Gene's participation before signing the Five Kellys.

Academically, at St. Raphael's and Peabody High, Gene and his older sister, Jay, did the best of the children. None of them were discipline problems. At each grade a grateful teacher would welcome the new Kelly, scrubbed and shiny, as an asset to the classroom, offering all sorts of ways to enhance the extracurricular program.

At St. Raphael's, even though Gene had not demonstrated a passion for entertaining others, the nuns simply assumed a talent because of prior participations by his older brother and sister. Much to his irritation he was cast in a series of school shows, the first being Victor Herbert's *Babes in Toyland*. The nuns were excited. He could be the dancer in the show—after all, he was the only boy in the grade who knew how to tap.

For such a star athlete—despite his diminutive size—possessing gifts that made him dream of cutting off ground balls for the Pittsburgh Pirates or pursuing a professional hockey career, standing onstage in a circle of light and doing a simple traveling timestep was a comedown. Certainly it did little for his status with the rest of the boys.

For the biography of Gene Kelly written years ago, the London journalist Clive Hirschhorn engaged the film star in conversation, and Kelly reminisced:

It was all right when I was playing football with them and being one of the gang. But when they saw me all dressed up on the stage—singing and dancing—that was a different story. And being a little guy you can imagine how self-conscious I was.

His mother would not hear his complaints and insisted that he and the other children each learn how to play a musical instrument. Gene elected the violin but was never really enthusiastic about his choice. Perhaps it was a symbolic connotation. For him it would never be the solo instrument of a star. It simply underscored that his role, inevitably, was to play second fiddle to the exploits of Fred. When he entered Peabody High School in 1926, it had to be something of a relief to be temporarily separated from his precocious younger brother. At Peabody, Gene was an outstanding hockey player and a varsity letter-winner with the gymnastics and football teams. He did appear in school plays, and his poetry was published in the school newspaper, *The Civitan*.

In the Peabody auditorium he and another student, Jimmy Brenner, a recent transfer from Philadelphia who showed talent, performed athletic dance routines that encouraged other boys to volunteer for the school shows. His mother was particularly satisfied when he was chosen for the Debate Club, on the path toward college, law school, and a lucrative white-collar career.

True to form, he proceeded to break his arm in a football game. He wore a plaster cast proudly for a number of weeks. It had one happy result: Harriet finally gave in to his protestations and allowed him to stop violin lessons. Whenever Gene was not the best at any activity, he simply looked elsewhere. Harriet insisted on his taking up the banjo.

By now Gene had discovered girls and something even more important: His dancing skills made them discover *him*. As he later said:

> Normally those girls wouldn't have given me a second look if I hadn't been such a hit in the school shows . . . most of those girls were head and shoulders taller than me. But it made me popular and I could get almost anyone I wanted to come to the school dances with me. Some of them thought I was bloody marvelous and pretty soon I began to believe them.

It was also the best way he knew to put his hand on a girl's waist and hold her close.

It was perhaps the first time he let himself consider the possibility of a professional career as a dancer. He became consumed with visions of performing all sorts of exotic steps onstage. He would try out ideas and bring fresh elements into his performances. It all came naturally to him. As had been the case with gymnastics, he was coming to realize that his height was ideal, and it was not too long before he developed a style that he sensed was truly original.

At home he began to drive his father and mother crazy by transforming the most commonplace action into a dance. At the dinner table, where they usually served themselves family-style, it was not beyond him to insist on dishing out the ever-present mashed potatoes in a balletic way, Gene-style. He tapped and pirouetted around the table as he scooped out the portions, to the laughter of his brothers and sisters. Unknowingly, he was adding to the pressures on his mother.

Much as she relished the stardust of the stage, it was apparent to her that the America of the late 1920s was edging into a depression. She had experienced at first hand the nickel-and-diming connected with seeking out gigs for the Five Kellys. She knew the odds were against making a decent living in show business. And there was always the immediate problem of continuing to pay for dance lessons. It was crucial to keep up with the styles and add new steps to the repertoires.

Her husband's sales commissions were starting to slide. There was always a shortfall of cash. Raising five children and making the mortgage on the Kensington house made Harriet dread the end of the month when she had to pay the bills. She had seen how her husband, away all week, was constantly under the pressure of making more sales. He was extended to the limit. He was drinking more. Liquor was on his breath when he returned from his sales calls for the weekend. There had to be an important change made, and it had to come very soon.

At this time, a man named Lou Bolton, who owned the dance studio where Fred took lessons, was also having a hard time of it. His business had a dismal credit rating. Suppliers insisted on cash up front. There were constant threats by the utility company to cut off his electricity. Instructors were never paid on time; angry, they might not show up for classes or form a picket line on the sidewalk. The plumbing failed. Toilet paper ran out. Bolton's checks bounced. Parents gathered in the reception room and complained. Many refused to pay. The place was a disaster area.

Harriet decided that the Bolton School of the Dance could use her services. She made an appointment with the harassed owner and talked her way into a job. She would be the person in charge of the reception desk. Bolton did not argue. Harriet would receive no salary but the Kelly children's dance lessons would be free.

Bolton was no fool. A now overweight former dancer who no longer could move very gracefully, he had an instinct for hiring teachers to put his ideas across, and he was very quick to see what a business and organizational dynamo he had hired. She was an immediate force for making his studio a serious institution. The key to the Harriet approach was strict discipline. As Fred Kelly recollects: "The teacher was king. . . . Came in with a big pointer and would tap on the ballet barre. There was always a row of long mirrors, usually purchased from closed barber shops, because beards and mustaches were going out of style, and men were getting shorter, quicker haircuts."

Now the teacher was never interrupted. The class was one hour and began and ended precisely on time. The students were not allowed to sit down. The Kelly children provided the demonstrations of the new steps. Tuition was collected or, if impossible to pay, services were accepted—cleaning or carpentry work or wall-painting. Gradually business improved, but very slowly. Newspaper advertising or perhaps a try at the new medium of local radio would have helped, and Harriet and Gene tried to convince the beleaguered owner of this. But ads, commercials, any sort of mail campaign, were too outlandish for Bolton's taste. He insisted they rely on word of mouth.

Despite the improved quality of instruction, sometimes it appeared there were as many creditors as students around Bolton. More and more he began to rely on Harriet. She, in turn, could feel Gene taking on a leadership role, as he did in everything that involved him.

One day, spurred on by Gene, she astonished Bolton by suggesting that he expand his school. Her favorite brother, Gus, who was living in Johnstown, sixty-five miles from Pittsburgh, was convinced that his town was ripe for a first-class dance studio. Fighting off bankruptcy with the Pittsburgh studio, Bolton thought the idea absurd. But Harriet and Gene saw the possibilities. Johnstown, a hardscrabble steel-mill town, already had a tap-dancing school (as did communities all across America) propelled by the surge of sound movies. But the Kellys knew the current competition was beatable. The owner of the Johnstown studio, according to Gene, "gave his pupils a little heel-and-toe and, after one lesson, convinced their parents their little geniuses were dancing. We taught them properly. We taught our kids to dance like professionals. We got them working at the barre and though it would take a month before they mastered a step, it remained with them for the rest of their lives."

With Gene and Harriet's persuasion, Bolton agreed on the Johnstown studio, so long as Harriet would assume the major responsibility. It seemed like a lot of trouble. It was a long trip across the Allegheny Mountains and over hazardous roads, often through ice storms, in the Kelly's warhorse of a coughing old Chevrolet.

They rented a room in the American Legion Hall, and Gene passed out flyers on the sidewalks. They managed to attract about a dozen pupils. Harriet scrounged a secondhand piano and persuaded an elderly lady in Johnstown to play it. She could not read music, but she could manage a few standard tunes. At the start Bolton himself would make the trek every Saturday morning.

But not for long. He was a New Yorker, urbanized and soft, not ready for the skidding drive over the mountains, in the freeze of winter. He soon rationalized the Johnstown venture as small-time. He began to miss sessions, giving very little or no notice. Gene would have to take over at the last minute and make the trip himself.

Within weeks he showed he could relate to children and now, ironically, Bolton's faith in word-of-mouth advertising proved to be right. The competing studio closed. Everybody was talking about the phenomenal teacher—still just a teenager!

Gene's success was disheartening to Bolton's pride. One day he just abandoned the Johnstown business and Harriet took over the operation, debts and all.

It was courageous of her. The crash of Wall Street would come soon. The unemployment numbers were spiking upward. The advent of radio had sufficiently eaten into the phonograph business for James Sr. to lose his job. He came home and took to drinking with a frightening bent. In his rare sober moments, he moped around the house to the bewilderment of the children. But Gene, sympathetic toward his father, believed he would recover to play a role in the family business. He encouraged Harriet to push ahead and take the appropriate legal steps to buy Bolton out of the Pittsburgh studio. Partly because of his intensity, partly because he was such a popular teacher, but mainly because there was nobody else—in those days it had to be a man—she renamed each of the schools, in Pittsburgh and in Johnstown, the Gene Kelly Studio of Dance.

He was all of sixteen, still in high school, in the graduating class. The Peabody High School yearbook ignored his business success but recorded Gene Kelly as "destined to be a great entertainer." His mother was still holding out for the robes of the Supreme Court, but she could not be so sure any more. Her Gene was growing up fast. He was his own man. He no longer confided everything to her. He had a way of holding to himself what he wanted to do.

Jules "Doc" Steinberg, his sole boyhood crony of the period, would later say: "We would discuss sports most of the time. We were both ice-hockey fanatics. Looking back now, I find it strange that never, in all the time I knew Gene, did he ever mention his interest in show business to me or his desire to be a dancer. It was something he kept absolutely secret."

Even to his family. He was always close-mouthed about his future. Harriet thought she no longer understood him. He was an enigma, she decided, no longer bristling with ambition, and every Sunday in church she would say some special prayers to straighten him out.

Her Gene was always to say: "If someone had left us a grocery store, we would probably have all become grocers." It was a mark of how, from an early age, Gene Kelly thought that chance, not the Almighty, determined destiny. Indestructible as she was, his mother was a religious woman to the core and this belief of Gene's always frightened her.

Because the video crew is poking around, still grabbing reaction shots, he removes the ridiculous oversized smoke-gray glasses. Suddenly his eyes sting like hell. Either globs of salty tears—his sentimental Irishness bubbling up—or something to do with the bad news his ophthalmologist had laid on him the day before: cataracts in both eyes. He would need an operation pronto.

But when all is said and done, what the hell does he have to be ashamed about? He's still in great shape, still ice skates and skis when he can get away to Klosters, and holds service against the club champ at the tennis court. He can still spike like crazy at volleyball.

So loosen up, let it be kissy-kissy time with the perfumed cheeks of some ladies he's done the deed with—dancing, that is. Take One rolling . . . and a strong and swift politico-style handshake for their sweat-shiny male accompaniment, bulging in mohair tuxedo, clapping hard for the designated AFI honoree as they consign him for good to the hardened concrete of Grauman's Chinese. Bastards! Those fat know-it-alls whose only form of exercise is jumping to conclusions! Like their predecessors, L.B. Mayer and Eddie Mannix and Harry Cohn. Nay-saying moneymen who ruled the roost when he and Betsy first came out here. "No, Gene." Or "Not yet, Gene." Or "Never, Gene!"

No green-lighting for Kelly ideas that stretched and broke the envelope, that didn't clone last year's top-grosser. Okay, maybe an amber light when they finally accepted his Invitation to the Dance. Then television came in and Invitation was out of the picture! Why the hell should a ballet fan plunk down hard-earned cash at the Odeon? The Kelly family curse—just like the "free" radio that killed his dad's phonograph sales, "free" TV more than satisfied what little public appetite there was for tutus and pirouettes.

And now he's in his assigned seat, having come past the huge blowups mounted around the ballroom, those familiar midair stills of himself in flight, as pirate or clown, musketeer or sailor, or just himself, the prime-time hoofer in khakis and roll-up short sleeves, and it happens again: the turbulent chemistry described in countless production meetings as his "Irish temper," sweet and full of gentle blarney one moment, angry to the point of terrifying the next.

"No, Gene. Not yet, Gene. Never, Gene!"—years later, the same intro for his swan song, when movie musicals had gone south, when there we are, dolled up for the 1880s on location in the Hudson Valley town of Garrison, not far from the Big Apple (where he shouldn't have left Pal Joey!). There in front of him is Barbra, talented as all-get-out, but with one, count 'em, one film in the can, there she is telling him—the Director—no, not yet, never when he wants to replace one of her shticks with a better bit of business. And yawping and bitching on the phone every night, calling producer Ernie Lehman (no pal of his), bad-mouthing Kelly, the old fogey, all through the night! Good night already, Dolly— it was Goodbye, Dolly! as far as he was concerned.

Okay, so he was long in the tooth for the Beverly Hills fountain of youth, ancient history, guilty as charged. Had he not joined the Hollywood scene just before World War II, and, after service with the Navy, returned to MGM to resume a promising career? Those were the burnished days of Cary Grant (who happens to be here tonight—surprising, considering how Grant went public with gossip about his and Betsy's marriage) and Joan Crawford, Gable and Harlow. And Astaire, silky and smooth in white tie and tails. Others too, the proud and lofty pride of MGM lions and lionesses, all endlessly glamourized and glitzed and reported on breathlessly by the Louellas and the Heddas. Stars, worshiped by millions, coiffed and shaped and forever smiling with capped-teeth dazzle, would sell souls for roles and credits, back-stabbing and double-dealing and double-crossing their way through the heated Hollywood game.

And into this vortex of competition and corruption had strolled—or rather, tapped— the would-be shortstop for the Pittsburgh Pirates. Confident and self-assured he seemed, his very style of dance a world away from Astairean elegance. While Ginger gave Fred sex, her partner gave her class. But the guy from Pittsburgh, Pee-Ay, was American mainstream, almost a blue-collar bulldozer, whose dancing captured the nothing-is-impossible postwar American mood.

STATE COLLEGE, PENNSYLVANIA, 1929

* * *

The letters for Gene, who had enrolled at Penn State, carried very little good news.

The world of the Victrola was sinking as the Depression took hold. James Kelly, Sr. never did recover his job of selling phonographs and records. It had been two years without a payday for the once-proud patriarch of the family. To curb his drinking, Harriet had insisted he take over the accounting responsibilities of their business.

Unfortunately, his meticulous spidery-thin handwriting was not very active on the INCOME side. At the Gene Kelly Studio, in Pittsburgh and in Johnstown, the demand for lessons was still there. The wherewithal to pay was not. Harriet tried to hold down the cost of tuition to fifty cents a lesson, but even then the IOUs were everywhere in the account books. At least the Kellys ate well enough from the tradeouts of home-baked bread or sacks of potatoes or products from vegetable farms. Harriet gave up coffee. The shortage of cash was the caffeine that kept her awake at night.

Gene did well at college his freshman year, with good grades despite a hectic schedule of classes and odd jobs to pay his own tuition and living expenses. "Working his way through" was essential. There could, of course, be no help from home.

He landed a part-time job as a laborer for a building contractor. Twenty-five cents an hour. Three nights a week he dispensed root beers and malted milks at an ice cream parlor. A BLT sandwich or a hamburger was the perk that served as his main meal. He pumped gas. He put in as many hours as he could get at the Firestone plant, taking tires off the production lines. He became known around the huge facility as the kid who could actually roll off eight tires at once.

Like his mother, he was indestructible, rugged, with energy to spare. He viewed the schedule as a challenge. His major was journalism, which he later shifted to economics, perhaps reflecting his concerns about money to get himself through college. Weekdays, there would be the classes, lectures, seminars, studying at odd hours between jobs, preparation of assigned themes. He was already developing a first-rate writing style. He was quick to come up with good ideas and could present them clearly and with verve.

Certain evenings he would be called by Harriet at the last minute to do gigs with Fred or enter amateur night competitions to try for the prize money. More and more, his talent as a director-choreographer asserted itself, and he made their routines more complicated and interesting, adding steps, even a "story-line" to involve the audiences. He wanted the Kelly Brothers to dance with a Gene Kelly stamp.

He realized there was money to be made in show business, no fortune but enough to help his family through the Depression. He and Fred would have to stay on the stage longer, give the customer real entertainment value for the money. He developed what he later described as "a beautifully corny master of ceremonies act" embracing a few jokes lifted from the touring acts of comedians visiting Pittsburgh. Occasionally Fred would extend and close the act with one of his magic shows. No dogs. Gene rigged up a tap routine on roller skates that won applause and, more importantly, cash prizes at the amateur nights.

He and Fred worked out their own method of notating a visiting professional's tap routine when something really new was presented. In a Kelly-invented choreographic shorthand Gene would sketch out the first eight bars and Fred would take down the second eight. Then they would watch the next two or three performances, make corrections, and improve their notes, until they felt they "had" the routine. The brothers became inseparable. There was a genuine fondness between them and no conflict about hogging the limelight. Fred by now had come to realize his brother's star quality and backed off comfortably into the supporting role. Gene was amused by his younger brother's attitude, his sheer delight in being onstage. Even when they played a gig in the seediest of Pittsburgh slum clubs—what a horrified Gene called a "cloop," an amalgam of "club" and "chicken coop"—Fred was cheery, unflinchingly upbeat.

"You would think Fred was like an accordionist," Gene used to say. "He never knew when to get off."

Saturday was no day off for Gene. From Penn State College, or from Pittsburgh in the event of a Friday-night booking in the city, he would drive to Johnstown and arrive at the studio before 8 A.M. Then would start fourteen straight hours of teaching and demonstration before the nighttime journey back to Pittsburgh over the mountains. Dead tired, he swigged from a thermos of coffee to stay awake. Occasionally Harriet would take pity and arrange a room at a Johnstown boarding house so he could stay over. But he was expected in Pittsburgh early on Sunday for Mass with the rest of the family. In the afternoon he would usually rehearse with Fred and spend some time with Harriet and his father going over the books.

But his priorities at the two studios that bore his name were not financial. He was a perfectionist, always doctoring and improving the methods of instruction. He had set up the idea of eight basic routines of gradually increasing complexity. Under his supervision his sister Louise wrote down the step-by-step sequence of each routine in almost military-manual fashion. It took several Sunday afternoons. Students were encouraged to take the dance layouts home and practice on their own. Gene's system called for Fred to work one-on-one with anybody who missed a lesson, to catch up with the class.

Now and then on a Saturday night when no stage booking turned up, there might be a surprise treat. Harriet would take the whole family to see the jaunty George M. Cohan when he came to Pittsburgh for one performance. Or Fred—now in high school—would tug Gene along to see one of the great black tap dancers, Dancing Dotson. Then they might copy a few routines.

"It's a way out of the cloops, Gene," Fred would say, and his brother could only hope so. He found everything in them third-rate or worse. The indifferent and careless piano and drum accompanists infuriated him. The listless audience paid far more attention to drinks than the dancing—except when he tried to give an intro, when, precisely at that moment, they all started to gossip, talk mob business, and tell dirty jokes. Most of all he despised the crooked small-time agents. They committed the Kelly Brothers to four or five shows a night for anything from five to twelve dollars, more often the former, minus commission. And one could never be sure the fee was really what the agent claimed.

Overall, the lack of dignity and respect for the performer clawed at his pride, so that, again and again, he vowed he would return to rolling tires off the Firestone line. Sheridan Morley and Ruth Leon, in their memorabilia book of Gene Kelly photographs, have quoted Kelly on the worst aspect of those raucous, rending nights in the "cloops":

> The audience . . . throwing coins on the stage embarrassed me terribly. The first time it happened I looked at the guy who threw the coins and was ready to punch him on the jaw. Then other people started throwing money and as I couldn't go around punching them all I just had to grin and bear it. . . . Fred picked up the money, flashed a smile and just went on dancing. But I was mortified. . . . I was just ready to die of humiliation.

Sometimes they were even hit by the barrage of coins. It was as though the audience had taken up a new game. Worst of all were the extremes of reaction after a number: either total silence or verbal insults, usually casting doubts on the dancers' sexuality.

One night a patron called them "fags." Gene jumped off the stage, pulled the offender from his barstool, and knocked him down. The two brothers then had to make a run for it, because the club owner and his brother, a murderous and mountainous pair, advanced on them flailing baseball bats.

Even harder to bear was the pattern for the closing of their act. As the Kellys froze positions, putting their last efforts into forced smiles, they always knew everybody in the place was waiting for the big-bosomed bubble dancer, who had done a striptease earlier, to come back and do an encore.

Mercifully, Monday morning found Gene back in the more civilized enclave of Penn State. Well-known on campus, he entertained at many college functions. He formed an act with a student named Jim Barry, a professional drummer as well as a dancer. When Gene did a solo he often worked in some self-styled moves and taps while Jim pounded out a percussive rhythm. The reception was much more favorable than in the "cloops."

His only gripe at Penn State was the fraternity system. There were special clubs with Greek names for Protestants, Catholics, and Jews. The initiation ceremonies he had heard about were juvenile, even sadistic. But more than anything, he thought, the segregation of religions fostered prejudice against students of other backgrounds. As he was to state later in any number of interviews:

> I'd come from a family where the word prejudice was never mentioned. In fact, I felt so strongly about it that with another fellow called Johnny Napoleon and a third chap, a Jewish boy called Eddie Malamud, we tried to take a stand against certain of the fraternities and formed ourselves into a triumvirate of rabid activists in the hope of being able to stop the sort of discrimination that was going on. But we couldn't fight the establishment and we lost.

By the winter and the collapse on Wall Street, his college life lost priority as the Depression raged to full force. The Kelly family and their dance studios were just managing to stay financially afloat, saved by the modest infusions of cash brought in by the performances of the Kelly Brothers. Gene decided to transfer to Pittsburgh University for his sophomore year. He would live at home, commute to classes, and be in a better position to take on gigs with Fred.

For the two young men it was grim going. Their price scaled down to five dollars for five shows a night. They were grateful to get what bookings they could in the "cloops." Often the backstage areas were so dingy and filthy that they had to undress in the cramped old Chevrolet parked outside. Shivering, they would put on the white trousers and frilly shirts Harriet had laundered and pressed, and sometimes tuxedos, when the nightclub owner insisted on a "classy" appearance.

Collections after the last show were a hassle. On one occasion an agent sent them deep into the tenderloin of Pittsburgh, to a mob-owned nightspot. Two shows for five dollars—a bonanza, they were told by the agent, who would not dare accompany them to the performance. After the speedy tap routine that closed out the second show, the owner paid them four dollars. Gene was tempted to take action then and there. Fred, indicating the bulky hoods all around, dissuaded him.

"Let's go. What do we have an agent for?" said the younger brother, tugging Gene away.

The next day Gene asked their agent to intervene with the owner. The agent's response was fast and direct: First, the agent wanted his commission. Second, driving Gene's blood pressure even higher, he insisted that the 10-percent cut be paid on the spot. Fifty, not forty cents. Gene's reaction was pure instinct. He stepped around the battered desk, tugged the struggling agent to his feet, and punched hard. There were two immediate effects: The agent hit the floor and Gene—as accident-prone as ever—broke one of his fingers.

In effect, as Harriet did not fail to remind him, the whole fee was consumed by the local hospital bill. As Gene left the emergency room, looking down at his splinted hand, he had to be thinking of concentrating all his energies on his pre-law studies.

It did not help his spirits to come home, where his father, with too few accounting responsibilities to perform, was unsettling Harriet more than ever with his heavy consumption of bourbon. The mood at the Kensington Street house was doleful. His mother was already scanning the real-estate ads, looking for a rental.

Then, as happens so often in the lives of significant show-business performers, the string of misfortune was yanked hard by a telephone call. It was from a retired theatrical booker in Pittsburgh, and a long-time friend of Harriet's. He said: "I've just had a call from the William Morris Agency, in New York. They represent Cab Calloway and his Cotton Club Band."

"So?" responded Harriet, always one for getting to the point.

"Calloway's been touring with the Nicholas Brothers as a special feature. But now, shit's hit the fan. The Nicholas boys have got a chance for a slot in a Hollywood movie. Cab's a nice guy, you know, he agreed to let them go."

"So?"

"So Cab's doing a gig in Altoona and the agency can't get a replacement act in time. They asked me if there are any good tap acts in Pittsburgh."

"You're calling the right person!" Harriet exclaimed. "How about—"

Her friend had anticipated and cut in: "Not a chance, Harriet, even in blackface! It's Cab Calloway, it's a Negro act they're looking for. I was gonna contact the Fish Brothers. You happen to have their phone number?"

"No, sorry, I've never even caught the Fish Brothers."

"Funniest damn kid act you'd ever want to see! A helluva routine! One colored boy dresses like a girl and the other one pats him on the head every time he jumps up, and they do splits, and they're just great!"

"Then if you want my advice, call William Morris right away and give 'em the Fish Brothers. You'll be able to track down the kids' phone number later."

"I sure will, Harriet. A commission's a commission these days."

With great difficulty Harriet let an hour pass before telephoning William Morris and reaching Calloway's representative. She asked whether the Fish Brothers had been booked for Altoona.

"No way!" The William Morris man was rattled as time was running out. "Cab won't hear of such a corny act on his bill."

"I see." Ethics having been dealt with, Harriet swung into action: "What about the Kelly Brothers? They'll stop the show! They're great!"

"Never heard o' them."

"They've played the Nixon and the Stanley and the Loews—"

"Look! We don't have time to horse around! The—what the hell's their name again?"

"The Kelly Brothers. Very professional and—"

"The Kelly Brothers should get their asses over to Altoona first thing tomorrow morning! If they're willing to spec it. Cab will have a look-see before we firm up the booking. Okay?"

"Okay." She rang off before he could change his mind. In the excitement of the opportunity—or so she explained later—she failed to mention the skin tone of the Kelly Brothers!

Fred was jubilant. Gene was cooler and more logical. He made the point to his younger brother that one look at their Irish mugs and out would come the hook and a not-so-free round-trip to Altoona for their troubles. But Fred was not about to be deterred by the bruising rough-and-tumble of show business. It was Altoona or bust! Surely, once Cab Calloway saw them dance, the famous bandleader would be stricken color-blind. Years later, Fred recollected for Rusty Frank's *Tap*, a series of interviews with leading tap dancers, what happened next:

> We were two kids crazy to get on that stage and perform. Gene and I took the Pennsylvania Railroad and arrived in Altoona at 10:00 A.M. and we went straight to the rehearsal at the theater. Across the front of the theater was a huge banner that read: CAB CALLOWAY AND HIS COTTON CLUB REVUE. Now, being just

a Pittsburgh kid, I wasn't too familiar with night clubs in New York. And I certainly didn't know much about the Cotton Club. All I knew was that Cab Calloway's music was hot and I wanted to dance to it. We just marched right backstage and asked for the manager.

A huge black man wearing a derby hat came out and looked down at the boys. "You kids are the Kelly Brothers?"

"Yeah," they responded, their high-pitched voices contrasting with the heavy bass of the giant who faced them.

"I'm gonna stop the rehearsal." The man crossed the backstage area and interrupted Cab, who stopped the orchestra.

They heard and saw the bandleader snap out angrily: "What the hell's so damn important you've stopped me in the middle of a run-through?"

"Cab," placated the man, sweeping off the derby to point at Gene and Fred. "Meet the Kelly Brothers!"

Calloway took a long disbelieving look. Then in a perfect rendition right out of the popular *Amos 'n' Andy* radio show, he pitched his voice in a rumble: "Somebody done make a big mistake!" He bent towards the Kellys. "Did you know this was an all-black show?"

Before Gene could take over the response, his brother, still a student in high school, responded enthusiastically, if somewhat off the point: "We've got your records at home! You guys really play with a beat. It'd be great to dance with it!"

The band members were enjoying this impromptu break. Through a medley of guffaws and wisecracks, Fred stepped over and handed over their music arrangements. Calloway glanced at the papers, nodding slightly. "Which of you kids is the fast dancer?"

They both answered in absolute unison: "I am!"

Now everybody in the orchestra broke up, and so did the famous leader. "What number do you dance to?" he asked.

"*Stardust*," Fred replied. Gene saw the expression on Calloway's face and now took over, knowing Calloway's penchant for pace and energy in his numbers. "Starting in half-time and then going into full-time, then double-time, then we quadruple-time to the finish!"

"Hey, this is something I want to see," said Calloway.

"Yeah, man!" called out a saxophonist, and others mumbled assent.

Years later, for Rusty Frank, Fred Kelly described the scene. It was short and very sweet: "Well, Gene and I danced the thing and as soon as it was over they all stood up and clapped and cheered. That was really something. The guys we were nuts about were applauding us!"

Realizing the Kelly Brothers had not eaten since arriving in Altoona, Calloway sent them across the street to a restaurant where he had reserved tables for his band. While they were enjoying the late breakfast, the boys saw two men in overalls emerge from the theater at each end of a ladder. They set it up just below the marquee. One of the men climbed up, the other handed him tin-backed letters one by one and, suddenly, the Kellys realized what was happening. The marquee was changing before their eyes.

EXTRA-SPECIAL ADDED ATTRACTION
THE KELLY BROTHERS

"That was it!" Fred said. "Now I knew we had made it! And Cab even held us over the next three days in Johnstown."

Shirley MacLaine, *the emcee, resplendent in a red gown, tells it well, which is no surprise in this world of storytellers, people with the skills to make the make-believe believable, who give real punch to punch lines, anecdotalists par excellence! He has heard her do her thing before at other Gene Kelly retrospectives, but bless her! She tells about their first meeting at the hit show* Pajama Game, *in May of 1953, when visiting celebrities would come backstage (not to visit her, of course, a mere dance gypsy in the chorus):*

"Many famous people came to see us. For example, Mrs. Eleanor Roosevelt came, and stars from Broadway and Hollywood. They were wonderful but, well, aloof. Untouchable. Then one night a gentleman came who changed all that."

Shirley paints the picture: the movie idol climbing over scenery, climbing over flats, over props, down the steel stairway that led to the basement where the girls dressed, wading his way through costume racks and piles of Capezio shoes.

"He came to see us! He introduced himself . . . as if he needed to."

She goes on deftly. The audience is with her. He can feel the heat on his face as those at nearby tables turn toward him. She describes how he moves through the cramped dressing room, radiating the ebullience of one who has just witnessed a happy show. Stopping in front of her, at her lowly position near the door. She was credited in the Playbill as Dancer Number Three.

"Then Gene looked down at me, picked up my ponytail, and said: 'Kid, you've really got something. Keep going.'"

Shirley holds up just a bit. "My eyes flooded with tears. I looked up and said: 'Oh, Mr. Kelly. You've got something too. You keep going, too.'"

She lets the delighted rumble of the audience play out and goes on: "Thirty years later . . ."—*she pauses for a face-scrunching wince, an easy "gimme" to draw a laugh, and he pushes up the laugh-meter by mirroring her expression (the rapid-fire passage of time is something this face-lifted group really comprehends)*—"I had my one-woman show at the Wilshire Theater, and he came backstage and did the same thing. Came to my dressing room, knocked, leaned in and said: 'Kid, you really have something. Keep going.'

"The one-woman show was killing me, and I responded: 'Gene! How long should I keep going?'

"You keep going as long as you find happiness and help people realize their dreams."

It is, he finds, a bit much. But Shirley is too much the pro to let the maudlin moment sit there and marinate and right away she's segued into a tender riff on how show people help show people and how Judy helped him when he first came out to Hollywood for For Me and My Gal. *That was before the era of film schools, when he was so green he didn't know how to find his mark during a take. When he still pitched his voice to reach the second balcony, nearly deafening the unsuspecting audio man, who wrenched at his earphones.*

All he can think is: Judy had been indispensable.

Shirley cues in the next run of clips. The room goes dark. Up there ahead are those kids Judy and Gene, doing Summer Stock—*Judy a bit clunky but born to dance—and he loses track for a moment but surfaces as Shirley makes another segue into her "dancers can't lie" shtick, making much of his dictum that his publicity stills were never to be airbrushed to hide the scar on his face. And as she says, "Gene Kelly tells the truth about our dreams," he thinks: No disrespect to Shirley, but maybe we should call in for a rewrite. He allows himself to tune out again. Bathed in the darkness he can at last let the smile fade out as a new parade of MGM clips fades in.*

PITTSBURGH, 1930

* * *

While not as ecstatic as his younger brother over the growing number of calls for their act, Gene began to give serious consideration to building a career on his talents as a performer or choreographer. His mother appreciated the money he brought in, but she did not pressure him toward show business. In her view, as an honor graduate of Peabody High (at sixteen), a stellar Penn State freshman, and now as a transfer student at close-by Pitt, he was right on track for the Supreme Court placement of her dream. Gene did think her ambition for him was a mite unrealistic, but he was comfortable with the pre-law program at the local university. Since his father was still unemployed and the dance studios were not resounding financial successes, his spare time, what there was of it, was taken up with more and more stage gigs.

Jay, his older sister, was now a public school teacher with a Master's degree. She and Gene would be booked for ballroom dance exhibitions at weddings, birthday celebrations, retirement parties, and elaborate bar mitzvahs. Ballroom dancing was not Gene's favorite activity until he began to work elements of jazz ballet into their performances.

To add to the seductive atmosphere of the foxtrot or tango, he and Jay would not admit to being brother and sister. Gene had a sense it made for an embarrassingly "small town" image, and being defined as Jay's brother would immediately instigate guesses as to his age. He would insist on a loudspeakered introduction as "the well-known professional dancing act now touring the country. . . ."

"I'm not sure if we fooled them or not," said Gene. "But we did make $150 some nights—apart from talent we had chutzpah, which was crucial."

The experience of whirling Jay around flower-decked hotel ballrooms earned something well beyond the fee for Gene. He now realized he would only be happy in a performance role when the venue carried some dignity. The "cloops" would be a thing of the past. The key was to avoid drowsy situations with gatherings of people half-watching while onstage he whiled away a few minutes of their time. He wanted—needed—respectful audiences getting involved in an organized act that would scream for attention. For him that meant dancing in his own way.

He had really begun to pursue these objectives in earnest at the end of his freshman year when he was hired as a counselor for the summer at the YMCA's Camp Porter. His task: to put on weekly shows. His fee: $150 for the season. It would be his first real experience as a director and producer of stage musicals.

There was a special challenge at Camp Porter. He had to motivate the worshipers of football and baseball stars to volunteer for the dance roles, brushing past the connotation that such activity was somehow feminine or sissified. He won the boys over by concentrating on the physical parallels between athletics and dance, a concept he would articulate throughout his professional life and the core of his own muscular style.

It turned out to be a productive summer for him. He was actually sorry when autumn came and Camp Porter closed down for the year. But the gap was soon to be filled by an unlikely source for a young man named Eugene Curran Kelly—the Sisterhood of the Beth Shalom Synagogue. "A heaven-sent opportunity," his mother called it when the temple, in the city's Squirrel Hill section, came into his life. At the time the synagogue, a conservative congregation, was having difficulty raising funds to pay the rabbi. Some spirited member came up with the idea of presenting an "original" musical show and selling tickets. Originally Lou Bolton had been hired. But he left town, so Harriet persuaded the synagogue to engage Gene for the producing responsibilities at a stipend of $15 a week until the performance dates.

He started at the Beth Shalom in September of 1931. He was nineteen when he stood before the group of giggly teenagers provided him as the cast for their Kermess, the congregation's first annual show. It bore the exuberant title (assigned by the rabbi, not by Gene) "The Revue of Revues." Tickets were to be 75 cents for children and $1.50 for adults.

Having gained confidence in his own methods at the YMCA camp, Gene held off barreling directly into dance instruction for the boys, who initially would not come near him. They were astonished when their mentor, in a Pittsburgh Pirates baseball cap, scheduled pick-up basketball games, touch-football scrimmages, or gymnastic lessons. Gene participated and excelled, stopping to point out that the demonstrated action wasn't very different from dancing. He understood how they felt, Gene told them, forced to go to dancing school when he could barely walk.

The parents at the synagogue, reflecting the kids' gathering enthusiasm for the show, redoubled their efforts to make the fundraiser a success. Concerned and attentive Jewish mothers were astonished at the breakfast tables—"not only our girls but our boys, can you imagine?"—when the children could hardly wait for the afternoon's rehearsals and dance lessons with "that handsome Irish fella." Kids came early and stayed late for exhausting sessions of tap, ballet, and acrobatics.

When a pimply-faced girl was embarrassed to try, feeling frightened and clumsy, Gene would flash a grin and take her hand and make her feel like his perfect partner, a Ginger Rogers. He had an innate sense of just what it took, in words and body-language, to raise her self-esteem. Home she would go, flying rather than walking, spilling over with euphoria and enthusiasm, maybe even puppy love, as Kelly-mania took over Beth Shalom. All the parents heard about was Gene Kelly, Gene Kelly, Gene Kelly. It seemed every boy and girl now wanted to participate. Gene managed to find places and routines for all.

It was by no means the first time he demonstrated his extraordinary affinity for working with children, his gift for surrounding an activity with an atmosphere of fun, laughs, and adventure. Many years later, in the San Francisco suburb where she lives now, Ruth Portnoy, the wife of a retired cantor, described how she and the other children of the Beth Shalom congregation worshiped their dazzling idol:

> It was something right out of the Pied Piper, the way the kids followed him around, would try anything he wanted them to try. I remember when Gene—as Irish as they come—taught me an Irish jig to perform for the Kermess. The next day I was in a hurry to get to the synagogue and I took a short-cut. I slipped climbing over a barbed-wire fence. I cut my hand. I had to go to the emergency room at the hospital, and when I saw Gene the next day, my hand was covered by a large cast. When I saw him, I said: "Gene, I'm sorry. I guess my Irish jig number is out."
>
> He made me laugh, joking about how he was even more accident-prone than I was. Then he showed me how to hold my hand behind my back during the jig and, at the Kermess, I did the whole thing. Although I was basically a klutz, he always made me feel I could truly dance.
>
> Sometimes he pulled in his brother Fred as an assistant. It was always a thrill to see them do a tap dance on roller skates. Gene's mother and sister would come to Squirrel Hill and help us with the costumes for the Kermess. I'm just really happy the Kellys were part of my life.

In all, the Sisterhood made $1100 with the first show and was able to retain the services of the rabbi. Gene, too, was held on and became a Beth Shalom institution, with the main mission of producing the annual Kermess until his departure for New York seven years later. The young congregation members like Ruth Portnoy followed his career after he left Pittsburgh, and whatever letter was sent to him from Squirrel Hill, an affectionate response would always arrive from New York, Hollywood, Europe—wherever in the world he was working.

During his final years in Pittsburgh, the rabbi, delighted with Gene's contributions to the morale of the congregation, allowed him to use one of the basement classrooms at no cost to take on private pupils. It was a major assist to the workings of the Gene Kelly Studio of Dance, because, in an almost magical reversal for the business, space had now become tight. It seemed every little American girl wanted to dance and dress like Shirley Temple, who, more than ever, was the reigning star of the movie houses. And what warm-hearted American parent could refuse?

Perhaps the worst was over for the Kellys. Would-be students of tap began to flock back. Performances of Gene and Fred around Pittsburgh were commanding attention. His remarkable ability to teach children was encouraging parents to forgo the competition and line their children up at the mirrored Gene Kelly barres.

In 1932, still pursuing college full-time at Pitt, Gene saw to it that his school would leave that rented American Legion Hall in Johnstown for a more spacious arrangement on Main Street. He was unusual for a "Depression kid." He understood it took money to make money. He made sure the new location was an attractive and welcoming center.

Success in Johnstown did not come immediately. It took some time for the clientele to build and, at first, Gene and Harriet worried about the additional investment and expenses. When hardly anyone appeared for the grand opening at the Main Street address and the cookies, candy, and soft drinks remained untouched, ready only for being carried back in the old Chevrolet to Pittsburgh, James Sr. fretted they had "gone too far, too fast." But for Gene the empty new studio was a challenge. He simply would not let the place gather dust. He realized he had taken over the responsibility for his family. It had been his decision. Influenced by the Beth Shalom experience he felt he was approaching a test of his capabilities as an adult; today was like *his* bar mitzvah, and he must be a man!

To put the Gene Kelly Studio of Dance on the Johnstown map, he applied every promotional idea he could think of. He arranged trade-outs with the town newspaper and radio station. Free lessons for the owner's children in return for ad space and spot time. He put together simple but effective mimeographed brochures. He hired high school students to place one flyer in every mailbox in town. Borrowing from his Beth Shalom success, he announced the coming production of a special children's show, an original musical extravaganza at a movie theater in the center of Johnstown. Admission for the townspeople would be *gratis*. Wanting to be part of so splendid an event, children pestered their parents to enroll them at the Gene Kelly Studio. The production turned out to be so popular that it was repeated seven times.

Gene paid another visit to the local newspaper. "No children's show anywhere has ever held an engagement that long in a professional, legitimate theater," he trumpeted to the editor. The Johnstown editor was overwhelmed by what he saw on the stage. "It cannot be surpassed anywhere on the Keith circuit!" he reported.

The show helped Gene's dance studio turn the corner, and was the first of a series of annual musicales requiring paid admissions: "Johnstown on Parade," "Gene Kelly's Kiddies' Vodvil," and "The Talk of the Town Revue." The entertainment ran the gamut from simple little ballet pieces to full-stage military tap routines, and teamwork kick routines were modeled on the famous Radio City Rockettes.

As always, Gene was uncanny in the way he could match up a student with a place in the cast. A senior on the gymnastics team could be trained to do an acrobatic number. Two sweethearts could be cajoled into doing an Apache dance, and the girl, if she showed some skill, would appear later on the program doing a toe solo. A spectacled, introverted girl, the valedictorian of her class, hanging back at the fringe of a crowd of beseeching teenagers, would be plucked out and assigned to take on the Dying Swan and, working with Gene, by opening night would bring the audience to its feet. Less grandly, if a youngster just wanted to learn the fad of the year—the Black Bottom, the Turkey Trot, or the Big Apple—Gene would embrace the number, apply his coaching skills and incorporate it into the show, often to the surprise of the reluctant youngster. He was obsessive about using all his students, aged four to eighteen (by 1933, there were 150 of them in Johnstown alone). His next step was to organize a full Johnstown Youth Orchestra, which became one of the town's most popular attractions, enticing even more new pupils to his studio.

For reasons Gene never understood—sometimes he would ascribe it to genetic or sociological factors or, jokingly, to the quality of the air or the drinking water—Johnstown was brimming with very pretty girls who could sing and dance. A number of his students went on to show business careers on Broadway and in Hollywood. Among them was a lithe, exotically attractive dancer named Jeanne Coyne, who became one of his key assistants in Johnstown and, in the process, developed a schoolgirl crush on him. It would flower into the most important relationship of Gene Kelly's life. But from the start he was not one to take advantage of his power in his relationships with aspiring dance partners or students and did his best to discourage any attitudes of adoration. He had already observed too many "cloop" owners using casting-couch maneuvers and promises as a lure to sexual involvement. His own upbringing with his mother and sisters had fostered an attitude of old-fashioned gallantry which was to stay with him all his life, despite constant temptations and a few regrettable lapses.

The organization of the Johnstown Youth Orchestra meant that, rather than making do with a pianist or recorded accompaniment, the Gene Kelly Studio gave kids an exciting taste of the big-time and lent stature to his productions. Gene bussed his shows on the road to play various dates in the small communities along an 80-mile stretch west of Pittsburgh, a cradle of stoical iron miners and steelworkers. The cost to the communities was $75 a performance. Cresson and Portage, Grove City and Slippery Rock, Meadville and Beaver Falls—these were tough, brawling towns, the kinds of places, in the words of the local school principal, "where you can be a successful neurosurgeon, but if you were a lousy football player as a kid, people still look at you funny."

But Gene always found a determined cadre of culture-seekers, led by a Harriet-type woman who would lobby the Veterans of Foreign Wars, the Order of Moose, or the local volunteer firemen to sponsor the latest Gene Kelly production as a fund-raiser. Gene was cagey enough to ride the Shirley Temple phenomenon for all it was worth. The cast received no cash, just candy and ice cream. They loved it. As his younger brother said:

> We couldn't stop it. So we went into it. In one of our shows we
> did a big Shirley Temple finale number. Mother went down to the

local department store and bought a gross of dresses, different colors. When the finale of the show happened, every girl came out in a dress that had a big bow on the back, all with their hair in bouncing curls. A stage full of Shirley Temples!

If not for his extraordinary energy and superb physical condition, Gene could not have taken on such responsibilities to build up what became a thriving business, all the time attending college and making very good grades. By graduation he had been accepted into the University of Pittsburgh Law School, which he still planned to attend. The financial prospects of a legal career still drew him and his mother, for working with his brother in the "cloops" had given him a sense of the realities of a backstage existence if public success is not attained as a performer.

Harriet was always a profound influence. And he was a workaholic, never one to waste time, or to lose his sense of purpose. Despite his schedule at Pitt and at the dance studios he managed to work out at the university gym. He sweated and strained at the exercise machines to develop upper-body strength, jumped and tumbled off the trampoline to enhance his sense of balance. He was a regular at the library, borrowing books on dance and ballet. He continued the study of French, vowing to get over to Paris as soon as he could swing it, and insisted on practicing the language whenever he met people with some fluency.

Gene was no prig. Now and then he would relax in a tavern, accompanied by his closest friend, "Doc" Steinberg. He would stand at the bar and have a beer or two and encourage a union steelworker to converse about his job. Gene was technically inclined; he was always fascinated by mechanical and scientific advances and he relished the descriptions, the more detailed the better, of real workers on the production lines. Then he and Steinberg would walk home along the deserted city streets, discussing the prospects for the Pittsburgh Steelers or the Pirates.

Whenever he could, he accepted a booking and performed, alone or with one of his sisters or with Fred, any time an agent proposed an acceptable gig. Every penny helped.

He and Fred spent their summer vacation in Chicago, which was preparing for the 1933 World's Fair. They would do from six to ten shows a day, often under different names. Because they looked so alike (although Gene had been blessed with a more theatrical look), they would often stand in one for the other, usually with Fred playing Gene's dates when Gene received a better offer elsewhere.

Gradually it became apparent that it was Gene who had the magical "star" quality, though Gene did not do anything to foster that differentiation. As Fred said: "We were never jealous of each other. Gene wasn't jealous of me, I've never been jealous of him. I've always been very proud of him and he of me. You know, we worked too hard to waste time on comparisons."

Fred was then only sixteen, but his youth played to their advantage. The Fair's Isle of Enchantment, a special area for children, was delighted to have Fred perform. He had his older brother's talent for recruiting, and Fred found a willing local youngster named Elizabeth Morgan who joined him in performing adagio numbers at various locations during the day.

At night, playing separately or together, the Kellys did the Chicago "cloops." The Windy City never ceased to be an eye-opening experience for the brothers. In Pittsburgh they were hometown boys, so the number always started on a bedrock of friendliness. At the World's Fair they were deep in the cold, professional world. Nobody gave a damn where they came from. Nobody asked.

As in the days when they were working on the rough edges of Pittsburgh, Gene was conscious of the drunks in the audience, more or less paying attention. Then came the flinging of coins and the obsequious bending down and retrieving. Gene felt he was an entrepreneur now. He deserved better, and he refused to style his performance toward what the audience wanted—those bastards, seen dimly in the dark, smoky nightclub, who showed no respect for a sophisticated dancer. They missed some of his best moves and would then clap at the most idiotic times, when he did something that could be performed easily by a new student at the Gene Kelly Studio of Dance. It was clear they preferred comedians and risqué jokes, the jiggling breasts and underdressed bottoms of the girl dancers. Invariably, they still would turn around and order drinks or go to the bathroom while he was dancing up a storm for his finale.

But by the time the World's Fair had closed he had learned a lot, mainly that the audience owed him nothing. It was his job, and his alone, to keep the audience interested and involved. This realization—an epiphany, really—did not come at once. He would gradually learn to take the verbal insults, guffaws, and hostile jokes. He throttled his temper, stopped shouting back at the men in the audience, and no longer jumped off the stage to seize a disruptive drunk by the scruff of the neck as he used to do. There was no feeling of payback in slapping a rude customer across the face or throwing a punch. He swallowed his pride and collected his fee.

All through the next semesters, his senior year at the University of Pittsburgh, he was tortured by the need to make a career decision. The law . . . or a dance studio entrepreneur? Harriet discussed with him the possibility of starting a chain of Gene Kelly Dance schools across the country. There was the allure of the Broadway theater as a producer, choreographer, or performer. And there was even another option: ballet. Not merely to infuse ballet into the routines he taught and performed, but to join up with an esteemed ballet troupe and work toward stardom in the kind of serious dancing that appealed to him most of all.

The dance studios, he knew, had grown to a point where he was no longer required on a day-to-day basis. His father had needed several years to ease the psychic pain of unemployment with alcohol. Spurred on by Gene and Harriet's prodding, James Sr. now ran the accounting side, a development that eased the worries of his concerned middle son: "My father found himself with a full-time job on his hands, for which I think he was very grateful, particularly as he had given up drinking and needed something to take its place."

Gene made all the artistic decisions and set the curriculum for the teachers and students, while his parents, especially Harriet, maintained strict control of the expenditures. Harriet even refused to reveal to him the cash-flow situation at the family business. Gene, Fred, and Louise received no salary. Harriet only doled out in small and separate payments what they needed to live on. Jay and Jim, the two oldest, now both over twenty-one and away from home, had the responsibility of earning their own livelihoods.

By now Gene had been discovered by the stage world in Pittsburgh, even as live theater continued to shrink with the rise of sound movies. There was no longer a reason to import a professional director or choreographer from New York. The Pittsburgh Playhouse regularly called on him to prepare a program of vaudeville entertainments combining amateurs and professionals. Inevitably, they insisted that he himself perform at least one number. The University of Pittsburgh, awaiting his entry in the fall of 1933 for law school, wanted him to stage the annual varsity show, the traditional Cap and Gown, which always concluded with burly athletes in female decolletage, doing the kick routines à la the Moulin Rouge in Paris, or so he told the footballers. His fee was $350, which Harriet promptly put away when he returned home. He was always the first to be called by the Junior League, the prestigious and socially connected club for young ladies, and so his final college year before graduation was busier than ever.

But he did not mind. Time on his hands only made him edgy, allowing doubts about law school to unsettle him. He welcomed his mother's initiative but was independent enough to see the pitfalls. The Supreme Court was *her* dream. Poking into his constantly was the allure of ballet.

Until now his interest as a choreographer had been combining the movements of tap and ballet. But was he being true to his god-given talents as a dancer? Was he, the economics major, selling himself short? Instead of tap dancing, showboating a few dazzling moves to awe the yokels, catering to audience taste with a bit of hootchy-kootchy, or the Turkey Trot or the buck-and-wing, why not the chesty and lofty *danse du ventre*, or even a charming quadrille?

Always the competitor, he resolved once and for all to find out how he measured up. In the summer of 1933, after graduating from Pitt with a B.A. at the age of twenty, he headed for Chicago again.

Vying with New York, Chicago had become a mecca of ballet instruction in America during the mid-30s. A number of prominent ballet dancers who had fled the Russian Revolution and managed to gain entry into the United States had fanned out west after finding the competition in New York intimidating. Many settled in Chicago to form what became serious academies of ballet. These were well supported by the wives of the new millionaires who lived on the shores of Lake Michigan with their passionate desire for the uplifting effect of "culture," to hide the grimy hardscrabble background of where the money came from.

The Chicago Association of Dancing Masters, whose members now included the finest ballet teachers in America, held master classes. Most candidates were turned away. Gene qualified for the summer session. The acceptance boosted his hopes that, by summer's end, he would be blessed with an offer from an active ballet company. But he was realistic and knew the odds were against him. Later on, he told interviewers why:

> When I studied dance in Chicago, I had this big dream of pursuing classical ballet. The problem was, there was nowhere to go after that. There were no big classic companies in the country. You have to remember we're talking ancient history here. It was right after the Chicago World's Fair, where I danced in 1933. But at that time, George Balanchine, founder of the New York City Ballet, had just arrived in the United States, and he didn't get his company really going until after World War II. Ruth Page had a company in Chicago, but she was already filled up with whatever talent she needed and there was just no place for me to work.

As was always to be the hallmark of Gene Kelly, he faced up to the challenge with every bit of energy and determination he could muster. He checked into a cheap hotel. Master status allowed him permission to attend as many classes as he could. His interest was insatiable.

His classmates were underage for ordering drinks in Chicago bars, which worked out to his advantage. At night he would visit the bars with the balletmaster, a Russian émigré named Kotchetovsky. Joining them would be the Spanish flamenco soloist Angel Cansino, who kept telling Gene about his own beautiful niece, a dancer named Rita Hayworth. Cansino took a fancy to Gene and gave him free lessons in his own specialty. But Gene would not swerve from his passion for classical ballet, and by the end of the summer he himself could measure his progress. He was offered a place with the touring company of the Ballet Russe de Monte Carlo.

He called his mother to tell her the news. She was too excited to hear him out. A bank had just informed her that it would extend a loan to finance the opening of an additional group of dance studios across the state. She was very emotional about giving Gene the credit; it was he, and only he, who had been the prime mover in building up what had become a thriving business. She could now visualize a chain of Gene Kelly Studios of Dance all across America.

She talked on, bubbling over with plans and hopes: Fred and his sister, with herself and her husband, could run the operation, and when Gene finished law school he could take over and certainly secure financing for the additional branches. She was convinced that even as an attorney giving part-time attention to the business, he could play the central role. And they needed him.

Not a word was spoken about the Supreme Court. Harriet finally rang off. He was late for his next dance class. When he arrived the male dancers were already at the barre in warm-up mode. The sight struck him with surprising force: They were teenagers—practically children!—with perfect long-legged bodies and a sheer energy and adolescent bounce in their movements. Ballet was their life; there were no distractions.

He, on the other hand, had already proven himself in different ways. As a student. A dancer. A choreographer. A business success. He was aware of the uncertainty of predicting ballet stardom in a competitive world where the exceptional proved the rule. But here in this suddenly strange place, this kiddie playground, looking around at the competition, he felt that if he was exceptional it was only because he was older. Would the future play out better for him? Even though he had developed a personal style—the blend of tap and modern dance that was quite unique, at least for Pittsburgh—ballet was another planet.

When the class took its break, Gene munched on a cold sandwich, alone in a corner. The kids ringed the room, their sweaty backs against the wall, chirping away gaily as they attacked the bagged meals. In two minutes the food was gone. A few boys and girls had nothing to eat. They rested, spoke to no one, their gaze stony against the opposite wall. That did it: The scene suddenly brought to mind what the absence of a dollar had done to the morale and self-esteem of Gene's father. As he was to say later: "I really couldn't see myself doing *Swan Lake* and *The Sleeping Beauty* for the next twenty years, living off $2 a week and a doughnut."

Back in his hotel room, he filled out his letter of acceptance to the University of Pittsburgh Law School. He turned down the offer of the Ballet Russe. He knew his mother would agree. She was probably, even now, searching out a set of used law books to buy at a discount.

Next on tonight's American Film Institute Salute to Gene Kelly, is (a flurry of trumpets) Baryshnikov!

He watches the double-cheeked kiss with Shirley MacLaine and now, facing him and the audience is one of the very few great talents: Mikhail Nikolaievich Baryshnikov. The forceful iambic ring of the name goes with the look. Serious. Those relentless, melancholy eyes are remote from the frolicking salute spirit. There will be none of the forced-festivity, can-you-top-this mouthing-off of just about everybody else. But somebody—some asshole of a speech writer, a TV sitcom jokesmith, probably assigned by the AFI—must have helped B. with his script, kudos not being a Russian specialité.

There is opening patter about him and Singin' in the Rain, rather stiffly delivered. Some guffaws sound out in the Hilton ballroom. He is already far away, his mind on this master of split leaps and cyclonic pirouettes. A true danseur noble of the ballet. Choreographer supreme for the great companies the world over. A paragon of twentieth-century dance. At one and the same time his attitude toward B. has been very complicated and very basic. He is jealous as hell.

"An unforgettable mix of entertainment and art. . . ," he hears and pulls himself up. Like the Volga, the accented voice is now carrying some serious freight, and that's fine, he can really let go. Turn up the heat on himself. Do what he always does when confronted by a formidable artist, compare. Match up. Give way to the tinderbox within him, that Irish competitive spirit. That's the game he and another B.—Betsy—used to play.

He really does not know Baryshnikov very well. If they bumped into each other on Rodeo Drive, would he call out "Hi, Mikhail" or "Hi, Mike," or even "Hi, Misha"?

But he has talked to a soloist at the Kirov Ballet, with knowledgeable people at American Ballet Theatre, critics who cover the New York City Ballet, and the parallels in their two lives—his and Baryshnikov's—are like whitewashed lanes at a track meet. They both are perfectionists when it comes to performing or staging a number. There is always the same remedy when the first faltering steps do not improve: Dance till the feet bleed! Their mothers, so strong and certain, charted the course from early on. B.'s mother had very little education but was a passionate theatergoer. Tickets to dramas, the opera, and ballet were as crucial as bread, and she always took her little Misha with her. Both, as choreographers, have carried a passion for marrying the purity of ballet to just about everything: jazz riffs, folk dances, tap, modern dance, and acrobatics, all the way to shimmies, bugaloo, even golf swings. Nothing is out-of-bounds.

Both fought the immediate establishment, barking back at the bosses. His: the Louis B. Mayers and the Harry Cohns. B.'s: the Artsoviet, or artistic committee, when the Kirov Ballet became a mini–police state, after Nureyev's defection. Okay, it's a stretch, but why not compare the McCarthy excesses with the oppression of the Communist state? Just as the Senator from Wisconsin breathed hot 'n' heavy on him, the KGB never let B. out of its sight after Nureyev skipped.

Parallels: They both have ranged beyond live theater, done TV specials, and movies. Movies that tapped into their sex appeal, B. cast as a roué, a womanizer. And him, the same, only the American way, the Pal Joey, the quintessential heartbreaker. Posters of them both hang in dorm rooms from Wellesley to Washington State.

(He has to admit: In real life, this Russky's libido is livelier. Some legendary attachments, the ballerina Gelsey Kirkland for one, a long liaison with actress Jessica Lange, others as well. With a clutch of children from different mothers.)

With his own actor-honed instinct for picking up a cue, he comes out of his reverie just in time to catch the Russian's gracious closer:

"We don't have dancers like Gene Kelly any more!"

And the gush of applause at the Hilton is like rinsing a sink of his thoughts. He smiles, goes thumbs-up toward B. up there, the grin reflecting what he is thinking: At least he's taller than B., who has done astonishingly well at a mere five feet, seven, who slept on a wooden plank as a kid starting in the corps de ballet because he'd been told this would help him grow faster.

Why didn't Harriet Kelly think of that? The question, not really serious, conjures up an even more radiant smile. The CBS cameraman is on him now like Willie Mays closing in on a fly ball. Again he does his thumbs-up signal as his own bellow of "Bravo, bravo, Misha!" is lost in the hullabaloo of the Hilton.

PITTSBURGH, 1933

* * *

It lasted just a few weeks until he gave up on Eugene Curran Kelly, Esq.

When it came, finally, it was an autumn afternoon and he was sitting in a lecture hall at the University of Pittsburgh Law School. It was a lecture on the relationship of torts and mercantile law. The droning of the professor just would not end. Fighting off the torpor, he could only contrast this moment with the excitement and passion of Kotchetovsky and Angel Cansino in the master dance class of his Chicago summer.

With a stab of remorse, he realized he would never be at the barre with the two of them again. He was surely a candidate for the wrong bar (he was always deft with wordplay, never one to let a chance for a pun slip by), and he decided, then and there, to hell with torts and mercantile law!

Before he could change his mind, he sold his textbooks at a loss and sacrificed the tuition money, later explaining in countless interviews: "I didn't want to be a lawyer or a businessman or head the chamber of commerce or be President. I just wanted to dance and create dances."

He held up on notifying his mother and hearing her disappointed reaction. Leaving the campus, he went for a long run to work off the nervous energy. As always, the physical effort was exhilarating. It brought to mind the pleasures he took from active sports and from dance, too, firming his resolve for the approaching confrontation with his mother. With each stroke of his sneaker he flowed through the encounter to come. Harriet was a great one for proverbs. Hearing his news would certainly bring out something testy, to the effect that with the Kellys, when the going gets tough, the tough get going. . . .

Well, he would remind her he had always been a first-rate student, graduating from high school at sixteen, going on with excellent college grades despite the press of show-business engagements, his responsibilities at the dance studios which bore his name and an assortment of less glamorous part-time jobs—*that's yesterday's news,* she would undoubtedly cut in.

Did she have any idea of the amount of work in law school, the preparation of briefs, the incredible reading assignments? She'd remind him of the boasts that he'd finished every book on ballet in the Chicago public libraries. Including those in French. Then she'd surely make him feel guilty about those beery nights with Kotchetovsky and Cansino, forcing him to change the subject to the interruptions bedeviling him at Pitt, the calls from the two studios, the rabbi at Beth Shalom, the sessions he could not avoid with out-of-town dancers passing through Pittsburgh.

And by this time her lips would be pressed together, brown eyes dark with disappointment. She would come at him another way. He was spending too much time at the movies! For professional reasons, he would respond (as he went into a final sprint). Watching Astaire and Rogers doing the Carioca and the Continental, for there was quick money to be made teaching ballroom dancing.

But even as he rehearsed his arguments, preparing for what was going to be an awful scene, he knew he was just doing a vamping intro, clearing his throat, not getting to the point. Two points, really.

He would have to tell her, though it would hurt, that he was not exceptional at the law. He was not going to be the best. And he must be the best!

Secondly, the competition, the law students at Pitt: Very earnest and well-behaved, desperately anxious to get ahead where the bucks were. And that was okay. But there was not the buzz and flash of creativity, the color and eccentricity of the show-business world he had left. There were—this time he would try to bring forth a nod of understanding from his dear, sainted mother—not enough laughs.

Later that day, the scenario well-rehearsed, he caught up with her in the kitchen at Kensington Street and started to tell her he had left law school and why. He didn't get far and he loved her more than ever. She had sensed his discomfort at Pitt. She was a woman addicted to the positive. It was fine with her. Now the two of them could put heads together and go national with the Gene Kelly Studio of Dance! With gathering force the exclamation points rolled into the peroration to her son. Nothing could stop them! The Depression was over! Roosevelt was in, Hoover out! This was the U.S. of A., not potato-dependent Ireland!

He never once regretted the decision to leave law school. He now had time and space for the family business and Beth Shalom and the touring professionals who had heard about "that Irish kid, the dance doctor" in Pittsburgh. People would pass around his name and phone number in a conspiratorial hush-hush manner, like drunks giving out the location of an honest speakeasy in Prohibition days.

His teaching talent was whispered around as a direct route to the big time, a source for glittering new steps or a new opener or a big finish, a single flourish or a complete makeover that would immediately add impact to one's performance. Typically, his phone would ring and an appointment would be requested for a session at his Pittsburgh location. The routine would be done in front of him. Gene's reaction was awaited.

What they would report, all the way back to New York, elatedly but still confidentially, guarding their discovery, was this: Gene Kelly was not at all like so many other dance teachers: puffy and out-of-shape drunks who wouldn't—probably couldn't—dance a step, or maybe hell-on-wheels with a cane jabbing the parquet floor, one and two and . . . motor-mouths yelling what to do with the right foot here, the left arm there, the hands like so. No, this Kelly would just stand there and watch what you did. Not say a damn thing until you finished. He might ask a question or two, then give an analysis, always terse and clipped, no B.S., not softened with phony accolades to make the dancer feel better.

Then, more likely than not, he would present his version of the "disaster" he had just seen. A silent rendition in front of the giant mirror, the piece presented, warts and all, crucial moves exaggerated, even burlesqued. Usually, at this point, the humbled visitor would want to pack up and leave.

But then Gene would move into a run-through with his commentary, supportive and encouraging, spurting out possible ideas with his lightning-quick movements—jetés and pirouettes, leaps, even handstands, sudden freezes of movement, whatever, embroidering and invigorating the dance that had been brought in. "Okay? Let's try it now from the top."

Again and again, he would demonstrate a move or step or tap sequence, perhaps in a slow count, in a way clear enough to be duplicated. Without any fuss or expression of personal inconvenience or concerns about the fee, he was prepared to stay all day, all night if necessary.

What the visitor didn't realize was that Gene Kelly was learning about himself, even as he was teaching. He was insatiable about watching as many dances as he could, "stealing from the best" as he absorbed new ideas for his own repertoire. And at the same time confirming something critically important to his self-esteem as a dancer, and certainly as a choreographer: *I'm better than they are!*

True, his thickset, square-shouldered body was not shaped in the balletic mode. In any case, he had started too late in the pursuit of a career in classical dance. But he sensed he was now onto something much more important: the integration of ballet, tap, modern dance into a fresh American idiom, buoyed by the work of popular composers like Jerome Kern, George Gershwin, Cole Porter, and Irving Berlin.

He would even generate some ideas with the kids at Beth Shalom, refining the numbers as he resumed his work with the Pittsburgh Playhouse and the University of Pittsburgh's annual Cap and Gown show. He directed and choreographed one musical show after another, often plugging his brother and sister into the cast, or taking on a starring role himself.

Local critics applauded. The people of Pittsburgh caught on to the pleasures of the well-staged musical. They hired babysitters and came in droves and enrolled their children in the Gene Kelly Studio of Dance. But for him, so insatiable for making a real imprint in the big-time, impatient for fame, it was still Pittsburgh, the provinces, not New York. He was pleased when an important Broadway choreographer, Robert Alton, came backstage at the Playhouse one night after a performance. Alton was a generous sort who had the character to appreciate the work of others and talk about it. He and Gene became friends and would stay in contact over the next years with frequent chats on the phone. The conversations followed the same pattern. Gene would report on what he was doing and Alton would always end forcefully with the conclusion that if anybody was "ready for Broadway" he was Gene Kelly.

But he stayed where he was, cosseted by a warm and loving family, rooted in a rhythm of productivity he was loath to give up. Suddenly the year was over, and 1934, too, went by in a flash.

He had a busy and varied social life. There was no problem in finding women anxious to please him, dance with him, or sleep with him, but the one-night stand was the usual experience. He was bored very easily. Beauty without brains had no appeal. He treated a new girlfriend as though he were directing her in a show. When the run of performances was over, he would close off the relationship. He tended to think the problem was the lack of intellectual parity. He encountered very few strong-minded, independent females in his line of work. It was always "whatever you say, Gene." There always seemed to be other priorities.

Of course, the inevitable show business rebuffs to him personally would periodically surface to shake him up and make him hesitate about leaving Pittsburgh, question his readiness for the career path Bob Alton had laid out. One particular setback jarred him hard. In the summer of 1935, he joined his family on a visit to relatives in southern California. While in Los Angeles, Gene did a screen test at RKO Pictures for an executive who had previously stopped in to see him in Pittsburgh.

When a run-through in front of a camera to check him out as a possible song-and-dance man had been proposed, Gene had no intention of participating in such a screen test. Acting was a different profession—he was a dancer, period. It would be like marking how Babe Ruth threw a forward pass or how Red Grange did at hockey. But then he made the mistake of telling Harriet about the test. Naturally, her response was to adjust the travel schedule and insist he use their time in Los Angeles to appear at RKO for the appointment. He still did not want to go. But it was apparent his mother now relished the idea of her son as a movie star—not quite a Supreme Court justice, but a worthy career.

The screen test was the ultimate "downer." As soon as the exaggerated makeup was applied, Gene felt he was in the running for a part in a Three Stooges short. The self-proclaimed director, younger than Gene, should have been directing traffic on Wilshire Boulevard. The session was brief, perfunctory, dismissive. A few lines spoken to the camera and out the door. Someone introduced him to Frederic March, which was the high point of his visit to RKO, but it did not salvage the day.

Back in Pittsburgh, he picked up on his daily routine. The blessing was that he no longer had to scrounge for money. His parents still controlled the dance studio accounts, and Harriet doled out allowances to the children. Louise and Fred, the two youngest, who had both graduated from college by now, worked at the family business with Gene and their parents. Jay, Gene's older sister, after one trial stint as a chorus girl with a traveling revue, had become a full-time public school teacher. Jim, the oldest, was now a commercial artist, no longer living in Pittsburgh.

By now Gene had developed a first-rate staff of committed dance teachers. He was no longer forced to break off what he was doing and dash to another appointment to give a one-on-one or one-on-twenty lesson. No last-minute drives over the mountain road to Johnstown, no working the "cloops" with his kid brother—he had left those harried days and nights behind. He would read and write and manage, build up the family business with clever promotional and publicity ideas, lay out advertisements, review Variety and the other trade papers for what was coming to Broadway, and cast himself to sing and dance in the local musicals. He made a point, though, of continuing to teach and demonstrate steps to visiting dance "gypsies" and children on the dance floor for the first time. (They were the ones he enjoyed most of all.)

Except when he would enter one of the rehearsal rooms at dawn or after shooing out the last student at night and locking the door, for then he had the luxury of working on himself. And on something new. Always the appeal was trying something he had never done before, working through the long lone hours and just letting go, maybe laying down a shuffle, then working the floor with the tap-dancer's metal, finding his way toward a fresh, workable routine. The huge mirror might reflect his closing out the session with swooping ballet moves, then witness an abrupt segue to a blistering gallopade, a cakewalk or a Charleston, maybe a lively rigadoon, first the man's, then the woman's part, or the "poor man's two-step" from the Louisiana bayous taught to him by a nameless black youngster who had appeared one day and never come back. At times, especially when it was very late, awash in his own sweat, he felt that his very nerve ends were all following his feet. Then it was time to stop.

There were times when he felt Pittsburgh was played out and he left town for a dancer's holiday in Chicago. He would always head for a place on the South Side. An African-American dancer had first put him on to the Snake Pit, a rehearsal hall where some wiseguy would invariably call out on spotting him: "Hey, anybody here seen Kelly?" Welcoming laughter would come from all sides. Dirty and seedy, the Snake Pit took up the entire floor of a tenement, perhaps fifty feet wide, seventy feet long, segmented and rented out as rehearsal alcoves. A doorless cubicle could be rented for a dollar. It was two dollars when a pianist accompanist was provided. One could even dispense with the pianist and bring in a radio. Or even a friend who just hummed. They had all come through the Depression and knew how few and far between paying gigs still were. The manager pretended not to see what was going on. He was sympathetic. He knew show business could be no business.

A huge number of young black dancers practiced at one time, learning and stealing from each other. There was no shutting out the barrage of taps coming from all sides. It gave Gene a headache but he felt at home here. Some lithe teenager, his T-shirt sodden against skin as dark as anthracite, might approach. They would slap hands. He would show Gene a step, maybe offer a few garbled instructions through the din that Gene couldn't possibly hear. It didn't matter; he got it. Bob Alton had told Gene often enough that he was a "mimetic dancer"—one of those rare ones who can master a new routine after a single demonstration.

As a thank-you, in pantomime he would invite his young dance donor out for a Schlitz. Together they would cross the rehearsal hall, paying only casual attention to the soloists in the cubicles who were preparing a performance, committed or imaginary: a harvest of supporting acts, Number Ones on the vaudeville bills when the seats were still mostly empty, when the audience was lined up for Coke and pop-corn and pissing before the show.

There might be a magician, a juggler, a belly-dancer, a snake charmer, a weight-lifter. Whatever. Whoever. Sometimes a coach or a manager or a relative, maybe just a kibitzer with a radio or phonograph was crammed into the tiny space, augmenting the spew of taps with static-flecked music. It was awful. But for Gene it was as good as it gets; he always sucked in the atmosphere as though using a straw.

By 1935 the two branches—others had not panned out—of the Gene Kelly Studio of Dance had 350 paying pupils. The Kelly standard of living—despite Harriet's cautious hand on the throttle of their spending—rose accordingly. New furnishings made the home more comfortable. Labor-saving devices previously unknown to Harriet now made her life easier. The old Chevrolet was traded in for a new family car. Soon the driveway at Kensington was filled with each Kelly child the proud owner of a first automobile—bought secondhand by Harriet after extensive negotiations with the dealer.

Gene couldn't understand why she was still so tight-fisted. Hollywood movie musicals were helping the dance studio business more than ever. Warner Brothers had put out *42nd Street*, a resounding hit. Secretaries and shopgirls identified with the sweet and innocent Ruby Keeler as she was propelled by Warner Baxter onto the stage and to stardom. Countless dancing feet headed for the real 42nd Street by way of hundreds of training centers across the country like the Kelly Studio.

What the rags-to-riches rise of Ruby Keeler didn't do, Astaire and Rogers did. Their *Flying Down to Rio* was the rage. It seemed everybody now wanted to glide glamorously across the ballroom floor. From the poor to the wealthy, at every socioeconomic level, millions of dollars in fees were extracted from ambitious parents speculating on dance careers for their children.

Wall Street was not slow to see the prospects. Investment bankers contacted Harriet, offering to finance expansion of the Kelly Studio from coast to coast. "Going national" was a heady and tempting idea. Harriet had tried once to set up a branch in Ebensburg, like Johnstown a hardscrabble Pennsylvania town not very far away. The venture had failed miserably. No boys would attend in the football-mad community. Spreading out for success had its pitfalls; without Gene Kelly's presence failure was possible. Wary of losing control and suspicious of the stock promoters and their unctuous, promissory ways, Harriet decided that if the business would grow it would do so slowly, as a family operation.

She and Gene did decide to move the Pittsburgh studio to a two-story building that could accommodate the rising tide of students. They hired a construction company to renovate the place. On the first floor there would be a large office where James Kelly, supported by a hard-working staff, would take over the administrative responsibilities. The entire second floor was devoted to tap, ballet, and ballroom dance classes.

Harriet felt she could slow down now that an efficient organization was in place. The Johnstown studio was doing even better than Pittsburgh's—fittingly so, for Kelly was a revered name there. In the 1850s a local man named William Kelly had developed a new method of making steel similar to the Bessemer process, rescuing the area from becoming a worn-out, worked-out mining town. William Kelly was no relation, but he was a Kelly and, accordingly, Harriet felt an emotional connection to Johnstown. It was as though God (and not her brother Gus) had chosen the locale for the second Gene Kelly Studio.

Her faith was to be badly shaken in 1936: A second great flood (the first, in 1899, occurred when the dam of the South Fork reservoir burst during torrential rains, causing more than 2,000 deaths) swept over the misbegotten community, taking twenty-five lives and causing over 40 million dollars' worth of damages. The Kellys suspended classes and turned both studios and even their Kensington house into emergency hostels for the families of pupils whose houses were washed away. The second Johnstown flood struck so unexpectedly that in a strange and apt way it was like a watershed in Gene's thinking. A misfortune—call it bad luck or happenstance—could suddenly rise up and strike one down—no reason, no logic; the flood confirmed the utter unpredictability of life. It reminded him starkly that there was no guarantee he could gradually rise in show business and achieve his ambitions. Time was not necessarily on his side.

Absurdly, at the age of twenty-four he was leaving behind his best dancing years. What to do? He knew he had to go to New York and enter the meat-market atmosphere of casting sessions and auditions. But still he stayed in Pittsburgh— a reluctance to leave that his boyhood crony Doc Steinberg simply didn't understand.

On the nights when Gene's schedule allowed it, the two of them would meet at Bakey's, a former speakeasy legitimized into a neighborhood bar. Gene had a fondness for beer, but he was a careful drinker, rationing himself, Steinberg believed, because of his father's alcoholism. Once in a while Steinberg could persuade Gene to share the specialty of the place, the owner's home brew (a product perfected during Prohibition years), at twenty-five cents a bottle. Gene then would look for someone who spoke French, usually with no success, but after a few more drinks he would try his rough gesture-supported Italian on the immigrant steelworkers bellied up to the bar. The two of them, Steinberg and Kelly, would often stay until closing time and leave Bakey's to walk the dark blocks to home, when Gene would pick up his habit of suddenly throwing out his arms for a series of pirouettes, singing the lyrics to a popular song as he launched himself off the sidewalk, not at all inhibited—as Steinberg was—by the suspicious looks of other midnight pedestrians and the fury of car drivers.

Despite all their conversations over the years, ranging freely from sports to politics to religion to movies to careers, back and forth, never once in Steinberg's recollection did Gene ever mention the possibility of a professional life as a dancer and choreographer. Said Steinberg, "It was something he kept absolutely secret. At least from me, he did. There was something very private and secretive about Gene. He didn't have many close friends—only acquaintances."

Yet, as always, the relationship was fascinating to Steinberg. He enjoyed the thrust of Gene's mind, the energetic interest in an ever-widening spectrum of subjects. He admired Gene's even temper as a Roosevelt man, "a working-class democrat" who saw some redeeming qualities in Herbert Hoover. Gene was verbal and articulate when he wanted to be, a natural persuader. But in a flash he could lose his temper at some slight and was ready to duke it out with his fists.

Steinberg always doubled over with laughter at Gene's use of Yiddishisms, a special vocabulary augmented by his stints at Beth Shalom. "Schmuck!" would be Gene's characterization of a competing dance teacher in Johnstown and when Gene said somebody had "chutzpah" it was high praise, indeed.

At the time, Steinberg later recalled, Gene was not particularly fond of going to a movie or flirting with the many girls who found him something of a local celebrity as a handsome singer–dancer. Offstage, what he enjoyed most, it seemed, was observing people: at the studios, in the gym where he worked out, at Bakey's, at church.

Steinberg wondered about his religious fervor: "He claimed he was an agnostic. But sometimes he'd leave Bakey's to go to Mass. When he had the Chevy, he'd then come back and drive me home."

Gene Kelly's apparent lack of interest in women, especially when related to his line of work, teaching and dancing—not exactly considered masculine activities in football-obsessed western Pennsylvania—led to rumors that he was homosexual. Miners and steelworkers expected every young man blessed with college opportunities to try out for such powerhouse squads as Pitt or Penn State, or at least to play for such local institutions as Slippery Rock College or Geneva College, in nearby Beaver Falls.

Gene had not lettered in football and gave no sign that he cared how people looked at him. When the wisecracks came and the innuendos turned ugly, Steinberg would always admire his friend's self-control. Gene would face the accuser, his body language immediately telling him to watch his language or pay the price. At Bakey's the men at the bar had witnessed his quick fists more than once. Gene would then joke that he never forgot the teachings of the old ring champion, Harry Greb. People might look at him funny but from then on they would do so behind his back.

Gene's ties to his family were incredibly close, Steinberg thought. But there were moments when a mischievous irreverence took over. Steinberg remembered Gene joking during a drive that all the Kellys were musically talented, dead-panning that his father could even play a song "through his rear end. It's the only musical instrument he can play."

Never would Gene say anything even remotely impertinent about his mother, who by this time, four years after his abandonment of law school, was wondering when she would welcome a nice Irish Catholic girl into the house as Gene's fiancée. Her hopes rose while Gene was producing and directing the latest of his annual Pittsburgh Playhouse revues. Gossip reached her that her son, surely the prime catch of Pittsburgh, was seeing an attractive young dancer in the cast after rehearsals. The thrilled mother set about to discover more about her Gene's choice. All she knew was that the name of the fortunate girl was Helene Marlowe.

Gene, true to form, said nothing about the relationship. Harriet was much too smart to confront her son with questions about the Marlowes, where they came from, what parochial school Helene had attended. No clues, nothing—and weeks went by with Harriet on tenterhooks until the morning when a neighbor came over with some definitive news.

It was not what Harriet Kelly had hoped for. Helene Marlowe was of Russian-Jewish background, which was bad enough. Worse, the Marlowes wanted nothing to do with the Kellys. For their Helene, a strong-minded and ambitious student of modern dance, they wanted a Jewish boy. An attorney or a doctor or a businessman might be suitable. But not an Irish dropout from law school!

To Harriet, a devotee of the trade paper *Variety*, this was the long-running Broadway comedy *Abie's Irish Rose* in reverse, but she was not amused. She had always been easygoing about Gene's friends, his leftist political positions, his missing Mass with occasional diatribes against the clergy. But for the Marlowes not to appreciate the unique quality and value of her Gene—enough!

Gene still had nothing to say about Helene, who was the first to resist his tendency to treat girlfriends as children. Introspective as always, he knew he had a tendency to take over relationships, to insist on primacy, to be the director telling the wannabe what to do. Helene would brook no patronizing. She came across as an original who had ideas and was not fearful about asserting them.

Some nights, after the curtain came down at the Playhouse, they would take supper together and Helene would come with him to the deserted studio. They had a common interest in modern dance, but not her work; no, it was always dance by his definition, done to the tune of popular composers such as Gershwin—no Stravinsky. What involved him had to be done in a new and exciting way that was accessible to the general public. He talked about his work with a passion she found thrilling in a way no other man's avowals had ever affected her.

Impulsively, she suggested they go to New York together. And when he held back she was hurt despite her toughness, and through her disappointment she pushed on: Was it fear of failure that kept him in Pittsburgh?

It was impossible for him to respond. Their relationship spiraled down until she went to New York alone to study modern dance with Martha Graham, Charles Weidman, and Doris Humphrey. There were letters, but he was never able to express any sort of commitment to her. Gradually Helene showed signs of giving up on him as he continued his full program.

Harriet was glad Helene had moved out of Gene's life, but she still worried about him. How many more Pittsburgh Playhouse musicals could her son do? Was there a world beyond the Beth Shalom Synagogue? There was the reality that Gene Kelly had reached a plateau. She wished she had some influential contacts to jump-start his career, more trustworthy than the local theatrical agents, always so full of talk and promise but empty-handed when it came to real opportunities. Gene would laugh if he knew she was again saying prayers for him at Mass.

Then—by her lights surely in response to her pleading with the Almighty—in the summer of 1937 Gene received an offer to choreograph a specialty number in a new Broadway revue. It was only a two-minute piece, not the whole show, and he was tempted to turn it down. Harriet, no longer feeling threatened by the Helene Marlowe possibility, persuaded Gene to accept the offer. Her son now seemed to be drifting in a sea of passivity that, in a frightening way, reminded her of her husband when he lost his salesman's brio. It was a condition she could not bear in anyone she loved, and she advanced him $200. He took the next train to New York.

On the first day of the casting call, Gene was informed in a casual matter-of-fact way, with no attempt at apologies or excuses, that there had been a misunder-standing. He would not be choreographing a number in the show. His duties were simply to dance as one of the boys in the chorus.

Gene protested. But the very idea that a choreographer, from Pittsburgh no less, would be imported for one number—the producer snorted that bizarre possibility away with the ash from his long cigar. Gene had to hold back from mashing the cheroot into the man's face. He stormed out of the theater, wanting to hit some-body. He wanted to call Helene Marlowe, but he took the next train home.

While he had been away, Harriet had taken a phone call for him from the head of the Pittsburgh Playhouse about Gene's next directing assignment. When her son appeared so soon at the door of the Kensington house, she knew at once the New

York offer had fallen through. Tirelessly upbeat, she spoke first in a rush to submerge whatever he had to say with good news: The upcoming Playhouse offering would be a fresh new production, what Gene had always wanted. Not a revival of some Broadway oldie.

"It's an original revue called *Hold Your Hats!*" she said.

He was too full of disappointment to respond and could only burst into an angry description of the fiasco in New York.

"Don't be upset, Gene," Harriet said. "Your chance will come."

"Don't hold your breath! Or your hats!"

He was surprised when she laughed—it was, after all, not much of a joke—but it helped to jolt Gene out of his depression. He was to work very hard on *Hold Your Hats!* He choreographed the dance numbers and the local producers insisted he star in the show. When it opened in April of 1938, he played in six of the comedy sketches, sang, and danced, and the evening was an unprecedented success. The critics in the Pittsburgh papers were ecstatic.

Bob Alton called and congratulated him. "Now you've got to pull it off in New York City. You showed what you can do with *Hold Your Hats!*"

And Harriet said with a wicked smile: "Maybe I can stop holding my breath?" And they laughed and hugged. "Okay," he finally said. "I think I'll go."

He was up early the morning of his departure, and after breakfast, when he had packed his one suitcase—he always believed in traveling light—she accompanied him to the railroad station. She gave him the usual $200 and the Pennsylvania Railroad ticket envelope.

He kissed her goodbye, promised to call, and got on the train. When the conductor came through, he opened the envelope. What he expected was not there. He found a one-way ticket to New York. It was much more expensive to travel that way. It was a message from his mother that he understood.

He blinks hard, a finger brushes across his cheekbone. He closes and opens his eyes, shakes his head slowly—a good bit of lost-in-thought business for a good TV cut-in as he watches Shirley introduce each of his partners from the film collage—except for Judy, of course.

Here is Cyd Charisse, here Debbie. There's Vera-Ellen. To the side is Leslie Caron, flown in from Paris for the occasion. Each, in turn, stands, turns toward him, blows a wristy kiss. Which he returns. Each is gowned exuberantly, the last word in Hollywood fashion, le dernier cri. Caron, his favorite, his discovery, remains standing for a moment. There is love in that look, he feels it, and, not for the first time this evening, he gives the thumbs-up signal and blows another kiss and mouths: "Merci bien, ma chère. . . ." All choked up, he cannot say more through the applause. Anyway, she can't possibly hear him, but it is somehow bolstering to speak French, reminding him of those frantic, funny days in Paris, his happiest professional times.

He warns himself to stop drifting off. He has already missed Shirley's introduction of Gregory Hines, whom he now sees onstage. While the applause plays out, Hines dances a little tap riff. Nothing fancy or acrobatic, nothing to show him up or certify that the dazzling days of the guest of honor are behind him. Black dancers never push the envelope unless they have to. Less is more, that's their dance mantra.

He has learned so much from them. Bill Robinson, of course. Buck and Bubbles. Bunny Briggs, Pops and Louis, the Chocolateers—and then the brother acts, the Hines kids, Maurice and Gregory, the Nicholas Brothers, who are here tonight, and—but he snaps to as Gregory starts to talk.

"A couple of years ago," Hines is saying, "a great thing happened. I created a step. I felt real good about it. A couple of months went by. One night I was looking at TV, seeing Take Me Out to the Ball Game. *And it was amazing, Gene! Funny thing! Somehow, you copied my step, thirty years before I did it!"*

As the laughter subsides, he goes on: "I want to thank you from here—" Gregory points to his shoes "—and from here." He points to his heart, and then walks off the stage.

The Nicholas Brothers, Harold and Fayard, now come on. Frail and dignified in crisp tuxedos, taking turns, they praise him for The Pirate, *in 1948. Going to bat for them with the MGM front office, insisting on a dance number for the three of them. Together. The brothers have the good taste not to make a big deal that it was the first time on the screen that a white joined black hoofers in the same routine. Old-timers in the audience must know that* The Pirate *lost some bookings in the South. Some theaters actually cut them out of the release print.*

"And here's a message for Gregory Hines," is Fayard's closer. "Don't fret about that new step that Gene copied from you thirty years ago. Gene done stole it from us!" The audience really lets go this time, a delighted bellow that churns into applause, mirrored by the grins of the elegant, coppery-faced old men.

In a way so at peace with themselves, a way always hard for him to attain, they are allowing the heartfelt compliment to ricochet back and forth along with the very best advice in show business: "Only steal from the best."

NEW YORK, 1938

* * *

He had planned his arrival to coincide with the summer auditions, as Broadway productions were being prepared for the 1938-1939 season. The temperature was well into the nineties. Never one to underplay the dramatic arc of his life, he made a mental note to remember the date when he left the railroad station. It was August 5, a scalding, humid afternoon.

Disdaining a taxi, he walked to the 44th Street Hotel, between Sixth and Seventh Avenues, advertised in *Variety* as an "inexpensive theatrical residence." The place, he had been told, catered to Broadway dancers. He thought it would be a good place to pick up leads on what new musical shows were in the pipeline.

The first thing he did after unpacking—it took him all of two minutes—was to check the *Times* listing of current Broadway shows. Very few were still running. The flops, the weak entertainments kept alive by promotions and half-price ticket offers, had sputtered out. The more durable summer holdouts from the season just ended were wending their own stubborn way toward extinction: Robert Sherwood's *Abe Lincoln in Illinois*, at the Plymouth Theatre, *Knickerbocker Holiday*, starring Walter Huston, at the Ethel Barrymore, and the wild and waggish *Hellzapoppin'*, at the Winter Garden. Nothing for him in the current crop.

He was not surprised. Bob Alton had briefed him well. Summer tourists from out of town constituted the bulk of the audience. New Yorkers who could afford the theater could also afford to escape the heat in Connecticut and on Long Island beaches, building up formidable suntans for the social schedule resuming in September.

The first dividend of his choice of hotels was a notice in the lobby about open casting for a new revue called *Sing Out the News*, with music and lyrics by Harold Rome. Gene had read about Rome's previous success with *Pins and Needles*, a satirical revue financed by the Ladies Garment Workers Union. The pro-labor bias of the show, as it danced and sang its way through a musical cartoon of capitalist buffoonery, fit comfortably with Gene's leftist politics. He resolved to try for Rome's new production. The audition was to take place the following morning, a Saturday.

He was keyed up and took a walk through the steamy city, intending to relax at one of the new air-cooled movie houses. On the way he had a sudden urge to phone Helene Marlowe. She was home and delighted he was in town. She made it clear he could have stayed with her and saved the hotel charges. It was the kind of decisive action she tended to propose.

He admired her spirit, but ultimately, her strength and certainty made him uncomfortable. During the separation he had brooded about their relationship. He was not proud of his behavior with Helene. It was in many ways childish, selfish. But he had come to rationalize his attitude as inevitable for a choreographer who spent days and nights telling attractive young females how and when to move. He simply felt more comfortable with a woman when he was the decision-maker. Not a laudable attribute, but at least it served to slow down his obsessive thinking about Helene.

There was also a pile-up of reasons warning him away from an "entanglement" with her, or anybody, for that matter. He wanted to keep his priorities straight. New York was expensive. It seemed his $200 stake was melting with every moment. Dating—even though Helene was a good sport about going "dutch"—would decimate his meager funds. He passed up the movie and ate a lone supper in the self-service Automat and went to bed early. He found it hard to fall asleep.

In the morning, his gloomy mood persisted as he crossed Times Square on his way to the audition. At Alton's suggestion he wore a T-shirt and slacks under a blazer and carried his best pair of tap loafers. He was struck by the enormity of the entertainment area extending south to 42nd Street. The giant crossroads was astir with traffic. It was difficult to work one's way through to the other side. The size and number of advertising signs and, even on the weekend, crowds on the move, searching for fun—here was a city, while Pittsburgh was a town, he reminded himself. He had been a big fish in a small pond. He rounded the corner and saw the long lines staked out in front of the rehearsal hall.

There must have been 300 dancers waiting for the doors to open. He was relieved that most of them were young women in leggings and leotards. Still there were far too many men for the few vacancies in what, after all, had been ballyhooed as "an intimate revue." These were the hoofers, the dance gypsies, clogging the sidewalk, each a freelancer anxiously awaiting a turn to do a quick series of tap and jazz steps that might mean coming off the unemployment listings for a while.

After an hour's wait on the sidewalk, in classic cattle-call fashion, they were herded into a rehearsal room in groups of twenty. As far as Gene could make out, he would be in the third or fourth group. He wished he had brought along something to read. There was some joking among dancers who knew each other, but nobody spoke to Gene. An hour passed . . . another hour. The morning sun came over the skyscrapers and the dancers who were still outside pressed against the building wall to benefit from the shade. Finally it was time for Gene's group.

A flamboyantly gay middle-aged man in a LaCoste shirt and tennis shorts announced himself as "the assistant choreographer." His briefing was short, and he obviously did not welcome any questions or interruptions. Each dancer would be given one try at the routine, which was then briefly demonstrated by two more "assistant choreographers," slick girl dancers.

Fortunately for Gene, he was not one of the first to be called upon. He was wet with perspiration. The room was not air-conditioned. The audition for singers was over and there was always the dispute: singers opting for warm rooms which went easy on their throats versus dancers pulling for lower temperatures because of their physical exertions. Whatever the case in the rehearsal room, Gene's body seemed to dry off magically as he saw what the test-routine was: a snap.

It was a simple buck and wing, which he had done long before the first pimple broke out on his face. He made sure, checking it out as the two dancers tapped away. Yes, his buck and wing. First his time step, then a triple wing, then back slides and then forward slides off. One full chorus, eight bars each: eight of his time step, eight of his wings, eight of his back slide, eight on his forward slide. C'est tout. French always seemed to come into his head when he felt great.

Seconds into the trial performance of the first chorus candidate, he felt even better. With each series of what he saw as faltering taps, his heartbeat was invigorated; it was as though a stone on his chest had slid away. But he reserved judgment until he watched some more applicants. With the rush of euphoria that was always there when competing—and winning—he rendered judgment: Amateur night, for chrissakes, bumbling hoofers trying to break through at a Pittsburgh "cloop"!

These hopefuls were not remotely in his class. Their routines were unsure, whatever personal touch they applied was banal. Why, a Beth Shalom bar-mitzvah boy could do better (okay, he checked himself, that is pushing it). These boys and girls could do with some time at the Gene Kelly Studio of Dance!

He was next. Nobody—nobody white, anyway—could pick up a short routine and play it back after just one look as he could. The hardest thing to do was to suppress his chuckle, his sense that this test was preposterously easy, and fight off the wish to show his confidence in a way that could annoy the assistant choreographer—in the event, always a possibility, that *Sing Out the News* would be going the gay route for the chorus boy contingent.

Not rushing the routine, watching the body language so his muscular style was underplayed, careful not to smile too enticingly at the two girl demonstrators, he did his version, first cloning their performances accurately before swinging into his own stuff, speeding up the count just a tad. He couldn't resist embroidering a few leaps, jumps, pirouettes into what he did; he would have done a hand-walk across the room but thought better of it.

"Thank you for entertaining us, sir," said the fellow in the LaCoste shirt, tugging up his tennis shorts as one of the two demonstrators applauded. Gene was concerned he had showboated too much, but he was asked to "wait around" and was not called upon to do any more dancing while the first cuts were made.

The unaccepted—drooping and dejected boys and girls—finally cleared out. The rehearsal rooms were suddenly brighter, as if a fresh coat of paint had been applied to the walls. A well-dressed man stepped up to Gene—one of the producers, Gene guessed—and told him effusively he would have "a feature spot" in the show.

At the end of the afternoon, it was confirmed he was one of the fortunate call-backs. Early Monday morning when he arrived, a desk had been set up in the rehearsal room and behind it sat yesterday's assistant choreographer in a gray business suit. He was all business.

"Kelly, your salary'll be thirty-five dollars a week."

"Thirty-five dollars?"

"That's the going chorus rate, dear heart."

It was ironic, he thought, that the producers of a left-wing revue like *Pins and Needles* should take on the classic capitalist role in their next venture. This . . . (he held back the adjective, gay-bashing not being his thing) *tennis-playing* "assistant choreographer" acted as though Gene was receiving a favor from on high. Where was the ebullient producer of yesterday and his feature spot? After all, he was the Gene Kelly who had built up a successful entrepreneurial career, a college graduate who had even been (admittedly for a short time) to law school—and here he was, being treated like some adolescent who should burst into tears for the opportunity of being on stage.

So Gene took a deep breath, coughed, and said words to that effect, but milder, and asked for seventy-five dollars. He was a business man. They would soon compromise to fifty dollars. Maybe he could even get sixty. "Goodbye, Mr. Kelly," was the response.

Now the nightmare darkened the moment for him: another failure on Broadway. Another somber ride back to Pittsburgh. He imagined the face of his mother as she opened the door. But, as he was to say later, a principle was involved. "I wasn't going to accept the same salary a chorus girl was getting for wriggling her arse when I was doing a helluva lot more in the show. They wanted to exploit me. But I wasn't going to have it."

It was a very long week. He resolved to see Robert Alton, the choreographer who had recommended he try his luck in New York. He caught up with Alton at the Imperial Theater, on 45th Street, rehearsing a group of dancers for a new musical comedy by Cole Porter called *Leave It to Me*. The show was already cast. There was no spot for Gene.

At a break Alton heard Gene out and immediately concluded he was too angry, too Irish to represent himself. Sitting not very far away was his own agent, a man named Johnny Darrow. Alton made the introductions.

Darrow trusted Alton totally and was so impressed by the dance director's assessment of Gene's talents and potential that he agreed to take Gene on. He watched Gene engage in gossip with the chorus boys and girls and was struck by his trim, athletic build and handsome matinee-idol profile. And Alton's imprimatur was icing on the cake.

Darrow and Gene walked out of the Imperial together, one measuring the other. Darrow did not speak, and Gene was conscious that Darrow was eyeing him carefully, looking him up and down. That height thing again, he thought.

"Look, Gene," said Darrow. "If I'm to represent you, the first thing I'd like you to do right away. . . ." His voice trailed off.

"And what's that?" Gene said guardedly. Perhaps Darrow had some special shoes in mind, orthopedic lifts he had seen advertised in trade papers. Murderous on a dancer's feet! Next, he could hardly believe what he was hearing from Darrow.

"Gene—that's a girl's name. First thing I want is for you to change your name."

"To what?"

"To anything," was the response. "How about Frank Black?"

Just the thought of a return to Pittsburgh, his sensitive mother thinking there was some shame in the name Kelly, some anti-Catholic stigma. He took a deep breath.

"No," he said finally. "Gene Kelly. That's good enough."

And that was enough for Darrow, who pointed up at the marquee of the theater they were walking past. Gene remembered the thrill of seeing "KELLY" when they played the Altoona gig with Cab Calloway's band. "I think I can arrange an audition for you with the Shubert Brothers."

Darrow came through for him, and an audition was arranged with the Shuberts' dance director. It took only a few minutes.

"We'll be in touch with Darrow. I like what I see."

"Well, thanks," said Gene.

"We don't want any swishing with our boys."

A beat or two went by before he could respond: "Whatever you say."

With just a few days in New York he was coming to understand the drill concerning gay hoofers. More often than not, being gay was considered something that came naturally with a dancing talent. The chorus lines usually made up a happy group. The more outrageously feminine you were, the more they loved you. If people had hangups about homosexuals in the cast, that was their problem.

But with some shows, chorus boys were selected for their "butch" characteristics.

Gene hated to get a job on that basis. In this case, in spite of Darrow's representing him in negotiations with the Shuberts, it turned out that he didn't. The Shubert lawyer offered $150 a week for Gene to appear in one of their shows. Darrow, anxious to demonstrate his superiority over Gene as a negotiator, responded quickly with a demand for twice that. "Gene Kelly's a real talent," he said.

"A nobody." The reaction was brusque. "No deal."

Darrow walked out of the Shubert office, irritated with himself for having overplayed his hand. After all, $150 was a lot of money in 1938, and Gene had never been on a Broadway stage. Gene was anxious to go to work. He still had no source of income and was fending off Helene Marlowe's invitation to share her apartment. Unsure of what to say, Darrow kept responding to Gene that he hadn't heard yet from the Shuberts. One day went by, then the next. Gene was persistent about calling. He had thought the Shuberts liked his style of dancing.

Darrow finally met with his anxious client. He was concerned with Kelly's temper. He had heard this Irishman was quick to use his fists. Darrow went so far as to make a lunch appointment at a prominent restaurant and requested seating in the front area, surrounded by other patrons who would come to his aid if Kelly went berserk. He finally came out with the truth: He had done poorly with the Shuberts and the deal was dead, and he should have had the courage to tell Kelly sooner.

He was relieved when Kelly took it well and said simply that he too had over-reached in the same way. Darrow decided then and there to represent Gene Kelly with all his energy as a prime and unique show business talent—straight, and a straight-shooter, too.

Within a week Darrow persuaded Alton to look past the fact that they were friends and engage Gene for a small featured role as a "specialty dancer" in *Leave It to Me*. This time Darrow did not quibble with the producers about Gene's salary.

The Cole Porter musical opened on Broadway in November of 1938, just as the threat of war was fading in the United States and Europe. Americans breathed a collective sigh of relief as headlines welcomed Neville Chamberlain's last-minute arrangement with Hitler for "peace in our time." Porter's show was a lightweight satire about a dolt of an American ambassador, played by Victor Moore, who was sent to Russia only to keep him out of mischief in Washington.

Gene was not only a news junkie—he subscribed to and avidly read the *New York Times*—but a serious reader of quality fiction. One morning early in the run of the show he was seated in the back row of the theater working his way through Aldous Huxley's *Point Counterpoint* when Cole Porter visited a rehearsal. The composer-lyricist was in his customary wheelchair; he had been thrown from a horse while riding at the exclusive Piping Rock Club on Long Island. Ironically, the accident had laid him low while he was churning out one successful song after another. "How'm I ridin'," he had written around then. "I'm ridin' high."

Several subsequent botched operations had left Porter unable to walk. Gene did not want to stare. He was caught up in the Huxley book again when he felt a tap on his shoulder. It was Alton and, behind him, Porter, who had wheeled over to chat.

At first Gene was intimidated. He had heard the theatrical gossip that Porter was an active homosexual and was jarred by the older man's obvious interest in him and what he was reading. What did he think about Huxley? He then asked Gene whether he had been to college and what his goals were in show business. He was more like a concerned career counselor than one of the nation's famous songwriters.

Alton told him Porter had asked to be introduced to that "unusual man" who was reading a serious book and not a trade paper or "making time" with the girls as the other young men were. A few weeks later Porter invited Gene to a luxurious party in his Waldorf-Astoria penthouse. He went, enjoying his taste of the high end of New York society, the elegance and dazzle of Porter's guests. Always competitive, always measuring himself, he was pleased that he could more than hold his own in the sparkling give-and-take of what he regarded as sophisticated conversation. The probability of America's entrance into the war, FDR's performance as president, the political future of Charles Lindbergh and the America First movement—from the serious to the gossipy, the young dancer's talk was trenchant, polite, well-informed, and quick-witted, as called for.

Porter was the perfect host, and he obviously sized up Gene as that rarity among chorus boys, with no interest in homosexual dalliances or kinky sex. Porter introduced Gene to his wife, the former Linda Lee Thomas, a rich divorcee he had married during his long sojourn in Paris after the First World War. She was considerably older and looked it, a woman of strength who disciplined Porter into ferocious work habits, while serving as a cover (or "beard," as it was known in show business) for his taste in young boys, which he just as energetically pursued. Bernard Berenson, the world-renowned art critic, had written that she had perfect taste in absolutely everything—including, obviously, amusing and sophisticated second husbands.

Her real genius was in keeping up appearances over the years, or, at least, trying to. As the self-appointed gatekeeper for Cole's boyfriends, she welcomed Gene, a handsome straight dancer, as a family intimate and another of the beards who could underscore to the world outside that the Porters were a happy heterosexual couple. It was a pathetic naive notion on her part, and Gene felt sorry for her, especially because he came to see Cole's relationship with Linda as a zigzag between an in-public effusive concern for her and an in-private chilly detachment from her. Which was more contemptible, Gene could not judge, but coming from his own close-knit family background, he could not abide such cruelty to an older woman. He made no effort to pursue the relationship with Porter, even though the well-connected composer made plain he could be helpful.

Now that Gene was part of the Broadway scene, a "chorus boy" measuring at first hand the influence of homosexual creativity in musical theater, he realized he was fortunate. It was no problem for him to make peace with the gay contingent in any production. If he was going to make his way to success, there was no other choice. The best choreographers ranged from deeply closeted to openly homophobic, as Agnes de Mille was. It was something always complained of and joked about when gay hoofers were on their own: They knew Americans went to musicals to see their fantasies onstage, refracted through the sensibilities of gay choreographers and gay performers. And all that was fine—so long as everybody kept quiet about it.

So generally—he was never one to be completely satisfied—it was a good period for Gene. Unlike many others who had come to seek Broadway fame, he had found a part in a show and it wasn't just an unpaid Greenwich Village showcase, either. But it was a "nothing role," in his judgment, just set dressing. His "big moment" was when he and five other dancers appeared as Eskimos while Mary Martin, a determined young woman from Texas in a sensational debut, sang one of her recitative songs, "Siberia."

In his first Broadway show, Cole Porter's Leave It to Me (1938), Gene (center) supported the sensational debut of another star-to-be: Mary Martin. (Courtesy of Photofest)

The number that was taking the town by storm was "My Heart Belongs to Daddy," in which Porter had a field day with double-entendres. It made Martin an instant star. Gene had absolutely no idea she ever noticed him. But wherever her heart was, Martin's show business acumen was also, and years later she recalled:

> There were six boys, dancers, who had to meet me wearing Eskimo suits and we did a dance number in which there were a lot of lifts, so the boys would pick me up, sling me around, and pass me from hand-to-hand. One of these Eskimos was Gene Kelly: He was just a kid then, on his first Broadway job, but I liked him from the very first day. He was so talented, had so much drive. I've never known anybody who worked so hard perfecting his art. Of all the boys, he was the one who came into the theater to work for hours and hours and hours on the stage. From the beginning I knew he was going to be somebody very great.

So did Johnny Darrow, who was determined to find something better suited for his client than an Eskimo costume. Gene was impatient to move on. Coming in every evening to lift Mary Martin was not much of a challenge. He was embarrassed by the silly plot with its anti-Russian implications. His acquaintances tended to be writers, stage directors, and academics, members of the New York radical intelligentsia who had been in a painful confusion when World War II broke out. The Soviet Union and Nazi Germany had been temporarily allied, but now, with Hitler's invasion of Russia, their allegiance to the American mobilization was suddenly strengthened. Gene predicted to Helene Marlowe that he would soon be drafted.

He had no trouble finding girls and finding himself in bed with girls, but these were momentary diversions. Helene was serious and pressured him toward marriage so incessantly he was grateful to her parents, who continued to object to what they saw as an undignified pursuit of a gentile husband.

Throughout his life Gene tended to regard the women he encountered, well-meaning as they were, as brakes to a career that demanded movement and progress. At times even his mother, blessed as she was, joined that restive group. While he was in the Mary Martin show he was all too aware—Harriet Kelly had a gift for making him aware—that he was not meeting her expectations. She simply could not understand why New York had not recognized the incomparable brilliance of her middle son. Her pressure was no help, and he, in turn, ratcheted up the urgings on Johnny Darrow.

The agent was a personal friend of John Murray Anderson, the director who was casting a new musical revue called *One for the Money*. As Gene did not have a run-of-the-play contract in *Leave It to Me*, he was able to leave behind the Eskimo suit, much to the displeasure of Mary Martin and Vinton Freedley, the producer. Freedley took it so badly that he publicly threatened that Gene "would never work again in this business."

To Gene's proletarian way of thinking, it was again the bosses wanting to take advantage of the worker. He told Darrow to ignore Freedley. The new offer, with a salary of $115 a week, twice what he had been earning in the Porter production, made it worth the risk. Freedley was bitter about the rebuff; he was perhaps the first of what would make up a long list of influential Kelly-haters on Broadway and in Hollywood. At the time, Gene couldn't care less.

In *One for the Money*, he would be singing and dancing in eight routines. He would also have some speaking lines, his first chance at dialogue. But as he was to reminisce much later, he jumped to the new opportunity because it really *was* one for the money: "In that second show somebody gave me a line to say and I realized they'd have to pay me more to speak. And I thought, hey, this is easy."

As a workaholic for whom it was impossible to stop and smell the roses, a perfectionist who found coasting an impossibility, Gene plunged into a heavy schedule of singing lessons and rented time at a dance studio in order to spend hours more working on dance solos for himself. And during rehearsals, he never took his eyes off the director: "I learned more about staging a show from John Murray Anderson than from anybody else in the business," he said. Anderson was very secure across the spectrum of practical knowledge needed by a top-ranked director. He seemed to know the intricacies of every job, and not superficially; Gene always had the impression that, in any crunch, Anderson could get his hands dirty—rig a light, apply a brush to a flat, and perform other needed tasks. Most important to Gene was Anderson's aggressive utilization of color and his creation of mood through the deft use of lighting. He was sensitive to an actor's needs; he would step forward modestly to make one simple suggestion and turn an adequate number into a show-stopper. Gene had finally come upon his role model as a director, adhering to his lifetime working principle of "only steal from the best."

As with his prior show, his social conscience was bruised by his participation in *One for the Money*. He carped now at the Republican tinge of the production, which was distinctly not to his liking. The opening line of the revue which he, as a member of the six-person ensemble cast, was obliged to sing at every performance, put it rhythmically and bluntly: "We think that right is right and wrong is left." It made Gene feel like a traitor to the working class, an attitude bolstered by his appearance in white tie and tails in almost every scene.

Another in the sextet of performers was William Archibald, who later had an important writing career, especially with his adaptation of the Henry James story "The Turn of the Screw" for Broadway. Despite Helene Marlowe's sulking, Gene decided to room with Archibald, and the two men moved into a pleasant Greenwich Village apartment.

The ensemble nature of *One for the Money* made it difficult to garner individual recognition for work in the revue. But Gene Kelly was now clearly a full-fledged professional, an active member of Actors' Equity, the performers' union. He had made his exit from the horde of stage wannabes and was regarded and talked about as very talented, handsome, bright, and ambitious—qualities that give buoyancy to one's popularity in the theater.

He began to make interesting friends, some of them very influential. When the show went on the road during the summer and settled down for a period in Chicago, he met Guthrie McClintic and Katharine Cornell, icons of the serious American stage. When he came backstage McClintic praised Gene's performance in the show. Cornell, his wife, showed an immediate interest in Gene and insisted he take elocution lessons to get rid of what he admitted was a "flat Pittsburgh accent." He had drinks with John Barrymore and Orson Welles. At a party celebrating their production of *Romeo and Juliet*, Laurence Olivier and Vivien Leigh chatted with him. It was pleasing that he was not patronized. He was accepted and well-regarded as a working professional.

While *One for the Money* was on the road, several cast members who had dance numbers dropped out for personal reasons. Since Bob Alton had other commitments, Gene was given the assignment to coach the replacements. He was flattered that John Murray Anderson called on him. It was not only a matter of recreating Alton's choreography; since several of the road replacements were basically actors who didn't know taps from time steps, Gene had to replicate the spirit of Alton's work with simpler routines. His years of experience in Johnstown and Pittsburgh, working with much less motivated and talented individuals, helped him through what was regarded as a difficult assignment. After watching the inserted numbers, Anderson told Gene he had done very well, without compromising Alton's work. His verdict gave Gene an enormous lift. As he was to say later: "The biggest compliment, certainly up till then, was his approval of my work on *One for the Money*.

I didn't know it at the time, but it was to lead directly to my first solo credit on Broadway as a dance director."

Now he was certain his career was gaining momentum. Even with the customary rebuffs of his calling—auditions with no callbacks, telephone messages unreturned, dangling promises that were forgotten, imposing projects to feature him that could not secure financing, and outright lies—he felt relatively serene. No question, he was going forward. The wind was at his back.

For the first time as an adult he felt he could afford to take a vacation. When *One for the Money* closed in Chicago, in June of 1939, Gene and Bill Archibald motored to Orr's Island in Maine and rented a weatherbeaten cottage by the sea. He and Archibald relaxed and ate lobster and mackerel and fish stew. There was absolutely nothing to do but loaf in the sun or, when he felt particularly daring, clamber up the rocky cliffs and dive into the icy water.

Gene being Gene, though, the sight of Archibald at his typewriter, pecking away for several hours a day, was a challenge. He thought it would be a perfect time to try his hand at writing a play. The work went smoothly at first. He made it to midpoint of the second act within a few days. Then, for no reason he could define, his progress stalled. The idea of the play, the flow of plot, suddenly seemed derivative, corny. He put the work aside and started a comedy, "a very sophisticated S.N. Behrman sort of thing"—but the curtain line on this writing project eluded him also. He surrendered after one act. Staring at a blank sheet of paper which remained virginally white for an hour, two hours, was torture. Writing was just too damned sedentary, leaving him with distracting energy to burn off. Writing was a lonely profession and he—so went his rationalization—was a "people-person." He needed a partner. Archibald and Kelly, or, rather, Kelly and Archibald—why not? He admired the work of George S. Kaufman and Moss Hart and other writing teams. Archibald, however, had no interest in collaborating.

The lazy Maine days became a trial for Gene. He told Archibald he had swallowed enough mackerel to last him a lifetime and wanted to get back to work. They went back to New York and went their separate ways, leaving Gene with the task of finding a substitute roommate.

The return from Maine was marked by two pieces of rather good news. The pupil enrollment in the two Gene Kelly studios was well past the 500 mark, Harriet reported. And Johnny Darrow had made plans with a major-league player on Broadway, the Theater Guild, for Gene to choreograph the summer season at the Westport Country Playhouse, in Connecticut, a well-known venue for trying out new material prior to Broadway. Westport was a manicured-lawn, upscale town with an active social life, and a young man unburdened by wife or companion could do very well with the ladies.

As it turned out, he was assigned one frantic project after another, and there was little time for parties and romantic adventures. The variety of tasks thrown at him affected his confidence, as he quickly realized working for the prestigious Theater Guild that there were very few aspects of show business he couldn't handle. He vowed to himself that by the end of the summer of 1939 there would be none.

His first assignment was to prepare the choreography for Eugene O'Neill's *The Emperor Jones*, starring Paul Robeson. Gene was handed the score of the organ accompaniment written especially for the production by the composer (and author) Paul Bowles. He had only a few days to design the dances and direct an all-black company from Harlem. His work was applauded as fresh, striking, and highly charged in a way to accent the exotic mystery of the play.

Robeson was very impressed. He quickly recognized the effective way this young man, unknown to him, directed a group of African-American dancers not disposed to go all-out for a white choreographer. For his part, it was a thrill for Gene to work with Robeson, not only for the magnificence of that mighty bass-baritone, but for the imposing actor's bravado: Robeson, an articulate Rutgers graduate, was outspoken in his political opinions, and while these were leftward of Gene's, the thrust for both of them was to make possible a progressive and liberal society. Gene respected Robeson's disdain for any attempt, however powerful the source, to keep black people undemanding and subservient.

Robeson's life-style was a revelation to the Irish Catholic mama's boy from Pittsburgh. Whenever he could, he watched Robeson onstage opposite Uta Hagen, the noted actress. She had already played Desdemona to Robeson's Othello, with her husband José Ferrer in the role of Iago. It was well known to the cast at Westport that Robeson and Hagen were lovers, which did not seem to bother Ferrer, as the three celebrities appeared to have settled into a comfortable *ménage à trois*.

The season at Westport accelerated Gene's immersion into the laissez-faire sexual behavior of the theatrical world. Sleeping with somebody—male-male, male-female, whatever, whomever—without intention of marriage or, at least, of pursuing a partnered life was indisputably the Westport way. Gene was one of the very few who did not partake.

It was not that he was uninterested in sex. His schedule and priorities simply did not allow time for it. He was caught up in Westport's Compo Beach build-up of excitement about the Robeson production. With every incoming tide on Long Island Sound, there seemed to be more rumors that the Theater Guild was going to open the production on Broadway in the fall.

But Robeson and Hagen never made it beyond Westport. Gene was disappointed, blaming the Guild's negative decision on a stuffy middle-class concern about the interracial liaison of the two stars. Robeson's constant pro-Russian public statements and incendiary appeals to the black population to rise up and be counted did not sit well with the general population in the turbulent wartime years.

Gene's next assignment at Westport was to choreograph a version of Lynn Riggs's *Green Grow the Lilacs* using traditional folk songs such as "Git Along, Little Doggies" and "Blood on the Saddles," as well as the title number. The production, like the Robeson one that preceded it, was a success. The decision was made to commit financial resources to the show as an ongoing project, which eventually led to the first collaboration of Richard Rodgers and Oscar Hammerstein II, *Oklahoma!*, and a Broadway run of well over 2,000 performances.

Along the way, the ballet choreographer Agnes de Mille replaced the Kelly dances. While Gene recognized enormous changes had been made in the development of the final Broadway production, he always resented that his contributions to *Oklahoma!* were never mentioned. The experience was a lesson to him. From then on he would always fight for credits and proper recognition and publicity. Anonymity, he concluded once and for all at Westport, simply doesn't pay.

His final show of the summer season had him in a performing role as emcee of a topical revue called *The Magazine Page*. The highlight of Gene's participation was a series of satires of how various dancers would negotiate an assigned routine. He developed the act, of course, from his observations of hundreds of students of all stripes and levels of talent at the Gene Kelly Studio of Dance and subsequent choreographic chores. His sketch concluded spectacularly and humorously, if illogically, with a dazzling combination of dance and acrobatics, as Gene sprang across the stage floor, bouncing on the palms of his hands.

Also on the bill was a foursome called the Revuers, an attention-getting act done by Betty Comden, Adolph Green, Alvin Hammer, and Judy Holliday that was coming off a successful run at the Village Vanguard, in New York. In Green's words, he and his cohorts were "knocked out immediately" by Kelly's performance, and a close friendship developed as the summer season wound down. Undoubtedly the coinciding of their left-wing politics clinched his relationship with Comden and Green, and they were to prove very significant to Gene's later film career.

In September, he went home to Pittsburgh. He was shocked by the aged, dried-out appearance of his father. The senior Kelly had done admirably as an in-house accountant; the dance schools, thanks to his joining forces with Harriet, were well-managed, a financial success. But in switching from swaggering traveling salesman to bent-over, green-eyeshaded bookkeeper, he had paid an emotional price. The pleasure of work had long since gone out of him, and he felt enslaved by the continuous drudgery of mastering numbers day after day.

Gene proposed that he and his dad go on a short vacation, just the two of them, Kelly father and son. It was almost a whim, but later on he considered it one of the most bountiful decisions he ever made in his life. It fit in with Gene's own desire to explore the America he had not seen. It also would serve as a way of bonding. His mother had always been in the forefront of his thoughts; now was his chance to really get to know his father. So by automobile they set out for Mexico via the Great Smokies. Without worrying about their daily destination, they followed the course of the Mississippi south via Louisiana and New Orleans and on down, across the border. It was a splendid trip in terms of what they saw and experienced together, but it was the change in their conversation that impressed Gene most of all. He was no longer just an audience for his father's baroque report about sales conquests. The fantasy was shoved aside. He probed the reality of his father's life and career. Especially the cavalier way James Sr. had been fired—the trauma of dismissal into the demoralized ranks of the unemployed.

Somehow, driving through Mexico, observing the poverty of the peasants in abject prayer at the churches, rich with gold and silver and jewels, he was sickened by the contrast. He abhorred the role of the Church in supporting the fascist Franco against the Spanish Republic. Now, seeing it firsthand, the failure of the Church, *his* church, to come to grips meaningfully with the physical and spiritual needs of the poor opened his eyes to the hypocrisy of what he called "organized religion." Feeding into his consciousness were his recent meetings with simpatico contacts who had influenced him with their outspoken attitudes—Robeson, Comden, Green, and many left-wing intellectuals.

On the return trip, long before they saw Pittsburgh looming in the distance, he made it plain to his father that he was now a complete agnostic. His father could tell Harriet or not, as he chose. But no longer would Gene Kelly be dominated by the wishes and preferences of his mother.

The time comes at every Hollywood fundraiser for the "freight," the pitch, about the worthiness of the sponsoring organization. In this case, the American Film Institute.

A handsomely gowned and well-spoken lady is at the podium, Jean Furstenburg, the head of AFI. In his judgment, she does the task very well. It is the first—and will probably be the only—serious speech of the evening. With the exception, maybe, of his own, when he will give the Closer.

Oh, how he would like to blow off steam, vent his fury at how the American film industry misused him, cheated him! But that's the way of the sore loser in Hollywood. Public complaints get you to nowheresville; flattery will get you . . . somewhere.

He has, of course, prepared a few words for his thank-you tonight. After so many Gene Kelly festivals and retrospectives across the years, after thousands (yes, thousands!) of interviews, he has it down pat. He knows what will be quoted by reporters, what anecdotes (true or invented) will draw laughs.

But he is talked out. It is, for god's sake, almost thirty-five years since Singin' in the Rain, and he has milked every drop out of the experience. He senses he is slowly sliding away from the events of the evening as his own thoughts continue to intrude. He tries to concentrate, sits up, and takes a deep breath. He curls his toes and forces himself to follow the line of Furstenburg's speech. He will do some ad-libbing when he is called up. Maybe she will say something he can pick up on.

She is talking about film as the durable art form of the twentieth century that will take us into the next millennium. Et cetera, et cetera. And he can only think of his own world, the Movie Musical. Jettisoned for good, or will it be around in 2001?

She segues neatly into how the AFI encourages new and fresh talent coming out of film schools. Et cetera, et cetera. And he can only think that those schools never existed when he was starting. He learned how to make movies on the set, thanks mostly to Judy. He learned how to cut film when he was in the Navy and the admiral assumed he knew how.

Dimly he hears Furstenburg coming out of et cetera, et cetera: "These young filmmakers are carrying on in your tradition, Gene Kelly!"

Pivoting with the audience applause she turns to him now. He is confused, snagged in his thoughts. Has he missed something? Worst of all: Is it his cue to stand up, go to the stage, do his Closer? He is already half-off the seat when, with enormous relief, he hears Furstenburg continue. She introduces the two winners of the 1985 AFI prize "for emerging talent" and a glowing pair stands up, a girl and boy about the age of his own Tim and Bridget.

Nobody notices his abortive move. He settles back into the seat again. A narrow escape. It could have been embarrassing. He remembers the Academy Award evening when poor Rosalind Russell must have dozed off and thought she had heard her name announced as the Oscar winner. She swept down the aisle to accept the award but, thankfully, someone grabbed her. Close call. But at least Rosalind, for a few magical euphoric seconds, exulted that she'd finally been awarded the Oscar she deserved.

No such luck. No such taste of a magnificent moment for him either.

NEW YORK, 1939

* * *

When he returned from Mexico, Gene was disappointed that Johnny Darrow had nothing. The agent, in turn, was irritated by his absence, which he took as a sign that Gene did not take his profession seriously enough. "Out of sight, out of mind" was Darrow's mantra, simultaneously his excuse and complaint; in show business going away with Daddy never pays off. But Gene never regretted the trip. Europe was afire with war. It was clear the United States would soon be in the thick of it, and he would be drafted. Time with those he loved was precious. Family—just the word itself resonated through him like a strong thrust of organ music—would always come first, and he was prepared to pay the price.

With the coming of autumn and the 1939–40 theater season, he was confident he could get back up to speed. He resumed the rounds of auditions. There were several callbacks but no job came through. He was not drawing any salary from the dance studios. He lived modestly with unemployment compensation his only source of money—about $15 a week.

As an economy move, he left his Greenwich Village apartment to share a small place on West 55th with Dick Dwenger, a freelance musician. Dwenger was in more precarious financial shape than Gene, and weeks came and went when he could not even pay his share of the rent. So they made a deal: Dwenger would play an out-of-tune rehearsal piano for Gene in a crumbling Masonic Hall building which Dwenger located in the Hell's Kitchen area.

The floor of what served as a rehearsal room was in fairly good shape. When not making the rounds, Gene did hour after hour of solo dance practice in his standard compulsive way. Dwenger, an affable sort who admired Gene, considered the arrangement completely open-ended. He was available at the piano on call, always cheerful and supportive. He and Gene became very close, one of the very few male friends Gene was to have. It was a relationship that had a short life, however—Dwenger's. He would be killed in action during the war.

One afternoon, taking to heart Darrow's scolding that by leaving Manhattan he had weakened his show-business contacts, Gene arranged to have a beer with the Theater Guild stage manager he had met in Westport the previous summer. Gene wanted to be invited to the Connecticut resort again for the Guild's season in 1940. After their 1939 Westport stints had been talked about and laughed about, the stage manager turned serious. He asked Gene if he knew what was going on with *The Time of Your Life*. Aside from knowing that the volatile Armenian-American writer William Saroyan had scripted the first offering of the Theater Guild's Broadway season, Gene didn't have a clue.

"Well . . ." said the stage manager, shaking his head, "the show's having problems." It was by no means an easy show to produce, he told Gene. Saroyan's work was very special, even unique. The gossip was that the playwright had dashed it off in six days. The play was set in a down-at-the-heels San Francisco waterfront tavern peopled by drifters with nowhere else to go. They bare their souls to each other in drunken monologues. The curtain comes down with the entire cast hailing as a hero a man at the bar who has just murdered a policeman. Saroyan called it "a comedy."

Eddie Dowling, the director and star, had come to the conclusion that the script was a confusing mess, a jumble of the author's opinions about social and political injustice. It was depressing, preachy. Dowling was concerned that the play would flop and wipe out the Theater Guild's investment.

For Saroyan, a man of considerable self-assurance, the play was nothing less than a masterpiece about a world suffering in the Depression barely ten years after the stock-market crash, while the planet was engulfed in war. *The Time of Your Life* was a spiritual affirmation to the playwright, showing the essential goodness of people even if pushed to the edge.

It was a creative conflict between two very strong-minded antagonists. Saroyan, the darling of the literati set, was no shrinking violet so thrilled to have a play on the boards that he would do anything and everything to please the Theater Guild. On the contrary, he wanted to take over the staging of his play from Dowling. The latter was a prominent director with a long track record, but, after a fiercely negative reaction to the tryout in New Haven, with boos and catcalls drowning out tiny spasms of applause from Saroyan admirers, he agreed to step aside for the writer to take over.

"And Gene, the first thing that mad Armenian is going to do is replace Harry the Hoofer," said the stage manager.

"Harry the what?" Gene broke in, really caught up for the first time in the traumas of the production.

The stage manager responded that in Saroyan's play Harry the Hoofer makes coherent the flow of events in the seedy bar. Harry is an out-of-work vaudeville tapman who tries to lift the spirits of everybody in the place with modest little dances. He was described by Saroyan bluntly as a "dumb young fellow whose philosophy is that the world is full of sorrow and needs laughter." The reason for the fiasco in New Haven, as Saroyan saw it, was that the actor playing the part of Harry was failing to make people laugh.

Gene was on the phone to Darrow as soon as the stage manager left. The agent was quick to call the Guild and was back to Gene in a few minutes.

"Sorry, Gene. They already considered you for Harry. Lawrence Langner turned you down. He said you were not at all the right type."

At once Gene knew the problem. Langner was the august, aristocratic head of the Theater Guild who had seen Gene's performance in *The Magazine Page*, the satiric romp with Comden and Green at Westport the previous summer. Gene had worn a tuxedo and danced and sung in a lighthearted way, playing the role of a young sophisticate.

"Can you find out when they're having the next audition for Harry?" he asked Darrow.

A few days went by. Gene read the play twice. He did not shave, and on Manhattan's Lower East Side, where secondhand clothing was bought and sold, he put together a wardrobe for himself: a coat much too large, pants much too long, everything else much too loose. The clash of colors was brutal.

On the morning of the audition, Langner and Dowling told Saroyan that a young musical performer named Ray Middleton was their candidate for Harry and should be the first actor to be looked at. About a dozen other would-be Harrys sat in the rear of the dark theater.

Saroyan, apparently determined to make peace with the jittery producers, acceded to the request. He had Middleton cross to the lip of the stage and read from the playscript. Dowling and Langner were in the front row with Saroyan taking a place just behind them. Seated in the rear, off to himself in a corner, Gene had to admit Middleton did an effective opening. But he was wearing a handsome blue suit right out of Brooks Brothers.

Gene had gone over the play very carefully, and his own attitude about the work was much more in agreement with Saroyan's. He felt Dowling's negative reaction was the typical Broadway nay-saying to anything daring, difficult, and untried.

The reading assignment handed to Middleton was a passionate speech with Harry, suddenly lucid and serious, exhorting the bums, sailors, prostitutes, cops, and assorted strays in the bar to rise up and be counted. Listening to Middleton, though, Gene felt the performer was neither making the best of the material, nor suited, literally, for the part. He hoped he was right in his judgment and not simply wishing the worst for his fellow actor, out of pique or jealousy. (It was possible; by now he knew well that competition always seethed in his blood.) Middleton's voice was somewhat thin, he thought, unable to handle the moments when Harry must yell passionately to arouse the drowsy and passive patrons of the bar. And from the way Middleton carried himself on his move downstage—though he was an assured, good-looking actor, more the male-lead type—Gene knew Middleton could not meet the essential demands of the part: He was no dancer.

When Saroyan asked Middleton to do it "from the top" again, Gene sensed instantly that the playwright had similar misgivings. Of course, he was not sure. But he had to do something, or his chance for the part was gone. It was now or never. Saroyan's memoirs relate what happened next:

Middleton would probably have got the part if he had been able to shout. But he couldn't. At least not well enough. Suddenly, from deep in the shadows of the Guild Theatre on 52nd Street, a voice boomed out saying: "I can shout!" Lawrence Langner, who was attending the audition, was most indignant and wanted to put the upstart, whose name was Gene Kelly, back in his place among the other waiting aspirants. But I said no, and I asked the man, who certainly looked right for Harry, to step forward and to shout out the monologue about who's behind the 8-ball and so on. He then did some tap and other dancing and I said okay, you'll go up with us to Boston, where I was putting the play into some kind of approximation of what I had originally intended it to be.

In a *Parade* magazine interview in 1983, Gene relived the moment when, dressed like a color wheel, he rose from his seat in the Broadway theater:

That was my first real break. The show took place in a saloon and I came in off the street and had to do a dance that I was supposed to make look like I couldn't dance. That's where I began to work on this idea of dancing through a characterization—making the character formulate the look of your body. The show won the Pulitzer Prize, and my dance was a huge success.

The Time of Your Life was a heady time of Gene's life. True, Harry was not a major role. The *Times* review might have been excessively laconic the morning after opening night when it concluded: "Some memorable scenes by Gene Kelly and William Bendix." But the word of mouth coming from the audience, the thunderous applause at every performance was loudly and gushingly positive. Harry the Hoofer served Gene very well. It made believers out of producers like Dowling and Langner and, through them, the influential Broadway community. The play ran for twenty-two weeks, a lengthy period for "a chant of love for the scared and rejected," in critic Louis Kronenberger's words, when war-weary ticket buyers preferred fun and games on the stage, with jokes, music, and half-dressed women.

From the start, as they chuckled over his costume adjustment and his three-day growth of beard to make Harry his, Gene and Saroyan took to each other intellectually and emotionally. Throughout the run of the show Saroyan always enjoyed their intense talks—helped, of course, by the reality that most of the words came from him-and what came through was his utter certainty that Gene Kelly was heading for stardom, without question. Had not Gene been the first aspirant to the role of Harry who understood the centrality of the part? He was not there as a vaudeville turn to draw a few laughs. His tap dancing, moving in and out of the action, represented the essence of Saroyan's comment on the state of the world. It was his Greek chorus on what was really going on. In the playwright's words: "The tapping of his feet was not unlike a drumroll at a funeral; an end that was both a loss and a welcome beginning of something else—almost anything else. Gene Kelly is a great man of the theater."

As for Gene, he relished their time together. He felt pride in a well-regarded playwright seeking him out as a friend. But more than anything else, he celebrated Saroyan's support for his approach to dance, which he was to espouse again and again: That there is no character—be it sailor or doctor or Harry Nobody—who cannot be interpreted by dancing. One must search and find the choreographic language. It is always there.

And still there years later, whenever he went to work. In 1985 when Gene Kelly was interviewed by the syndicated film columnist Margy Rochlin, she asked if, in his view, dance was an art form he was "attempting to masculinize" over the course of his career. He responded:

> Well, it fit into my scheme of things for many reasons. At one time it was true that male dancers were looked down upon, and it was true that a lot of male dancers were effeminate. But what I was really trying to do was develop something that would be American. At the time the quickest way to establish yourself as an American was to throw a little bit of tap into your dance—even when it wasn't called for.
>
> But what also helped me was the fact that I was dancing in roles that I had played. If I played a tough kid on the street I couldn't go out there and get into fifth position. I had to dance like a tough kid on the street.
>
> See, I never played a rich man, I never played a prince. And to play a sailor or a longshoreman you had to make your dance more eclectic and varied, but still keep it indigenous to your nationality, upbringing and background.
>
> In the 1930s there was this tendency in Hollywood to portray everyone as rich. Even if they were doing a poor man's dance, they were all so nicely clothed, gowned, coiffured. That's why I decided to wear white socks, loafers, T-shirts and blue jeans. I had a socio-political context in front of me: I was a child of the Depression who danced in a way that would represent the common man.

It was the stated passion of his professional life. For a time during those fulfilling months of *The Time of Your Life* he tended to be obsessive about articulating his ideas about the essence of choreography.

Even Helene Marlowe, whom he had taken up with again, wished he would go easier on the subject, or, at least, bestow an equal passion on their relationship. He did to a point, and they became intimate again. But still he preferred not to move in with her and, what was worse from her point of view, never mentioned the possibility of marriage. When she pressed him—as, not always to her advantage, she tended to do—his excuse was always his total involvement in the career which, from her perspective, was going grandly. Now another offer had come in that he could handle simultaneously with *The Time of Your Life*, a chance to do what he missed terribly despite the plaudits for Harry the Hoofer: design dances, be a big-time New York choreographer at long last.

While he felt secure about his work as an actor and dancer, he was realistic about his chances to achieve top billing as a stage performer. He was, after all, getting a late start; he was pushing thirty. Only a few brief mentions in a critic's review would come his way. But conceiving dance numbers—the exhilaration of creating something fresh and dazzling—*there* was where real pleasure for Gene conjoined with opportunity for the fame he now lusted after. Bitterly competitive, he could not ignore the gathering attention and respect being given to choreographers such as Agnes de Mille, Jerome Robbins, and George Balanchine. Even just a taste of that sort of notoriety was what he needed now.

Not far from the set of the San Francisco bar where he was Harry for six nightly performances and two matinees every week was a hugely successful nightclub, the Diamond Horseshoe. It was owned by a shrewd, diminutive, exceptionally talented ex-songwriter (and champion speed-typist) named Billy Rose; here was a man of many disparate gifts and an enormous ego. He had recently produced the theatrical success of the New York World's Fair, a spectacular water show called "The Aquacade," staged by John Murray Anderson.

With the closing of the Fair, Rose turned his attention again to his nightclub and decided to freshen things up with a new girlie extravaganza. He wanted Bob Alton to do the choreography, but Alton was busy with another assignment and suggested Gene Kelly. Rose also asked Anderson if he could recommend anybody, and the director, who had worked so well with Gene in *One for the Money*, seconded Alton's suggestion.

Rose had seen Kelly's performance as Harry the Hoofer. It was not quite what he had in mind for his club. He reminded Anderson that he wanted somebody who could handle "tits and asses, not soft-soap from a crazy Armenian like Saroyan." But that night, for the second time, Rose went to see *The Time of Your Life*. A Broadway character to the core, he always insisted that his seat allow an absolutely unobstructed view of the stage, taking into consideration his height of just over five feet. It was Broadway legend that until he became rich enough to command the seat of his choice, when seated behind a tall person he would think nothing of leaning forward to ask, only partly as a joke, "Pardon me, sir. Would you kindly remove your head?" Now that he could well afford it, he always bought four seats in the orchestra for any performance, one pair for himself and the beauteous young blonde he usually escorted, and a pair directly in front of them, which remained empty. He made the usual arrangement for his tickets and observed Gene's Harry the Hoofer very carefully.

Seeing the play for the second time and really paying attention to Harry for the first time, he was struck by the way Gene had "grown" the role. It was now nuanced and sensitive in a way that made Saroyan's world work for him. It was an involving, emotional evening of theater for Billy Rose, and he thought of going backstage. But he decided against it, preferring to enter a negotiation in an aggressive state of mind.

The next day Rose brooded about whether to contact Gene who, he surmised, was too "arty" and "intellectual" to shape up the Diamond Horseshoe chorus line. But Rose was a brilliant judge of talent. He sensed that Gene would take a fresh approach to the choreography and not present him with the usual watered-down version of Rockette kick routines or Moulin Rouge cancans.

At the end of a busy day he finally decided to make the call. He reached Gene in his dressing room at the theater a few minutes before curtain time. Rose explained the job he had in mind. "Kelly, can you handle it?" Gene was quick to say he could. He would have liked to put off the discussion until the next day—but there was no putting off Billy Rose.

Rose briefed him on what he wanted for the next Diamond Horseshoe show and, then and there, insisted on Gene going through a "mental audition," as Gene later described it. What was Kelly's approach? How did Kelly conceive the choreographic elements? Did Kelly have any particular theme in mind?

The stage manager for *The Time of Your Life* was knocking nervously on the door of the dressing room as Gene, who had never visited the Diamond Horseshoe, launched into an attack on the banality of most nightclub acts. He was glad Rose had questioned him about the theme, because that was precisely the point: first, nightclub or no, a theme had to be decided on. Then and only then could the show be constructed. It almost called for a full-fledged script, like a Broadway show. It could not be treated as a ragtag bit of vaudeville.

As Gene reported later: "The silence from the other end of the phone line was deafening. I thought Billy Rose had fainted or something. Or maybe tiptoed quietly out of the room."

But the diminutive showman had heard the final pleading of the stage manager. He cut in to say he thought Gene might be on the right track. He offered a contract as choreographer with a salary of $100 a week. "Now go for it, Harry!" he said as he rang off.

Much to Rose's surprise, Gene made no effort to contact his office the next day. It was left to Rose to make the call and finalize the arrangements. But Gene had thought it over. The offer was too low.

"We have a deal!" protested Rose.

"The hell we do! You didn't even give me a chance to respond last night."

"Hey, do you know who you're talking to?"

"A capitalist bastard! Who throws out a low number with a take-it-or-leave-it ultimatum!"

Back and forth went the insults and put-downs, louder and louder until, all at once, Rose burst out laughing and came up to an offer of $135 a week. "Take it or leave it, Kelly!"

"Okay, I'll take it, Rose. Now let's get on to something really important—the theme of your show."

They spoke for two hours on the telephone, and when Rose hung up, he knew he had the right choreographer.

The priority for all Billy Rose shows was to enlist the youngest and prettiest showgirls in New York. Just as Gene was starting to organize the casting for the

Diamond Horseshoe, a competitor, the International Casino Supper Club, abruptly went dark. A cooperative friend in the District Attorney's office tipped off Rose that the manager had absconded with a month's receipts. The casino would file for bankruptcy.

The major asset of the International Casino did not show up on a financial statement: it was the breathtaking, long-legged, slim-hipped casino chorus line. Rose immediately sent every woman in the casino show a postcard invitation to audition for his club. The tryout date was printed in red within the outline of a long-stemmed rose.

One of the dancers who received Rose's postcard could not attend and gave the audition notice to a sixteen-year-old dancer from New Jersey named Betsy Boger. Her stage name was Betsy Blair. She came from a modest background, the daughter of parents who both worked, one as a teacher, the other an insurance clerk. They worried about Betsy, who was always going off to New York, trying to break into show business as a dancer or an actress. The truant officer of her high school was constantly calling her parents with the prediction that Betsy would never gain a diploma; her spotty attendance record was a sure route to unemployment and damnation. But the Bogers had confidence in their daughter and respected her drive and ambition.

New York, not a small town in New Jersey, was the place for Betsy Blair. She borrowed a cousin's inherited fur jacket, and a friend supplied a pillbox hat, modeled on one worn by Ann Sheridan in a recent film, to enhance the best outfit she could put together and, impatient and excited, on the appointed morning she went to the Diamond Horseshoe.

She was surprised when she reached the place. There was little splendor about a nightclub during the day. It was empty, even eerie. Gloomy shadows darkened the room. Chairs were piled high on tables. She had intended to arrive early, but now knew she had arrived way too much in advance. She turned to go, perhaps to walk around the block to calm down. Suddenly a voice called out: "Can I help you?"

The speaker was an attractive young man, unusually pleasant and well-spoken for someone who was lifting a table onto a riser at the front of the room. She told him she had arrived for the dancers' audition.

The young man responded that she had come a day early. She pulled out the worn postcard and saw that he was right. She was furious at her mistake. And she had gone to the trouble of borrowing special elements for an impressive outfit. The fur jacket, she had been told by her cousin, would not be available the next day. She would have to call her friend for some leeway with the hat. Betsy the boob! It was a worse feeling than being turned down. She gave out a long sigh and headed for the exit.

"Wait a second," she heard. He did not look at her. He placed some chairs on the riser. "Are you a good dancer?"

It seemed a rude question, but perhaps he was trying to enlarge and extend their meeting. Maybe it was his way of trying to arrange a pickup, and the possibility made her feel better. But then she felt even more angry with herself. She had come here on a serious job search and the possibility of a date with this stagehand charmer had thrown her off like a silly school girl! There was a very hard edge to her response.

"Actually, I happen to be a very good dancer."

"In that case," he said, straightening up from his labors on the riser and looking at her, really for the first time. "I'll see you tomorrow. Early. It'll be a mob scene. Mr. Rose has invited just about every pretty girl in town."

"Oh?" She felt she could die on the spot for the tongue-tied way she was handling this conversation. His smile was rattling her, that was it. He was not as tall as she had thought at first—and older too, maybe even thirty or so—but his trim, athletic build showed to advantage in a T-shirt and slacks. He was wearing a pair of loafers, so he surely was not one of the dancers. Certainly he was on the lowest rung of the Rose production staff, a backstage flunkie making a play. Handsome, she had to admit, with his strong, even features and large brown eyes.

And that big smile never wavered. It was like a flashlight beam connecting them. Was she crazy? Suddenly she felt warm and clammy in that damn borrowed fur jacket. For sure, he was trying to encourage her to stay and chat awhile, but she could not; she could still get back to school and ward off another call from the truant officer.

"I gotta go," she said. It was an awful exit line, she knew instantly. "Hey, where do I find you tomorrow?"

"Here, there, everywhere," he said, and now he could see the furious expression come over her face that she made no effort to conceal. He knew why. His airy response had been taken as a dismissive put-down.

"Thanks a lot," she said.

"But just ask," he managed to get out his final words, cheery and upbeat, before she turned and was out of the room, "has anybody here seen Kelly?"

He's always glad to see Jimmy Stewart, a past winner of the AFI's Life Achievement Award. For a low-key guy like Jimmy, this sort of over-the-moon adulation is murder.

In the only Western he's ever directed, Jimmy was the leading man, co-starring with Hank Fonda. Sort of a geriatric trio facing up to the onslaught of the Sunset Boulevard Youth Movement. But it had been a decent learning experience for him and did reasonably well at the B.O. Jimmy's stepson had been killed in Vietnam during the filming. Ever the trooper, the decorated Air Force officer hung in and did his scenes before going home to mourn.

What the hell, just as he had done when Betsy took off when he was on location with The Happy Road. Made sure it was a final wrap, then headed home. The mark of a pro.

He cautions himself: Better think happier thoughts! The kid with the video camera, still hungry for insert shots, would just love to catch old GK, all teary and trembly.

But there's a sight for sore eyes: In the third-row aisle seat, not having impatiently left the premises as he often does, Baryshnikov is watching the film clips, listening to the kudos for Kelly. He is flattered. The Russian's presence is, in a very real way, a certification that he has been more than just a hoofer. He's still worthy of some respect in the world of ballet. Not as a dancer, okay. He's the first to admit he never had the classic physique for that. But as a choreographer of fresh, innovative work—that's another story!

And to hell with the critics and a big red-inked Chapter 11 for the assholes at MGM who held up Invitation to the Dance for years! The best work of his professional life could not get distribution, despite his yelling and screaming. They had treated him like a musical-comedy Orson Welles, a wild buffoon with budgets, allowing Invitation to be seen as a huge failure when, to this day, he knows in his gut it's a breakthrough film. And yes! Baryshnikov staying here makes it so.

His mouth feels tight with resentment. He'd better be careful. The video crew is near him now. He has to keep smi-i-ling, with plenty of sunny, teethy, Kelly grins, hard to maintain when he spots Cary Grant in the audience.

He is still pissed off at Cary, a guest of him and Betsy so many times at the house on Rodeo Drive—a quirky word man like himself, who dazzled everybody at The Game that put the Kellys on the social map: Charades, Kelly style. Cary's also big on making up word games himself, such as Cary's Fractured French: Coup de Grace for lawn mower. Vin Ordinaire for Volkswagen bus. Cafe au Lait for whorehouse. Not bad. A lifelong Francophile is Gene Kelly; he enjoys kidding around and parlaying in français himself.

Then there is Cary's "The Name" Game: Gregory Peck is Gregory Bushel. The long-reigning child star was Shirley Synagogue. Ha Ha. But this is what really sets his teeth on edge: Somebody—he doesn't even remember who the hell it was—who told him about a Grant party (with him and Betsy conspicuously uninvited) when Cary had unfurled his newest inspiration: Unlikely Couples. And right after Tennessee and Esther Williams had come . . . Gene and Betsy Kelly.

Apparently it had gone over very well, lots of chuckles in the old Cary corral. God knows he could have reciprocated, put the squeeze on Cary, given distribution to the gossip about that elegant son-of-a-bitch, to the effect that he is (certainly) gay and (maybe) Jewish. But that's not the Kelly way.

Bad enough so many guests in their home recognized Betsy's talent and drive and intelligence—amazing in a kid that young!—but they made too much of her neurotic tendencies and left-wing ideas. Especially during the McCarthy days. It had cost him, nearly drowned him. Water over the dam now—but he suddenly finds himself breathing deeply, coming up for air.

He looks around, relieved that the lurking cameraman has stepped away for a moment to shoot some audience inserts of a kid nearby with an awful lot of hair. A rock star, he guesses, but he's not sure.

NEW YORK, 1940

* * *

Betsy Boger took Gene's advice and was on an early bus to New York the next day. She was stunned when she rounded the corner near Times Square and saw the line of young women stretching a block from the Diamond Horseshoe. She took her place at the end and almost immediately additional auditioners spread out behind her, like ivy sprouting out of control. In both directions now all she could see was a restless and unformed group of rivals. The odds of being chosen—considering her youth, inexperience, and, she was desperately aware, modest bosom—were dismal. It was a chill morning, and she wished her cousin had not insisted on the return of the borrowed fur jacket.

An hour later she was closer to the Diamond Horseshoe but still outside. By twos and threes, others made their exits. They did not look very happy. Some of them were astonishingly pretty by Betsy's standards, a perception that rocked what little confidence remained.

It was only her brief contact the previous day with Mr. Kelly that somehow stopped her from skulking back to New Jersey. Once inside, she saw him. *Gene Kelly*—she had made some inquiry calls the night before, so she now knew about *The Time of Your Life* and Harry the Hoofer—was on a riser with two other men. He was in a canvas-backed director's chair, leaning forward, his profile every bit as perfect as she remembered it. He was looking up at the man talking to him, a tiny fellow atop a high stool. That must be Mr. Rose, Billy Rose, she assumed. Ever so often, Mr. Rose would break off his conversation, slide down off the stool, stride to the lip of the riser in powerful short steps, and stand there like Napoleon viewing a battle in the valley below. Then quickly he was at Gene Kelly's side, standing his tallest over him now, as he pointed at one or another of the tap-dancing chorines who were trying out. When an assistant blew a whistle over the crackling din, the third man on the riser—he was John Murray Anderson, Betsy guessed—politely thanked them for coming and called for the next group.

Each of the candidates was allowed to do a short piece of her own choosing. If she was deemed satisfactory, she would enter the next round: the group tap routine, led by one of the assistants with a spectacular variety of steps. The men on the riser clearly were looking for adaptable dancers, quick learners of new routines. But to "make the cut" the survivors had to deliver the other requisites. The assistant would parade around each candidate left on the floor as she was asked to turn around slowly, raising and lowering her arms. An odious experience, she felt, the much complained-of meat market, where she and the others were like sides of beef hanging from hooks, their body parts the choice cuts: pillowy breasts, curving rumps, legs, the longer the better.

She was, as she had told Gene the previous day, a good dancer. And pretty enough, but not in a conventional way. Just one glance at the little man on the riser made it evident who carried the day when it came to making the final decisions, and she was no rose in that person's eyes. But she was a scrappy fighter who gave the try-out effort everything she had. She heard later that John Murray Anderson thought (what else?) she was too skinny and flat-chested for a glamorous Billy Rose revue. But Gene Kelly had insisted she had the potential for bringing something special to the show. He could work with her. When she made the final cut and was told by another chorine about his surprising intrusion, the thought crossed her mind: Work with her? He might want to play with her, too. Well, she would deal with that; she was only sixteen but no innocent.

Rehearsals started at the Diamond Horseshoe. The schedule was designed to fit around the choreographer's performances in Saroyan's play. For Betsy, Mr. Kelly became Gene almost from the start, but with a mixture of relief and disappointment, she saw quickly there were no advances for her to deal with. He was the complete professional. He was so helpful and encouraging that she developed a teenage crush in no time. It thrilled her when Anderson made a joking reference to "Betsy, the teacher's pet" as he gave some general notes to the assembled cast.

She applied herself more than she had ever done at school where, despite the truant officer, good grades had come her way. She changed her rehearsal clothes twice a day and, as she was to say later, "couldn't have been cleaner, fresher, or more hard-working. I wanted Gene to like me and I wanted him to like my work."

Gene was beginning to think his status called for a better place to live, a more prestigious address. He had managed to place Dick Dwenger, his apartment mate, as the rehearsal pianist. Now that he was receiving a regular paycheck, Dwenger, too, wished to leave the cockroachy place they shared. But the pianist was very surprised when Gene moved in with Helene Marlowe.

Dwenger was attracted to Betsy and made no secret about it. But she made him know quickly it was Gene who interested her. One day, shortly after the opening of the new Diamond Horseshoe show, Dwenger asked Betsy if she wanted to join them—him and Gene—for lunch. Betsy was overjoyed, even more so at the restaurant when Dwenger left after one cocktail, saying he had an errand to do. She waited for the invitation to Gene's apartment. She had no idea he lived with Helene.

It seemed interminable as Gene made a fuss about guiding her choices from the menu. Her mind was not on food but on whether she should accept. She had a canny sense that playing hard-to-get with this man was the way to go, especially when he insisted, since she was below the legal drinking age, they both have Cokes.

The first course came, but the invitation to his new apartment didn't. The lunch was going well enough, she thought, although she was somewhat put off by his fatherly way of offering what seemed like a nonstop stream of advice:

That if she wanted to get ahead in show business, he said, she should get out of nightclubs, cavorting in tights, and into musical comedy where she could act, emote, deliver lines. "A speaking role, Betsy. That's where the money is!" (What did that mean? He no longer wanted to see her around the Horseshoe? He didn't like the way she looked in tights?)

That she needed to leave her parents' home in New Jersey and move into the city so she could promote her career full-time. "Betsy, out of sight is out of mind in this business!" (What was he really getting at? Was this, at last, the beginning of a pitch to get her to move in with him?)

That in consideration of budget she might think of taking a room at the Henry Hudson Hotel, on West 57th Street, a women's establishment where many theater professionals lived. (The Hudson, for heaven's sake! Men could not set foot above the lobby, but could only phone from the desk and await the descent of their dates. A cloistered nunnery for showgirls!)

Confusion and tears brimmed her eyes at this. After coffee and a brisk kiss on the cheek, she was sent on her way while he proceeded in another direction. Before the evening performance she was crushed to find out from Dwenger that Gene was with Helene Marlowe.

While the major critics for the *Times* and *Herald Tribune* did not deign to review nightclub shows, the crowds at the Diamond Horseshoe flocked in and lived up to Billy Rose's expectations. He and Anderson were very pleased with Gene's work and talked about hiring him for the next edition.

Betsy gave up on her pursuit of Gene, while taking his advice to heart. Her parents agreed that commuting from New Jersey was difficult, and she moved, presumably at their insistence, to the protective enclave of the Henry Hudson Hotel. In her free time she explored New York, delighted in what it offered, especially in the way of libraries, museums, lectures. She was proving to be an authentic intellectual, needing no school course to prod her. There was no shortage of men encountered as she tapped into the city's cultural advantages. They were writers, newspaper journalists, unemployed poets, academics, Philharmonic musicians—unusually bright fellows who did not hold her age against her. She avoided men of show business like the plague. But she kept track of Gene. Her dates would always make jokes about the Hudson lobby being like the Maginot Line of the war raging in France, holding the Germans at bay, though in actuality the Hudson was far more resistant to breakthroughs; no man ever reached the second floor.

Which was just as well for Betsy, who always danced at the Horseshoe with a special manic energy when Gene came by to check on a performance. A couple of weeks into the run of the show, he and Helene Marlowe slipped into the club after the curtain went down on *The Time of Your Life*. As always, the dancers were charged up by Gene's visit. Now and then Betsy was able to glance at the slender, dark-haired woman with Gene. A handsome couple, she had to admit, their body language easygoing and animated with each other.

When the Broadway run of *The Time of Your Life* had run its course, Gene decided not to join the touring company of the play. He wanted to remain in New York, for Darrow felt he was on the verge of some important offers. Eddie Dowling held special auditions to find another Harry the Hoofer and was disappointed at the quality of the turnout. Nobody gave the play Gene's spark. "You're not going to believe this," Gene finally told Dowling, "but there's only one person who can do it."

"Who?"

"My brother Fred."

Dowling brought Fred to New York and tested him for the role. Fred was not blessed with Gene's looks, and there were certain differences in style between the two brothers, but Fred was able to model his steps on Gene's work, beyond giving his own likable spin to the role. Dowling declared him satisfactory and engaged Fred for the nationwide tour.

Gene's decision to stay in New York lifted the hopes of Betsy Blair, who was still trying to grow into the woman in his life. Then she found out his topsy-turvy relationship with Helene Marlowe had faltered and he was now living on his own once more. She took a deep breath and called him. They began to date. Soon they were regulars at his favorite hangout, Louie Bergen's tavern, on 45th Street, where the talk was stimulating, even if the food wasn't.

Gene introduced her to the other regular patrons. Saroyan was one of them, but Bergen's was a far cry from the drifters' San Francisco bar of his now-touring play; indeed, it had an atmosphere unique for the Times Square area, attractive to an intellectual set whose political compass swung strongly to the left. At Bergen's, just being politically liberal—say, a Roosevelt New Deal Democrat—was like being a Republican. Lubricated by drink—often starting with beer and wine before going on to harder stuff, usually vodka ordered by the more voluble and emotional Soviet sympathizers—the subjects for discussion were never sports, but always serious, if not sober: the Spanish Civil War, the concern about Hitler, the conundrum of Stalin, the chances for Henry Wallace. To a New Jersey girl not yet seventeen, Bergen's was a fascinating arena, far more absorbing than any class she had ever attended. She couldn't help noticing she was one of the very few females in Bergen's who participated, and she always glowed happily when she and Gene left the bar, arm in arm, with the feeling he approved of her.

Still, she needed more. "He treated me like an angel, almost," she told an interviewer years later. "Very gently—as if I were someone to take care of and educate." Prodded by Gene, she tried for a part in a new musical called *Louisiana Purchase*. In a heavy-handed but laugh-provoking way, the show launched satirical jabs at crooked New Orleans politicians, so Gene and Betsy felt, at least, that it had some redeeming social value, as well as a possible speaking role for her. She was rejected, however, on the final day of tryouts. She broke into tears when she did not make the cut. She had left the Diamond Horseshoe to pursue theatrical opportunities and was now in the position of needing a job, any job, to pay the rent at the Hudson.

Gene, aware he had been responsible for Betsy's unemployment, spoke to Bob Alton, who saw to it that Betsy was hired for *Panama Hattie*, Cole Porter's latest musical. It was a place in the chorus line, but it boosted her morale nevertheless. If you were an "Alton girl," it was a message to Broadway that you were the *crème de la crème*, having risen to first class in the gaudy, spangled world of high-kicking chorines. In the line with Betsy were June Allyson and a dancer who had taken the stage name of Vera-Ellen.

Panama Hattie, starring Ethel Merman and Betty Hutton, drew favorable reviews and long lines in front of the theater and settled into a lengthy run of more than 500 performances. It was a major success for Porter and, for a time at least, stabilized Betsy's working life. She continued to study acting and pursue speaking roles, and then William Saroyan told her, elbow-to-elbow one night at Louie

Bergen's, that his next play had the perfect role for her. Indeed, he swore he had modeled the character after the real-life Betsy.

As the months went by, Gene, as dance director of the Diamond Horseshoe, came to chafe at his job, which was largely to train replacements and maintain the high level of performance Billy Rose demanded. It was hardly an all-consuming task. He resolved to make the best of the situation, using his considerable free time in a productive way. Despite his boredom with rote exercises, he kept in shape by working out daily at the gym. Much more to his taste were the long solitary runs in the early morning through Central Park.

On days when *Panama Hattie* gave no matinee, he and Betsy visited museums or took in the art galleries on 57th Street. They were both readers and would spend time in his apartment, enjoying books and records. There was some hand-holding and kissing but (to her frustration) no sex. He continually made a point of her tender age, as if that was the barrier that prevented intimacy. From time to time he made jokes about the federal Mann Act, which prohibited the movement of minors across state lines for purposes of sexual activity. And she came from New Jersey, he reminded her. While she thought Gene had a beguiling sense of humor, those attempts at being funny did nothing more than distress her.

For his part, he had to remind himself constantly she was only seventeen. He delighted in the quality of her mind, always alert and questing, much like his own, he thought, or perhaps even better.

In the evening the pattern was for him to pick her up at the stage door, and they would make their way through the crowds of Times Square to Louie Bergen's. She would wait for him at the bar while he made what seemed like his hourly call to the answering service, hoping for some positive news from Darrow. She never remained alone for long. Somebody—it might be Saroyan or one of the straight dancers from *Panama Hattie*—would insist on buying her a drink. She was popular at Bergen's, part sexy woman, part darling of the group, and everybody thought Gene lucky to have her.

Gene would return from the phone booth, signaling at Betsy with a shrug the absence of any meaningful calls, and they would join a table for an evening of some food and more drink and, above all, political arguments. Gene always seemed to lead into the more serious subjects. He would look uncomfortable when there was trivial shop talk and gossip about show business. His career had stalled. The goings-on at the Diamond Horseshoe were unimportant and depressing to him.

Long after midnight he and Betsy would leave Bergen's and walk through a deserted Times Square to the Hudson, and the goodnight kiss.

That's what it was, just a goodnight kiss, as though he too were a teenager returning his prom date to her home. Gene knew she expected more of him, in every way. She was beginning to panic about their relationship. On the lone return to his apartment he debated within himself whether to break it off, for her sake. Set against her passionate feelings, expressed in so many endearing ways, sometimes even flaunted in girlish desperation, his own lack of ardor had to be unsettling and cruel—and hurting her was the last thing he wanted.

At Bergen's a drinking buddy, a young psychoanalyst of all things, had put her on to reading Freud. She had hinted that Gene could benefit from those fifty-minute hours. Gene wasn't insulted; he was touched by her concern and the way she always tried to cover it up, to be amusing and flip and light-hearted. When she made him laugh, a glint of triumph shone in her eyes; it was far better than receiving her high-school diploma!

Through it all, despite her youth, Gene knew Betsy was a no-nonsense judge of talent, and he was bolstered by her repeatedly expressed faith in what he offered the theatrical world. Coming from her it was like a nightly mantra, like breathing: "Gene, just as you came into my life at the Diamond Horseshoe and everything changed for me, so will something . . . or somebody come along for you."

Something did, he did. It—and he—was Pal Joey.

The composer Richard Rodgers had been to see The Time of Your Life before the run ended on Broadway. As he wrote in his memoirs, he had been especially impressed by one performance. And Rodgers was not easily impressed. Dour, subject to periods of depression which would eventually send him to the Payne Whitney Clinic for prolonged treatment, Rodgers was initially bored by Saroyan's play. Only his vocational interests as a composer kept him from walking out. He perked up when a song and dance was done by a character named Harry the Hoofer, "by an especially engaging young man named Gene Kelly. The stage was aglow with life whenever he appeared."

The next day Rodgers sent a note to the noted writer John O'Hara, his current collaborator. O'Hara had been a mainstay of The New Yorker for many years, most often with stories about the fictional owner of a down-at-the-heels nightclub, Joey Evans, a.k.a. Pal Joey. In the weekly magazine, passionately followed by the New York intelligentsia and a significant readership across the country, O'Hara recounted his anti-hero's adventures, or misadventures, in a mordantly acerbic style with densely packed realism and gritty dialogue. The essence of Joey was that he was a user of women to get ahead, never aware of the pain he caused them.

They were excited about the project. They—along with lyricist Lorenz Hart—knew the show was to be a landmark, a turning point in the development of Broadway musicals. It took a more realistic, hard-edged tack than other shows. Pal Joey was not the usual Cole Porter musical material; it would venture out of the bland white-tie-and-tails, anyone-for-tennis WASP world to take in that of the cynical, seedy, money-hungry denizen of cool users like Joey Evans.

In Gene Kelly this brilliant team of collaborators found their Joey. One morning Rodgers, the spark of the project and the most organized of the creative team—at least when compared to Hart and O'Hara, who too easily could be attracted by other temptations, usually involving alcohol—called Johnny Darrow. He had one question to ask. He wasted no time with the agent before getting to it: "That guy Kelly. Can he sing?"

"You betcha!" Darrow responded with classic agent ebullience, wanting to keep the conversation going so he could find out what Rodgers had in mind. The composer, however, was close-mouthed and would offer no more information.

Darrow had his Broadway sources. Swiftly he sniffed out that Rodgers had Kelly in mind for the lead in his new show. He and his client made the decision that Gene would cut down on his regime of conditioning, including long-distance running, and dance practice. A singing coach was engaged. One week passed, two weeks, as Gene and his new teacher prepared for the audition. The lead song he would offer was one of Rodgers' most beautiful—and difficult—numbers. The second song was faster and peppier, a rollicking Irish ditty he had often performed in the "cloops," where real Pal Joeys hung out, waiting for a break. He wanted Rodgers to know that Joey was no stranger to him.

Still, the famous composer–producer did not call. But at least the singing coach was building up Gene's wavery tenor. The lessons did not come cheaply. Gene was worried about how he could possibly pay the bill. Daily he pressed Darrow to arrange the audition and, at long last, a Saturday morning session was set up. On Friday night he did not meet Betsy but went to bed early, only to be rewarded by a tossing, sleepless night.

In the morning he met Darrow and the singing coach in front of the Century Theater. They nodded and entered without a word. The creative team for the production was already there, concluding a meeting Rodgers had called. Now in the role of jurors, they scattered, taking separate places in the darkened orchestra. Watching from the lip of the stage, Gene was reminded of baseball players running out to their positions for a new inning. But this was a game he never enjoyed. It was like a screen test without the camera. The singing coach seated himself at the piano and was ready. O'Hara had come in from his home in Bucks County and was lost somewhere in the shadowy back rows. George Abbott, the director, went even farther away, preferring to watch from the standing-room section. Were they concerned that his voice would not carry?

Rodgers, though, placed himself in the first row. "Mr. Hart couldn't be present this morning," he said sourly. "So go ahead, Mr. Kelly." Hart's absence was a blow to Gene's confidence. He had counted on Lorenz Hart as being his only "friend in court." Years later, Sheridan Morley and Ruth Leon quoted Kelly on the tension in the Century Theater that day:

> I remember a terrifying audition for Rodgers and O'Hara and Abbott. The only one of the team who was absent was the only one I already knew. I had gotten to know Larry Hart in local saloons, not Sardi's or the Stork Club, but the cheap bars around Eighth Avenue and 45th, where Larry could easily be found. . . . I got to know him, not closely but in a fun kind of way. He'd come in and we'd be around the bar and he'd tell us stories, chomping on his cigar . . . he always had a real audience. We all looked up to him.

All at once Gene wanted a drink of water, but he did not dare even to clear his throat. Pal Joey would never give off such a sign of being intimidated. He nodded at his singing coach, who did an intro into "I Didn't Know What Time It Was," a Rodgers classic. Gene did not know he had already sinned in the judgment of Richard Rodgers, whose unwritten law for auditioners was never to offer one of the attending composer's songs. To the composer it was a sneaky form of pandering, currying favor, "kissing ass." Break the Rodgers rule and risk being summarily ordered off the stage! But there was no interruption as Gene did the number as well as he could, concentrating on projecting into the far reaches of the house. When he finished, there was no reaction, visible or audible, and he found himself backing up slightly as though he'd been standing on a precipice, eyeing a dangerous gap of silent, threatening darkness.

Then Rodgers spoke, with no great enthusiasm, Gene thought. "Can we hear something else?" Gene did the "It's the Irish in Me" ditty, agonizing now that it was absolutely the wrong choice, ridiculously corny for these highbrow observers in front of him. He had resolved not to segue into the jig he used to do in the "cloops" because his singing was the issue here. Unadorned by an exuberant dance, he felt the song came out flat and silly. And for the first time it occurred to him: Would O'Hara be put off by what he considered an ethnic putdown, or pandering? Mercifully, it was soon over.

He and the singing coach had prepared a few more pieces, but he was not asked. He was unstrung by the lack of feedback; not the slightest courtesy had been extended. He felt anger building within him like phlegm in his dry throat. He wished he had the guts to spit at them, these capitalist fatcats who put desperately hard-working proletarian actors through this torture for their own amusement. He was convinced Rodgers and the others had already picked their Pal Joey but had agreed to hear him, ever so briefly, only because of Darrow's pesky urgings. He helped the coach gather the scores, and they were already walking off the stage when, like a clap of thunder, a hoarse voice came out of the darkness. "That's it!" It was John O'Hara from the back of the theater. "Take him!"

At that moment one Irishman could have kissed another. Before the day was over, Darrow has secured an Equity contract for Gene. The salary was $350 a week, far less than a Broadway starring role called for. Darrow remembered the rebuff by the Shuberts in bargaining for a better payout. He would not play tough now. *Pal Joey* would do more than pay Gene's bills; it would unveil a new star on Broadway.

The producers were aiming for an opening on Christmas night. There was a lot of work to do on the script. Gene agreed with the expressed concern of George Abbott, the director, that the challenge was to hold true to the cynicism of the original O'Hara stories, but at the same time not to allow the ruthlessness of Joey to keep the public away from buying tickets to the show. Abbott put pressure on O'Hara for rewrites, and Rodgers put pressure on Hart to fine-tune the lyrics. The real challenge was the framing of the protagonist. For all of Joey's bravado as he has one sexual encounter after another, he is actually a kind of innocent who operates so blindly or gullibly that at the curtain he will be blackmailed out of his own club and left penniless and deserted by his wronged woman. The role of Joey and the flow of the story demanded the best from the writers and from Gene. The show was light-years away from a typical one-dimensional musical-comedy role; Pal Joey had to be rendered in a nuanced, sensitive way—not all good, not all bad, surprising and unpredictable yet ultimately understandable.

The test would be in the Philadelphia tryout before the Broadway premiere. Amid the frenzy of revisions Hart and O'Hara sometimes buckled. Hart was an emotional man tortured by his unattractive appearance and harrowing intimacies with young male pickups. On bad days he would remain in bed and drink himself into oblivion. Just when Rodgers would give up on him, cursing not only his partner's misdirected "queer and faggy" passions but his utter lack of professional responsibility, there would come the breakthrough morning when Hart would suddenly reappear, bleary-eyed and gray-faced, a cold cigar butt lumped in his mouth, and present a set of glittering lyrics that were all the composer could have hoped for, a divinely inspired marriage of Hart words to Rodgers music.

The working habits of O'Hara, as well, presented problems. He drank a good deal—though never with Hart—and periodically withdrew to ply himself with scotch and wonder how the hell he had been sucked into doing a musical for Broadway. In his absence, George Abbott would make needed revisions, trying as best he could to keep the production afloat and emulate the unique style of one of America's most popular writers. Abbott was competent, but only O'Hara was O'Hara, and Pal Joey paid the price.

The constant ferment of a work in progress, rather than a finished play, was hardest on Gene. During the Philadelphia tryout, it would fall on him to do the performance with the then-current script du jour. Returning from the theater around midnight, he would be handed a packet of colored pages which conveyed the changes for the following evening's performance. He would be up till the early morning hours, absorbing the reworkings and memorizing the new scenes.

In the daytime, before the next evening's performance, he concentrated on his dance numbers, aided by Alton, who let him take the lead in designing his own choreography. Gene was grateful for his help. The two of them managed to craft dances that conveyed the essence of Joey Evans in a wordless, gutsy way. It was Gene's passion: His dances were not to be set pieces, independent of what came before and what would come after; instead, his numbers were there to catapult Joey toward the dramatic, turnaround finale.

As the clock wound down to the Broadway opening, there was always yet more work to do—on the book, the songs, Gene's dances—and it was a furious race to get everybody and everything in place by Christmas Day, 1940.

Vivienne Segal was playing Vera Simpson, the fortyish society lady slumming in the nightclub circuit who is attracted to Joey and agrees to help him. Veteran performer that she was, Segal knew the show was in trouble. So did June Havoc, who was making her Broadway debut. And only Gene, in the lead, could pull it up to the level of a hit. Van Johnson, a dancer in the chorus line, felt much the same way, as did the youngest member of the cast, a precocious and ambitious South Carolinian named Stanley Donen also making his debut on Broadway. The latter,

not yet seventeen, was an unusually cool-headed observer, but at the time, as he was
to tell Clive Hirschhorn, his feelings came close to hero worship:

> I remember being impressed by Gene as soon as I saw him on the
> stage. He had a cockiness, a confidence in himself, and a ruthless-
> ness in the way he went about things that, to someone as young
> and green as myself, was astonishing. I also found him cold, egotis-
> tical and very rough. And, of course, wildly talented. He was the
> only song and dance man to come out of that period who had balls.

At the time, of course, neither Kelly nor Donen could possibly conceive a future
where their lives would be intertwined, professionally and emotionally. Donen's
admiration would be severely tested over the years in their complicated, puzzling
relationship, which would bring much gratification yet, in the end, mutual rancor.

Right now, before both the star and the chorus boy, was the curtain's rise at the
Ethel Barrymore Theatre. *Pal Joey* had arrived on Broadway.

*He can't find Stanley Donen in the crowd at the Hilton. He may be out of the country—
conveniently. Stanley's still pissed off. Probably thinks he never gets enough credit for
Singin'. . . But it wasn't Stanley, it was goody-two-shoes Gene who did the goddamn
number, jumping around in puddles with a temperature of a hundred one and counting.
Well, so long, Stanley.*

*Right now he has an immediate concern, impossible to swat away, like a horsefly in
the sun. That damn video crew, hanging around him for the cut-ins, not letting him be
human, even breathe, relax, belch, roll his eyes or—my God, no!—close them for
a moment. And he's sagging. He knows the signs, does he ever! The tiredness settling over
him like a blanket of humid Pittsburgh air, weighing down his energy. He's seventy-three
years old, for chrissake, he has attended GK retrospectives all over the world and then
some, and what he wants more than anything else is to be home on Rodeo Drive, in his
bed, reading or watching "Movie of the Week" on TV. Long ago and far away—hey,
there's a song title right there!—are those nights when he and Betsy would give those
weekend parties, when they and their guests (people of talent, too, mostly lefty New
Yorkers with IQs to make the nose bleed) would play the famous Kelly Game and Judy and
Frankie would sing songs with Bernstein at the piano, and a little deli food and lots of booze
and shop talk would carry them through the night. In the morning hungover bodies littered
the rooms, like a battlefield. But he'd be out there on his volleyball court with mostly young
chorus boys (straights) and some specially invited recruits from UCLA varsity teams. They
were years younger, but he'd run and jump and spike every damn ball in sight! A Mozart
of the volleyball court!*

This hovering video crew, these hippie bastards, want candids showing him as Methuselah, not Mozart. Closeups of the old man dozing off are to die for!

NEW YORK, 1940

* * *

Gene felt little of the joyous Christmas spirit, the day of the opening. What he was going through in his room at the Hotel Woodward, on 55th Street, was tension, pure and simple. It was building and ticking within him, a time bomb. There had been so many insertions of colored pages, signaling last-minute rewrites cobbled in by O'Hara, Rodgers, and Abbott, the script was more patchwork than play. The possibility of blowing a line putting pressure on the whole cast. He would have to be alert, ready to ad-lib his way out of trouble and—worst case—God help *Pal Joey* if the music cues got screwed up!

His mother and one of his sisters, Louise, were in from Pittsburgh for the opening. He was obligated to spend the day with them, forming a Kelly tourist trio window-shopping around Rockefeller Center. Harriet was disappointed she would not meet Betsy Blair until after the performance, when Lorenz Hart would be hosting a combination Christmas and opening-night party at his Central Park West apartment. Gene had to tell his mother several times that Betsy was still appearing in *Panama Hattie*, so the two women could not meet during the day. He knew Harriet was as nervous about Betsy as he was about Joey Evans. That thought, oddly, served to relax him a bit.

There was a stack of Western Union telegrams and call messages at the hotel when he returned, from Bob Alton, Helene Marlowe, Jules Steinberg, the nuns at St. Raphael's, his brother Fred. He put the rest aside, unread, as he began to feel the pressure again. It was not his own performance he worried about. It was the breakthrough quality of the play—would it be appreciated or scoffed at? He had to face it: despite the fix-ups, there was still no romance in *Pal Joey*. The show bristled with sexuality and Hart's naughty double-entendres, but he and his co-star Vivienne Segal never embraced, not once. And there was only one love song, the very beautiful "I Could Write a Book." But will the audience believe a lowlife like Joey Evans can mean what he is singing?

Nobody recognized him as he walked to the Barrymore Theater. The elderly man who handled the stage door let him in and, after raving incoherently about his performance at the final run-through the night before, actually said in a voice throbbing with emotion: "Gene, tonight you'll walk out of here a star." Shades of the Brothers Warner and Ruby Keeler and *42nd Street*. But he knew better; *Pal Joey* was not a safe entry into stardom.

It was still early when he finished checking his makeup at his dressing-room mirror. He resisted the urge to examine his script one last time. It might shake loose the shards of panic. Meanwhile the door was constantly being opened. Heads jutted in to wish him good luck or—knowing he was a committed Francophile—*merde*, or break a leg or some dumb joke or just a speechless thumbs-up. He wished the parade of support would end. But knock-knock and there they were, probably the whole cast, one after another from Vivienne down to that bright teenager Stanley Donen who had impressed him. Johnny Darrow came by and hugged him, and there were separate visits from George Abbott, John O'Hara, Richard Rodgers, and others, with much hand-shaking and arm-squeezing, and little talk. It was too late for talk. He did not expect Lorenz Hart. By now he was probably settling his nervous stomach with a bellyful of Dewar's at Louie Bergen's. The proprietor had sent over a bottle of champagne with the wrapper reading FOR PAL JOEY FROM PAL LOUIE.

Finally there was quiet, not only in his dressing room but all through the labyrinthine passageway to the stage, where he took his position for the curtain. The setting was very familiar. Not for the first time he thought of the irony. Joey Evans' crummy nightclub was the "cloop" Gene Kelly had sworn to escape.

Pal Joey was the first Broadway musical to open on an empty stage without the traditional chorus. He took a last-minute swig of club soda from a bottle on one of the tables, by arrangement with the stage manager, to whom he now nodded. Ready. From the orchestra pit, he heard the quietly confidential tsk-tsk-tsk of the tapping baton of Harry Levant, the musical director. Then there was music, a quiet progression of soft notes, and the curtain went up and he was into "Chicago," his first song, almost an *a capella* introduction for a few seconds that felt endless to him. Then the orchestra was there, caressing and surrounding him, and with a gathering swell of confidence, almost euphoria, he took the number all the way. Coda!

He didn't need the applause to tell him. It was like scoring the first goal in ice hockey; getting off to a good start was what he needed. Then he and *Pal Joey* would do all right. He was certain of it, saying later on:

> It was just a case of being the right man in the right place at the right time and having the tremendous luck to play a part like that. With a script by John O'Hara, songs by Rodgers and Hart and a director like Abbott. I think I did well in it because it gave me a chance to use my own style of dancing to create a character. I wanted to dance to American music and at that time nobody else was doing it. And Joey was a meaty character to play.

True, Rodgers, Hart, O'Hara, and Abbott had created what would have been a satisfying evening in the theater, but it was Gene's portrayal of Joey that carried the show. His chillingly unsentimental portrait of a man out for himself was a revelation: "He was completely amoral," said Gene. "After some scenes I could feel the waves of heat coming from the audience. Then I'd smile at them and dance and it would relax them." Through the character he did more than manipulate the audience; he allowed them to see into his soul, care for Joey while hating him. Unsure whom to root for, as the curtain came down they responded with passionate and sustained applause.

The night was a vivid, memorable triumph. Surrounded by well-wishers in his dressing room, Gene saw his mother trying to push through. The cast members, sentimental to the core, always pushovers for an emotional family scene, especially at Christmas, parted instantly. Mother and son embraced. Her tears actually drew tears from him. Some wag in the room started chanting "When Irish Eyes Are Smiling," and the cast joined in as Harriet held on, her hair tousled, her cheeks wet. She had always been a controlled and controlling person, not one to show feelings very easily; but now there was no way she could hold back her happiness and pride.

At that moment Betsy, having bolted from *Panama Hattie* the moment the curtain came down, rushed into the loud, champagne-popping crowd. Finally he managed to introduce them, the teenage chorus dancer and—as he always referred to her, not quite in jest—his sainted mother. Betsy looked especially radiant, and he was pleased with the way his girlfriend, so well-spoken and supportive, helped Harriet through the emotional moment.

Then they were all swept up in the festive mood as they went on to Hart's apartment for the Christmas party—and to await the verdicts of the drama critics. The first reviews, phoned in by reporter friends in the newspaper city rooms, were very favorable. But what concerned everybody was the opinion of the noted Brooks Atkinson in the all-important *New York Times*. Because it was Christmas, the *Times* review would not come out until December 26. So while the party was an exhilarating bash with laughs and liquor flowing, there was still an undertone of suspense.

Hart, already well fortified with spirits, found the tension hard to withstand and retreated to his bedroom with several bottles of scotch, as though to live up to his reputation. (In *Time* magazine he had been described as "cigar-chewing Hart, the pint-sized genius with the two-quart capacity.") O'Hara went back to Bucks County. Rodgers and his wife stopped in for a quick visit and then were gone. The others—Abbott, the backers, the cast, family members and friends—stayed and drank and danced till dawn, ecstatic with their connection, spiritual and financial, to the newest hit on Broadway.

They celebrated too soon. Hart was not to leave his bedroom and bottles for several long days. The opinions of the critics turned out to be mixed, and dominating as ever was Atkinson of the *Times*, who set the tone of his review immediately with: "How can you get sweet water from a foul well?" Atkinson's answer to his own question was decisively negative and, even more crushing because of the tease of faint praise, was the critic's conclusion: "*Pal Joey* offers everything but a good time. If it is possible to make an entertaining musical comedy out of an odious story, *Pal Joey* is it." It was the nightmare Gene had worried about from the instant he had signed his contract for the role: that a musical about a heel would be considered tawdry, a melodrama gone haywire.

His feelings were only partially soothed by the reactions of the other critics, such as Burns Mantle, in the *Daily News* ("Mr. Kelly is able to give the part personal attractions that justify the O'Hara picture.") and Richard Watts, Jr., in the *Herald Tribune* ("It was a happy stroke of casting that placed Mr. Kelly in the title-role. . . . *Pal Joey* is a hard-boiled delight."). The prestigious *New Yorker* magazine, where O'Hara's original stories had appeared, was steadfast in repeatedly praising the production. And the dance writer for the *Times* took the unusual step of countering the opinion of fellow critic Atkinson by going public with strong praise for Gene: "A tap-dancer who can characterize his routines and turn them into an integral element of an imaginative theatrical whole would seem to me pretty close to unique. He is not only glib-footed, he has a feeling for comment and content that both gives his dancing personal distinction and raises it several notches as a theater art."

Regardless of the pros and cons, or perhaps aided by the debate and controversy, *Pal Joey* managed a decent run of 250 performances in the first season and returned the following year for another 104 performances—a middling result that barely reimbursed the backers for their investment. For the creative participants, though— whom Gene Kelly in his movie days would define as "above the line"—it was a monumental boost to their careers. A *succes d'estime*, he would forever term it in his ubiquitous French. Not just a series of specialty numbers stitching together a meandering and predictable plot, the book, music, lyrics, and essential Kelly dances of *Pal Joey*, conveying a sexy world of corrupt Chicago nightlife, made it a memorable experience in the theater. Gene thought it would be a great movie. And nobody deserved the role of Joey more than the actor who had created it at the Barrymore. That was for the future; now he meant to enjoy the limelight of being Broadway's newest star.

Though he was underpaid for the role and the producers made not even a gesture toward raising his salary, he was earning more than he had ever made in his life. But the self-styled Depression Kid, child of a woman who still counted pennies, saw to it that the checks went directly into the bank. He drew on the account sparingly, and splurged only to upgrade his room at the hotel. For the first time in New York, he now had a private bath.

Johnny Darrow felt that Gene was engaging in an excessively spartan style for a star. He looked for ways to augment his client's income. He booked Gene into a late-evening performance at a well-known night spot, the chic Rainbow Room. It would not only mean extra bucks; it would unveil another Gene Kelly to prominent movers and shakers of the theatrical world. Darrow wanted to display a more ingrati- ating public side to Gene, separating him from the nasty Joey Evans persona.

After his performance at the Barrymore, Gene and Darrow hurried to the Rainbow Room. It was a packed house which was fine, just what they wanted. Everything else was wrong. The orchestra leader introduced Gene as George Murphy. The musicians couldn't get the tempo right. The acoustics contributed bizarre sounds. Worse, the after-theater crowd talked and smoked during his performance. Nobody threw coins at him, but it was as bad as the "cloops."

In the elevator going down from the top-floor club, they both knew Gene would not be asked back. In his assuaging agent way, Darrow started to explain the dismal audience reaction: Gene's work was not "superficial and social." But the evening had been such a fiasco, Darrow could not finish; both agent and client broke up in laughter before the ground floor was reached.

The experience firmed up a Kelly resolution: From now on, he would never depend on anyone else for arrangements. He would check and double-check in advance that the setup met his specifications. People would continue to call him a perfectionist. In his judgment, the apt word was "professional." He had considered the Rainbow Room a kind of audition, a scrutiny of his talents. But the circumstances were unfair and undignified, and he was past the point of enduring these psychic tortures.

Soon, however, he was gratified when Darrow reported a flow of inquiries from the major Hollywood film studios. Yet every one of them was attached to a requirement that he appear at some grimy locale in Manhattan, New Jersey, or Long Island City for an ill-prepared screen test. He had never forgotten the ridiculous session he had been put through at RKO, when he and the Kelly family were in California. So now, when Darrow telephoned about a studio's interest, if a screen test was required Gene cut off the agent before the deal could be described. Darrow thought his position was overreaching, but his client was adamant: If you want to see what Gene Kelly can do, buy a ticket for *Pal Joey*.

Betsy was not eager for Gene to accept any offer that would spirit him away to the West Coast. Saroyan, true to a pledge made to her at the bar of Bergen's, had cast Betsy in his new play *The Beautiful People*. She was replaced in *Panama Hattie* by a young woman named Jeanne Coyne, a Pennsylvania dancer new to New York, who had originally studied at the Gene Kelly Studio of Dance. Gene remembered Jeanne—they always kidded each other about the same first name—and liked her, believing her to be talented. So did Betsy, who was thrilled to leave the musical for a speaking role, brief as it was, in a serious play.

Betsy Blair visits Gene in his dressing room during the run of Pal Joey. *(Courtesy of Photofest)*

Gene and Betsy were now full-fledged working actors, and they had less time to be together. On a day when there was no matinee, they might take in an art exhibit or a lecture somewhere, but the only relaxed, unhurried hours were at Bergen's after showtime. She continued to be amazed at what a serious, purposeful person Gene was, constantly presenting a book he wanted her to read or clippings from the *Times*. At Bergen's he would steer her into the company of men and women he regarded as interesting intellectuals, usually with extremely left-wing ideas. Here in the dizzying atmosphere of a crowded bar, the impressionable seventeen-year-old concluded that the New York intelligentsia was exclusively composed of communists and socialists. While Gene, beer in hand, drifted off to join other groups—she knew it was part of his educational effort on her behalf—she would be forced to engage in debate. At Bergen's she first regretted her lack of formal education; dropping out of school might not have been a good idea. Despite the crash course of reading Gene encouraged for her, she felt unlearned. Karl Marx could have been one of the Marx Brothers, as far as she was concerned. She intensified her program of study, especially regarding the grave issues facing the world in wartime. There were plenty of active political radicals in the vicinity who were only too anxious to guide the attractive, receptive teenager. She began to be a regular reader of *New Masses*, the Communist party journal. She joined in heartily when, always just before closing, a group would start singing the Russian anthem, "Arise, Ye Prisoners of Starvation." Thanks to her omnivorous reading, she came to hold her own in spirited disputes.

"Before I knew it," she told an interviewer years later, "I'd become interested in socialism myself—so much so that I even attended some Marxist lectures which Gene didn't. In that area of my life it was really a case of the pupil overtaking the master."

Those at Bergen's who attracted her were men who took the most fiery anticapitalist positions, displaying a passion she found magnetic. It was just the out-of-control quality she still missed in her relationship with Gene. They still had not slept together. Any number of times she suggested they go to his hotel after leaving Bergen's. Gene would have none of it; she was, he made clear, still underage, barely on the cusp of adulthood. Perhaps, she was beginning to conclude, his reluctance to advance the erotic aspect of their relationship represented some sort of old-fashioned gallantry, or a Catholic hangup. Assuredly, he was not gay; she even had the notion that, on the nights when they didn't see each other, he had a few drinks and enjoyed one-night stands with other women reassuringly closer to him in years. He could then satisfy himself sexually with no guilt feelings.

She did not press him. Time was on her side. What with the role in the Saroyan play—minor, but a real start for her acting career—and the exciting diversity of New York, she had to admit she was enjoying her independence.

One night, though, her composure was shaken when she arrived at Bergen's. There was a message that Gene had to cancel their date. Judy Garland had come backstage at the Barrymore after a performance of *Pal Joey* and invited him for supper. No apologies from him, no explanations. He didn't make her feel any easier the following afternoon when they had coffee together and he spoke glowingly of the movie star's visit. One delicious detail after another came across the table at Betsy;

he could not stop. The huge retinue surrounding Garland—mother, press agents, manager, security guards, others he could not identify. People at adjacent tables in the posh restaurant applauding as they came in and sat down. A pair of twin girls in their teens, at a birthday celebration with their parents, standing and chirping "We're off to see the Wizard . . ." And going to the Copacabana where he and Judy danced till 1:30 A.M. Betsy nearly choked; offstage, he'd always been reluctant to dance with anybody, even her!

Gene was too wrapped up in his narrative to notice Betsy's discomfort and went on: How Garland had asked her mother for permission to ride in a horse-and-buggy carriage with Gene through Central Park. (Imagine, Betsy steamed, having to ask her mother.) How during the ride Judy praised his performance in *Pal Joey*. It was his "big break"; she classed it with her own in *The Wizard of Oz*. And the wonderful way she had said goodnight when he returned her to the hotel. "It would be great if we could make a picture together," he quoted, his eyes on Betsy but surely not seeing her. "Great," she lied, convinced that Gene would soon be off to Hollywood, leaving her to defend the policies of the Soviet Union at Bergen's.

He told her of Arthur Freed, producer of *The Wizard of Oz*. "He came backstage to see me one night after seeing *The Time of Your Life*. Arthur told me I'd be great in pictures." "Great," she said again; he had recounted Freed's visit more than once. But it had a different context now: Gene was already tired of repeating his performance in *Pal Joey*, over and over again, and had never been one to sit back and enjoy success. The *next* project would always be the captivating one.

That night with Garland in 1941, the expressed desire of a major movie star to team with him, was now pointing Gene Kelly toward film, toward Hollywood, and away from New York—and, Betsy thought, herself. The bloom was off the rose in his feelings about the New York stage. Gene now saw the drawbacks of live theater. It was not like a solo dance where he could constantly improvise, change a step or movement, and keep himself challenged and interested. In *Pal Joey*, if he did something different one night, there was always the danger of throwing off another performer. The stage manager would be upset, and Richard Rodgers, always taut as a kettledrum, would be furious. And while he was repeating himself nightly and at matinees, week after week, the opening of a new musical would always steal the limelight. The hottest show in town was always the newest; any day now *Pal Joey* would be left dancing in the dark.

One night a writer named Fred Finklehoffe, then doing a project for Arthur Freed, came backstage at the Barrymore and told Gene that Freed had recommended that L.B. Mayer, operating head of the MGM studio, see the show on his next trip east. "Whether it's to put in a bid for the movie rights to *Pal Joey* or interest in you, Gene, I really don't know," said Finklehoffe. "My guess is it's you. It's a great show you're doing here, but it's too grim, too down-and-dirty for L.B. He'll never okay it for a Metro musical."

"That figures," responded Gene sourly. He had never met Mayer and did not like what he had heard, though Judy Garland had spoken surprisingly well of the MGM boss. As an executive producer, Mayer seemed interested only in churning out fluff about an America that existed only in his immigrant imagination, a storybook land where there had never been a Depression and everybody was white, warmly housed, fully fed, lived with close-knit families, went to church on Sunday, and lived happily ever after. Mayer was also, not incidentally, a hefty contributor to the Republican party.

Sure enough, a week later Mayer's assistant contacted Darrow and made an appointment for Gene. "Alone, if you don't mind, Mr. Darrow. Just a get-acquainted session." Gene arrived for the appointment with Mayer unsure of what he wanted and what was possible. His dilemma was that, clearly, the most stylish and admired film musicals were being produced at MGM by Arthur Freed. He was ushered into the office always reserved for the MGM chief on trips to New York, a vast and luxuriously furnished suite with a breathtaking view of the city. Mayer was in a conference, a secretary told him, and would be out shortly. Gene went to the window and took in the high-angle panorama of Manhattan. He had just managed to locate the small and shoddy Hotel Woodward when Mayer entered.

"Mr. Kelly," the movie magnate said, advancing to shake hands. "Mr. Mayer," Gene responded with equal force. When they were seated, Mayer congratulated him for his performance in *Pal Joey*. It took him by surprise, and he responded almost automatically with a "thanks, Mr. Mayer" and immediately regretted his own tone. Obsequious. Was he trying out for the part of Uriah Heep? He was no Harry the Hoofer any more, dammit, no starving actor hungry for a job.

His thoughts were disrupted by Mayer's abrupt question: Would he like to work for MGM? Mayer was ready to contact Darrow and work out "a favorable deal."

Gene reported on the meeting years later in an interview for *The World of Entertainment*, a movie history by Hugh Fordin: "I was sure Arthur Freed was behind all this. But I didn't want to make a test in New York—everybody had warned me the work was inferior." To his bewilderment, the subject of a screen test never came up with Mayer. "I saw you and I'll sign you," the movie mogul said expansively. "You're fine . . . fine."

When he left the building Gene immediately phoned Darrow. The agent had been worried about his client's hostile attitude toward Mayer. Now he was exultant. "Great! I'll close the deal when he calls me. Next stop for you, boy, is Hollywood!"

A few days later, however, reality—or perhaps MGM inefficiency—surged in with a vengeance. A company staff man in New York telephoned to arrange for a screen test. "There must be some mistake," Gene responded irately. "Mr. Mayer made it clear: no audition, no screen test!"

"Sorry," was the unbending response. "I have in front of me a memo from the home office in California. What they want is—"

"I don't give a bloody damn what they want! Mr. Mayer said no, repeat, no screen test!"

It actually was a mistake. Somehow a request by Freed "for a set of stills of the Kelly boy," who was being considered for a role in *Strike Up the Band*, had been garbled. Had each party remained calm and only picked up the phone, the matter would have been cleared up within minutes. But such was not the Kelly way.

Perhaps he had to live up to his already notorious Irish temper. He did not consult with Johnny Darrow. He sat down immediately and wrote a sulphurous letter to Mayer. It had the tone of a manifesto of a true man of the people, concluding with a triptych of in-your-face declarations: "I'm sorry. I won't work for you because you lied. I'd rather dance in a saloon!"

No one was happier than Betsy Blair that Gene had quashed the possibility of working for Mayer, "the right-wing punk who had lied to him." She did think Gene might have overreacted a bit. Although she was by now well to the left of Gene politically, she was more practical about the value of important contacts in show business. The head of MGM was not a good choice for an enemy. But at least Gene's outburst kept him in New York and kept the possibility of marriage within reach.

With all the strains of dealing with a person whose attitude toward lovemaking was baffling, hurtful, and unnatural, she was determined that when and if Gene went to Hollywood, she would be with him. She would even go *now*, with not a word about marriage, but what was the point with this Catholic conformist, this mama's boy? He gave absolutely no indication that he wanted her to go west with him. In her most bitter moments she brooded that the part of *Pal Joey* had gotten to him; he had become a user of women without any sense of commitment. Every few days, it seemed, Gene was having meetings with a representative of one Hollywood studio or another. Darrow was frequently on the phone with him. On the late night walks through the summer heat from Bergen's to the Henry Hudson Hotel, that irritating citadel of her virginity, all Gene could talk about was this possibility at Warner's or that one at Paramount. And not a word about them!

She began to date other men, and she made sure Gene knew about it. One night at Bergen's, when she was there with a bearded editor of *New Masses*, Gene came over and there was an exchange of small talk. Gene mentioned that Darrow had set up a meeting for him with David O. Selznick, the producer of *Gone With the Wind* and *Rebecca*.

"Isn't he the son-in-law of Louis B. Mayer?" Betsy asked.

"I'll try not to hold it against him," Gene replied. And, as it happened, the following day when he met Selznick he liked the producer on sight. Selznick spoke highly about Gene's performance at the Ethel Barrymore. "I saw you. I like you— and I want to sign you."

"Just like that?" asked Kelly.

"Just like that."

"That's what Mr. Mayer said, and he lied." He told Selznick how the experience made him wary of Hollywood producers and their "devious ways." Selznick took this with considerable calm; he'd heard about Kelly's temper. "Well, I won't order a screen test for you. What I saw at the Barrymore was more than enough."

"I hope so. I hope I can trust you. You sons of bitches are all alike."

It was, of course, outrageous, but since Kelly's diatribe had been instigated by the father-in-law he detested, Selznick was disposed to let it all pass. "Have Darrow get in touch with me and we'll set the deal."

The agent, always feeling buffeted from all sides when making arrangements for

Kelly's screen career, settled with Selznick quickly. A contract was worked out for a seven-year period with a starting salary of $750 a week. The contract with Selznick would begin officially in November. Gene had three months to clear up his affairs in New York. *Pal Joey* had been put on hiatus for the summer. The producers intended to reopen the show in the fall. When Gene notified George Abbott he would not be available, Abbott countered with another proposition that would bring a substantial increase in income. Gene would work with Georgie Tapps, his successor in the role of *Pal Joey* and, in the time he had remaining in New York, would choreograph a new Abbott show, *Best Foot Forward*, with a book by John Cecil Holm, lyrics and music by Ralph Blane and Hugh Martin. Like a Judy Garland–Mickey Rooney "Let's put on a show!" musical, it was a silly story about a famous movie starlet who accepts an invitation from a student to attend his school prom. It was a plot that made Gene wince, exactly the kind of absurdity Hollywood and Broadway were disgorging one after another.

It was not coming along well in rehearsal. Gene conceived new dance numbers which delighted Abbott, who invited him to assist in the overall direction of the show. Gene persuaded the producers that a rollicking story of a high school needed an infusion of fresh youth, and this gave him the opportunity to recruit several of the more talented graduates from the Kelly studios in Pennsylvania. The best of these was Jeanne Coyne and, again, she came into the orbit of his life. Jeanne was a superb dancer and very attractive, too, in an appealing, perky way. Betsy knew her well—she had taken over Betsy's place in *Panama Hattie* when Betsy left for *The Beautiful People*. Whenever Jeanne worked with Gene, they were homonyms in harmony; an extra effort was always there that implied an intimacy, a long-time closeness between them. Seeing the adoration in Jeanne's eyes whenever Gene was present, Betsy felt twinges of jealousy. But for her there was no turning back from the decision to let Gene go.

While *Best Foot Forward* was in rehearsal, Abbott pleaded with Gene to resume his role in *Pal Joey* after the summer hiatus. The director even spoke to Darrow about delaying Gene's move to California. Perhaps an adjustment with Selznick was possible? Darrow declined. The agent was certain that film was Gene's pathway to stardom. However, an agreement was reached that Gene would play the first two weeks when *Pal Joey* resumed, with the aptly christened Georgie Tapps in the wings, studying his performance carefully before taking over.

Those two weeks, starring in the show at night while serving as assistant-director to Abbott by day, left Gene barely any time to prepare to go to California. But he felt good about himself. He had created the starring role in a breakthrough show. GENE KELLY was on the marquee. And the Playbill for *Best Foot Forward* credited him as choreographer. On all counts, he had accomplished his goals in New York.

He managed to arrange a quick trip to Pittsburgh. All was well with the studios under the direction of his parents and his brother Fred. Best of all, Harriet was still relishing the memory of seeing his name in lights. What more could be asked for? When no one else was present, his mother did bring up the subject of his girlfriends, or lack of them. He was, after all, nearing thirty—getting up there for a Catholic boy. Blessedly, that Jewish Marlowe girl, once a worry, had gone her own way. But what about that bright young thing she had met at *Pal Joey?*

Indeed, what about Betsy? On the train back from Pittsburgh he found himself thinking about her and, amid the rush-hour crowds of Penn Station, he headed for a phone booth. At the very sound of Betsy's voice, the effect on his racing heart, his suddenly thickened words and inability to make sense, made him wonder why he had been such a jackass as to let her slip out of his life.

The next day was Saturday, with two performances of *Pal Joey.* He met her at Bergen's after the evening performance. She was alone. He had much to tell her and, for once, it wasn't all about his problems with *Best Foot Forward* or her problems with *The Beautiful People* or even the problems of the world—it was about them. At 5 A.M., outside the Henry Hudson Hotel, he proposed. He couldn't help thinking, ever the showman, that in a play or movie the moment called for a song. And a dance. Betsy had an immediate idea. *Best Foot Forward* was starting a trial pre-Broadway run in Philadelphia. Gene was required to be present to review the show one last time. She would go with him, and they would elope. Simple.

He knew elopement was out of the question. Betsy was seventeen. Without her parents' consent, a marriage license would not be granted. In any case, Harriet would never sit still for a nonreligious civil ceremony. The first step, clearly, was for Gene to buck up his courage and call Betsy's father and withstand the mumbles about her being too young and win his consent.

When he called later in the morning, Betsy's parents were thrilled. Yes, Betsy was amazingly precocious but still a teenager and a constant worry besides, what with her impulsive left-wing notions. What better for their daughter than the support and protection of an established star? They swiftly made arrangements for a Catholic ceremony.

Gene and Betsy were married at St. John's Church, in Philadelphia, on September 24, 1941. Mr. and Mrs. Kelly came over from Pittsburgh for the ceremony. As it turned out, after a few more conversations between them Harriet was not enthralled by Betsy. She found her restless, adventurous spirit disquieting—but then no woman of Gene's choice could ever bring forth her enthusiasm. Still, Betsy was attractive and intelligent, and her parents were decent people, eager to cooperate. So, always convinced Gene could have done much better, Harriet accepted her new daughter-in-law as best she could.

It could never be soon enough for Betsy but, at last, *Best Foot Forward* had its opening night. Gene truly didn't think much of the show, even though he had given style and polish to the dances and received Abbott's hearty praise. To Gene it certainly did not have any sort of serious creative aspirations, as did *Pal Joey,* so he was honestly surprised when *Best Foot Forward* opened to almost unanimously excellent reviews. The show would play 326 performances, 56 more than his Rodgers and Hart vehicle. Now there was a round of parties and what seemed an endless series of goodbye toasts at Bergen's. William Saroyan sidled up to the bar, gave Betsy a long farewell kiss, and promised her a part in his next play. Most of the attention was centered on Gene. There was excited talk he would be doing the film version of *Pal Joey*. Nothing could have pleased him more, of course, and he urged Johnny Darrow to do whatever he could to make that happen.

Jeanne Coyne came by on the final night at Bergen's to tell Gene she intended to try her luck on the West Coast. Betsy broke in to invite Jeanne to be sure to contact them. She sensed her new husband would want it that way, and she even felt a leftover tinge of concern. She made the identical invitation to Stanley Donen, who was also planning to go west. She knew Gene thought Donen was talented and could be helpful to him as an assistant choreographer. For her part, she found Donen very appealing. She was sure the attraction went the other way, too.

On that last night at Bergen's it was a struggle to hold back the tears. Betsy would miss New York far more than Gene. It wasn't the music, the shows, the libraries. It was the diverse collection of extraordinary people—the originals, the wackos, the brilliant, the clever, the opinionated—she had met here with excitingly fresh minds that had forced hers to grow. Now, on the eve of their departure, there was a foreboding that California somehow would diminish her, as if the steady, boring sunshine would melt her down. Her role would not be side-by-side with Gene Kelly but forever trailing him. That it was, after all, Gene Kelly's world, not Betsy Blair's, was a hard feeling to shake.

He *is watching the big screen, and there they are in sailor suits, bouncing through clips of* Anchors Aweigh *and* On the Town, *Sinatra now and then sneaking those ol' blue eyes down at his feet, unsure of the steps. Sinatra was never one for rehearsing, and it shows.*

It strikes him, not for the first time, that a sailor suit is the ideal tap outfit, snug enough to limn the body, not too tight in the crotch, nice and full for those quick moves. But after Pearl Harbor it felt squirmy to wear that uniform on screen when on the Murmansk run and the Coral Sea kids in uniform were facing the real thing. So he'd enlisted. Subtitle: HITLER, HERE I COME!

But the Navy's like MGM. It calls the shots. GK's an officer and a gentleman, but of course! So, in a hurry, boot camp serves up a thirty-day wonder. Assignment Washington. In a hurry! Still going through his share of chicken-shit, when to get up, when to eat, when to turn out the lights. In a hurry! Then Lieutenant Junior Grade Eugene Curran Kelly is awaiting assignment and waits and waits. Super subtitle for life in the military: HURRY UP AND WAIT!

The same subtitle is apt for the movies. Or, at least, for David O. Selznick. Christ, like a maniac he had rushed everything to wind up his activities in New York, his final performances in Pal Joey, *his choreography for* Best Foot Forward, *a breathlessly arranged marriage with an impatient teenager hot to trot, sober goodbyes to his mother and drunken ones with his buddies at Bergen's—a blur of departures with its own bristling subtitle inscribed across his mind: HOLLYWOOD, HERE I COME! Yeah? Five months later and he still isn't facing a camera. No subtitles. A blank screen.*

LOS ANGELES, 1942

* * *

On October 2, 1941, Gene and Betsy drove into the Lincoln Tunnel and left New York behind. On the trip west, Gene was true to form. At every overnight stop, he insisted on keeping in touch with the Selznick office by phone. He was worried about being late for an assignment. No matter how Betsy tried to relax him, there was the fear of missing a casting call. He was rattled when he got through to the producer—which was by no means every time—by Selznick's casual reaction now that he and Betsy were finally Hollywood-bound. "There's no hurry, Gene. You kids should enjoy yourselves."

Betsy expressed delight with the prospect of prolonging what she regarded as an extended honeymoon. She added more stops to the itinerary, more sights to see, as it became apparent no shooting script awaited her husband in California. With some trepidation he agreed to her route changes and they cut south to New Orleans, where (after another unproductive call to the Selznick office) they boarded a banana boat for Vera Cruz. Then back in the States, calling California every second day now, it reached the point where he would be chuckling as he pushed out of the phone booth, his thumbs up, a jubilant signal they needn't bolt to California just yet but could continue their deliciously haphazard way. And so they went on.

They toured national parks, joining tourists at popular attractions or making their own quirky choices of sites, all the way to Oregon. Betsy was radiantly happy, most of all because she knew he was. They were thrilled to be alone together at last, able to reach for each other free of inhibition, far more eager to make love than to eat or drive on. With every distancing mile from his mother and the Henry Hudson bastion of virginity, with every day and night, Gene seemed to become an even more tender and passionate partner, in every way fulfilling Betsy's hopes and fantasies. For his part, she was more than just a precocious teenager; he found her a beautiful, blooming young woman, even more unpredictable, funny, and quick-witted than he had believed in New York. Her mind challenged his. There was a touch of the original about every perception, an ability to grasp the essence of a new experience, serious or silly, with a speed that awed him.

Above all, she had the precious gift for giving pleasure and wanting it. If she only could—he joked with her—she would keep him traveling whimsically for the rest of their lives. She didn't deny it. She was at him, especially in bed, constantly making fun of his solemn workaholic ways, talking of the need to relax. Their honeymoon was a unique opportunity, and she used every argument, logical, seductive, or preposterous, to rein him back. Knowing that the writing team of Kaufman and Hart was a favorite of his, she pointed out they had written *Once in a Lifetime* and *You Can't Take It With You*—"and, what's more, Gene, Kaufman was born in

Pittsburgh"—all as some sort of supporting argument for leaving the highway to explore an out-of-the-way barbecue joint revered by blacks, a President's birthplace, an Indian reservation. She was a flame igniting his energy.

From Oregon they drove to San Francisco for a visit with William Saroyan. Mischievously, Betsy inquired about her part in his new play and Saroyan responded with a cackle of laughter. He had just completed a one-act script called "Hello, Out There," and it contained parts for both of them. Gene and Betsy had no idea if Saroyan was serious, but somehow Gene's mood was affected by the exchange. The light-hearted conversation about plays and parts seemed to rev up Gene's career concerns again, and he abruptly insisted they leave and head for Los Angeles. After all, they had been away, out of the show business fray—in his Francophile vocabulary, *hors de combat*—for six long weeks.

Their enchanting interlude, breathlessly brief, was over now. On the Pacific Coast Highway toward Los Angeles Gene's body seemed to hunch forward over the wheel, which he gripped with both hands. No soft squeezes of Betsy's shoulder, no intermittent caresses; an interior motor was humming. He brought up the name Selznick in every other sentence. She showed her irritation by evincing no interest, once they were in Los Angeles, when he made a flamboyant declaration that they were at the crossroads of the movie colony.

They had barely checked in at the Roosevelt Hotel when he was at the phone trying the Selznick office, then Darrow, then other contacts in town—friends like Van Johnson and Keenan Wynn from New York. Nobody was in.

Betsy sat down without unpacking. Gene said, "I don't mean to be hogging the phone."

"It's okay, Gene. Go right ahead." She was depressed, he could see—suddenly a teenager who had opened a beribboned Tiffany package only to find a mundane gift certificate inside.

They went to dinner at Musso and Frank's, saw the Brown Derby, and walked around Grauman's Chinese Theater, the motion-picture fantasy palace built in the 1920s. They drove past the homes of stars and moguls in the canyons of Bel Air and Beverly Hills and nearer the sea at Malibu. He tried to find a studio to show her but he did not know his way around, and the important companies were some distance away; MGM was ten miles or so to the southwest in the suburb of Culver City. For the first time in their relationship she told him she was tired and wanted to close off the evening.

Gene shared Betsy's mood when they returned to the hotel. There had been no signs of movie-making, and they had not spotted even one film star. It could have been Pittsburgh. All the way across the country he had raved to Betsy about the constant sunshine. Now the day had ended in a smoggy dusk and the residual smell of burned fuel was everywhere. It had not been a Grand Entrance.

Worst of all was her reaction to what he told her as they undressed for bed, in an effort to offer a kind of reassurance: "You know, Betsy, Hollywood is less a place than a state of mind." She managed a pathetic smile of appreciation. He was ashamed of himself for letting the aphorism stand without a credit, as if it was his original thought and not a cliché that Darrow had heard and had passed on to him. (Many years later, interviewed in *American Film Monthly*, Gene Kelly described the typical reaction of Broadway actors arriving on the Hollywood scene: "When I came out here, I thought of the famous Fred Allen line, 'Who wants to make love to an orange?' The New Yorkers who came out here hated the movies. We came out to make some money.")

The next day he left Betsy at the hotel to investigate a more permanent living arrangement and was in the reception room of Selznick's office when the producer arrived. Much to Gene's relief, Selznick was affable, and there were warm greetings and friendly questions about the trip as they stepped into Selznick's private office. For Gene the meeting went downhill from there. It was apparent they had differing ideas concerning his career. He was shocked that Selznick, who had signed so expensive a contract, had no plans for using him. There was no production-ready script. Having poured his energy into a succession of enormous hits, *A Star Is Born*, *The Prisoner of Zenda*, *Rebecca*, and *Gone With the Wind*, Selznick was in no rush to start another picture. And—certainly the most crushing point to Gene—Selznick had no particular interest in involving himself in a musical; given his success in elaborate narrative films, he had no disposition to change. Indeed, what had drawn him to hire Gene was Gene's potential as a dramatic actor!

Furious, Gene drove back to the Roosevelt, intent on telling Betsy to pack up for the return to New York. That possibility held on for perhaps a mile before reality stopped him like a red light. He had cut his ties to Broadway. Georgie Tapps was now Pal Joey. He and Betsy would have to stay. He would see if he could work something out, if not with the bewildering Selznick, perhaps with another producer.

Johnny Darrow operated a small real estate agency as a sideline. He found the Kellys a charming, if tiny, house in Laurel Canyon, on quiet Lookout Mountain Drive. It was furnished solely with a bed and a ping-pong table. Betsy, whose buoyancy had been restored by a good night's sleep, saw a metaphorical significance in what had been left to them by the previous tenant: a start-up residence with a place to make love and a place to play. Gene thought she was just being Betsy, but his own spirits were raised by her positive attitude. It reminded him—he did not dare tell her—of his mother. But Betsy being Betsy was just what he needed and wanted. What he specifically did like about the place was something that would not please visitors or Betsy: From the driveway, it took a climb of more than a hundred steps to reach the front door. Bounding up and down them was an ideal way for Gene to keep in shape.

Selznick's plans remained a mystery, but his checks arrived every week to finance the furnishing of their rented house, piece by piece. Betsy, a newcomer to domestic duties, took on these responsibilities with the zeal of a bride. Her omnivorous reading now narrowed to cookbooks. She concentrated on the dishes Gene favored, especially Harriet's fish stew, a Kelly perennial. The first letter from his mother to their new home carried the recipe.

As someone who had been a bachelor through his early adulthood and had never lived, while away from his parents, in spaces that allowed for playing host—it had usually been grungy apartments that he had shared—Gene was eager to start inviting his New York friends and the people they began to meet in Los Angeles. It was not just a matter of seeking show business contacts to jump-start his career. It took only a short time to realize that Hollywood's entertaining, unlike New York's, was done at home. His desire to have guests over to Laurel Canyon was blocked, though, and not just by the maddeningly slow way the cottage was furnished. He was embarrassed by his lowly status in the film colony, really his nonstatus, with no assignment or film debut to talk about. What was there to do at parties except nod at the gossip and good fortune of others? An excruciating position for him; he simply could not bear it.

Gene turned down invitations to play at Hillcrest because he really didn't like golf, eighteen holes to fill with conversation. He found tennis, by contrast, no venue for shop talk, and he picked up the game and quickly became rather good. He and Betsy came to know the best bookstores—Martindale's, Hunter's, and Stanley Rose's on Hollywood Boulevard—and evenings were passed in reading, especially now that Betsy's cookbook phase had come and gone. They shopped for breakfast at the Farmer's Market and pursued a yen for Nova Scotia salmon and Jewish pastrami, which made them homesick for Manhattan.

Darrow's mantra "out of sight, out of mind" in this context meant not begging any questions affecting the weekly arrival of Gene's check, but Gene persisted in calling the Selznick office almost daily. Selznick did not appear to be bothered. On the contrary, he had time on his hands now, his working schedule had slowed down, and he enjoyed Gene's company, especially as a drinking partner. He would schedule his meeting with Gene as the last appointment on his calendar; then they would repair to a bar for drinks which would extend to dinner and whatever evening plans Selznick had in mind. The fights at the American Legion Stadium were always a favorite, followed by a postmortem brandy or two or three in some hideaway favored by Selznick. Wherever they had been, it would be very late when Selznick's limousine dropped Gene at home. Sometimes, despite the late hour, Selznick would follow Gene up the dizzying cliffside steps as they made their way to the house. Wheezing, the producer would grin sheepishly at the teenage wife wearing a hastily donned dressing gown and who served some much needed coffee.

When Gene first introduced Selznick to Betsy, the producer was taken with her and made a point of constantly congratulating Gene on his choice. Selznick sent her flowers more than once. One time, referring to her bravado in appearing without a touch of makeup after being awakened, he sent roses with an accompanying note: "To an unretouched angel, for her courtesy to drunks at dawn."

The stairs rising from Lookout Mountain Drive were not to exercise Gene and challenge visitors for long. Torrential rain started a mudslide, and they had to move. After a stay at a temporary rental, the Kellys moved again to a more substantial home on Alta Drive, subleased from lyricist Yip Harburg, one of their left-wing acquaintances from New York who had written the Depression-era song "Brother, Can You Spare a Dime?" Along the way, Betsy announced that she was pregnant.

Right now they could afford these dislocations, thanks to Selznick's continuing largesse. In terms of cost they were living in a housing heaven, compared to Manhattan. In the early '40s a furnished two-bedroom house in West Los Angeles with a decent front lawn and even a flower garden rented for $85 a month the first year and $75 the second year if the tenant chose to stay. And, for the first time in her life Betsy now had some disposable income; Gene gave her a weekly $100 cut of his check. (She had never earned more than $35 a week.) Moreover, Gene took care of the bills for any clothes she bought on a charge account and he got her a used car.

Back when Betsy had come to New York and met radical intellectuals she was shaken by their vivid accounts of the Depression, and reading *New Masses* and other Communist journals and attending demonstrations at Union Square had opened her eyes to the squalor and hopelessness of millions of Americans. As a child of middle-class parents on fixed incomes, she had endured tortured discussions about money at the breakfast table every day and she became determined never to let money or the lack of it rule her as it did her mother and father. On her cross-country trip with Gene she had seen the "one-third of a nation" that was ill-fed and ill-housed according to President Roosevelt's fireside chats. Now, in a disorganized way, spurred on by her emotions and whoever was the latest to ask for help, she wrote out checks to movements or fund-raising organizations that promised to change the political and economic system.

Gene respected her leftist sympathies; to a degree her political direction matched his own. When he felt she was not applying cool logic to the overheated screeching of the Communist Party chief Earl Browder, of *The Daily Worker*, and of *New Masses*, he blamed it on Betsy's youth. Every now and then—especially when one of her checks was returned by the bank, marked "Insufficient Funds"—he discussed with her the need for budgeting and an awareness of expenses. She listened, and she tried. But a talent for handling money was not hers. The need to economize was clear, but so were the needs of the destitute. Gene knew that if it were not for his cautions, she would give away what he was giving her. As the weekly check from Selznick International made things easy, so a serious decisiveness about their financial state became elusive.

To this point, thanks to Gene's unpredictable producer and drinking pal, Hollywood was a never-never land of easy come, easy go. Still, there were pressures. When the news of the Japanese attack on Pearl Harbor came over the radio, many men in the Hollywood community enlisted—stars and stagehands, production workers, technicians, and back-office staff. Gene was tempted to join up too and discussed it with Betsy. Now in the early stages of a difficult pregnancy, she certainly did not want to be left alone on Alta Drive, but the U.S. and the U.S.S.R. were allies now, and Hitler's armies were advancing on Moscow. It was hard for her, she admitted, to peer out the window on a sunny day and see her robust husband mowing the lawn while the world was imperiled by fascist aggression. It was difficult for Gene to stay calm in the face of her inconsistency. One day she would make the sacrifice and wanted him to enlist. The next day there was the wonderment: How could she possibly get through the birth of his child without him?

Meanwhile Harriet Kelly's letters and phone calls did not help. By this time

Harriet was impatient for news that her son had finally been cast in an important movie. She did not want him to rush into uniform. He would soon be a father and, anyway, wasn't it enough that Fred was now in the Army?

Soon it would not be a matter of choice. Local draft boards were swinging into action. Deferments were harder to come by. Gene half-expected to be called into service. He hoped to hold it off until the baby was born. Meanwhile more and more items in the local newspapers reflected the many faces of Hollywood at war. The Republic Studios, where gunfighting westerns were ground out weekly, volunteered to turn over most of its warehoused stock of small arms to Civil Defense and received an official commendation from the War Department. The Producers Association called a special meeting to discuss the need for "morale-building" films. The Army, Navy, Air Force, and Marines vied with each other to offer logistical help at no cost—training barracks, parades, target ranges, aircraft carriers, pilots and planes, regiments of uniformed extras—all for the making of movies that glorified the military.

At the studios, the use of night locations, arc lights, and spotlights outside the blacked-out soundstages was no longer permitted. Japanese-Americans were wrenched from their homes and moved to camps in the interior of the country, and it was now hard to find qualified Asians to play the enemy in combat scenes. Want ads called for chorus boys who were draft-deferred by being "legitimate 4-Fs." With all the difficulties, the movie industry was thriving as Americans flocked into cinemas across the country for a respite from the worries of wartime. Though the studios had lost personnel to the military, production stayed active, mostly on B pictures of modest budget, the second halves of double bills. For expensive productions each studio seemed to take a different tack in making its special contribution to public morale. 20th Century–Fox was emphasizing musicals—*Moon Over Miami, Springtime in the Rockies, That Night in Rio*—places people couldn't easily visit anymore, with stars like the Scandinavian skater Sonja Henie, the motor-mouthed siren from South America, Carmen Miranda, and the GI's favorite pin-up, Betty Grable. Reflecting the close relationship of the Warner family with FDR and the Democratic Party, Warner Bros. was early into supporting the war effort in almost every film. The major musical on the Warner lot during 1942 was a biography of George M. Cohan, *Yankee Doodle Dandy*, with James Cagney. It was drenched in patriotic fervor, but Cagney made it work—as did *Casablanca*, with Ingrid Bergman and Humphrey Bogart, a sentimental portrait of a world that Roosevelt and the Warners were determined to save from the rampaging Axis forces.

As for MGM, toward which Gene felt hostile largely because of his bumpy dealings with Louis B. Mayer, it was the wealthiest and most influential of the studios. But, Gene thought, it did not put itself on the line for the Allied cause; what was coming out of Culver City was a parade of wholesome family entertainments: the Andy Hardy films with Mickey Rooney, exotic escape-extravaganzas like *Random Harvest*, with Greer Garson and Ronald Colman, and the musicals to which Gene paid special attention. These were humdrum features with such safe and predictable performers as Jeanette MacDonald and Nelson Eddy, Ann Sothern, Red Skelton, and Eleanor Powell, whose rat-a-tat tap dancing was the closest evocation of a machine gun permitted on the Metro lot.

Gene was convinced by now that Selznick would never use him and would simply discover one day—or would be informed by a zealous bookkeeper—that a lot of money had been dribbled away while Gene had not delivered one role. To keep his client sane and calm, Darrow delicately persuaded Selznick to arrange for Gene to visit the major studios "and get to know the environment." Gene was relieved to have a place to go in the morning. He watched the best actors perform, saw how they hit their marks, and observed the technique of the big-time directors.

If his survey of the various studios had one high point, it was Gene's introduction to Fred Astaire at Paramount, where he was co-starring in *Holiday Inn* with Bing Crosby. Gene was flattered that Astaire knew of his work in *Pal Joey* and had some generous things to say in his usual low-key way. Gene tried not to be effusive but, as was often to be the case when he and Astaire were together, he felt uneasily inadequate, unable to be completely relaxed in the presence of the famous dancer to whom he was already being compared. As he left the Paramount lot, he felt depressed, even angry with himself, mentally rewriting his lines in the encounter with Astaire. A clear case, he knew of *esprit de l'escalier*, as the French would put it, always thinking of the perfect thing to say just when the moment has glided past.

He knew Astaire was probably a dozen years older. About the time Gene was doing a warm-up act at the Penn State junior prom, the team of Adele and Fred Astaire did a command performance for the King and Queen of England. Despite Astaire's head start, the contrast between his and Gene's current status was almost unbearable. What pegged Gene even more as a nonentity was something petty but pinching: Paramount's security staff had refused him a parking place on the lot, and he had to walk three long blocks into a residential section to his car. Naturally, the windshield was flagged with a parking ticket. It was that kind of day.

He was in a sour mood when he returned to Alta Drive. There was, of course, no message from Selznick or Darrow. He saw less of Selznick these days; the noted producer was attending to the worldwide distribution of his blockbuster films, traveling abroad, doing deals or doing mischief—Gene had no idea which. But surely, there was no progress going forward with any casting of Selznick's former drinking buddy in a part, any part.

Since graduating from St. Raphael's, it was the longest period Gene had ever gone through without gainful employment. The arrival of the check in the mail every Monday morning, welcome as it was, now scoffed at his manhood, his talent. At times, he would complain to Betsy, he felt like one of the many Okies who had migrated from the Dust Bowl to California, a jobless recipient of relief payments kept afloat by Roosevelt's New Deal. Because Broadway, under wartime blackout conditions, offered dim prospects, and Betsy's pregnancy was very much on his mind, he considered going back east to resume his responsibilities at his dance schools. With his brother Fred now away on tour with the soldier show *This Is the Army*, returning to Pittsburgh made sense. Pittsburgh was not heaven to Betsy; when he brought it up with her, she was aghast at the prospect.

Somewhat to his surprise, absorbed as he had been in his pursuit of Selznick, she was building a busy social life. He had noticed she was often away at meal times. Strangers, male and female, made frequent calls. Despite his reluctance, she insisted that they put on parties, and she proved to be a deft and popular hostess, not only providing the requisite buffets of food and drink but introducing what she called with mock grandeur "The Game" to spark up an evening. (She had developed a proficiency at this form of charades in the chaperoned lobby of the Henry Hudson, where it had helped to hold carnally minded male visitors at bay.) But Gene's juvenile embarrassment at his so-far lackluster film career was hampering her rise on the social ladder, she told him acidly. But it was Selznick's fault, not his! Where oh where was the tough-minded man she had married? By this time their decibel level had spiked upward in the loudest argument thus far in their marriage. What's more, she lamented, once the baby was born she had every intention of resuming her own career as a film actress, for admirers were telling her she had something really special to offer—in Hollywood, not Pittsburgh or, God defend them, Johnstown! And with that shouted declaration she turned and raced tearfully up the stairs.

To calm himself Gene went for a long run, but without the usual steadying effect of physical exercise. He stopped at a diner for coffee. He couldn't get through a cup without stepping over to the newsstand near the cashier. Anything—even a lousy tabloid or *Variety* to read as an anodyne—to help him stop thinking of the mess he had made of his own prospects and his marriage, of his rotten luck at being tied to that madman David O. Selznick. Being in Hollywood, the stand contained no real newspapers. There was a group of real-estate folders, tourist brochures, and trade-paper throwaways he didn't recognize. He picked one up when he saw on the front page: NEXT FOR SELZNICK: KILTS? The gist of the article was that Selznick had returned from Europe, having optioned *The Keys of the Kingdom*, the best-selling novel by A. J. Cronin, and that a film adaptation had already been completed. Selznick had high hopes for the project. Gene hurried to a bookstore and bought a copy of the Cronin work.

When he returned home Betsy embraced him at once, apologizing, and he could barely respond no, no, it had been his fault, he was so goddamn jumpy lately. But now he had a feeling his luck was changing, and he pointed to the book in his hand. "Selznick. He's back in action again."

"I read the novel," Betsy said. "He's turning it into a musical?"

"God knows. Either way, I've got to be in the cast. Got to! The guy's made my life miserable. He owes me."

Gene stayed up late that night to read the novel and found it a throbbing, engrossing story. Not trusting his own judgment in his currently distracted state of mind, he had Betsy look over it again. She agreed with him, and the next morning he was on the phone to Selznick's office. The producer took his call right away. "I guess you read it in the trades. About my picking up Cronin's book?"

"Yes."

"Well, there's a great part in here for you, Gene. A wonderful part. Start off your film career with a bang." Gene said nothing. "It's the lead, the missionary priest."

Gene had thought it through. Careful not to make too much of it, he expressed his appreciation of Selznick's faith in him, then explained why he was sure that the part was not right for him. Or, more accurately, that he was not right for the part. He could not—yet—carry a lead dramatic role. After all, he emphasized, *The Time of Your Life* was the only "straight acting" he had ever done. And that was on the stage. He was half-hoping Selznick would brush aside his reservations. But the producer countered, with an immediacy that bothered Gene: He could play the part of the Scottish doctor. Selznick was being extraordinary thoughtful.

"That's more like it, David. To tell you the truth, for a lead role I'm worried about the accent. But to carry one or two big scenes—"

"You'll be fine. After all, Gene, you've a hell of a talent for languages. Your French is pretty damn good, and you haven't even been near Paris. I'm going to put you onto a Pasadena vocal coach we use. In a couple of weeks, no one will believe you're not some guy from Glasgow."

Gene had his doubts, especially when he started to work on his lines. The Scottish doctor proved to be a more difficult role than the missionary priest. It involved a couple of long speeches and some tongue-twisting medical terms. It was difficult to sustain the accent and the rhythm of the sentences. Every day he commuted to Pasadena, the eager student of an expert on dialects who, it developed, had never been within a thousand miles of Scotland.

After ten days Selznick phoned him. The mood was businesslike. Selznick no longer invited him out for drinks; the post-midnight appearances at Alta Drive for Betsy's coffee were history and he was showing none of the camaraderie of their drinking-buddy period. "Before we go into production, Gene, I'll have to arrange a screen test for you. That would be helpful, considering the accent problem."

Selznick's request was legitimate, but Gene felt uneasy. "Whatever you say, David."

At least after all the delays there was now a sense of movement. Even a bit part in *The Keys of the Kingdom*, done with skill and sensitivity, could finally jump-start his film career after all these frustrating months.

The producer did him the courtesy of being alone in the executive screening room of Selznick International, in Culver City, when Gene arrived to see the "dailies" of his screen test. Gene had not slept well the night before, worried that the test had gone badly. Selznick did not say a word but gestured for him to take a seat in front while he remained at a desk lined with black and red telephones, high in the steeply raked mini-theater. Selznick pressed a buzzer. Instantly there was a stream of white light from the projection booth, then a chalked slate appeared. G. KELLY TEST, he read. Then there was a project number and the date. The spareness of the slate, the no-nonsense of it, was a light-year away from the Broadway marquee bearing his name. All at once he felt stripped naked in the darkness, a nobody without his accolades from George Abbott, Richard Rodgers, and John O'Hara. He felt like, well, a beginner, like the terrified teenager who had walked into his life at the Diamond Horseshoe—and before he could organize his thoughts there he was on the screen.

He looked all right, considering the makeup that had been slathered on him. But the editor had not synched the soundtrack properly! Words did not match picture, his lines were way off, and then, with gathering horror, he saw his mouth writhing and heard animal-like sounds—he was talking goulash. He couldn't hold back any longer and burst into nervous laughter over the sheer comedic tour-de-force of his accent. Suddenly conscious that Selznick, a few rows back, was reacting the same way, he now knew, with a clarity that shocked him but could not stem his own cackles, that he had been set up. He was just a pain in the ass to Selznick, a weekly drain on the bottom line of Selznick International and, in a typically overpriced and elaborate Hollywood way, the producer was telling him to get lost.

When he arrived back at Alta Drive, he tried to explain the traumatic moment to Betsy. All she could feel was Selznick's treachery. "Not at all," he said, burying his real feelings. "You can't expect him to subsidize us forever."

"What's going to happen now?"

"We sell a hell of a lot of furniture, right after the baby comes. Then we start back for Pittsburgh."

"Ohh, no, please, Gene!"

"Well, maybe Darrow will have a better idea." He still could not believe Selznick had sunk him without a trace. A month later he read in *Variety* that Selznick had sold off the "package" of *The Keys of the Kingdom* to 20th Century–Fox as a vehicle for Gregory Peck. The ethnically correct Thomas Mitchell would play the Scottish doctor.

Selznick would always be a mystery to him. The weekly parade of checks did not stop. Gene never found out why the producer suddenly turned cold. Why the abrupt banishment from drinking-buddy status? And why, in the first place, had so canny a producer inveigled him to come across the country to this callous, ball-breaking Hollywood?

They stayed in California. They told themselves it was because of her pregnancy. That they loved the steady sunshine. Or that there was the remaining lease on the Alta Drive house. There were many reasons they lobbed at each other across the living room, avoiding the one that counted: For Gene Kelly, afire with ambition, to go back empty-handed without even one screen credit was inconceivable. How could he face his mother?

One Monday, shortly after he opened the mailbox to find the Selznick check—expected but still the weekly pinprick at his pride—a call came from Johnny Darrow. Promising news: Arthur Freed at MGM wanted Gene for his new musical *For Me and My Gal*. There was a key part in the film supporting Judy Garland and George Murphy. Darrow was nervous his "wild Irishman of a client" would walk away from the opportunity. Kelly had made no secret of his snappish letter to Louis B. Mayer about the screen test (a perfectly reasonable requirement, in Darrow's opinion). In the Alta Drive living room the agent had heard both Kellys inveighing against Mayer—"Mr. Republican." From the way Gene's outspoken young wife sounded off, Darrow thought she had to be a Communist or at least a Socialist. But the agent knew, above all, that Gene Kelly had been unemployed long enough. His real love was his work. And Gene assured Darrow he would do everything possible to win the role in *For Me and My Gal*.

As he told his English biographer: "I was very tempted, in spite of how I felt about Louis B. Mayer. Well, I was older now and not quite so headstrong as I'd been on Broadway. Besides, I was anxious to work and the thought of doing a picture with Judy Garland really excited me."

Darrow was quick to work out a deal with the suddenly and bewilderingly cooperative Selznick, who "did not want to stand in Gene's way." A loan-out was arranged. Gene's draw of a $750 weekly salary was now taken over by MGM. "I think we can do a little entertaining now," Betsy said.

"Don't send out the invitations just yet," was his response. He still could not cope with being a Hollywood host as an unemployed actor. Anxious to get the first film under his belt, he would breathe easier after the first day of shooting and once he knew he wouldn't be fired.

For Me and My Gal was his initiation into the movies. Except for Judy Garland, who had probably persuaded Freed to take him on, nobody on the set would be disposed to help him. "At that time," he recalled later, "I was constantly being thrown by the piecemeal way in which pictures were being made. I knew nothing about playing to the camera, and I didn't even know whether I was being shot close, medium, or long or about the intricate business of hitting all the marks laid out on the studio floor for the movements of the actors."

In For Me and My Gal, *Judy Garland and Gene helped each other through some difficult moments. (Culver Pictures)*

The day before shooting was to start, Darrow sat him down for an urgent review of the situation. There would be tensions on the set, the agent warned. First of all, there remained the sticky matter of Gene's letter to Mayer; it was inconceivable the irascible MGM head would not exact some revenge, if not directly (fearful of upsetting the fragile Garland) then through his assistants, Sam Katz, executive in charge of musicals, and Eddie Mannix, the studio manager. Already, both men had weighed in with negative judgments. Mannix, indeed, had told the agent directly:

"I don't see any motion-picture potential in Kelly. I certainly don't see him as Harry Palmer."

Gene had a negative reaction to the shooting script, starting with the time frame of the story, the years embracing World War I. It was typical of Metro, he thought, to avoid the reality of the battles now raging in Europe and turn a sentimental, chauvinistic light on past victories. His part, Harry Palmer, was that of a pushy, opportunistic hoofer whose only ambition was to play the big time at the famous Palace Theater in New York—a character much like Joey, which was probably the reason Freed wanted Gene for the role.

Judy Garland was cast as Jo Hayden, a talented but naive vaudeville performer who falls in love with Harry and teams up with him in a new song-and-dance act. She breaks off her engagement to Jimmy, her longtime loyal partner, played by George Murphy. The newly formed duo of Hayden and Palmer is an immediate sensation. There is a tidal wave of bookings. Just when starring at the Palace is within reach, Harry receives a draft notice. He is determined to stay and play the Palace. He will not be sidetracked from his dream, war or no war. He slams a trunk lid down onto his fingers to become 4-F, physically disqualified for military service.

Meanwhile Jo's kid brother leaves school to enlist in the Army and is killed in action in Europe. Grief-stricken, Jo turns on Harry for his cowardly, unpatriotic action. She scorns his reasons and tells him tearfully she will never perform with him again. Harry is ashamed and, after much brooding, has a change of heart. He manages to get overseas as an entertainer doing a solo act for front-line troops and returns to New York in time for a grand finale of Hayden and Palmer at the Palace.

Even as a song-and-dance vehicle, Gene didn't think much of the script. And here he was being cast again as a cad, typed as a resourceful but dirty-playing Pal Joey.

Darrow did not want Gene to report to the set the next day in a dispirited mood. He tried to close their talk on a cheerful note. "Gene, you've got a damn good part in *For Me and My Gal*. Hey, at the fade-out, it's you who gets the gal!"

"Big deal," responded Gene sourly.

"That's what it was to George Murphy. He wants the part of Harry Palmer. It's more juicy than good ol' Jimmy, who's left at the altar. Murphy pitched Berkeley and Berkeley agreed—agrees with him." Busby Berkeley, the director and choreographer, would make the film. Gene was no admirer of Berkeley's approach to dance, another reason he could not show Darrow the enthusiasm the agent was trying for.

"Dammit," Gene snapped. "If Berkeley and Mannix and the MGM brass don't see me as Harry Palmer, then why the hell did Arthur Freed hire me?"

"In two words, Judy Garland. Murphy was supposed to have that part. That's what Busby Berkeley promised him. So now they're both pissed off!"

Gene said, "There's nothing like a happy set."

The next day, the first date on the shooting schedule, he drove to the MGM studios at Culver City. Darrow's briefing had not been brief—the agent had stayed on for several hours telling Gene all he knew about Berkeley and Murphy gleaned from gossip as well as reliable firsthand sources. They were a formidable pair with friends in high places. Gene would have to tread lightly.

He had been at MGM before, when circumstances were very different. During the period of what he and Betsy called "the Selznick sabbatical," he had kept a low profile on his visits to the various studios. Even though the Selznick office would call in advance, he had been sensitive about being an unemployed observer and stayed out of the way on a sound stage when observing a director at work or a cast in rehearsal. Unobtrusively, he would take a seat behind an editor cutting a workprint at the Moviola and was always scrupulous about asking for permission first. Now, as he pulled up at the entrance gate and one of the security guards approached, clipboard in hand, he knew it was time to shed his introvert persona and be Pal Joey again. He was an arriving star, here to play a role opposite Judy Garland.

He would deal forcefully with Berkeley and Murphy, two old-timers whose day was done. He would not be intimidated by them or—his eyes swept over the complex that surrounded him—the walled city that was MGM. It was a variegated, vast enterprise providing jobs, temporary lodging, and meals for a huge number of employees—3,000, Darrow had told him—actors, executives, secretaries, gaffers, best-boys, makeup specialists, audio technicians, carpenters, drivers, scenic designers—a seemingly endless list of categories ranging from the most prosaic to the most exotic. There were sound stages, recording studios, post-production centers, office buildings, warehouses, a rendition of New York's Lower East Side, and a Western street, complete with tethered horses and fifty extras waiting to witness a gunfight between a sheriff and a man in a black hat. There was a hospital and a commissary and a string of barber shops, a headquarters for the MGM police, and dressing-cottages for the stars. He was early, so he paused to admire the fourteen-room Spanish-style bungalow paid for by William Randolph Hearst, Mayer's good friend, as a present for his mistress, Marion Davies. It brought to mind, painfully, his overheated letter to the MGM mogul. He would pay somehow, and dearly—he knew it.

Busby Berkeley was contained and polite when Gene arrived for the first meeting of the cast principals. Everybody present knew what was at stake for the aging director. Berkeley was fighting to hold onto his position and was troubled by alcoholism and poor health. Arthur Freed had given him what was really a last chance to revive a fading career. The director had come early to Hollywood when the coming of sound attracted scores of dancers and singers. In 1929 and for several years thereafter, dandified young men and cute chorines pranced for the camera in the manner of Broadway—a second-rate Broadway, that is, of directors bereft of ideas on how to stage dances for film—and by the early '30s movie musicals had lost favor with the public. But Berkeley revived them, making his initial reputation with a glittering series of Warner Bros. musicals—*42nd Street*, *Golddiggers of 1933*, *Footlight Parade*, and others. He excited studio executives with the potential of dance on film, the Busby Berkeley way: elaborate visual confections, platoons of dancers in flower-like geometrical formations, dazzlingly inventive kaleidoscopic patterns with illuminated violins or swaying pianos—there were seemingly no limits to his imagination.

But not in Gene Kelly's judgment. From the start he saw Berkeley's dances as set pieces, standing apart from the rest of the film, giving a surreal air to the musical number and the flow of the movie. Berkeley's choreography had nothing to do with furthering the plot or developing the characters. Worse, because Berkeley's numbers were so elaborate, to hold them within the scope of the realistic motion-picture medium, it was almost always necessary for the writer to design a plot around the production of a gargantuan stage show. It was the only way to give an essence of believability to the presentation. Swaying pianos did not belong on Main Street; only the likes of Madison Square Garden or Yankee Stadium could contain the fantasy numbers. Berkeley's technique, Gene felt, put a heavy-handed restriction on musical comedy.

Though there was a conflict in the creative outlook of the two men on the set who knew and cared the most about dance, only days into the production Berkeley—already plagued by fatigue and alcoholic tremors—realized what Gene had to offer. It became clear that Gene could design his own dance numbers, particularly the solos and the more intimate one-on-ones with Judy Garland, to give a warmth and energy to his relationship with her and to the overall film. Berkeley found ways to give signals to Gene that it was okay with him. Deserving of his recognition as one of the greatest of all dance directors in film, ironically, Berkeley himself could not dance and had to hire somebody to do the demonstrations for him. He was gratified when Gene stepped in to take over that role in an easygoing, unpretentious way. Drunk or sober, by the third week of shooting Berkeley realized that Gene was not only a unique talent but was saving an old man's job.

For his part, Gene recognized Berkeley's unique strength and learned from it. Berkeley was best at arranging large groups of performers in colorful, inventive ways, then placing and moving the camera to cover their moves in a boldly abstract way. As Gene would relate to interviewers: "I would just watch what Busby did with the camera. The camera was the most important dancer. We could move it anywhere we wanted and that gave us all the advantages."

Berkeley's initial coolness toward Gene changed to admiration over the weeks of hard work, but George Murphy never wavered in his undisguised hostility. The veteran song-and-dance man had hoped *For Me and My Gal* would top off what he regarded as a distinguished career. A plum role had been snatched from him for reasons he couldn't fathom (unless, as he continually hinted with some rolling of the eyes, there was some hanky-panky between the newly married Garland and the newly married Kelly). Murphy's role, Jimmy, was the perennial, smiling sidekick who didn't get the girl at the end. Murphy's had been no easy climb. He had started in show business at the age of twelve, when he formed a self-taught dance team with a neighborhood girl. Teamed as Johnson and Murphy, the pair had caught on in the happy-go-lucky years before the Depression, playing the best of the speakeasy circuit and then cabarets, including the famous Cotton Club (they were one of the few white acts to do so). Murphy felt strongly that his Johnson and Murphy period qualified him for the role of Harry. Known for dancing with a lighthearted charm, he had a controlled elegance that embraced both tap and ballet. In 1934, tall, handsome, and debonair in white tie and tails, he had moved from stage musicals to movies, initially cast as a singer, then as a singer-dancer. He had appeared with Astaire, Eleanor Powell, Shirley Temple—and now he was supposed to smile and make way for a "nobody" like Gene Kelly?

Murphy may have played acquiescent as Jimmy, but he was no patsy on the set. He recognized Busby Berkeley as an icon among dance directors but was quick to let Eddie Mannix know that the numbers could be done more efficiently with less cost. He had no shortage of choreographic ideas. He would present them forcefully to Berkeley, often coming to the studio with a diagram of a dance number he had concocted. He was persistent and charming, but there was steel behind the smile. There were a few times when the fatigued, hungover director said with exasperation: "Let Murphy shoot the number."

"I think he was being sarcastic," Murphy said. "But I said: 'Okay, I will.' And you know what? I did the number and we got it done in no time." Murphy would then go on to say—as he would relate years later when he was Senator Murphy of California and a prospective Republican candidate for President: "I'd like to be a producer. And I'd take charge of all the musical numbers. And I would take ten percent of what I could save the studio as my salary. I tell you, I could own the studio in two years."

Gene was obliged to hold his tongue during those off-camera pronouncements by his embittered rival. Darrow reminded him that Murphy was a favorite of Mayer and Mannix because of his conservative politics; he was considered a restraining influence on the newly organized film unions that were bringing headaches to the MGM executives. Gene felt good about For Me and My Gal except for his reservations about the script and the contacts with Murphy, and, seeing the reactions of those on the set, he was certain his dancing would be a high point of the film, especially his two favorite numbers, which Berkeley had essentially ceded to him. One was a solo early in the story, when he did a deliberately hammy vaudeville routine climaxed by bouncing across the stage on the palms of his hands. Even more, he was pleased by the first meeting of him and Judy in a railroad station diner, where he sits at an upright piano and they talk, dance, and sing. When they recorded the audio track for the song a few days earlier—in the scene, they are on the cusp of love singing hopefully about a possible future together—her voice, so mellow and tender, had seemed to bring a strength to his own, often so shaky and insecure to his own ears. Days later on the sound stage when they danced to the soundtrack she was so appealingly hesitant against his quiet confidence, his sexy intensity, that the rapport was something magical. The overall master shot of the dance drew handclaps from the usually unresponsive crew when Berkeley yelled, "Cut and print!" Gene had put in many extra hours coaching Judy through the dance steps. It was the least he could do by way of saying thanks. He enjoyed the times with Judy so much he was certain the chemistry between them was right, their interplay easy and natural, just the way it had to be.

He would forever be telling interviewers, when questions were posed about the psychological stability of Judy Garland: "Without her, my first few weeks at MGM would have been more miserable than they were." The problem was that he had to learn film-acting techniques on the job, and Berkeley, with no gift for dramatic direction, could not help. As Gene Kelly later told *Interview*'s Graham Fuller, describing his first attempts:

> They weren't very good; as a matter of fact, I think they were pretty bad . . . but I could see that there was some kind of cinema know-how. I quickly learned that with Judy in my first picture, *For Me and My Gal*. She was so good. I sort of followed her around on those little vaudeville routines we did.

With others in the cast—Murphy, Ben Blue, Richard Quine, Keenan Wynn, and the very professional Marta Eggerth, he tended to overact, punching out words, mugging as though he were still trying to reach the rear balcony of the Barrymore. Understatement—the essential quality of a real film actor—was something he did not pick up easily.

Unlike a stage show, motion-picture production logistics allowed him and Murphy to perform their tasks separated one from the other. To the final wrap Murphy felt cheated of the plum role he deserved, but there were no blow-ups. The shooting went smoothly enough even though Garland took sick and was unavailable for four weeks. MGM was hopeful for a box-office winner.

Gene felt his first movie had gone reasonably well, and Betsy found the domestic atmosphere much less tense. Gene was impatient for the post-production to be completed. He felt his status was still "up in the air." The preview would be a key part of the whole process before any mass order of release prints could be effected. It would decide his future with MGM.

The location of the first public screening was always kept secret until the last minute. The unveiling of *For Me and My Gal* was held at a cinema in Westwood Village, not far from Louis B. Mayer's ranch. As a representative of Gene's interests, Johnny Darrow felt Westwood was a lousy choice. Many producers at Metro argued that the theatergoers there had become spoiled and surfeited, nonchalant about new films, and not at all typical of moviegoers across America. The word around the studio was that Mayer didn't want to be away from his horses any longer than necessary. Consequently, Westwood ran more "sneak previews" than any other cinema. Darrow managed to get seats for Gene and Betsy in one of the limousines amid the flock of MGM executives converging on the theater and entering in a deliberately low-key way. It was a weekend audience. When the manager of the theater announced the surprise preview of a major MGM musical, contrary to Darrow's prediction there was a buzz of excitement. Patrons looked around to see what stars were in the audience. Judy had called in sick and was not present. Neither was George Murphy. Nobody paid any attention to Gene.

Now that he had made his mark as a working film performer, a co-star with Judy Garland no less, he felt more relaxed about Betsy's determination to become an important player in the Hollywood social scene. It seemed every weekend was Open House at the Kellys', initially at her insistence, but he came to enjoy their parties, too. They helped keep his mind off the editing cubicles at Metro, where he felt his future was being decided. He had tried to stay clear of gossip about the film and speculation about how it was shaping up in post-production and its box-office prospects. Since the shooting wrap on the set, he had talked to nobody in the cast. There was nothing in the trade papers. Once he had tried to call Judy but she was away, involved in her divorce action against the film composer David Rose. It would have been nice to feel her friendly presence at the Westwood. Darrow, meanwhile, was passing along no job offers; there was not even one inquiry as to his future availability. "It's all going to happen after the preview," the agent assured him. He envisioned Judy, just as she had bolstered him throughout the shoot, standing up with her timid smile and taking in the applause of the audience after the closing credits. Then she would surely introduce him: "My co-star Gene. . . ." No such luck.

Now the opening titles flashed on. At least it would give him a chance to look over the film and his performance with a fresh eye. The scenes with Judy worked for him. But not much else. He was embarrassed by the inadequacy of the script and seeing it played out larger than life on the screen. He squirmed at one corny, predictable line after another. The periodic insertion of ringing patriotic sentiments was shameless. And again, except for his scenes with Judy, his overheated performance as an ambitious, dancing draft-dodger made him swear to bury Pal Joey for good. He was even startled by the sequence when he purposely maimed his hand; it may have been intended as a note of realism but it was completely out-of-touch with the blithe quality of what was, after all, a musical comedy.

"They love it," Betsy whispered, not for the first time. Somehow her enthusiasm made him scrunch down even further in his seat, eyes closed. But the audience's pleasure at certain moments came through to him: especially his and Judy's rendition of the title song and the jazz dance "Balling the Jack." His hand-standing dance was a triumph. When the lights came on he turned to Betsy and seeing her so wide-eyed and excited, he could not spoil her mood, and he said: "They like it."

"You idiot! They love it!" She hugged him, and as the audience around them stood and applauded, peering down in wonderment, he wished he could tell them the excited woman was not just a teenager, but his wife.

The reaction cards were passed out. He and Betsy left the theater and, outside in the lobby, were congratulated by a number of MGM executives. Mayer had already been escorted to his limousine, but Freed stayed and Mannix, too, involved in a quietly buoyant conversation. Busby Berkeley, perhaps a tad drunk, was very emotional and kept shaking Gene's hand until Freed came over. "You know, Gene," said Freed, "when we cast you, Eddie Mannix told me he did not see any motion-picture potential."

"So I heard," said Gene.

"Well, word does get around in this town. But you know what Mannix just told me?"

"Arthur, word doesn't get around that fast."

The producer laughed. "Mannix said to me: 'Arthur, remind me not to tell you how to make pictures.' That's his way of saying you were great, Gene. And that means Mayer feels the same way."

"We'll see soon enough," said Gene.

Along with the MGM executives in the lobby he knew their boss would not commit himself until the reaction cards were collected and analyzed. The following morning the findings of the *For Me and My Gal* preview—columned, analyzed, summarized—were conveyed to Mayer. At once the euphoria of the Westwood lobby was gone. A full 85 percent of the respondents reflected disgust that a "draft-dodger" was the hero of the film. The self-inflicted disfigurement of his hand to avoid military service was despicable. George Murphy, not Gene Kelly, deserved to win the affections of Judy Garland. "What the hell were we thinking?" Mayer was heard to moan, sending immediately for Freed and Mannix.

Johnny Darrow had a friendly informant in the Metro office and heard about the reactions as early as Mayer did. His call woke Gene, who was thunderstruck. Darrow was blunt: It was the worst possible scenario. Mayer would order a rewrite and reshoot. "With your pal Murphy as the Golden Boy who gets the gal."

"Ohh no, can't be!"

"Ohh yes, gotta be! Mayer won't let the picture go out this way. It's un-American! Say what you will about the bastard, he wraps himself in the flag. He's more 'America First' than Lucky Lindy!" Darrow liked his client too much to remind him of the infamous letter, the ultimate reason Mayer would never lift a finger on Gene's behalf. Harry Palmer would wind up on the cutting-room floor. Gene slammed the phone down bitterly.

Everybody involved, as it happened, was not disposed to give enough credit to the resilient Louis B. Mayer, who ordered Freed to do a repair job. Freed called in a pair of new writers who added two major sequences to the shooting script: Harry Palmer, a volunteer entertainer of American troops on the battlefields of France, is trapped in a combat zone as the German enemy advances. Ignoring his civilian status, he seizes some hand grenades and enters the fight, demolishing a crucial German machine-gun nest, paving the way for the successful American counterattack. Now an acclaimed war hero, Harry joins Judy at the Palace for the grand finale performance—without George Murphy. Between the new scenes, film editors placed vivid combat footage lifted from King Vidor's MGM production *The Big Parade*, creating a montage of an intrepid Harry always advancing, always throwing grenades, never retreating.

The last-minute conversion of Harry Palmer from heel to hero did not come cheaply. It involved twenty-one days of additional shooting and months of additional post-production activity, boosting the cost of the movie to slightly over $800,000. *For Me and My Gal* was a resounding success. In its initial release the film grossed $4.5 million. And it made Gene Kelly a household name.

The MGM publicity department, headed by the highly regarded promotional wizard Howard Strickling, took out a huge advertisement in the *New York Times* proclaiming the arrival of a great new star. And what pleased Gene almost as much was that he, not Murphy, got the gal!

He got another, too, younger and much more meaningful to him: About the time *For Me and My Gal* was released, his and Betsy's daughter was born, on October 16, 1942. Gene wanted to name her Bridget. Betsy thought Bridget was too cloistered, had too much of an Irish-Catholic scullery-maid connotation. He replied that his mother would like Bridget. She told him she didn't give a damn. She wanted a name that "had a lilt to it," that reflected energy and ambition. She proposed Kerry. Gene did not wish to fight or quibble; he was finally in a wonderful mood. So they compromised. Kerry Kelly it would be.

Gene was now signed by MGM for seven years, with options at a salary of a thousand dollars a week. He had a beautiful baby, a lively if provocative wife who was ready to resume her own career and the parties that were to establish them among the creative elite of Hollywood. True, he was thirty years old, too old to become a ballet star. But coming to Hollywood had been the right move. There was plenty of time ahead to sing and dance in movies the world was waiting to enjoy.

God knows he has paid his dues at these glorified goodbyes. Dumping his usual slacks and shirt to put on a tux, the cummerbund pulling at his belly. . . . Now the montage of film clips gives him a chance to check out the audience, even in the half-light. Astaire was last year's nominee, so of course he's here. Next to Hank Fonda is Jimmy Stewart, now returning his thumbs-up with a jovial military-style salute. Good to see you, General!

Where are the others on the A-list seated? Like the prizes in Cracker Jacks, not clumped up but scattered. Toward the front, on the aisles, where the hand-held videocams can get at them for the network cut-ins. Gracious as always, doing a bit of business for the "photogs," Astaire now throws back his head and laughs at something his new young wife is saying. Why is it that dancers—those few of us who go for girls, that is—so often rob the cradle when we marry?

Astaire versus Kelly. The PR flacks at the studio always tried to build up the contest. Remember the old Bob Hope gag that Reagan had the chutzpah to use, last year at the Kennedy Center? "Every time Gene Kelly starts dancing, Fred Astaire starts counting his money." But it never really took hold, the rivalry. Fred is older, a different generation, with a totally different style. Fred—dressed to the nines for the Delmonico crowd. In the same costume Gene Kelly's a truck driver going to meet the mayor. Fred and he always danced to different drummers. It's that simple. And Fred's career peaked in the early pre-war days, when television was not around to offer a feast of dance through the week. For free, if you didn't mind those steady drumbeats of praise for Alka Seltzer and Buick. And millions of moviegoers didn't mind and stayed home.

He watches Astaire watching the screen, intently waiting for the clip from Ziegfeld Follies. The only time they danced together. "The Babbit and the Bromide," words and music by the Gershwin Brothers—looking at the damn clip now, he still has to agree that Pauline Kael's review was right on the mark. It looks as though he's trying hard to show Fred and Gene having a wonderful time. Trying too hard.

All at once, as though a gofer were knocking on his Winnebago dressing room, he comes out of his drowse. The houselights come on along with his expression of delight—remember that video crew—and Shirley MacLaine is at the podium again, looking just great in her smashing red gown. As interested as he is in words, in writing, and in talking with precision, he can never describe a woman's outfit. Shirley's is deliciously red and she looks fantastic. His mood brightens. And it's icing on the cake when he makes out another Fred—the most important Fred in his life, his brother. With the rest of the Kellys. Now, almost as if some higher power—surely, his sainted mother!—still were connecting them like a family magnet, Fred and the rest of them are not peering ahead at Shirley. They are all turned toward him. Those Kelly smiles glittering even in the blurry light. His eyes fill with tears. He needs to wipe his glasses. But first, he gives the thumbs-up signal. The sign he always used on the set when the shot was okay for Cut and Print. It's a wrap and a move to another location for the next scene.

Los Angeles, 1943

* * *

None of Metro's other current song-and-dance projects had a suitable role for his second film, but Gene now had plenty of work. There was no shortage of assignments, yet at first none drew his passionate interest. As he told the magazine writer Graham Fuller: "After *For Me and My Gal*, I was pushed around for a few years doing films where I didn't have dancing partners—little program pictures, which I was glad to do because I liked to work."

What he termed "little program pictures" were to be Gene Kelly's creative output for the next two years. Not at all in the languid Selznick style, MGM was eager to keep him working for his salary and, influenced by Selznick's dogged opinion that Gene's future was not limited to musical roles, put him in narrative films as well.

Gene was quickly developing a reputation for a flaring temper; he was considered a talented but tough-minded actor with ideas of his own, unlike less lustrous, less troublesome contract players such as Van Johnson or Dan Dailey. MGM was like a major-league ball club sending him to the minor leagues for further seasoning. So Gene was next cast in a wartime B movie.

It was better late than never for MGM to get on the bandwagon with the Warner studios to support America's war effort. Although intended as a routine programmer, *Pilot Number 5*, with an original script by David Herz, had been pushed by the influential Dore Schary, head of production and an active liberal firmly in the Roosevelt camp. (Within a few years it was known that Schary would replace the aging Louis B. Mayer.) Schary felt that though it was budgeted as a B picture, it showed every promise of outgrossing some of the A pictures—and he shortly persuaded Gene of this.

Pilot Number 5 was an episodic drama directed by George Sidney, the son of Mayer's key assistant, L.K. Sidney. Told in flashback, it concerns an ambitious young lawyer who becomes involved with a fascism-inclined politician. To Gene the reference was to Huey Long, the dictatorial governor of Louisiana. The lawyer, in his uneasy partnership with the politician, is forced to do more and more depraved actions, until he sacrifices a promising career to enter the Air Force and continue his fight against the enemies facing a democratic America.

Gene was cast just below the star, Franchot Tone. He played, curiously enough, a moody, philosophical Italian-American. His voiceover—fortunately, no accent was required—narrates the tale, which leaves Louisiana behind and is set in Java under Japanese attack. To Gene and, even more, to Betsy, the film would at least register as a strong statement against fascism, drawing a parallel between corrupt political power in the United States and the threat of Germany, Italy, and Japan.

Gene worked hard on the film, but he was not happy about the experience:

> We intended a warning against fascism at home, based on the memory of Huey Long and the danger of one man gaining control of a state. But MGM lost its nerve about taking any kind of a political stand at that time, which is not hard to understand: We were in the entertainment business, and this was wartime. So the script was totally defanged.

Gene's own performance did not meet his standards. But, never one to waste his time, he labored hard on his lines and moves with Sidney, sensitive about his lack of experience. There were no flashy dances to call attention to himself. He felt the constant pressure of raising the level of his performance in scenes with Franchot Tone and Marsha Hunt, two intelligent and talented actors. Gene realized Tone was always holding back, underplaying, proving that film acting is a province where less is more. Later on, he analyzed his performance in *Pilot Number 5*:

> I was trying to give a performance all the time, and that's about the worst thing you can do. I looked fine in the long shots but the close-ups weren't any good. In fact, I've never learned how to do a close-up the way, say, Spencer Tracy did. . . . I had a tendency to overact.

Critically, his performance in the film was at best patronized, and he wanted to leave it behind and get on with the main thrust of his career. He knew by this time it would be musicals. Responding to the pressure that Gene was never reluctant to apply, L.B. Mayer—who never tired of joking to his fellow executives about Kelly's absurd letter swearing he'd never work for MGM—saw to it that Gene was next assigned to *DuBarry Was a Lady*, the movie version of Cole Porter's Broadway hit starring Ethel Merman and Bert Lahr, from late 1939. For MGM *DuBarry* was a "showcase" film, one of many tapping into "more stars than there are in heaven"— Mayer's proud boast, except when he was in an irritated mood, when he would add: "except that damn mouse owned by Disney."

In its usual cavalier fashion, MGM spent a fortune to buy the Broadway show, then made the decision that Merman and Lahr would be fatal for the film and replaced them with Lucille Ball and Red Skelton. Worse, Metro emasculated Porter's score, using only three of his numbers and pulling in six songwriters to replace the show's seventeen other songs. From the outset, there was no particular idea undergirding the film; the point was to stack it with nothing but entertainment and hang it all on a bare-bones plot. Gene was given third billing. He immediately rendered a complaint, confirming his growing reputation as a disgruntled, radical, left-wing troublemaker among studio executives. But at least it was a musical, and he was happily assigned two of the three Porter originals that survived: "Do I Love, Do I?" and the chorus number "Friendship."

From the start, he showed his unhappiness with the dance direction of Felix Seymour. Gene knew instinctively in the first moments of his meeting with Seymour that their ideas did not mesh. Seymour was, in Gene's eyes, an elderly man whose day had come and gone—a Berkeley without that visionary's use of the camera. He marched into Freed's office and suggested that Seymour be replaced by his friend and benefactor Bob Alton or by Charles Walters. (It had been Walters who, a few years earlier, had proposed Gene for Harry the Hoofer in *The Time of Your Life* on Broadway.) Seymour protested and complained bitterly that Gene was only swapping favors. Gene was adamant, but he simply talked about his conceptions of the dances.

Freed was very sensitive to people of talent and saw that no personal animus was involved. Convinced that Gene had the interests of the entire production at heart, he agreed that, working with Gene, Walters would do a first-rate job. The latter, put under a staff contract to MGM, ended up working there for more than twenty years.

Yet Gene was glad when the *DuBarry* experience was over. It ended up as a frothy concoction of eighteenth-century French court comedy and twentieth-century nightclub highjinks. The *New York Times* credited it with "eye-filling opulence and splendor." For Gene it was a waste of time, though he did enjoy playing the derring-do of the fabled Black Arrow, a revolutionary Robin Hood calling for the overthrow of Louis XV and Madame DuBarry.

He tried to rationalize that there was some social significance in the part, but he didn't get very far. Indeed, the silliness of the whole effort impelled him to give more thought to enlisting. The reigning male stars at MGM—Clark Gable, James Stewart, Robert Taylor, and others more or less on Gene's level—were away and in uniform by now. He was becoming increasingly uncomfortable with Betsy's forays into Hollywood left-wing circles; her constant drumbeat was that the main thrust of the war against Hitler was from the Soviet Union. When would the U.S. start the Second Front?

Now that Kerry was a healthy, delightful baby, Betsy agreed that Gene should serve. He spoke to Darrow about a possible abridgment of his contract with MGM. The agent reported back that Mayer would have none of it: "Kelly, he's a father now, yes?" He could best serve his country by staying home and starring in morale-boosting films.

As if in response to his unsettled state of mind and as proof of Mayer's point of view, MGM kept him busy during 1943. In an active but, professionally speaking, unfulfilling year, Gene made two more films that the studio somehow considered wartime contributions, beginning with *Thousands Cheer* (not to be confused with Irving Berlin's stage hit *As Thousands Cheer*).

Gene played a circus star drafted against his will. Shades of *For Me and My Gal* made him worry about type-casting at this early point in his film career. He falls in love with Kathryn Grayson, the daughter of his camp commander. She volunteers to put on a show for the troops who are about to depart for the war in Europe. Her lineup of acts made the film essentially a parade of MGM players; the plot was buried beneath the song, dance, and comedy numbers that came on one after another Mickey Rooney was the emcee of the camp show and did impersonations of Clark Gable and Lionel Barrymore. Red Skelton mugged through a sketch with the child star Margaret O'Brien about who could eat more ice cream without getting sick. Lucille Ball played the wary patient of a doctor who was examining her much too closely. The big bands of Kay Kyser and Bob Crosby made a splashy appearance. As a surprise, Judy Garland teamed up uneasily with Jose Iturbi, the classical pianist, to do the jazz number "The Joint Is Really Jumpin' in Carnegie Hall." (It didn't.) Lena Horne did her best on a sultry version of "Honeysuckle Rose," and "A Little Spanish Town" was rendered by a trio of three pretty newcomers, one of whom was June Allyson, Betsy's former neighbor at the Henry Hudson in Manhattan. She and Gene shared some laughs and anecdotes about the fortress mentality of the all-girls' residence, so far in distance and attitude from the free-flowing sex of the movie colony.

Gene's participation was to be the climax of the film, an aerial act with his circus family. Much to Betsy's dismay, he offered to do the trapeze work himself, but an aerialist from Ringling Brothers was recruited by producer Joe Pasternak to do the actual stunt.

While *Thousands Cheer* was shaped into a rough cut, George Sidney, the director, was bothered by the rather predictable, metronomic, one-after-another rhythm of the film. He thought a dynamic element was needed for insertion as a change of pace—a solo dance by Gene Kelly. He inquired if Gene had any ideas. It was like asking if Hershey had chocolate. Gene returned the next morning with several interesting conceptions, but he favored one and pushed it so hard that Sidney could only agree. What fascinated the director about Kelly as a choreographer was that, first and foremost, Gene thought in terms of the film's overall story. He approached the number as would a scriptwriter, as integral to the flow of narrative. What Gene proposed was that there be a scene where he was confined to quarters for insubordination and, as punishment, was ordered to mop down the camp's post exchange. On the wall was a War Department poster depicting a target built around a portrait of Adolf Hitler. The core of the dance would be Gene aiming his mop as though it were a gun, bayoneting, and firing at the portrait.

Now, really for the first time since arriving in Hollywood, Gene took over and designed his own choreography, the total conception, not just a patch-up or takeover of someone else's work. Sidney was thrilled, and Pasternak allowed Gene to design and execute the number without interference. In the first of the ground-breaking Kelly solos, he dances, he mops the floor, he sees the enemy, he is a soldier in combat. His steps are superbly coordinated with the mop wielded in his hands, now a deadly weapon, now a dance partner, his Ginger Rogers.

Astaire, of course, had worked with props, and perhaps there was nothing in Gene's routine that surpassed the older dancer's brilliant solos. But, for the first time, he was to achieve recognition as an innovative choreographer and dancer; now he was in Astaire's league. And what he was doing was tangible. As a choreographer he had proven his ability to make anything dance in character, even a mop. And he was, finally, contributing to the war effort as a morale builder and motivator, as he administered violent revenge on the Führer, the very face of evil.

Thousands Cheer (1943) was one of the films in which Gene danced with his favorite partner: himself.

Gene was pleased with the number. It represented advancement and growth on his part and showed what he had to offer as a film choreographer-dancer. But, as was to be his fate many times in his career, he was angered by the way the finished film came out. He had been told that the concluding number would be his circus aerial act. It was understandable that the playing order would be changed when the mop dance was completed and scored. What an exciting finale! What better way to give emotional force and substance to a wartime film? Instead, probably for political reasons, namely, pressure from Washington to honor our Soviet allies, the decision was made that the finale would be "The United Nations Hymn," a pompous work specially composed by Dmitri Shostakovich and sung by Kathryn Grayson to the accompaniment of an army orchestra. Gene was concerned that his two dance contributions to the film would be swamped by the other star turns.

He was wrong. His mop dance easily stood out in a film that went on to be one of the top money-making musicals of 1943. He was gratified by the review in the New York Herald Tribune, stating that he dominated the film and "saves the picture from being merely a parade of personalities."

By the time Thousands Cheer was in release, he was well into the shooting of The Cross of Lorraine. He had lobbied furiously with the MGM executives to cancel his contract so he could join up with the military. As if to make up for its ostrich-like avoidance of the war early on, the studio sent him directly into his third consecutive film with a wartime story. As a healthy civilian, he felt embarrassed wearing a uniform only by courtesy of the MGM costume department. Still, he found the storyline of the film appealing. He played a Frenchman who joined the army at the outbreak of the war to fight the invading Germans. He is no hero; without putting up much of a fight, he and his unit quickly surrender. But his defeatist mood changes as he observes the brutality of the Germans toward the prisoners and local civilians. Although he is a humble enlisted man, he is able to lead a breakout from the German camp. He and his unit join the French Resistance to continue the fight and help liberate their country. It was a workable platform for a solid anti-Nazi propaganda picture. Gene was attracted to the script by his feeling for France, a passion of his since high school. He was happy to help cast a better light on the French, who were being castigated for relying on the Maginot Line, then giving way helplessly to the Germans.

But somehow, as *The Cross of Lorraine* was rewritten and shot and edited, there was a watering down of the thrust, of the message about the need for steady courage under adversity and the power of democracy in the fight against fascism. MGM's temporizing and tampering with the script hurt the film badly. Director Tay Garnett's loose control of the actors, especially Peter Lorre as a bizarre renegade Nazi, threw everything off-key in such a way that audiences laughed.

Gene's was not a large part, but it did present a strong challenge: He had to show the after-effects on someone who had undergone gruesome torture. In one of his usual dispassionate postmortems he felt he had done tolerably well, but, as before, he was still dissatisfied with his closeups.

By late 1943 he had five films in release. He was well-known, not quite a star, not quite "bankable," but *en route* to being a name above the title. The musicals had been popular at the box office, but the two war dramas had created no stir. He tortured his agent with an avalanche of requests to find him a musical. "I gotta dance," he would say again and again.

It had nothing to do with a desire to increase his income. During the strained months when Gene had been unemployed, except as the drinking buddy of David O. Selznick, the Kellys had been living well. Pregnant—with no friends, job prospects, or interest in housewifery—Betsy had time on her hands and, seeking a social life, organized house parties, originally in the quiet, almost seclusive way Gene had preferred. But once *For Me and My Gal* was in production, he had loosened up and encouraged her to invite guests who were "intelligent and talented." Hollywood being Hollywood, word soon got around concerning the guest specifications for the house on Alta Drive. Evening at the Kellys became the mecca *du jour* for many in the film colony who were absolutely certain they qualified. There was also the bizarre attraction of The Game.

Saul Chaplin, the songwriter and musical director, had recently arrived in town. At his first meeting of Gene, he and his wife were invited to the Kelly home. "Just a few folks, some booze, and The Game."

"The Game?"

Gene just nodded. Chaplin said later: "Kelly gave me the address, told me to come any time after ten, and said the dress was casual. We arrived at the house at about 10:30 and rang the doorbell. No one answered. We tried the door. It was open, so we walked in. We were in a room packed with a lot of noisy people." Despite the decibel level, the Chaplins were impressed by the guest list that inaugurated their first of many Kelly parties: Judy Garland, Frank Sinatra, Lena Horne, Mickey Rooney, Johnny Mercer. The tempo of doorbells and entrances sped up. The comedian Phil Silvers, Tyrone Power. Hugh Martin and Ralph Blane, who had done the words and music for *Best Foot Forward*. David O. Selznick barged in, attended by an entourage which included several lissome young beauties. A working duo entered who had just arrived from New York, Betty Comden and Adolph Green. Chaplin found Gene, "who introduced me to his pretty, energetic red-headed wife Betsy. Before we knew it, my wife Ethel and I found ourselves on different teams—one captained by Gene, the other by Betsy. And The Game turned out to be charades, but we had never seen it played this way."

The Kelly version called for two teams to be organized and placed in separate rooms at the far ends of the house so one group could not hear the other. A hired high school teacher served as the umpire. He was paid by the Kellys to prepare a list of celebrity names, film, stageplay and book titles, advertising slogans, proverbs, clichés, aphorisms, famous sayings through history. One by one, from one team and then the other, contestants would be called up to receive a slip of paper from the teacher bearing the next item on his list. The teacher watched the stopwatch carefully. The challenge was to pantomime enough clues so teammates could guess, as quickly as possible, what was being acted out. The team completing the teacher's list first was declared the winner.

It was clear to Chaplin that in the Kelly world, games were played only to be won. Losing was unacceptable. As he put it: "It was scary watching our easygoing hosts turn into veritable storm troopers right before our eyes. The time between games was taken up with post-mortem recriminations. Gene would yell, 'If it weren't for you—,' naming the unfortunate who was slow coming up with the answer. It could be a movie star like Tyrone Power or a quick-witted comedienne and writer like Kay Thompson; Kelly didn't care. 'We would have won in a walk!' Somehow everybody bore up under Gene's verbal abuse, maybe because Kelly was clearly the champion player."

The host was amazingly quick at coming up with the strained-for answer. More surprising to the guests was Betsy's performance. Whatever the provenance of the mystery word or phrase, she was usually a close second to Gene and sometimes even faster. So seriously was The Game taken by the movie colony that an invitation to the Kelly evening was soon considered "the hottest ticket in town" by gossip columnists, not only for the exciting competitive event but for what was to come after it.

Selznick, having unloaded the Kelly salary burden, had become a favored friend again, and when in town he often participated in The Game. To his embarrassment he did quite badly, and he reacted with classic Selznick overkill. He recruited a team of recent New York arrivals, very *au courant* and sophisticated screenwriters and directors. He briefed them carefully and ran them through some practice sessions. He actually hired the Kellys' high school teacher to give his team actual experience at playing The Game. It was even rumored that Selznick had gone so far as to offer a bribe for the teacher's "cooperation." But when Selznick and his imposing group appeared at the Kelly home to challenge a team organized around Gene and Betsy, the visitors trailed badly and lost.

There was an open bar on those evenings. No bartender, just a table laden with liquor and simple sandwiches—Betsy was not one for frills as a hostess. The heated competition of The Game made guests thirsty, so the Kellys ran up a liquor bill, typically, of more than $200 a week.

The food and drink were not the drawing cards but, ultimately, neither was The Game. It was the remarkable talent: On the night of Saul Chaplin's first visit, through the din he heard Judy Garland's unmistakable singing. All at once everyone became quiet. The Game was over. The guests sat down, most of them on the floor. Judy sang "The Boy Next Door," from *Meet Me in St. Louis*, with one of the song-writers, Hugh Martin, at the piano. Ralph Blane, Martin's collaborator, then slipped in, and the two songwriters performed the highlights from that film. Johnny Mercer took over and sang his "One for My Baby," from an upcoming Astaire picture. Then it was Lena Horne's turn, then Sinatra's. Then Gene would step forward, cracking a few jokes about the miserable fate of anyone scheduled to sing right after Ol' Blue Eyes. With a fast riff of click-clackety tap dancing Gene embellished the perfor-mance of a few pieces from *Pal Joey*. Chaplin, a deft pianist, was encouraged to accompany Phil Silvers in a wild, make-up-as-it-went-along patter song about the sunny dullness of Beverly Hills compared with the devilish excitement of New York.

So it went on through the night, unpretentious and informal, an impromptu parade of performers. Few departed; the less hardy would find a place to lie down and rest awhile. Stanley Donen, now on the Coast job-hunting, located an empty bed to catch a few hours of rest before the *next* Kelly event, scheduled for dawn. As Chaplin described it:

> As soon as it was light enough, some of the men adjourned to the backyard, where they started a volleyball game. Suddenly the gaiety disappeared and all the tension of the charade game returned. Volleyball was played with the fierceness of war. It was unbelievable that here were ten or twelve men who less than an hour ago had been crowded around a piano singing and laughing and now were reduced to hurling insults at each other. . . . the master of the merciless putdown was Gene.

By far the best athlete there, no matter what side he was on, was Gene. While the others were logy and unslept, he was all over the place, showing no effects of an active night of drinking and performing. Not timid about hurling his body around, he would usurp shots arcing down at his unskilled teammates. Sending an aggressive message about his height, he would jump high over the net and end a rally with a crunching spike. Those who came to watch or play with him were used to his incredible athletic skills. Word had gotten around: Here was a one-man team.

Some guests might hang on to play with him for a few games until seven or eight in the morning. Then Betsy, as active, wide-awake, and bubbly as Gene, served up some juice and coffee, and it was finally all over. Shaking their heads at the Kelly energy level, the guests would disperse to their cars and be on their way. If it was a working day for him, Gene would have a quick shower and drive to the "call" at whatever studio where he was working.

His own efforts, not his agent's, would eventually get him back on the musical track, but it wasn't easy. It started off with a ringing disappointment. When *The Cross of Lorraine* was in post-production, he was in rehearsals with Eleanor Powell for MGM's *Broadway Melody of 1943*, but the project was abruptly canceled. He was given no explanation. He demanded an appointment with Mayer but was rebuffed. Always sensitive about his height, or lack of it, he suspected that Mayer and his cadre of "lickspittle toadies" had "done him in" by deciding that Powell was too tall for him as a partner. Or perhaps Mayer, a man who rode an emotional roller coaster every working day, was simply now paying him back for the outraged letter he had sent from New York. Since his arrival at Metro the MGM head had never once mentioned the letter to him. There was also the possibility—it had come to be Gene's desperate hope—that his choleric outburst had been lost in the mail. But whatever the case, he had to confront Mayer with an ultimatum: Use me or lose me . . . to the Navy! Contract or no, he was prepared to enlist immediately.

Johnny Darrow had heard through the grapevine that Gene's next assignment would be in a loan-out, for a film with Deanna Durbin, the former singing prodigy whom Universal Pictures was trying to build into an adult star. Durbin would sing, and he would not dance. Gene felt it was absolutely the wrong move for him at a pivotal time in his career. Swallowing his pride, he made the rounds at MGM, bullying the secretaries of producers who did musicals to find him "face time" with their bosses. Arthur Freed, of course, was his first preference, but he had no place for him. Joe Pasternak, for whom he had done *Thousands Cheer*, was sympathetic but, as Gene told Graham Fuller of *Interview* years later, "Joe was very helpful, but he was only interested in singing. . . . there was nothing I could do with a high C."

Alone in his study at home, he was thinking insightfully about the marriage of musicals and movies, generating ideas for distinctive dances. He tried his best to be productive, but he found himself in a constant state of depression. Yet again, the dreary days of waiting for the right phone call came and went, sapping his resolve and spoiling his pleasures with his daughter and wife. Betsy had taken to describing his periods of unemployment as manifestations of the evils of capitalism. While he felt she was going a bit too far—he was not quite yet one of the "prisoners of starvation" she sang about at fund-raisers for Russian War Relief—he wondered if he was gradually being radicalized toward her more extreme positions.

His own opinion of Mayer was like an elevator: *Down* it had first plummeted with the double-cross about the screen test; *up* when Judy had told him about Mayer's many unpublicized kindnesses to her; *up* farther to the roof with Mayer's heroic salvaging of *For Me and My Gal*. Now, after making money for Metro with his work in three musicals and performing solidly in two wartime morale-boosters, he was hat in hand, begging Mayer for the chance to live his dream with his tap shoes on again. He bluntly described his feelings about Mayer to Graham Fuller: "I can't use four-letter words because you might print them. But at that time, to give him as good a face as I can, he was more interested in his racehorses than in new talent."

Then, during that bitter period, there happened a miracle, an MGM miracle: The Kellys received an invitation from Mayer to a dinner party at his home. It was surprising and baffling. They were not remotely in the Hollywood power circle, despite Betsy's frenetic efforts at creating a talked-about social life. The Game at Kelly parties was a world apart from the black-tie formality of the Mayer mansion:

> We were just a group of entertainers amusing ourselves. . . . We'd play charades . . . chat or talk politics. We were all, with a couple of exceptions, left-wingers, all Roosevelt people. We—the Kellys—never got invited to the upper-crust socials in Hollywood. . . . we were the working stiffs. L.B. Mayer once had us to a party for *Gone With the Wind* because Vivien Leigh and Laurence Olivier asked for us to come. That's the only time I was ever in Mayer's house.

He didn't want to accept the invitation. Telling Mayer the Kellys were entertaining at home that night would be a way of showing the contempt he felt for the Metro head. Betsy talked him out of that with a caustic "Who's the teenager here?"

"I don't like the bastard, you know that!"

"Don't you want to see Vivien Leigh again?"

He had told her about meeting Olivier and Leigh while on tour with *One for the Money*; the show had been booked for a stretch at the Selwyn Theater, in Chicago, and nearby the famous British theatrical couple was performing a repertory of Shakespeare. They, and especially Vivien, had taken to Gene, and he had found her beautiful and endearing. He now wondered if her mammoth success in *Gone With the Wind* had changed her. David O. Selznick, who had produced the blockbuster, had been a mite catty about Vivien, claiming she was emotionally fragile, even ill. No longer did he heed the judgment of Selznick; he'd see for himself.

"Okay," he said. "Let's go."

And facing Betsy, holding the vellum invitation in his hand, he had the image of being embraced by the guest of honor, clearly the Number One film actress of the day, thereby impressing the bejesus out of the host. He would then escort Mayer into the library, close the door, and make his declaration: He had been a productive actor. He was a recognized song-and-dance man already in the Astaire league. And a dancer's life is short. So, to the ultimatum: Use me or lose me! The Navy awaits!

He would finally find out what was on Mayer's mind. As it happened, at that party for Vivien Leigh and Laurence Olivier he would also find out what was on his own. The first discovery would set him on a course toward film immortality. The second discovery would be even more important.

Funny, he thinks, rousing himself after yet another run of film clips: Nobody has the faintest idea what a worry-wart he really is. They would rather label him a perfectionist. It's because of his brash image. "Look Ma, I'm dancing!" whatever the obstacle. Even by himself, in spite of the rain and a wary policeman, or with Songbird Sinatra, in spite of Frankie teetering and almost falling in Anchors Aweigh. Where he even tapped like crazy with a spunky rodent, for chrissake. (Allowing him to get a lot of ink from over forty years of press conferences when he joked that Jerry the Mouse was his favorite dancing partner!)

The girls here in the Hilton don't mind. They can take a joke, go with the flow. After all, they are very special, not special-effects. Now each of them—except Judy, God rest her soul—is called upon by Shirley MacLaine to say a few words: Debbie Reynolds, Cyd Charisse, Leslie Caron. Betty Garrett (her husband Larry Parks, so roughed up in the McCarthy hearings!) is on last; she's grateful for being paired with Sinatra in On the Town, *she says with just the right amount of ruefulness, but she never did get a chance to dance with Gene Kelly.*

He flash-forwards to his Worry of the Week: that, after the final speech, a side wall will slide open and there will be a dance band, Peter Duchin's or somebody's, and the evening will climax with a pairing-off of guests and sure enough, some woman will approach him and ask for a rhumba! Or worse, the husband will come over to him and say something like: "Hi, Gene. Would you mind going over to my wife and asking her to dance? Beatrice would just love to dance with you." And the husband goes around and tells his friends: "Beatrice is gonna dance with Gene Kelly." Suddenly, there's a crowd of people standing around expecting they're about to see Fred and Ginger. They think it's show time. They're shaking with anticipation at the thought that Gene Kelly's about to lift up Beatrice and whip her around, toss her, and catch her, too! He remembers that time with Vivien Leigh. He still cringes when he thinks of it.

He looks again for Astaire, who must be pressured the same way constantly. Fred looks cool, and that helps. Better yet, there's a break and he has a chance to glance at the glossy AFI program. He's listed last: Acceptance of the AFI Award by Gene Kelly. Time for him to get it together. Then go home.

The program's thick with ads and testimonials. He closes it and sets it on his lap. The front page seems to be shivering. It's either a cool blast of air-conditioning, or his nerves, or his very long exhalation in relief. No rhumba with Beatrice tonight.

LOS ANGELES, 1944

* * *

The party at Mayer's mansion was sheer perfection, from the subdued efficiency of the valet parking to the exquisite *tarte Tatin* served at the end of the meal. A small combo started to play for dancing. A butler tapped Gene on the shoulder to pass along an invitation to join the host in the library. "For just a moment," the butler said. "If you please."

Mayer shut the library door, offered him a post-dinner cognac and a cigar. They lit up. "I understand you've been wanting to see me, Gene."

So far, it was going just as he had hoped: a chance to clear the air between him and the unapproachable head of MGM. Dispassionately, avoiding any intensity or trace of hype, Gene quickly reviewed his record at the studio: Five films, three of which were musicals and substantial successes; the other two largely propagandistic war films. Mayer broke in: "We all have to do our part in the war effort."

"Exactly. And that's why I'm here, Mr. Mayer. I want to enlist in the Navy."

To which Mayer responded yet again with his version of the Dorothy Parker quip: The movie business is one of the very few where all of the assets go home every night. "We've lost so many people to the military, especially our stars—Gable, Stewart—we can barely function. We have to depend on the secondary performers to step in and hold the fort."

He bristled at the category where Mayer had consigned him but held himself in check. "If I'm to stay, I'd like to go on and do musicals. I'm primarily a song-and-dance man—"

"Like Astaire?" Mayer's face hardened.

"Well, okay, like Astaire. And if—"

"No," Mayer spoke out flatly. "Get with it, Kelly. You're no Astaire!"

"Whatever you say, Mr. Mayer. I still—"

"No Astaire, not by a long shot. You need seasoning, seasoning. That's why we're sending you down to the minors."

"Minors?"

"A loan-out to Columbia. Crazy Harry Cohn has a film going with Rita Hayworth, and he's in a fix! He started principal shooting before he had his ducks in order—imagine! But this is Crazy Harry, remember? The asshole's in production but he's got nobody to play opposite Rita!"

Mayer drew heavily on his cigar. He spoke over the blue-gray plume of smoke in a way that seemed to freight his words with sudden heat and hostility. "That's Crazy Harry for you. Kelly, if you think I'm inconsistent, that I don't stick to my word—"

"If you're referring to my letter, Mr. Mayer—"

"—then wait'll you have a taste of Crazy Harry! For starters, he's already told me you're too damned short to be in the same frame with his beloved Rita."

The atmosphere had turned vicious. Mayer's dislike of him was so obvious that, unless he left the room right away, he feared he might throw a punch at the old man. Then through the pounding of his blood against his skull, he heard Mayer say more quietly: "But that's not why I asked you here tonight."

Gene did not even try to speak.

"I saw the way the Oliviers greeted you out there." Mayer gestured toward the door. "Vivien told me they had met you in Chicago when you were doing a show.

And she liked you in *For Me and My Gal*."

"Good. Well, Mr. Mayer, I'll let you get back to your party and—"

"You can do me a favor."

"Oh?"

"Ask Vivien to dance. That's what Larry says would make her happy. She's been depressed lately. Has even seen doctors about it." Mayer went to the door and opened it. "I'm doing a favor for you, you do one for me."

When he returned to their table Betsy's smile faded as she saw his exasperated expression. "Was it that bad?"

"Well, at least I know. That letter of mine, he received it."

"Oh oh."

"But we're back in business, kiddo. They're loaning me out to Columbia."

The exuberant smile came back. "Tell me, tell me!"

"I will. First, I have to ask Scarlett O'Hara to dance."

"But you hate that sort of thing!"

"Just being social." The band had started up again, a suitable foxtrot, slow and simple. He crossed the floor to the head table, a beehive of conversation, where Mayer had reseated with the Oliviers. One of the MGM executives was exuberantly talking to Vivien and, laughing, she threw back her head and brought it forward to sip her champagne. It was an awkward interruption but he had no choice. Conscious of Mayer's gaze, Gene leaned over and asked her to dance.

"Thought you'd never ask, Gene." She slurred the words as she got to her feet uncertainly, and he knew at once, with the clarity of one who had grown up with an alcoholic father, she was drunk. "There's only one thing left for me to do in Hollywood. That's to dance with Gene Kelly."

He had to hold her hand tightly as they walked out on the dance floor. Of course, most of the guests had already turned to watch. Even though these were mostly movie people aware of the preparation needed to do a cinematic dance number, Gene sensed an expectant glaze over their eyes as he put his hand upon Vivien's back. She rocked forward into him. He bobbed back and forth gently—and knew it would be impossible, as he later told his English biographer:

> As soon as we began to dance, I realized she couldn't follow me too well. We were both too nervous about it, I guess, and simply out of synch with each other. Maybe we both had had a couple of drinks too many, but it just never worked out, and after a while, I did something I've never ever forgiven myself for. I asked her if we could sit the rest of it out. Well, of course, I hurt her feelings terribly. It was a cruel, thoughtless thing to have done to any-one—let alone someone as lovely and gracious as Vivien Leigh— and I wanted to kill myself the second after I'd done it.

It was the look on her face that he always remembered. Disappointment, of course, and wonderment, inadequacy, pain. Hand in hand, she almost tugged him back to the table and her drink while he was smiling his best, as though having enjoyed a grand time. The whole experience was heart-rending, and, if the encounter with Mayer hadn't poisoned the night, his callousness killed it. He was in a funk and hardly spoke to Betsy all the way home.

He knew he had treated Vivien Leigh so rudely because he was irate with Mayer and wanted to send the Metro head some sort of tough and ballsy response, something consistent with his pious declaration about enlisting. He slept poorly that night.

The next day was a Saturday and he received an early-morning call from the Columbia producer Arthur Schwartz, verifying the loan-out for the movie *Cover Girl*. Schwartz emphasized that he wanted Gene not only to do the romantic lead opposite Hayworth but to take over the choreography—"God knows, we need you, Gene!" They talked awhile about Agnes de Mille's work on the stage hit *Oklahoma!*, which Schwartz admired. It was a good sign, as far as Gene was concerned; he also thought de Mille's work was extraordinarily creative, very much in the way he wanted to go, integrating dance into the body of the story. A meeting was called for Monday morning at Columbia.

He would have liked to spend time with Kerry, but a glance out to the garden showed her nanny and his daughter happily involved in a game. Betsy had an appointment somewhere. Abruptly he decided to go to the USO Hollywood Canteen. He was honest with himself; surely, it had something to do with his going into *Cover Girl*, not the Navy.

He drove to the hospitality center and for a few hours signed autographs and chatted amiably with servicemen and -women. From time to time he participated in entertainments at the Canteen, usually serving as emcee of an MGM-sponsored show. Each of the major studios had taken on the responsibility for a night's entertainment. It had started on a small scale, a deliberately informal evening where GIs could relax, drink Cokes, and dance with pretty girls supplied mainly by the film companies. But each studio head, congenitally competitive, had passed down the word that his studio's reputation depended on the quality and elaborateness of the entertainment provided. Each studio wanted to be the most popular at the Hollywood Canteen. Stars were ordered, not asked, to be present, and even rehearsals were held. Word that Warner Bros. had enlisted a bevy of stars and put on a fantastic show on a particular Wednesday night would have the other studios calling an emergency meeting on Thursday morning. Strong appeals would be made. Those who could not sing or dance could "chat it up" with the audience. The idea was simple: Give the boy in uniform a taste of the Hollywood myth.

Gene thought the effort was wildly overblown and spoke his mind forcefully at Canteen committee meetings. What a GI wanted, he insisted, was a girl, a girl, a girl . . . to do the Lindy Hop with, or to hold as close as possible and dream of the impossible. While he worked hard on his Canteen nights, he preferred the group visits to training camps and area hospitals. He wanted to give priority to men wounded in action or about to leave for combat duty. Too many servicemen at the Canteen held cushy noncombat jobs in the Los Angeles area. Betsy felt that way too. She rarely came to the Canteen with Gene, preferring to put her time and effort behind other causes. Right now, she was busy working on a fund-raising concert by Jascha Heifetz and Vladimir Horowitz on behalf of the Russian War Relief campaign.

When a Wave officer asked him to dance, he decided it was time to leave the Canteen. He did a turn with her—she was, as usual, nervously expecting him to put her through some ornate steps—and made a special effort to be charming and gracious. A line of women—Waves, Wacs, nurses—immediately formed.

"Sorry, girls," he called out. "This has to be my last number. I've got a bad knee from doing a stunt in *Thousands Cheer*." But to make up for the fib he stayed an extra hour to sign autographs on glossy headshots supplied by the MGM public relations office. Then he escaped.

When he reached home he found the *Cover Girl* script Schwartz had sent over. There was no time to study it. The front porch light was on—Betsy's signal to the world that guests were welcome. Another open house at the Kellys, and he wasn't in the mood for it. He preferred to go over the scenario carefully, play with Kerry, or just sulk in isolation until the simmering rage he carried against L.B. Mayer wore off.

But Betsy needed the excitement and attention due the hostess of a string of successful parties. She was fiercely into the routine of making contacts now, striving for dramatic roles. He had come to realize she was every bit as ambitious as he. The disparity of their career movement was creating tension between them. She was becoming even more high-strung. Staying home and rearing a family was not what she wanted. She was no Harriet Kelly.

He came out of the shower and couldn't resist sitting down on the bed a moment with the *Cover Girl* script. Already the caterer downstairs was preparing the cold cuts and sandwiches in the kitchen. Through the clinks of liquor bottles and glasses being set out, he scanned the pages. Yes, he would have second billing, sure enough, but more than making up for that deficiency, he was the choreographer. It would be his first film credit in that capacity. As he read on, he was conscious of the tingling of excitement, as though a shivery draft were coming from somewhere. The script was not exceptional, no new territory was explored, but it would be graced by the evocative music of Jerome Kern and the clever lyrics of Ira Gershwin—reflecting a Columbia production *not* minor-league, as Mayer had harrumphed the night before.

What pleased him now was that the choreography sections, left virginally without detail, tersely marked *Dancing Follows*, were positioned at key moments. His dances would meld with the storyline, driving the characterizations and plot forward, not interrupt as set pieces always did. Of course, besides the second billing, there was another down side to his part. One he could live with, apparently had to live with: the return of a Pal Joey type. He was cast yet again as the owner of a seedy nightclub. He would never get away from the "cloops"! But in *Cover Girl* he was a sympathetic figure in love with one of his dancers at the club, played by Hayworth. Minor-league indeed, Louis B! Rita was a major-league beauty if ever there was one and, *en plus*, the niece of his old Chicago friend and dance teacher, Angel Cansino.

Every few minutes the doorbell sounded, and he knew he was needed downstairs to help Betsy. There was a changing guest list to open house at the Kellys. As

Gene ascended the Hollywood heights, the prestige and notoriety of the visitors rose in tandem. The usual suspects still came eagerly for The Game and the music and the excitement, always augmented by other celebrities arriving for the first time.

Joan Collins, a charming and bright British actress just starting in Hollywood, became a frequent open house guest. She was attracted to Gene. "He was charming with a zany sense of humor and tremendous energy and vitality," she recalled. "I first met him at the Beverly Hills Tennis Club, where he played a vicious game of tennis with the club pro. We were introduced, and he invited me on the spot."

What impressed her more than Gene's athletic abilities were the guests he drew: "The door was always open, and I found the guests always fascinating. They were not just pretty faces. Some of them were considered to be intellectual giants." Perhaps because of her British background, she was partial to the likes of Noël Coward and Margot Fonteyn, who, when they came, participated in The Game with spirit, if not with the quicksilver reactions of Gene and Betsy.

Fortunately for the hostess, on the night when Gene would have preferred to study the *Cover Girl* script, the guests were all from the younger creative community and more mischievously inclined. It was the perfect occasion for Betsy to play a trick on Gene, an idea she had harbored for a long time because, as she told Saul Chaplin: "Gene's given you guys too much abuse over The Game, bawling you out and all." She announced that she would captain one team, Gene the other. It seemed eminently sensible; they were the best players. Chaplin was placed on Gene's team with four other guests, all taken aside by Betsy and briefed on the plot. As Chaplin described later: "When it was Gene's turn, he was given the song title 'Tramp! Tramp! Tramp! The Boys Are Marching.' The five of us on his team were supposed to guess the title, led to it by his clues. Gene, confident as always, sprang to his feet and quickly pantomimed the appropriate sign to get us started."

"Song!" his teammates shouted immediately and then, in response to Gene's indications: "Seven words . . . and the first word is. . . ."

So far so good, Gene nodded. He stamped on the floor. Chaplin called out: "March!"

Gene shook his head. When no other response was forthcoming, his smile dimmed. He shook his head in wonderment at his team's stupidity as he now marched vigorously in place.

Somebody on Chaplin's side said: "March" again, and then there was a flurry of other guesses: "Hike!" "Proceed!" "Parade!" One after another the words were advanced, with Gene more angrily red-faced with every contribution. From the other room came a cheer and whistling. Betsy's team had already come to the response that was eluding Gene's partners.

Now Gene, utterly frustrated, brought up his stiffened right hand and added a salute to his marching and there came the shouted responses: "Soldier!" "Officer!" "Private!" "Uniform!" Somebody even said: "Hitler!"

Gene was enraged now. He pounded the floor. He glared as his team continued to offer the wrong answers. As Chaplin said: "Chances are that if he hadn't been so angry, he would have realized he'd been set up. Because we should have guessed 'Tramp! Tramp! Tramp!' almost immediately. We strung out the torture as long as we could until we couldn't hold it in any more and began to laugh uncontrollably, started by Betsy."

The timekeeper proclaimed Betsy's team the winner. Gene stood stonefaced, almost in shock. Chaplin and everybody else were quick to see that Gene took it very well—for him—when Betsy described what they had done. He joined in the laughter but he was never one who could be the butt of a joke for very long. "Our moment of glory was short-lived. Gene reverted to his abusive attitude in the very next game," said Chaplin.

In any case, dominating his thoughts and creative energies now was *Cover Girl* and what he could give to the film. On Monday morning he drove to the Columbia studio for an orientation meeting with Arthur Schwartz. Compared to the sprawling MGM assemblage of buildings and shooting areas, the Columbia lot struck him as crowded and small. Was this what Mayer meant by minor-league? But at least Schwartz had arranged a privileged parking space. Gene resolved to be as constructive and upbeat as he could; he would not be cranky, negative, belligerent—perhaps Betsy's "Tramp Tramp" joke over the weekend was her way of telling him something about himself.

He liked Schwartz on sight and appreciated the candid briefing about *Cover Girl*. It was to be a lavish Technicolor musical, directed by Charles Vidor. With his legendary impatience, Harry Cohn, the bristling head of Columbia, had gambled by green-lighting the start of shooting without casting the leading man. Cohn's plan— if, indeed, he'd had a plan—was to "shoot around" the absent male star until the appropriate partner for Rita Hayworth could be signed. But Cohn's luck had run out. No song-and-dance man already under contract to Columbia could be sprung loose, and it had been left to Schwartz to pursue the loan-out from another studio. The candidates were either working, anticipating another production, away in military service, or terrible for the part, in Schwartz's view. Except for Gene Kelly.

This state of affairs pleased Schwartz. An admirer of Gene's work, he was a tactful executive. At this point he skipped the reaction of Cohn to his suggestion that they tap MGM for Kelly. Cohn's blistering response had been too destructive to pass along: "What? That tough Irishman with his tough Irish mug? You couldn't put him in the same frame as Rita! Nothing doing. Besides, I saw him in *Pal Joey* and he's too goddamn short!"

But Schwartz, increasingly desperate with the passing of each shooting day, dared to bypass Cohn and negotiated with MGM (who assumed he had Cohn's permission) for four weeks of Gene's time, the best MGM would do. With a sick feeling in his stomach, knowing he had to face the meanest and toughest of the Hollywood rulers, Schwartz returned to Cohn's office and blurted out his accomplishment before he lost his nerve: "Harry, I've got our leading man!"

"Who?" Cohn bellowed.

"Gene Kelly," responded Schwartz, wondering why he had ruined his professional life for such a whimsical assertion of independence. He doubted even one studio would grant him an employment interview after Cohn had cursed him out and fired him.

All Cohn said was: "Thank God!"

Having related this, editing out the insulting details, Schwartz led Gene into Cohn's office for their first meeting. Gene was surprised at the luxury of the place, since Columbia was considered somewhat on Poverty Row in the community of motion-picture studios. Cohn was badmouthed as a skinflint who clucked over every outgoing penny, but his office was a vast, Persian-rugged, high-ceilinged room with plush sofas along two sides. A white baby grand piano was opposite the sofas in front of three huge bay windows overlooking the entrance. It was well known, and Cohn made it no secret, that he frequently checked the arrival and departure times of Columbia employees, even spying on their comings and goings from the parking lot directly across the street. Seated on a raised platform in the center section of an enormous three-part desk, Cohn was illuminated by a bright overhead spotlight which spilled over a dozen or so glistening Oscars displayed behind him. He brusquely gestured the visitors toward one of the couches.

When seated, Gene's view of the Columbia head was extremely low-angled; Cohn looked mountainous. When he finally tossed some papers into an "Out" basket and stepped down to greet Gene, he carried himself erectly, as though reinforced by a steel rod. Even then, he was barely Gene's height. As they shook hands, Cohn's eyes seemed fixed on Gene's forehead. Then Cohn nodded, turned to Schwartz, and said heavily in what was almost an expression of relief: "All right."

When they left the office, Schwartz did not attempt to explain exactly what was all right. But Gene knew.

Schwartz brought Gene into the screening room and showed the *Cover Girl* footage already shot, some of which Gene felt was acceptable, some of which he hated, especially the musical number at the film's opening called "The Show Must Go On." It was set in Danny McGuire's nightclub to establish it and the dancers, including Rita Hayworth.

"It's a lousy opening, I agree, Gene," said Schwartz, almost in apology. "But Cohn won't swing for the bucks to reshoot."

"Who said anything about junking it? We do a quick cutaway of me in the wings, looking over the number. I have an expression on my face, something like this—" Gene's face contorted as though he'd bitten into a lemon—"and at least that sets me up as Danny McGuire and also jump-starts the story."

Ever since *For Me and My Gal*, Gene had shown a constant audacity, even a bristling resistance to the accepted pecking order of feature-film production that was remarked upon again and again in many Hollywood circles. Schwartz had heard the rap on the mick from New York, always involving himself in every facet of the production, not just his dances, wanting to convert every production into a Gene Kelly film—the Orson Welles syndrome. But here in the Columbia screening room, Schwartz knew he was with a straight-ahead creative contributor, someone who cared deeply about the overall project. He realized Gene would not, could not, hold back. It pleased him. It also frightened him.

In the days that followed, Gene was not afraid to take on the hallowed music and lyrics by the big-name team of Kern and Gershwin. He felt several of the songs were too long and, while ideal for the stage, carried too many choruses for the screen, where the pace had to be faster. Cuts were discussed with Kern and Gershwin, then made reluctantly after a frigid meeting that took all of Schwartz's tact. Gene's eloquence finally turned the tide; the two legends of stage musicals came to trust his instincts for what would play.

After the reworking was done and scored, Kern agreed that Gene had been right. A few days later a package was delivered to the Kelly residence. It was from Jerome Kern. Betsy opened it and found that the composer had sent her husband a silver-plated plaque: TO G.K. WHO IS O.K. WITH J.K.

Not every one of Gene's contributions was received in that spirit. He spoke out in the cutting rooms, criticizing the rough cut of the already-shot main production number, an elaborate confection glorifying the American cover girl. Across a background of giant blowups of leading mass-circulation magazines, slim, tall fashion models paraded to a musical accompaniment. Gene thought it was low-rent Ziegfeld and did not hesitate to say so. His comments did not sit well with Felix Seymour, originator of the number, with whom he had previously disputed while working on *DuBarry Was a Lady*. Seymour was furious and complained to Charles Vidor, the Hungarian-American director. The latter had never served in that capacity before and was more at home with straight-narrative films; insecure and temperamental, Vidor merely sulked about Gene's interfering in areas where others had responsibility.

For the new material to be shot, Gene proposed a number of script revisions. Some of these were incorporated into the scenario by Virginia Van Upp, possibly because, as an experienced screenwriter and a professional, she knew *Cover Girl* was not one of her best. She did wish Kelly would offer his ideas about new lines and situations in private meetings, not on a working set with cast, stagehands, and a furious director standing by.

Van Upp's script dealt with a nightclub dancer who runs away to become a model, as her grandmother (both roles played by Hayworth) had done before her. But she finally returns to Danny McGuire, the man she loves. The 1940s story is told in parallel with a series of flashbacks to the turn of the century, when the dancer's grandmother made the same decision to reject the glamorous life for one of simplicity and honesty. Love is more important that success—hardly a fresh theme. Gene thought he must do what he could to liven things up.

The gossip got around Columbia that Kelly was Trouble on the Set. Vidor was appalled by the way Gene made no effort to restrict his creative contributions to his own work as an actor and dancer. As a European filmmaker used to working in a controlled environment where responsibilities were clearly defined, he thought Gene was a force for catastrophe and chaos. Far from trying to dissuade him, Gene was outspoken and public about what he thought was decent and serviceable and what was beyond salvage. No sweet talk; lousy was called lousy. And he thought Vidor was wrong for the film because the director had no sense of humor.

The comedian Phil Silvers, also in the cast, agreed with Gene. After all, the film was to be airy and funny and easy to absorb, not a melancholy meditation on American values—besides, Vidor never laughed at his jokes on the set. Vidor could handle Silvers, who did not have an even remotely threatening manner. But every now and then, Gene's temper would spill over, and though he would usually hold back from the aggrieved Hungarian émigré, once there was even a fistfight between them, broken up by a nervous production manager. Cohn had to be called down to the set to settle the dispute which he did in his own churlish way. "Wanna fight? Go challenge Joe Louis. But not on my time!"

Cohn, a legendary womanizer and brawler with a volcanic temper easily set off, soon recognized a brother in spirit with an Irish temper fairly akin to his own. As the production took shape, he came to be fond of Gene and respected the extra effort he put into the film. More than that, he had the instincts of a superb show-man. He had the sense that *Cover Girl* was no longer a lemon being improved to lemonade; thanks to Kelly's talent, even genius, there was now the possibility of a winner here. Perhaps another Oscar would join the others in his office to glow in the spotlight with him.

Creatively speaking, Gene knew he and Harry Cohn were on very different wavelengths. He described his experience at Columbia years later:

> Half the time I realized Harry Cohn didn't know what the hell I was talking about. But I must have been pretty convincing because he'd listen with a blank expression on his face, then say 'All right. Go ahead. Just get the hell out of here.' I think he knew I wouldn't nag him for something if I didn't believe it was possible to achieve.

For all its script weaknesses, conflicts between the director and leading man, and tight budgeting of Cohn, *Cover Girl* would turn out to be more than an achievement; it was surely one of the freshest, most original musicals of the '40s. An interplay of many factors contributed to this, but three, above all, turned the troubled project around: The driving influence of Gene Kelly on the entire production team; the presence and persona of the spectacular Rita Hayworth; and a Kelly dance masterpiece, with, quite possibly, his favorite partner: himself.

Saul Chaplin, by now a close friend of Gene's, was for the first time working with him; Chaplin was hired by Columbia as the music director for the production. The shooting was well along when Gene asked Chaplin to prepare some new comedy material for Phil Silvers, a patter song based on an idea Gene had when he realized that the entire film should be "lightened up." Vidor, once again, protested, but Cohn backed Gene. Silvers, a longtime crony of Chaplin's in New York, warned the songwriter, according to Chaplin, that "working with Kelly probably wouldn't be easy because Gene had definite opinions about everything, wasn't reticent about expressing them, and was very articulate." Since the number would have to be done in a rush, Chaplin caught up with Gene while he was coaching Rita on a new dance sequence. Chaplin wanted to know where in the film the new Silvers bit would be plugged in. "Now Gene, where," he asked, holding the latest shooting script, "what page does this new stuff for Phil go into?"

"Saul, please," said Gene, toweling off perspiration, "read the whole thing again. The whole script. So the new stuff really fits." Gene went over the points he thought Chaplin should consider: the overall flow and structure of the story, the preceding sequence and the one to follow, the essence of Silvers' role, his own presence in the scene as a listener to Silvers, how he would be reacting, how the cinematographer would compose the master cover shot—and just before returning to rejoin Hayworth, emphasized the importance of what Chaplin was preparing. Chaplin was taken aback by Gene's energy. He had expected to be given a page number in answer to his question with, perhaps, a hurried few words of orientation. Gene was flooding him with valuable insights. Late that night Kelly phoned him at home. Chaplin never forgot what was said on that occasion and his own reaction:

> Gene got right into it. He said: "Saul . . . I didn't mean to palm you off when you came around today about Phil's new bit. Listen, I've thought it over. Just make Phil as funny as you can and don't worry about me. I'll take care of myself. . . ." I was amazed. I had never met such an unselfish actor. He was interested in the picture as a whole . . . and his attitude never changed. He was always concerned with the entire project and was indeed able to take care of himself.

Thankfully for *Cover Girl* Gene made it his priority to take care of Rita Hayworth, too. On the surface it would seem Hayworth needed no support. She was, after all, the American Beauty of the era, worshiped by the public. She was blessed. Everything about her was visually stunning: her strikingly lovely face and figure, the delicacy and grace of her hands and feet, her gentle and endearing demeanor. She was a true movie star.

But at the core, she had no self-esteem. She was a battered woman. Her personal history was a morbid one: Abused as a child by her father, involved in a hideous marriage with her domineering agent, Ed Judson, who made every decision for her career and her life, she was now trying to divorce Judson to marry Orson Welles. Judson had threatened to have his mob contacts pour acid over her face if she left him. She went from day to day fearful whenever a stranger came close. Mustering all her will power, she managed to glow on camera, but at the director's call of "Cut!" a wan smile tried to shield her internal torment.

And Cohn himself—on the all-Hollywood varsity team when it came to womanizing and couch-casting—made advances almost daily. When, despite his powerful position, she rebuffed him (just as Marilyn Monroe was to do years later) he reverted to his role as a congenital humiliator. During the making of her first big hit, *Gilda*, witnesses had been present in the Columbia screening room when rushes were run of the previous day's coverage of a Hayworth dance sequence. The Columbia head picked up the phone, they recounted, and made a phone call to her: "Rita? That you? You still sleeping? Big night, last night, eh? Well, baby, I just ran your dailies. Yeah, the dance scene. You look awful, you've got a big fat ass!"

Kelly warned Cohn there would be "mucho trouble" if he talked to Rita that way again. He then made a short call to Ed Judson promising a personal visit. He arranged for Judson to be barred from the Columbia lot. Then he and Phil Silvers made it their project not only to lighten the mood of the film but the atmosphere surrounding Rita at Columbia. Once Saul Chaplin entered the sound stage when Gene, Phil, and Rita were rehearsing. The three of them had stopped and were overcome with laughter at one of Silvers' quips. All Chaplin could make out through the chuckling and sniffling was the comedian's punchline: "Rita, darling, Orson's gonna do to you what he did to Hearst in *Citizen Kane*." Chaplin didn't get the joke, but Rita found it very funny—and that, he knew, was the important thing.

Within a short time after Gene's arrival at Columbia, she was a different Rita Hayworth, relaxed and cheerful, clearly enjoying what she was doing even though (or perhaps because) the two mischievous co-performers, dancer and comedian, never gave her a moment's peace. One of them always had his hands on her, and when they were working out steps as a trio, the two men would clown around, one ahead and one behind, and make what they called a "Rita sandwich." She, and they, too, loved every second of the tomfoolery needed to erase her fears.

She was a quick study, and they worked in harmony. She picked up on Gene's ideas and danced superbly, with gusto and panache. With her dress billowing out, the music track a build of romantic arpeggios, it was as if she flowed, not danced, around and around vast circular ramps, poised for flight into the heavens. She never looked happier on screen.

Gene had lost touch with her uncle in Chicago but he knew Angel Cansino would be pleased with how his niece was coming along.

Cover Girl offered Gene the opportunity of his movie lifetime. It would mark his leap from hoofer to dance legend. With one gloriously original achievement, he would be the creator of a seminal moment in film musicals: his alter-ego sequence—if he could bring it off.

The plot of *Cover Girl* moves relentlessly to the point when the heroine jilts Danny McGuire. He wanders out into the street, discouraged. Van Upp's script, not very helpfully, simply called for *Dance*, but Gene saw the importance of the moment within the context of the film. He needed to express the mood changes Danny was going through: the anger at being rejected by the cover girl, set against his responsibility for her unhappy position. Her face on a magazine cover has made her a goddess. She has everything, but it has come to nothing. She feels her chances for happiness have been destroyed, and that is why she will abandon the life of a cover girl. He has a guilty conscience for having caused her this trauma.

It is likely Gene's concern for his own marriage contributed to his dance conception, a fight between Danny and his own conscience. For Betsy, a teenager from New Jersey, had been carried off by him to Hollywood, catapulted into a constellation of stars and celebrities, the Wonderful World of Gene Kelly. But what was there for her? She was in the position of the cover girl, whom happiness eludes. He, too, felt a sense of guilt at what he has done to Betsy.

For Van Upp's *Dance*, Gene's concept took form as an internal struggle between Danny McGuire and his conscience. On his somber walk down the city street, Danny spots the conscience, another image of himself, a double, in a shop window. The conscience comes alive and dances with Danny. Their moves speak to each other: The conscience is competitive, hostile, angry. Danny, at first, is guarded and defensive. They try to outdo each other, leaping over each other's head. Finally, in desperation, Danny heaves a garbage can into a store window that reflects his image. With the shattering of the glass the conscience is finally gone and the dance ends as Danny quietly walks away, as so many of Gene Kelly's numbers do.

With the framework for the dance number worked out, Gene now bit the bullet and went to Cohn's office to seek the Columbia head's okay. As Gene said later:

> Cohn had to be convinced about everything before he gave the go-ahead. He automatically said "no"—and left it up to you to see if you were strong enough to persuade him otherwise . . . but when we came to selling him the idea of the alter-ego number, it was a battle because he couldn't visualize it. After all, how do you tell a man with not very much creative imagination that you're going to dance with yourself for five or six minutes, and that the dance is meant to represent a man fighting with his conscience? The only way to do it was to be as persuasive as you could—then threaten to walk out if he said no.

If nothing else, Cohn was a gambler. Gene must have been convincing. Over Vidor's protests, the Columbia head approved the additional budget for the special-effects work in creating the alter-ego number.

In the 1940s, of course, computer imaging did not exist. Now facing Gene was an obstacle course of technical difficulties. He decided he needed help. Perhaps this was the time to hire the "kid" who had followed him out to Hollywood and become a fixture, if a sleepy one, at the Kelly open house: Stanley Donen. Here began one of the most productive partnerships in the making of motion pictures, and though it would end on a very different note, it started in an atmosphere of sweetness and light. As Kelly described the early relationship: "Stanley was a chorus boy in two of my Broadway shows and came out here as a chorus boy for MGM. When they fired him, I said 'Come on down to Columbia and work as my assistant on *Cover Girl.*' He was like a son to me."

Donen quickly proved his value and took on additional responsibilities. Gene had set a lofty goal for their joint effort: to translate his brooding, internalized emotion into exciting Technicolor footage. The camera was locked into a stationary position. The first step was to shoot Gene dancing as himself on the street set, no easy task, because he had to hit precise marks in relation to the invisible movements of his alter-ego. Then the entire set was painted and covered in black. With Donen behind the camera operator, the camera rolled again with Gene now dancing the part of the alter-ego. In post-production, the coverage of the alter-ego's dance was printed with Gene's original performance within the same frame. Each dancer's moves could not invade the other's dancing area or, of course, it would look grotesque, as if two bodies were occupying the same space. And when the two Genes were supposedly dancing alongside each other, if the alter-ego slipped behind Gene's prime character ever so slightly, despite all the ministrations of Columbia's Special Effects Department the alter-ego would have the surreal appearance of floating and the entire laboratory printing process would have to be redone.

A very special effect for the time: Gene competed with his own conscience in Cover Girl (1944). *(Culver Pictures)*

It was not always high-tech. There were moments of low comedy, unintentional snafus that left them laughing. During rehearsals, it was Donen who danced the alter-ego role when Gene played himself. In the chase section of the number, Gene had to pursue Stanley and come as close as possible without actually catching him. The difficulty was that Gene's natural movements were much faster than Donen's. Over the taps and slides, there were the constant verbal assaults from Kelly: "Move your fat ass, Stanley!" or just "Dammit, move!"

Then there was a dramatic slide down a telephone pole. Stanley, in the rehearsal, would start his slide but Gene was so much quicker that he would wind up sitting on Stanley's head when the ground was reached. For all his flashes of temper and calling out of invective, Gene respected the contribution of his young assistant:

> I certainly couldn't have done "alter ego" without Stanley Donen, who would call out all the timings. We worked for a month on that dance, shot it in four days, and then spent a great deal more time editing all the double-printed footage. Having been told that

technically the double-image could not be done, I was delighted to bring it off.

Harry Cohn was miserable over the cost of the insertion of the alter-ego number; it was over $100,000, an item not included in the original budget. But when the film editor ran the rough-cut for him on the Moviola and he finally grasped the enchanting sequence Kelly had provided to *Cover Girl*, he knew the gamble had paid off. He admitted to himself—he was not one to go public with praise, for it always ended with performers beseeching him for more money—that he had a winner. Another Oscar was in reach. Hayworth was radiantly beautiful, a Vogue cover come to life. Kelly's rendition of Danny McGuire was riveting and his dances made Cohn catch his breath. Even Silvers' jokes set him laughing.

Cohn put on a giant uproarious "wrap" party to commemorate the end of shooting at a Hungarian restaurant on the Sunset Strip. Phil Silvers did a long patter song, written especially for the occasion by Saul Chaplin. It made fun of everyone: the dictatorial Cohn, the perfectionist Kelly, the sex symbol Hayworth, the scrambling Donen, even the often apoplectic Vidor. All took the kidding in good spirit. The lucky ones went on to new projects, the others to unemployment insurance.

In the period between the shooting and the release of *Cover Girl*, MGM, still not comprehending what a resource it had in Gene Kelly, continued to loan him out on a profitable basis. He went directly into a nonmusical role at Universal Studios, supporting Deanna Durbin, the former child star, in *Christmas Holiday*.

On the evening of the sneak preview of *Cover Girl*, as luck would have it, Gene was on call for a *Christmas Holiday* exterior-night shoot, so he could not be at the Crown Theater in Pasadena, where Cohn had arranged the first test showing. The Crown's feature attraction was a new film with Edward G. Robinson called *Flesh and Fantasy*. Gene, barely keeping his mind on the Durbin project, drove home rapidly when his night scene was completed. Donen was to phone him right after the sneak preview. His assistant had not yet called when he arrived at Alta Drive, which was surprising and disconcerting to Gene.

The next two hours were difficult to get through. He tried Donen's apartment. No answer. Finally, toward midnight, the phone rang and Gene snatched up the receiver and burst out impatiently: "Stanley?"

"Yeah." Donen sounded a bit harassed.

"Well?" Gene was suddenly tight with breath. "How did it go?"

"The film went beautifully. But . . . but . . . ," he stammered. "There's a big but, Gene."

"Go on."

"The alter-ego number. It bombed."

"What?"

"For some goddamn reason, people burst out laughing."

"Laughing!"

"The moment they saw your double in the window, the audience hooted and howled, Gene." Donen waited for Kelly to say something, then went on gloomily:

"I don't understand. As you can imagine, neither does Cohn. He's upset about his hundred thou."

Overcome by disappointment, they were too sick at heart to talk much longer. Their talents had been tested and found inadequate. When Gene rang off he knew he'd be getting a call from Cohn. The Columbia chief would emulate L.B. Mayer after the *For Me and My Gal* sneak preview and order a complete redo, undoubtedly dropping the alter-ego number. Betsy could do nothing to cheer him up.

Cohn did not call during the night. Nor the next day while he was at Universal. But around noon of the following day an urgent message reached the Universal switchboard: Could Gene Kelly come to see Harry Cohn at Columbia as soon as possible?

Robert Siodmak, the director of the Durbin film, was sympathetic enough to rearrange the afternoon's schedule and let him go. Gene drove rapidly to the Columbia lot, considering what fate was in store for him. The alter-ego number was an all-or-nothing experience. If some element within it made an audience laugh, he was in serious trouble. So he was in serious trouble!

The security shack at the Columbia entrance had been alerted. He was let in to see Cohn immediately. To his astonishment, the burly studio head jumped up when he entered, came around his desk, stepped off the platform that extended his height, and nearly knocked Gene over with his hug. "Congratulations, Gene! We did it!"

"What—what's going on, Harry?"

"The sneaks—the results are terrific!" He saw the look of astonishment on Gene's face. "What? That's not good enough for you?"

"I heard—" He didn't want to mention Donen's name. "The audience laughed . . . laughed out loud during the—"

"Ohh, *that*," Cohn cut in. "The Crown Theater manager called me. Apologized for the laughing, explained it: The theater was running Eddie Robinson in *Flesh and Fantasy*. Well, it happens there's a sequence in it when Eddie is walking down a New York street. It's night and, guess what, Gene? Eddie sees a reflection in a shop window and goes toward it. It's a reflection of himself! Then we hear Eddie Robinson giving out his voiceover, his thoughts. It's a major sequence, Gene! What a coincidence! Because, naturally, when Eddie's picture is over and out comes our sneak preview and there *you* are, bigger than life, looking into a shop window— whaddya expect? The audience laughs like hell! I ran another sneak last night in the Valley. No Eddie Robinson this time. Just a Gene Autry western to go along with our *Cover Girl* and, y'know what? We're a smasharoo! Let's have a drink!"

"I can't, Harry. I'm working."

"You bet you are! And will be! I've been talking with Mayer, your esteemed boss."

"Oh oh."

"I know, he's a prick and he's driving me crazy, the price he's asking for you."

"Price? For me? What—"

"For my *Pal Joey*." Cohn nodded, very proud of himself. "This morning I called New York and bought up the rights. You're gonna do it in the movies! A Columbia production starring Gene Kelly. I just have to get your release from that dickhead Mayer. Who's asking a pretty penny. But you'll be in my *Pal Joey*, believe me!"

"I believe you, Harry!" He was back at work with Deanna Durbin in the afternoon, hardly remembering the drive through traffic back to Universal. He did dimly recall a lot of exultant laughter coming from him on the Freeway. There was plenty to be cheery about. His dream was to be Pal Joey on the screen. His dream had come through, and why not? It was inevitable. After all, who, if not he, *was* Pal Joey?

By *now, almost everybody in the Hollywood branch of the Gene Kelly Fan Club has been called on by Shirley MacLaine. The above-the-title titans, the still-bankable biggies, anybody who's anybody, has stood up to gush what a four-star genius is GK! Almost everybody. Who's counting? It may be dirty pool to figure out who's not paying their respects tonight. Or fun in a pleasure–pain way, like picking at a scab.*

There's Donen, for instance, who should be here watching what are his films, too. But who can blame him? Stanley's marriage to Jeanne went south in 1949, lasting less than a year and, face it, you-know-who had a lot to do with their divorce. If only Betsy had hung around more, it might have been a different story. The poor guy had to grin and bear it— the red-hot team of Gene and Jeannie—through all those films, with people putting Stanley down as GK's gofer, GK's stand-in, GK's cuckold! Well, beneath that shit-kicking, shucks-fellers Southern boy-wonder is a brooding, tough competitor, and when It's Always Fair Weather didn't make it, he saw his chance for himself and cried out: Enough already!

No, this AFI salute is supposed to be a love-fest. Donen wants no part of it. Sinatra's not here either, but he's on a concert tour in Europe. (Singers last much longer than dancers!) Took the trouble to call from Rome, did the kudos bit in his usual dry style. Betsy hated Vegas, and Jeannie was a homebody, so he never joined Pal Frankie's "Rat Pack."

Alas, Frankie had been no help in his tiff with L.B. Mayer. He'd wanted to get out of his own deal with MGM and grab that great part in From Here to Eternity. When one of Mayer's ponies tossed the big boss into the hospital with a broken leg, Frankie had made that awful crack about L.B.'s companion: "L.B. didn't fall off a horse, he fell off Ginny Simms."

Then he had yelled at his friend: "You stupid dago bastard! When are you going to learn to keep your mouth shut?" He was mad because Simms was certainly no bimbo, but a dignified woman with talent. L.B. found a way to break Frank's contract and, wouldn't you know, Ol' Blue Eyes ends up at Columbia with an Oscar for Eternity.

So L.B. didn't take it out on Frankie. Guess who he took it out on?

LOS ANGELES, 1944

* * *

Despite his dream, stardom in the film of *Pal Joey* was not immediately forthcoming.

Typically, as in the case of previous recipients of Gene's phone barrages, David O. Selznick and Johnny Darrow, he hounded Harry Cohn. He was impatient for the Columbia head to arrange the loan-out deal with MGM for his services.

"Hold your horses," Cohn would tell him. "Mayer's asking a price for you that makes my nose bleed! I offered him the max I can do. But the bastard always asks for more, more."

In another call, Cohn told him he had even offered Rita Hayworth later on, in a trade for Gene, but Mayer's response was that he didn't need any more female stars. "And then he goes into that 'there are more stars at MGM than in heaven crap.' But don't worry. I've bought the film rights to *Joey* and you're m'man. I'll work it out with Mayer yet."

Cohn's determination was encouraging. Gene felt, at long last, that after seven films he had progressed as a motion-picture actor. He was ready for the dramatic demands of *Pal Joey*. By now he had completed *Christmas Holiday* with Deanna Durbin, no musical sleigh ride despite the blithe title, but a constant challenge to his abilities. The screenplay was loosely based on a Somerset Maugham short story about a psychopathic murderer, played by Gene, and a naive wife-victim, Durbin's role. On his own initiative he had played the part as a homosexual—no cartoon, nothing homophobic, but a sensibly, sensitively drawn character. Robert Siodmak, the director, had thought Gene's approach was brilliant; indeed, it served to disguise the inability of Durbin to handle her first adult role.

The film turned out to be notable. It not only made money as one of Universal's major successes in 1944; it also contains the only scene in Gene's career when he steps onto a dance floor with a partner (the victimized Miss Durbin) and the film immediately cuts away to the next scene at another location.

His participation in *Christmas Holiday* was under a loan-out arrangement, a trade with Universal for the more Asian-looking Turhan Bey. Due to the War Department's forced evacuation of Japanese-Americans from the West Coast, no Japanese actors could be secured. Bey was needed for *Dragon Seed*, Metro's adaptation of Pearl Buck's novel about a Japanese takeover of a Chinese village. Gene was pleased with the exchange on two counts: It showed Mayer had no ongoing prohibition against loan-outs. And it was evidence that Metro, better late than never, had finally awakened to its patriotic obligation and would now support the war effort more energetically.

He returned to Culver City, determined to cooperate fully with Mayer and keep his hostility under control. He expected Cohn and Mayer to wrap up his loan-out for *Pal Joey* within a few days. But it soon became clear Mayer was not going out of his way to benefit Gene Kelly, at least via the career pathway Gene was desperate to follow. He would now go to work, Mayer mandated, on a new MGM production. Arthur Freed wanted Gene to co-star with Mickey Rooney in *Honey Boy*, the life story of George "Honey Boy" Evans, one of America's most popular traveling minstrels. Rooney would take on the title role, Kelly would be Evans's closest pal, a fellow performer. He barely had time to react to the announcement before newspapers and radio broadcasts reported Rooney's induction into military service. The project was postponed.

Just the thought of the tiny, nonmuscular Rooney heading overseas to combat while he, tougher and stronger by far, remained pampered within MGM's protective walls, reinforced Gene's desire to join up. Especially because the pursuit of the loan-out for *Pal Joey* was not going well. In fact, it was not going at all. Mayer was adamant, his decision made: If Kelly had any thought of continuing a career in pictures, his scenes could follow only the logo revered by Mayer, the roaring MGM lion.

A young up-and-coming MGM executive, speaking for Mayer and Eddie Mannix, explained the decision to Gene and did it coldly and crisply, brooking no protest. Gene had played a military man in the majority of his films. Thus he was consequently serving as an important role model for young Americans. He was doing significant work as a morale-builder. Period. Now it was 1944, MGM's twentieth anniversary and, Gene was told, the studio had two important assignments for him during the banner year. A musical extravaganza, *The Ziegfeld Follies*, "which the boys will appreciate, especially those overseas" said the executive, making the case for Gene's wartime contribution.

Gene persisted: "What did L.B. say about my loan-out with Columbia for *Pal Joey*?"

The executive acted as though the question was unheard. "Then we finish out the year, our anniversary year with a real war film."

"That so? What's it about?"

"A war film's a war film. It's called *Anchors Aweigh*."

Whenever MGM ran out of ideas for new musicals, it seemed there was always one dependable source, one treasure trove to turn to: the legendary showmanship of Florenz Ziegfeld. MGM had already tapped into Ziegfeldiana for *The Great Ziegfeld* (1936) and *Ziegfeld Girl* (1941). Both pictures had made money for MGM. It augured well for another reshaping of the material, and so was born *The Ziegfeld Follies*, Gene's first assignment since returning to the MGM fold.

It was not a storyline film but a throwback to the sumptuous, glittering, all-star, all-singing, all-dancing Broadway stage revues, a prewar favorite by now somewhat diminished in popularity. Prefacing the hodgepodge of acts was a languid on-screen performance by William Powell, the cinematic Great Ziegfeld himself, now no longer of this planet but ensconced in a luxurious penthouse apartment in heaven. There he is found planning a new show. But what MGM stars will participate?

The question is dealt with by Ziegfeld's assistant, Fred Astaire, still happily alive and kicking on earth. Astaire works out the list of participants. Then follow twelve sketches or musical numbers, of which the less forgettable feature Lucille Ball as a circus ringmistress leading a female extravaganza "Bringing on the Beautiful Girls"; the inevitable Esther Williams and her water ballet; Astaire dancing with Lucille Bremer to "Limehouse Blues"; Judy Garland doing a surprisingly sophisticated parody of an uppity Greer Garson holding a press interview; and, as a climax, Astaire and Kelly dancing and singing "The Babbit and the Bromide," a song Fred and his sister Adele had originally performed in the 1927 Broadway musical *Funny Face*, by George and Ira Gershwin.

Outside of another small taste of their dancing teamwork, much later in *That's Entertainment! Part II* (1976), it was the only time Gene and Astaire were to dance together. As if he realized the rarity of the occasion and its place in film history, from the start Gene was disappointed with Astaire's choice of material. The latter, usually low-key and not one to push his weight around, had been unusually effusive in recommending the number. It involved two very ordinary, even boring, people meeting in a park. Behind them is a statue of a rearing horse, the rider pulling at the reins. A motionless covey of airbound pigeons completes the background.

The men meet first as youngsters. Then they encounter each other by accident, ten years later, and have the identical pro-forma exchange:

"Hello."

"How are you?"

"How'za folks?"

"What's new?"

As though they care for each other, which they obviously don't. They go through the same routine with the same exchanges of "How are you?" followed by a rapid dance circuit of the park. A decade later they meet again for the same social ceremony. Nothing has changed except that they show signs of age. In the final section, they meet in heaven and go through the tedious business again, sporting gray beards, harps in hand as they dance tra-la-la through the park.

Vincente Minnelli, the director, left the choreography to Astaire and Kelly. His contribution was to insist on the aging of the statue, including the horse and the pigeons, with each meeting of the dancers, a bit of stage business that the sketch could well use. The relationship between the two dancers was clearly competitive but overwhelmingly polite, with neither ever criticizing the other. As Minnelli put it: "It was quite fascinating to watch."

Out of Astaire's hearing, Kelly told Hugh Fordin for his encyclopedic volume, *The World of Entertainment: Hollywood's Greatest Musicals*: "The number I really wanted to do was 'Pass That Peace Pipe,' an original song written for the film by Roger Edens, Hugh Martin, and Ralph Blane. I thought Fred and I could have fun with it and it would be different."

He was usually quick to assert his opinion, but not to the dance icon of the moviegoing public. "When it came to Fred saying I'd like to do this or I'd like to do that, I deferred out of great respect and admiration. I hated the third section. I thought I looked like a klutz."

The problem with Astaire's choice, Gene thought, was that it presented only one joke: the numbing banality of the same conversations. The joke was tired from the beginning, and Gene was much more tired after rehearsing it for six long days, in the middle of May of 1944, on MGM's Stage 21. The meticulous archives of the company still convey why it took four more days, even more grueling, to get the number finished and "in the can." It was not because of Astaire's high standards. It had nothing to do with Kelly's insistence on perfection. It was Murphy's Law—that insidious disrupter of motion-picture schedules: If anything can go wrong, it will.

It is 8 A.M. and Vincente Minnelli is ready to shoot. Kelly and Astaire sit down on the park bench, waiting for "Action!" George Folsey, the veteran cinematographer, suddenly looks up from the eyepiece. "No, no!"

"What's the matter?" asks the director, as the two waiting stars finger their red neckties.

"Need to powder the left side of Mr. Astaire's nose, the left side only."

Instantly, a makeup girl jumps up and does the repair work. Everybody stays frozen in position. But Folsey points out next that one of the wires holding an airborne pigeon in place is visible. A piece of cotton has somehow adhered to it. Minnelli orders the lights to be cut. The dancers try to relax on their bench, in idle conversation. They realize it is as aimless as the script, so they use the time for a last-minute run-through of the exchange between them.

"Hello."

"How are you?"

"How'za folks?"

They break off as the grips bring in a long ladder. One of the stagehands climbs after the bit of fluff and accidentally breaks a wire supporting one of the pigeons. The stars are released to their dressing rooms as four grips crawl into the rafters to arrange the dropping into place of a new wire. The morning is half over and not a foot of negative has gone through Folsey's camera.

They are ready to go again when Folsey notices something. The pigeon fixers have nudged the bronze statue slightly out of line. Men are assigned the task of correcting the position. Another hour passes.

Folsey steps to the side and Minnelli takes a look through the camera. He complains: Four leaves on the left-hand bush are shiny. He wants these to be dulled down. He does not want any undue light reflection.

The Property Department sends the leaves to the MGM paint shop to be sprayed. To make use of the time, Minnelli calls for a camera rehearsal of the action. Astaire and Kelly return. They sit down. When they spring up to dance, Astaire sports a black streak on his white pants. Similar defacement has been done to Kelly's.

Folsey curses the grips. "Don't you guys know we're shooting Technicolor?"

The Wardrobe Department supplies substitute trousers to the stars. The idea of a last rehearsal is bypassed. They will "go for it" now. Minnelli is quite concerned about the total nonproductivity of the morning. Folsey is bending over the camera again. He lifts his face from the eyecup, frowning at something he sees. "Joe!"

"Yes, Mr. Folsey?"

"Powder the left side of Mr. Astaire's nose, the left side only."

And so it goes. Or doesn't go. Someone is now wiping the bench with a large towel. Grips are tearing up the camera track, responding to a problem best known to themselves. Electricians install fresh carbons in the arc-lamps. The two stars, professional to the end, wait patiently. They understand the organized chaos of movie-making.

Kelly "versus" Astaire in Ziegfeld Follies (1944), the only time these friendly but uneasy rivals shared the screen. (Culver Pictures)

Still, in release-print form, "The Babbit and the Bromide" winds up as an amiable romp, the two stars pleasing the public with their easy grace. One understands why Astaire is so insistent on his choice. It is clearly his dance, while Kelly strains a bit, presses, force-feeds the impression that a good time is being enjoyed by both men. Overreacting, the pressure of the moment getting to him, he comes through sweatily in comparison to the dry Astaire, as pointed out in the much-quoted comparison of the two dancers by the distinguished *New Yorker* film critic Pauline Kael:

> The difference starts with their bodies. If you compare Kelly to Astaire, accepting Astaire's debonaire style as perfection, then, of course, Kelly looks bad. . . . Kelly isn't a winged dancer. He's a hoofer and a man—a hurting man. Now Astaire is impervious to emotion, no matter what calamity he has to face with Ginger, it's an oh gosh, oh gee emotion he gives out, and he handles it in a stylish fashion . . . whereas Kelly is a suffering human being. Kelly bleeds and Astaire doesn't.

Over the years, Gene's temper inevitably flared when journalists compared them. In interviews, his dislike of the top-hat-and-white-tie look became almost a set piece:

> I tried to be completely different from Astaire. I had an objection to the kind of dancing I saw on the screen in those days. There was a lot of great dancing but the trouble was, everybody in those films seemed rich. As a Depression kid who went to school in very bad years, I didn't want to move or dance like a rich man. I wanted to do the dance of the Proletariat, the movements of the people.

An attitude with an incendiary vocabulary that did not put him closer to the conservative Louis B. Mayer. *Pal Joey* and Harry Cohn might be beckoning, but Mayer was not about to do a favor for an antagonistic employee prone to spout what Mayer considered Communist jargon. Aware that Gene was now golden at the box office, Mayer and his successors were determined to hold Kelly to his MGM contract. For the next fourteen years and twenty-one films, he was never to work again for another studio. Of course, in 1944, never one to give up easily, he was still lobbying Cohn and Mayer to actualize his own dream of playing Pal Joey on film.

It was an election year, and President Roosevelt was campaigning, for an unprecedented fourth term, against his challenger, Governor Thomas E. Dewey of New York. Gene and Betsy were fervently pro-Roosevelt. They were furious that the MGM front office, spearheaded by Mayer, was the controlling force of the Southern-Californian Republican effort to unseat Roosevelt. Mayer, as he always did, contributed heavily to the G.O.P. campaign, and pressured his associates and underlings to do the same—even modest-salary workers. The Culver City studio buildings were garnished with posters of Dewey's mustachioed face and anti–New Deal slogans. Mayer assigned studio personnel to handle the logistics for Republican Party mass rallies, the largest of which took place at the Memorial Coliseum. Cecil B. DeMille directed a glittering outdoor show featuring a bevy of stars, preparing the way for an emotional exhortation by the keynote speaker Ginger Rogers, the vice chairman of the "Hollywood for Dewey" group. She called the event "a mobilization against the New Deal."

The response from the other side was swift. Gene and Betsy gave liberally of their time and energy to the Democratic effort, despite Gene's work on *Ziegfeld Follies* and pre-production commitments to *Anchors Aweigh*. With his usual energy and insistence on an insider's decision-making role, he was soon at the center of the Democratic planning group. Shortly after the DeMille Republican extravaganza, the "Hollywood for Roosevelt" organization, chaired by Jack Warner, Samuel Goldwyn, and Katharine Hepburn, honored FDR's running mate, the bespectacled and relatively unknown Senator from Missouri, Harry Truman, at the Shrine Auditorium. Afterward, at a fund-raising dinner for the Democratic National Committee at the Ambassador Hotel, stars, producers, and wealthy liberals in the Los Angeles area were entertained by Groucho Marx and Danny Kaye. The hit of the duo's performance was a female impersonation, a comic dance in drag designed and choreographed by Gene Kelly. His experience in Pittsburgh at putting together what were essentially "amateur shows" came in handy now, despite the fame of the current casts.

Soon Gene and Betsy were leading voter-registration drives and boosting a slate of left-leaning candidates for national, state, and municipal office. They signed petitions and made many speeches (usually Gene but sometimes Betsy) at public rallies for a more open foreign policy, support of the Soviet Union's fight against the Nazis, pro-labor laws, and "full rights for all racial and minority groups." Betsy's efforts were centered on helping the Russians. More local issues involved Gene; it was his personal response to the increasing tensions in Los Angeles, which was changing from a small city of transplanted white Midwesterners into a sprawling, multiracial urban center with associated problems: unemployment, housing shortages, job discrimination, and the reappearance of the Ku Klux Klan. The year before, 1943, had seen the infamous "zoot-suit riots." Mobs of servicemen tore through the streets assaulting Latinos, while police looked on, reluctant to stop the rioting. Democrats had called for an investigation. Republican officeholders blocked any action to punish the rioters.

Involved as Gene was in the Roosevelt campaign, constantly harangued by Betsy to contribute more time and money to left-wing activist causes, his priority still was his career. He was relieved that MGM had finally green-lighted *Anchors Aweigh*. It pained him that Betsy considered his movie work less important, and he knew a severe personal problem was heating up: Their marriage was coming apart. Now, though, first things first; he looked forward to working with Frank Sinatra, whom he regarded, unstintingly, as a major talent. And Frank, like him, was "against the system."

He knew producer Joe Pasternak would give him liberty to design his own dance numbers. He was ready to try out many ideas which, later on, would be repeated in other Kelly vehicles, especially *On the Town*. Gene had third billing behind Sinatra and Kathryn Grayson, which rankled him a bit. But he was assuaged by the delicious opportunity to choreograph and appear in three original dances.

Anchors Aweigh sets Kelly and Sinatra out on their ever-present search for female companionship—as in *On the Town*, the plot centers on sailors looking for girls, but here the search takes place in Hollywood, not New York. They are only getting started when they run across Dean Stockwell, who, despite being woefully underage and a truant from school, wants to run away to join the Navy. Naturally, the duo will have none of that, and they return the boy to his home and an anxious aunt, played by Kathryn Grayson. The story from then on is even more predictable, but done with a who-gives-a-damn panache that is ultimately pleasing. Of course, one has to accept the distinct impossibility of Frank Sinatra, the bobby-soxers' favorite, needing help to score with a weekend date. Once that hurdle is jumped, it is full-speed ahead with *Anchors Aweigh*.

In pre-production, Gene was determined to create cine-dances that would be impossible to do in any other medium. Far from being intimidated by motion-picture technology, he would use it, facing the challenge of the dramatically different way a dance looks on the two-dimensional screen, versus the way it looks on Broadway, where it is a fully three-dimensional experience.

Gene's former girlfriend Helene Marlowe had studied with the modern-dance pioneer Martha Graham and had once brought to his attention an interview with Graham's male star, Paul Taylor, who expressed a common frustration of preparing choreography for film. Said Taylor:

> It still to my eye does not look like live movement. The moment
> you commit yourself to dance being in the screen, so much
> changes. It looks flat and little. For the camera, if you stay on

a long shot too long, the dancers' figures are so small that they look like bugs. So you have to keep finding ways to get closer.

Gene knew, of course, he could zoom in or cut to a close shot. But then the background goes out of focus, owing to the technical limitations of the camera. Worse, the eye of the camera is not akin to the human eye; there is no peripheral vision. The close shot will enclose only a small area of the setting behind the dancer. The atmosphere of the full environment is lost. It is a sterile, unsatisfying moment.

"To keep finding ways to get closer"—the choreographer's responsibility as Paul Taylor saw it—was now Gene's constant objective, and he worked very hard to retain the overall environment one finds in the theatrical experience. His dances embraced movements toward the camera, from long shot to close shot, with the camera holding position or pulling back slightly to embrace the sense of movement. When his cameraman needed to track or pan with a moving dancer, Gene called for the placement of specially designed vertical props, strategically separated, in the background. The effect was like trackside telephone poles underscoring the sense of the speed of a moving train.

Speed, quickness, vitality. The pick-up refreshment that a film needs most, Gene had learned in his first screening of the dances with Judy Garland in *For Me and My Gal*. What lasts on the stage for five minutes is interminable on screen, deserving (at most!) one minute of screen time.

These considerations were factored into the three Gene Kelly dances in *Anchors Aweigh*. One is a fantasy sequence which finds him making a play for Kathryn Grayson on a movie sound stage. All at once, where the script says only "MUSIC: IN FULL" in a vaguely promissory way, a magical transmutation takes place, thanks solely to Gene's creativity: The set is now a sun-dappled Spanish courtyard. Gene, practically giving off sparks in a gold shirt, red and black cape, and black trousers, does an amazing fandango that has him leaping over parapets, scaling battlements, and taking a Tarzan-like vine-ride from a 50-foot-high rooftop to the balcony of his beloved. Entirely in the tradition of Douglas Fairbanks, a Kelly hero from childhood, the number demonstrated the gymnastic skills that stood him so well since his days at Peabody High and signalled his beginning in this vein; he would continue to create this kind of athletic number as the choreographer of *The Pirate* four years later.

Another number, the Mexican Hat Dance, he would have preferred doing on location—ideally the real Olvera Street in the Mexican neighborhood of Los Angeles. But Joe Pasternak, along with almost every Hollywood producer or director, believed movies had to be made in the studio, especially musicals. Unless one could control all the elements—sound, lighting, crowds—the shooting day could be a nightmare of chaos, overtime costs, and liability lawsuits. No, the first order of business was to see if any of the standing sets on the back lot might serve the purpose: Broadway, Main Street, Night Club, Western Street. . . . No? Then they would *build* an Olvera Street, where he could dance with little Sharon MacManus. In another highlight of the film, they linked their arms, adult and child, and rigadooned around the fountain in the middle of the square. Gene could not hide his disappointment that the location wasn't authentic, but nobody else seemed to care; Pasternak and the MGM executives thought the number could not be improved upon. Not so his daughter Kerry—when she finally saw the film, she was jealous her father had not danced with her! It was a difficult explanation to labor through.

In the preparation of this number, the young Stanley Donen, following Gene over from *Cover Girl*, demonstrated a number of gifts but showed no special affinity for child performers. For Gene, working with children was hardly new, given his experience at the Gene Kelly Studio of Dance back home. Little girls and boys like Sharon MacManus always responded to his Pied Piper quality and found him endlessly funny. To keep kids happily involved and amused he was not above doing anything and everything—from standing on his head to wriggling his derriere. One of Donen's tasks, not always appreciated by Gene, was to teach Sharon her new routines, primarily one involving a skipping rope. Donen remembered one particularly hideous day of work with her, when she was game enough, but did not find his more arid personality an adequate substitution for Gene's flamboyance. Donen spent three hours on the rope routine, took a quick break for lunch, and then came an additional four hours of rehearsal of the needed step while the California social worker assigned to little Sharon was lured elsewhere. Every thirty seconds, it seemed, Gene stuck his head into the rehearsal room: "Stanley, does she have the rope bit yet?"

Donen, exhausted from the effort, the countless demonstrations, the aching need to maintain a continuous smile, could only respond with a glowering "No." It became like a comedy routine from hell. Gene would call him and say something to the effect that he, Donen, must concentrate more on the tiny pupil still standing by, indestructible and impassive, peering up at him with wary suspicion: "Stanley, you've got to make believe you love little Sharon."

"But I loathe little Sharon, Gene!"

Little Sharon began to loathe her teacher just as much. Both of them were rescued on the morning of the shoot, when Gene was there, fresh and smiling and playful in a blue-and-white-striped T-shirt and a beret with a red pompom, instead of the grumpy Donen in his grimy sweatsuit. If only to spite Donen, the adoring child worked beautifully with Gene and the scene was filmed with few retakes.

For the third Kelly dance that was to make *Anchors Aweigh* so special, Donen was far more than a reluctant babysitter; he was central to the conception and production of the famous "The King Who Couldn't Dance," when Gene was partnered with Jerry, the animated-cartoon figure from the famous MGM Tom and Jerry series. Though Donen was to constantly brood that Kelly never gave him enough credit in their collaboration, in interview after interview the star would describe the Eureka moment in the same way: "Stanley Donen and I sat around for a couple of days trying to think of something, and after one long period of silence Stanley suddenly said: 'How about dancing with a cartoon?' That was it."

It was not the first filmed dance to combine live action with animation. Combining the two had been done as far back as 1917; it had been credibly accomplished in Max Fleischer's *Out of the Inkwell* cartoon series. But the difficulties for Kelly and Donen involved the use of color and the synchronizing of Gene's dance routine and an animated figure. It was far more complex than any previous marriage of the two forms, and it had to be vigorously sold to the quizzical Louis B. Mayer and Eddie Mannix. Like Harry Cohn with the *Cover Girl* alter-ego number, the executives found it difficult to visualize what Gene and Donen were going for—indeed, whether the final effect was possible. The grim fact that doing the number would pile on another whopping cost to an already swelling budget was of concern. Producer Pasternak was charmed by the vision of Gene tapping away with the popular Jerry, and since Gene's films had always made money, Mayer could not dismiss the idea out of hand. The cautious Mannix suggested that Kelly and Donen visit Walt Disney and run through the technical procedures with the recognized guru of the animation field. Disney at the time was also combining live action and cartoons for his *The Three Caballeros*, but Gene knew the Disney production was not nearly as complicated as what he and Donen had in mind. He would forever be grateful to Disney for his support: "Walt gave us his blessing. And the fact that Disney considered the idea feasible helped us to persuade the MGM cartoon department to do the job. . . . that was all Mannix and Mayer wanted to hear. And they gave Pasternak permission to go ahead."

For Kelly and Donen, it was a tortured trial-and-error process. The basic scheme was for Gene's solo to be photographed against a neutral blue background. As he danced, Donen, with the cinematographer, called out the intricate movements and timings. The challenge for their cameraman was to compose a pleasing two-shot when one of the dancing duo, the mouse, was absent from the frame. Then the action of the dance was tracked frame by frame for the animators' reference. They filled the area around Gene with the appropriate renditions of Jerry—in more than 10,000 painted images—moving in harmony with him. The mouse danced alongside Gene, and even around him, when a composite picture was finally made by a newly designed optical printer. The entire cartoon sequence took two months to complete. It played four minutes of screen time.

In the end, man and mouse come together seamlessly as teacher and pupil in a charming dance class. We see a Gene far removed from the Gene Kelly Studio but a captivating instructor nevertheless. We see a Jerry gliding and cakewalking his way out of gloom. They are comrades enjoying a new experience, enchanting the audience whenever *Anchors Aweigh* is shown.

Even though he was aware that the script was not exceptional, Gene, fired by his own enthusiasm for the dances he created, worked unsparingly to improve the overall film. As he had demonstrated particularly during the filming of *Cover Girl*, he didn't recognize any separation of creative departments. He sought out Isobel Lennart, the film's scriptwriter, who realized that Gene was a source of fresh ideas. After a session with him she invariably found herself at the typewriter doing some rewrites of a line or even a sequence. She respected his sense of plot construction, too, though his blunter criticisms sometimes hurt.

Pasternak, the antithesis of Gene, was inclined to coast as a producer, satisfied if the basic story idea was commercial and he had some recognizable stars with a few promising song numbers. Let well enough alone and things would work out, and, for him, they usually did. He avoided Gene, who seemed to be constantly at him like a terrier with calls for revisions and improvements. Director George Sidney, similarly unblessed with an adventurous spirit, considered it a good day when he met his quota of camera setups. At scene run-throughs involving the principals, Gene would have recommendations concerning the placement of the camera, reblocking of the action, succession of cuts, and reaction cutaway shots, and a dread of overtime— a no-no of L.B. Mayer—would hang over Sidney like a guillotine.

The head of the film editing department would have complained to Mayer that Gene was a constant and unwelcome visitor—except that the cutters at the Moviolas always found his ideas helpful.

It was something of a trial for Gene to work with Frank Sinatra. He liked Sinatra enormously as a human being and respected his talent—"except that he set dancing back twenty years in *Anchors Aweigh*," as he joked. Though Sinatra was not lazy, he did not believe in rehearsing and would disappear, adding to the hysteria of Sidney and Pasternak. Sinatra was convinced that his first take, when the material and performers were both fresh, would prove to be the best. But with Gene, who was his instructor for the rather simple team-tap routines they had to do, he was locked into a room over the course of several days, a lifetime for the singer, who would say later: "Apart from being a great artist, Gene's a born teacher. I felt really comfortable working for him and enjoyed his company, in spite of his manic insistence on hard work."

For Gene, there was nothing bizarre in not going home to Betsy and Kerry and staying overtime in the studio or on location over a span of sixteen hours, and then go on day after day with that same blistering regime. He remarked:

> I suppose there's a certain masochism in it. But in a way I like the training period, the weeks and weeks of endless rehearsing much more than the actual shooting. There was something about achieving a perfection during rehearsals which I found even more exciting than committing that perfection to celluloid, and I imagined everyone I worked with felt the same.

But everyone didn't. It was a constant misjudgment on his part, the blithe certainty that his convictions were always mirrored in the minds of others. It reflected the need to control which, ultimately, hurt him in the work arena and eroded his marriage to Betsy.

For something was going wrong at home. He could feel it. But he was not one for introspection; he always focused on the challenges of his career and, even worse, discouraged Betsy's attempts to talk about her—and their—personal problems. Years later, when interviewed by Clive Hirschhorn, Betsy described the difficulties of living with "the most marvelous man a woman could have. . . . he treated me like some strange phenomenon that had constantly to be watched, cosseted and protected. . . .

that's exactly how Gene saw me—as something special, and he was protective and very fatherly about his possession. I was only twenty at the time, I needed his guidance and concern."

With the birth of Kerry, Betsy had temporarily shelved her own career aspirations. Her plans were still to resume her professional efforts when Kerry was older, but on the stage. The cinema's 35-millimeter film was not unkind to Betsy, but her unconventional, atypically photogenic looks stood in the way of gaining movie roles, and somehow in screen tests she appeared overburdened with an unsettling tension that casting directors frowned upon. She continued to exercise every day with a personal trainer and took dancing lessons regularly in an effort to reestablish her slim figure. But in the Lana Turner era, Betsy Blair didn't shape up, and she knew it.

Gene had a sense she regarded his Hollywood films as unimportant. The stage was where the hearts and minds of Americans could be changed—and at political rallies, too, during the 1944 campaign, not just those promoting the Democrats and FDR (Gene attended with her whenever he could) but also those conducted by various Communist-front groups. From Gene's standpoint, when he thought about it—which wasn't often—she had fallen in with the same sort of leftist intellectuals she had been close to in New York. She had become known around Hollywood as an outspoken radical, a fixture on the speakers' platform at Communist gatherings. She attended performances at the Actors Lab, a leftist theater group that was considered the West Coast version of New York's Group Theater.

And when Actors Lab performers came to Kelly parties, it was difficult for Gene to debate the redeeming social value of *Anchors Aweigh* as against the urgent plays of Clifford Odets or the the impassioned Marc Blitzstein musical *The Cradle Will Rock*.

Especially when Gene was working late or was on location somewhere, it seemed to him she was always out, if not at Actors Lab, then at a political rally or a committee meeting. It concerned him that his baby Kerry was being raised by a governess. When he confronted her, Betsy was insulted and defiant; for her, the real subject was their difficulties as a married couple. Again, she would propose therapy—psychoanalysis or, at the very least, a marriage counselor. He would have none of it. To him it was simple: they were going through the inevitable tensions that exist between a husband and wife who are both in the same profession when one is well along the road to stardom, and the other doesn't yet have a foothold.

She shrugged and gave up. What could she do with this intractable man she loved so much? She knew, even if he recognized the marriage was showing signs of slippage, it was not in his nature to let it sink. Divorce, the multi-marriage pattern of Hollywood actors, was anathema considering his Catholic background. After all, as Betsy had been told so often, his sainted mother had managed to hold his parents' marriage and family together despite very serious troubles—despite the Depression, a lacerating poverty, the scourge of alcoholism. What did Betsy have to face, that she couldn't get a part in Saroyan's new play?

Late in the fall of 1944, just as *Anchors Aweigh* completed shooting, Gene was called by the Democratic National Committee for some more radio work. It was a relief to leave the domestic arguments of Alta Drive behind and immerse himself in the preparation of a national network broadcast, "The Roosevelt Train." The program was produced and directed by Norman Corwin, the most revered radio writer in the country. True to form, Gene helped shape the show and worked hard on the production. The concept was clear: nonprofessionals, "ordinary Joes," would make their own statements, coaxed out by skilled interviewers, as to why each one was for Roosevelt. Interspersed were more smoothly delivered exhortations, presumably from the Roosevelt campaign train, by James Cagney, Judy Garland, Groucho Marx, Rita Hayworth, Talullah Bankhead, Irving Berlin, Claudette Colbert, Linda Darnell, John Garfield, and other stars whose testimonials were recorded at various locations and inserted into the body of the program.

Gene wrote and delivered his own participation. It was puzzling to Betsy when she heard it over the radio. It was aggravating to Louis B. Mayer. It was blunt and short: "This is Gene Kelly—Army-bound but not before I vote for Roosevelt."

It was—and continues to be—a bewildering statement. Gene had been discussing a direct commission in the Navy as a Lieutenant Junior Grade (he had gone through Naval Reserve Training exercises at college). He may have changed his service assignment for the broadcast because, with his showman's sensitivity to the mass-audience reaction, he thought the truth would be off-putting. Becoming an officer and a gentleman, a "thirty-day wonder," he was bypassing the gob's sailor suit he always wore in the movies. It was elitist. It was not the Kelly way.

Or most likely he felt, again as a gifted performer, that the bluntness of being "Army-bound" was quicker, faster, had more energy—Kelly hallmarks in any public presentation.

As it turned out, "The Roosevelt Train" contributed mightily to FDR's re-election in 1944. But the impact of the speakers, famous or not, had less to do with the Democratic triumph than something else: timing. Success in broadcasting—the attraction and holding of a huge audience—is a matter of timing, a truism well-known to the veteran New York–based media buyers working for the Republicans. Concerned by the anticipated audience for the Democrats' radio appeal, they made what they thought was a shrewd move and paid a premium price for the hour slot immediately following "The Roosevelt Train," with the intention of derailing it with a persuasive response. Then they made a further move in the all-out war between political parties.

Wishing to have a sure bet, the Republican radio strategists, using certain conservative channels that were never divulged, pressured the final speaker on "The Roosevelt Train," the popular Jimmy Durante, to withdraw from the show. Norman Corwin had scheduled the comedian to present a wacky but wily comparison of the two political parties in his inimitable honking, nasal way; his monologue would be devastating to the Republican position. With absolutely no notice, at the last minute, Durante pulled out, leaving Corwin's program four minutes short. Corwin thought instantly of plugging in another rendition of Judy Garland's rollicking "You've Gotta Get Out and Vote." Instead of finding a substitute for Durante, Gene Kelly and Humphrey Bogart had another idea. Why not let "The Roosevelt Train" run short? Sacrifice the extremely expensive four minutes of network time! Corwin, a very quick study, saw the point. He would now fill the blank time with a dreary medley of organ music, ideal for a funeral home. The Republican show could not go on the air until the hour was struck.

"America turned off its radios and went to bed" was the concise way Corwin described what happened next. The national audience for the Republican program plummeted with every second of aimless organ music. The next day, FDR had his fourth term, winning a total electoral vote of 432, to Dewey's 99.

There was a special open house at the Kellys' that night. For once, The Game was not played, but Judy Garland and Lena Horne sang. There was champagne.

"Did I hear you right on the radio program?" Betsy said, as she and Gene clinked their first toast. "That you're going to—"

"Betsy," he said, "that train's already left the station." He had finally wangled a leave of absence from Mayer. The MGM head, certain that *Anchors Aweigh* would be an enormous hit and would be nominated for Best Picture of 1944, was not about to risk a public scandal, "especially with a maniac like Kelly and his Irish temper" asserting MGM was not a loyal supporter of the war effort.

The night before Gene left for the Navy, there was another party at the Kellys'. This time, by unanimous vote, The Game would wait until Gene had returned from his tour of duty to harangue the players again. Phil Silvers and Saul Chaplin had rehearsed and now half-improvised a forty-five-minute cantata tracing Gene's life from his birth in Pittsburgh to *Anchors Aweigh*. Everybody stood to sing the rousing Navy theme, glasses held high.

Then Silvers did a patter song he claimed to have written "just for Betsy." He turned toward the young hostess and said, his voice heavy with emotion: "I call it 'Betsy with the Laughing Face.'" Actually the comedian, never disposed to stick with the boring truth, always made it a practice to do the song, with adjustments to the lyric, for every wife or sweetheart left behind by a departing film star. Everybody in town knew it was a standard Silvers shtick, by now almost a tradition at Hollywood parties. But Betsy hugged Gene as if the song were for them and them alone, and there was not a dry eye on Alta Drive as the party ended early.

No guests slept over or waited for the volleyball game in the morning. Only the two of them were there when the alarm clock went off before dawn and he left their bed for the San Diego Naval Base and boot camp.

The applause is the loudest yet, and he snaps to. Jimmy Stewart, a past recipient of the AFI salute, is at the podium now. In that rambling, endearing way of his, saying nice things about him and The Cheyenne Social Club: "Hank Fonda and I were once making a Western up in Santa Fe and we looked behind the camera and there was this guy Kelly directing. I guess there's nothing he couldn't do in pictures."

And so on, from one of the class acts in the business. Brigadier-General Stewart, U.S. Air Force, who flew bombers over enemy territory in the Big War and lost a son in Vietnam. A true war hero on screen and off—not quite like Lieutenant Junior-Grade Kelly, U.S. Navy. Oh, in interviews while at boot camp he had mouthed the requisite let-me-at-'em lines from B movies. But sure as hell he'd curbed his tongue when the brass sent him to Washington to act in a film about Navy personnel suffering from battle fatigue. He wasn't risking his life, but to make up for it, he gave it the old Kelly try and persuaded his boss to set him up at a naval hospital near Philadelphia as a combat-ravaged seaman needing psychological support. Absorbed the routine: the physical therapy, the drab meals, the bull sessions with the guys, the docs playing with his head . . . and mostly, the hours in bed, staring at the ceiling, remembering. Some tough war—beating off the mosquitoes in San Diego, D.C., and Philly!

A funny bit: Some paparazzi busybody spotted him and snapped a candid shot, and the next day's newspaper carried the story that Gene Kelly, returned from overseas, was suffering from battle fatigue. AP and UP sent it over the wires. Created consternation (and confusion) in Betsy. Same with Mayer and Company in Culver City.

He still feels his performance as a shellshocked Navy gunner was the best he'd done on film. So did the Navy. He was formally assigned to the Photographic Division of the Naval Air Force in Anacostia, near Washington. Where he met the loyal and lovely Lois McClelland, still with him after forty years. He was assigned a series of films to produce—ssh! top secret. The first one (now it can be told) documented a crucially needed test of new firefighting foam for aircraft carriers. A big shoot, worthy of DeMille: Twenty inoperative planes drenched with gasoline and filled with explosives. Ka-boom! Covered it from thirteen camera positions as the experimental foam was hosed over the inferno. Learned a hell of a lot about film-making!

Then filmed the installation of new radar equipment on the cruiser Fall River. About radar or boats—didn't know shit from shinola, starboard from port. Helped out by a kid from Pittsburgh who'd worked for him in a Cap and Gown show. Navy pleased. Learned a hell of a lot more about film-making.

Then ordered to the Pacific for the invasion of Japan with a film crew of eleven and a camera for a weapon. The A-bomb was dropped. Stopped in Hawaii. Sent back to Anacostia.

Still more work to do. A recruiting film on the submarine service. Going underwater is hell for a dancer, who needs space as much as oxygen. Like being trapped in an elevator.

A documentary about the huge aircraft carrier Benjamin Franklin, under repair at the Brooklyn Navy Yard. He would be back again someday to use the location—and very soon after his discharge. On the Town, when he'd been un-Hollywood enough to let Donen share his director's credit. Dumb move. Stationed in New York on that last assignment, finally able to join up with Betsy in an expensive Central Park South apartment sublease. She'd landed a job on Broadway, gung-ho for her career again! Kerry, no longer a baby, had become a vivacious, bright daughter.

And he, a hell of a better film-maker.

He is suddenly conscious that all around him the guests, so dapper in tuxedos and *evening gowns, are standing, and Jimmy's walking away from the mike. Now he struggles to his feet, too, unsure whether it is, well, kosher, for him to applaud—after all, Jimmy's probably been extolling him all the while. So he settles for the thumbs-up signal, even though there's not a chance Jimmy can see it through the crowd.*

NEW YORK, 1946
* * *

Gene's last assignment while in uniform was editing *Navy Screen* magazine, a weekly newsreel distributed to the fleet. He also did the voiceover commentary, a task valuable for sharpening his own screenwriting skills. But the real, immediate bonus of the job was its location, New York City. He could be with Betsy again.

Shortly after Gene's enlistment, Betsy had given up the house on Alta Drive and returned with Kerry to her parents' home in New Jersey. They lived close enough to Manhattan that Betsy could audition for parts in the resurgent Broadway theater, and she was successful in landing one as understudy to Julie Hayden, in Tennessee Williams's *The Glass Menagerie*. It was by no means an exalted role but it encouraged her to intensify her efforts as a serious actress.

Without discussing it very much—both felt uncomfortable about the decision—Betsy and Gene decided that Kerry, now of school age, would remain with her grandparents in New Jersey, leaving the two of them alone for the difficult adjustment to life as a married couple again. Neither had forgotten they had parted in California as the relationship was turning shaky; now, almost in the spirit of a New Year's resolution, a postwar restarting, they would each try to make the partner happy and content.

Gene felt pangs of conscience that Kerry could see her father only once a week, not nearly enough for him. It seemed selfish, unfeeling. But in the short term, his priority had to be cementing the marriage. Later on, he would rationalize the arrangement, but the sense of guilt never departed: "I guess Betsy and I fancied ourselves as Zelda and Scott Fitzgerald and just wanted to have a good time. A child would have been in the way."

It was like old times for a while. There were the lazy afternoons of drinking with the same old lefties at Louie Bergen's. Betsy joined in on the late-night rendition of the Soviet "Internationale," as off-key as ever. Until the liquor got to people, the conversation was stimulating. They attended premieres of new plays and caught up with revivals and the avant-garde scene downtown in Greenwich Village. Julie Hayden caught a cold and Betsy had the chance to play her role for one night; Gene sent flowers and champagne, and she cried when he said her performance was "luminous." From the grandstand behind third base they rooted for the visiting Pittsburgh Pirates at the Polo Grounds, with special yells of encouragement for slugger Ralph Kiner, just back from the Navy Air Corps. She consoled Gene when the Oscars were announced and *Anchors Aweigh* and Gene were ignored. (Ray Milland won Best Actor in the Best Picture, *The Lost Weekend*.) He cheered her up when *The Glass Menagerie* ended its run. They walked past the Henry Hudson Hotel and traded off-color jokes. They visited the Bronx Zoo and held hands on the subway all the way back.

Good times they were, but no movie; it wasn't great, and when he was notified in April he would be discharged in a month, he held his breath and told her they had to go back to California. He was tired of Navy billets and double-deckers, shipboard crowding and BOQs, and even flashy apartments with a view of Central Park. He wanted Kerry back. He wanted to live as a family again. He wanted roots.

To his relief Betsy agreed there was no way he could reassume his career and remain in Manhattan. He phoned Johnny Darrow, now a successful real-estate agent in Los Angeles, and said he wanted to buy a house. Betsy and Kerry would fly ahead to California, and he would join them as soon as his discharge came through.

Darrow knew Betsy's sentimental taste. She was one for atmosphere. The agent took her on a drive. "It's the last existing farmhouse in Beverly Hills," he said. "It needs work, but it's a steal at thirty-seven five." Betsy walked through the house, which was on North Rodeo Drive, only once. She didn't check the plumbing, never asked Darrow about the roof or went to the basement. She didn't quibble about the price. She did enter one of the bedrooms on the eastern side and went to the window to get an idea of what dawn would look like. Then she walked around the grounds, sat under a tree, and looked at the house. Her house. Gene's dream house.

She called him that night. Almost out of breath she described what she had seen, and, mainly, what the view would be with the sun's first light. "Oh, Gene, I've got great ideas for furnishing it!"

He didn't have the heart to tell her there was no money for frills like furniture or roof repair. Her enthusiasm was intoxicating. He called Darrow with instructions to make the purchase, and it was only when the agent reviewed the schedule of payments that he started to worry he had gotten in over his head.

When he rang off with Darrow he called upstate to Rochester, the hometown of Lois McClelland, recently discharged from the Waves. She had been his secretary when he was working out of Anacostia.

"Loey," he said when she picked up. "This is Lieutenant Junior-Grade Kelly."

"Gene!"

"Found a job yet?"

"Not yet."

"How are you with a paintbrush? As good as you are with a Remington typewriter, government issue?"

"I . . . I suppose so. Gene, what's—?"

"How would you like to come to California?"

The brief call was memorable to the young and attractive Lois; she was to consider it a turning point in her own life. Gene's presence had charged the air with excitement from the very beginning of their relationship:

> We girls in the secretarial pool were thrilled when we heard from
> our CO that Gene Kelly was coming to join our outfit. I had just

seen *Cover Girl* and that night another girl and I drove thirty miles—the heck with gas rationing!—to another town where *Anchors Aweigh* was playing. The next day he reported in, looking just great in that officer's uniform with that smile of his. He went out of his way to come by where we were—we were not officers, of course, so the Navy didn't encourage that kind of informality—and he introduced himself: "Hello, I'm Gene Kelly." As if we didn't know!

The presence of a movie star made for some logistic problems:

> There were so many letters from his fans he couldn't fit into his cubicle of an office. What struck me right away was that he tried to answer each and every fan letter with something personal, cheery, and upbeat. I offered to help him, and he hired me as a secretary to work for him off-duty. He asked me what I would charge. I said nothing, it would give me pleasure, etcetera, and he insisted I give him an hourly rate. When I did he shook his head. He said something New Yorky like "pleasure, schmeasure," and doubled my rate and said: "Now that the business is out of the way, let's really get down to business" and we got to work.

She was struck by the way Lieutenant Kelly never "pulled rank." Gene would get together with three or four of his co-workers who could sing, and at night in some-body's home they'd sing songs from Broadway and film musicals; he would never hog the spotlight but would insist that the others do the solos. When Betsy visited him in Washington she came to the sings, too—even though she had less than a great voice. Lois and Betsy took to each other, and Kerry grew fond of Lois, too. She was to be "one of the family" until close to the end of Gene's life—when circumstances she could not control forced her out.

In May of 1946, when Gene was released from Navy service and she accompanied him to the West Coast, Lois had no idea she was starting on a lifelong commitment. It was to be a glamorous adventure in sunny Southern California. She would be working for a man she idolized. Gene even arranged for Lois to live, rent-free, with Saul Chaplin and his wife on Orange Grove Avenue. Her first task sounded like fun: to help Betsy get the North Rodeo Drive house in shape.

Early on her first morning, she arrived with a small toolkit in hand, ready to pitch in with what Betsy had described on the phone as "some minor fix-up work . . . a patch here and a patch there." The house empty, Kerry at kindergarten, Lois found herself alone. Betsy had landed a small part in a movie soon after the return and would be away all day. Gene, wasting no time on his first morning back, had gone early to MGM to pin down what film project was next for him. Lois gazed upon a house in deplorable shape. Plumbing, caulking, painting, grouting, roofing, gutter repairing, electrical rewiring—in her efficient way she started on an inventory, and

OFFICER PERSONNEL SEPARATION CENTER

Naval service completed, Gene headed back to Hollywood and a new home. (Culver Pictures)

the list of needed renovations was long. When Gene returned she started to talk to him about the need for hiring a professional crew, but his grim mood stopped her from spelling out what had to be done and the probable cost involved.

He had immediate money problems, he now told her. The purchase of the house and the legal bills at the closing had sucked up everything. He was still under contract with MGM and would soon be drawing full salary, but for the time being he had no funds for improvements. He admitted he was not very sophisticated about handling money, like so many others of his age who grew up during the Depression. He hardly knew anything about stocks and bonds, and had never invested in real estate, as had so many of the wealthy Hollywood community. (He had heard that Bob Hope owned a large portion of the San Fernando Valley, Malibu, and Palm Springs, he told Lois.) Though he had been paid "decent money," in his view— a huge salary by her standards—the checks went directly into the bank, never augmented by deposits of dividends and capital gains. He was going to change; he would engage a financial adviser.

Now he summoned up a haggard smile, peering around at the empty, scarred hallway of his new home. "So right now, Loey, you and I, we tighten our belts. Do what we can, ourselves."

"Aye, aye, sir." She would do anything to hold that smile there, even bring it out more. But it was already gone. The news at MGM, it turned out, had been dismaying. It was as if *Cover Girl* and *Anchors Aweigh* had never happened. It was the Selznick tease, all over again. Or Johnny Darrow's out-of-sight, out-of-mind. She didn't quite understand what he was talking about, and the names were foreign to her, but she did get the idea: His dream of returning as a big star was in shambles. Gene Kelly would have to start all over again.

Eddie Mannix at MGM had been good enough to meet Gene that morning and discuss his future with the studio, what little there was to talk about. The eighteen months he had been away had erased his name from the list of "bankable" talent, actors regarded as drawing cards for the mass audience. The box-office star in 1946 was Judy Garland. Behind her, in descending order of ticket-buyer popularity, were Bing Crosby, Ingrid Bergman, Van Johnson, Gary Cooper, Bob Hope, Humphrey Bogart, Greer Garson, Betty Grable, and Roy Rogers. For the studio—or for L.B. Mayer—Gene carried a special problem: The majority of the Kelly films to this point had featured him as a serviceman in uniform. It was Mayer's contention that his image was linked to wartime. Now, in peacetime, he was somehow out-of-date, a painful reminder to the public of casualty lists, gas-rationing, and blackouts.

Then Mannix—speaking on behalf of Mayer, he made clear—stated that MGM felt obligated to give priority to other contract players who had served MGM longer and had entered military service earlier than Gene. They, too, were eager to resume their careers, stars like Clark Gable, James Stewart, Robert Taylor. . . .

"Gene, why don't you check with Freed?" Mannix said, walking him to the door. "See if there's a musical for you on his horizon."

"I have, Eddie," Gene replied. "And there isn't." What really hurt was Gene's inability to gain a film assignment at a time of incredible prosperity in the movie business. War had brought a windfall to the studios. Box-office receipts for 1946 would approach a record-breaking $2 billion. More than 500 films would be released before the calendar ran out, an unprecedented number. Most relevant for Gene was another statistic: 600 actors and actresses were on full-time studio contracts. With the average ticket price of 40 cents, 90 million people went to the movies at least once a week. On weekends, crowds lined up at more than 20,000 cinemas across the nation. Garland, his "gal" from their first film together, was drawing them inside and earning $6,000 a week for her efforts.

All the while he held his breath that Mayer would find some way to close out his contract, leaving him to wield a paintbrush and a hammer on the oldest farmhouse on North Rodeo Drive. He thought of how his handling of fix-it tools was emblematic of the way things were going: His career, like his house, was falling into ruin. He had returned eagerly to civilian life but was now tempted, he swore to himself, to re-enlist in the Navy. He wasn't really serious, but 1946 was that kind of year.

That *house*—not the famous open house of the pre-Navy Kellys, but the ailing farmhouse Betsy had found on North Rodeo Drive! It certainly lived up to the real-estate mantra of location, location, location, after all, smack in the middle of the very tony Beverly Hills. Who could ask for anything more? But was there a single day that year when no professional visitors called—contractors or carpenters or plumbers or well-diggers, whatever the arcane specialty—to perform their mystifying and expensive duties, thereby draining what remained of his checking account? The Kellys became fixtures at garage sales. With the uncountable hours he and Lois put into renovation work, everything from designing and building much-needed furniture to cleaning up the mess left by the professional visitors, the project seemed to balloon into a mammoth one more fit for the Corps of Engineers than a modest make-over at *chez* Kelly. An exaggeration, perhaps, but it was that kind of year.

Betsy's film career started in 1946 with a role in *The Guilt of Janet Ames,* and then a flurry of other films came her way, with small but attention-getting parts. Now it was Betsy who drove away early to be on time for the studio call; Gene remained at home to see Kerry off to school. Between Betsy's film work and her political activism—meetings, rallies on behalf of various left-wing organizations— he still didn't see very much of her. A pattern in which each was getting used to the absence of the other.

Just when he was adapting to a looser schedule which allowed him to spend more time with his daughter, MGM unexpectedly came through with a picture assignment for him. Exuberantly titled *Living in a Big Way,* it was described as a comedy but, more accurately, it represented the emergence of Marie "The Body" McDonald as the studio's new sex symbol. At the time, MGM was mysteriously ignoring a young woman named Marilyn Monroe, who already was on the payroll at $100 per week. The choice of McDonald undoubtedly had something to do—Gene felt it with a bitter certainty—with Louis B. Mayer's nomination of the curvaceous young woman, reflecting an interest that was much more personal than professional.

Though Gene had to feel grateful for the assignment, he knew it was an awful way to resume his career. First of all, he was once again cast—typed!—as a man in uniform, a serviceman who meets and marries a woman (McDonald) the night before he is drafted. When his tour of duty ends, he returns to find that she's a millionaire, regrets the marriage, and seeks a divorce. Summed up briskly or detailed scene-by-scene, the script made no sense and was a bore. Gene could not suppress the suspicion that casting him opposite McDonald was a continuation of Mayer vendetta against him. He described his co-star as a "triple-threat: She could neither sing nor dance nor act."

All the same, his assignment included the choreography of a dance for the two of them. The director was the well-regarded Gregory LaCava. He wanted to pair Gene with the unsteady McDonald in the hit song "It Had to Be You," to convince the audience that the serviceman and the millionaire loved each other despite the disparity of wealth. It was a huge weight to put on one dance number, made worse by the obvious mismatch of talent. Gene was determined to make the piece work and put McDonald through the usual torture of his long and frequent rehearsals— but the results were and are forgettable.

Under LaCava's gentle hand (he had just done the successful *My Man Godfrey*) Gene avoided a stereotypical characterization, minimized the sentimentality, and again showed a comic flair that producers forgot when considering him for a part, largely because of his intense preparation before shooting. But McDonald, unfortu- nately, could not hold up her end, despite the ministrations of LaCava and Gene's support. When the rough cut was viewed in the screening room, LaCava himself realized that Gene was right: They were headed for a box-office catastrophe. He asked Gene to design and perform three more musical numbers—"dances *minus* McDonald," LaCava said—that would be seeded into the film to stir audience interest. It was directly counter to Gene's conviction that dances should be woven tightly into a musical's storyline, but he liked LaCava and agreed to do his best.

There was also a personal consideration: The last thing he needed at this precarious point in his career was a box-office dud.

Again he called on Stanley Donen to help him with the trio of requested dances. The first result was a curious but effective piece in which Gene danced with an astonishingly well-trained dog. Gene felt he was upstaged by the animal, but the dance was entertaining. The second number partnered him with a large female statue with whom he is supposedly enamored, even as he is rejected. The statue appeared to show more animation than McDonald. LaCava was pleased, and Gene wasn't, but in preliminary form the dance conveyed a situation, steps, and ideas he would later develop and use.

The last, desperate insertion into *Living in a Big Way* indicates where Gene's work was heading. Built around a series of children's games and set in a half-completed apartment building, it makes exciting use of available props—metal rings, stepladders, wooden planks. Gene dances amid a gaggle of enthralled kids in an easy, nonpatronizing way. Clearly, he is having fun, and so are the kids.

So did the paltry-sized audiences that ignored the critical rejection and saw *Living in a Big Way*. Surprisingly, so did the famous choreographer Martha Graham, who favored the piece with the judgment that it "represents Gene Kelly's best work." Nevertheless, Gene was dead-right in his original judgment. The film was a box-office bust. Dazzled by Marie McDonald's fleshly charms, Mayer had made a big mistake; his loving in a big way brought no financial reward to MGM.

It was a bad film encountering bad luck in a year when nothing seemed to go right for Gene, for to make matters worse, the International Alliance of Theatrical Stage Employees (IATSE), the powerful alliance of craft unions, called a strike. While some sequences remained to be shot in *Living in a Big Way*, all production employees at the studios walked out and joined the picket lines. LaCava's film was stuck in the never-never land before release prints could be struck off and sent into distribution, gaining at least some return on MGM's investment.

Wallowing in post-war prosperity, the major studios quickly were able to meet the demands of most of the craft unions—with one exception, the Carpenters Union. The industry executives looked around for someone who could serve as an intermediary with the union, whose recalcitrance was costing a fortune every week. Somebody thought of a man whose image was ideal: an intelligent, well-spoken, persuasive union activist whose wife was a passionate defender of labor's right to strike. A man of the people, Gene Kelly could talk with carpenters and not be laughed away as a dilettante or a tool of the capitalists.

Even if his absence would hamper the completion of *Living in a Big Way*, MGM was far more concerned with ending the strike. Gene was flattered, even honored, to be chosen as a mediator. He agreed to go to Chicago.

Thus began a chaotic period, two months of shuttling back and forth between Los Angeles and the head office of the Carpenters Union. There were long meetings lasting into the night, often over weekends when Gene was unable to return home. The drafting and redrafting of position papers was an endless process. He sat and talked and listened to steely lawyers' sedate, polished phrasing; in contrast, there were yelling matches with burly men just off the picket lines, threatening to darken every theater in America. Mostly it was a matter of giving in here, demanding something there, of staying calm and tacking toward a compromise. He was good at it. Perhaps, he thought not for the first time, he should have been a lawyer.

When, hoarse and sleepy, anxious to be with Betsy and Kerry, he landed at LAX with the final agreement of the Carpenters Union, IATSE called off the strike. Production resumed at the studios. Salary checks were paid again to the employees.

He was rewarded for his efforts in a way that shocked him: MGM and the other studios assailed Gene Kelly for championing the strikers. It was not a fair settlement, intoned the spokesman for the studios. More insidious than the press briefings and public interviews was the buzz of tut-tutting, the I-told-you-sos over telephones, on golf courses, and at executive staff meetings where the word was passed around: Big mistake to send Kelly. What else can you expect from a lefty with a Commie wife?

It was partly Gene's fault. He had been incredibly naive and had taken on a huge responsibility without first grounding himself in the facts. The movie industry did not play honestly with him when he was urged to mediate the strike. He did not know that a slush fund existed for bribing purposes—to pay corrupt union leaders for "sweetheart" contracts, to buy them off from striking and settling to the producers' advantage. The union side was not peopled by angels. Gene was aware that, in 1945, both George E. Browne, president of IATSE, and Willie Bioff, the union's Hollywood representative, were convicted for extortion and conspiracy. He had read in newspaper coverage that during the late 1930s, the golden years of IATSE, Browne and Bioff (as in *Buyoff* was the grim joke among renegade unionists) would shake down studio executives regularly in return for limiting union demands.

MGM alone—as Louis B. Mayer and the Schenck brothers, operating presidents in the New York home office, would concede in later testimony—had saved $15 million through illegal and corrupt actions. It was, then, a murky and sordid arena that Gene had plunged into so innocently. Fortunately for Gene, though, his activities as mediator brought him to the attention of Roy Brewer, who replaced Browne as the IATSE leader. They liked each other immediately, not least because Brewer was a fan of *Cover Girl* and *Anchors Aweigh*. Although Gene was put off by Brewer's voluble and relentless pro-American attitude and his anti-Communist fervor, they became good friends. Gene had no way of knowing that Brewer's distasteful flag-waving mindset would, a short time later, save his film career from extinction.

Feeling somewhat misused and unappreciated for his mediation efforts, Gene was further disappointed to find no project awaiting him at MGM. But Betsy had news that cheered him up: She might be involved in a movie project in Europe, starring Montgomery Clift. Neither Gene nor Betsy had ever traveled abroad. He welcomed a temporary departure form Hollywood with the hope his luck would change during his absence.

Leaving Kerry under the care of Lois, with full-time domestic help, they left for a holiday in Rome, London, Paris, Florence, and Venice. They saw the sights tourists were supposed to see and many others they vowed would bring them back to

Europe. Gene, the Francophile *in absentia* all his adult life, felt immediately at home when they clambered into a taxi at Orly Airport and his instructions in the native language were met with a cheerful, unquestioning "Oui, monsieur!" The time together was good for them, even though Betsy was not cast in the Clift film.

More than making up for that disappointment, at least in his eyes, was the telephone call from his agent, who welcomed him back with sensational news: Arthur Freed had cast him in the lead role opposite Judy Garland in the blockbuster Irving Berlin musical *Easter Parade*.

"It's about time," Gene declared to Betsy. "Let's bring back open house at the Kellys!"

The old group, augmented by newcomers, delighted over the return of a Hollywood institution: drinks, food, good talk, music, and The Game at the Kellys'. Lenny Bernstein had gone back East, but now to play the piano there was André Previn, who worked in the MGM music department, not yet the famous composer and conductor. Judy Garland, though in the midst of another divorce action (against Vincente Minnelli), would somehow manage to shape up, stop by, and sing. Carol Haney, part of the dance team brought to MGM by Gene, along with Jeanne Coyne and Stanley Donen. And Comden and Green, trying out new material written for Freed.

The atmosphere, open to anything, was less frenetic than before. Perhaps The Game was losing its allure, or maybe it was Gene, feeling like an out-of-synch gymnast on a trampoline since his arrival in Hollywood: the baffling unemployment; the successes of *Cover Girl* and *Anchors Aweigh*; being blocked by Mayer from enlisting; then punishment for being at the tail-end of the list of returning stars; *Living in a Big Way*; and then, absolutely the last straw, the trashing by studio heads of his strike mediator's role, at the same time he was catching hell from many of the unionists he had put back to work.

He felt he was aging too fast. He wondered if that was inevitable with men who married much younger women. It seemed to underline the reality that he had started his career as a professional dancer and film actor well past his prime. The Game was for brash kids like Betsy. At their parties he now preferred to carry his drink over to someone who had something to say, like Arthur Freed (about orchids, Freed's passion) or Spencer Tracy (about Katharine Hepburn). Later on, when she came into Gene's life, Leslie Caron, though young and unformed, would describe his changed stance as a host with Gallic precision: "He did the Irish thing for Saturday night: He drank his whiskey and talked."

Gene was becoming close to Spencer Tracy, whose less-is-more approach to film acting he admired. He was determined to modify his own style accordingly, and was anxious for any role that would allow him to underplay. Unfortunately, that was almost an impossibility in musicals. When Hepburn was not in town, Tracy would visit and share a bottle with Kelly—Coca-Cola, as Gene would tell interviewers over the years: "We'd invite him to our place and he'd come and sit quietly and he'd sip his Coke. He'd chat amiably enough and after two hours he'd leave. He sure was a sad, lonely guy when Katie wasn't there." An alcoholic battered by health problems,

Tracy, with help from the irrepressibly positive Hepburn, would pull himself together to more than hold his own on the movie set. He enjoyed and respected Gene, whom he found the perfect listener, never one to open up about his own concerns. They were both, at least nominally, followers of the same Church, and that encouraged Tracy to speak frankly about his difficult situation. As a Catholic with an ailing wife, he couldn't possibly divorce to marry Hepburn. Now, he told Gene, because Hepburn was convinced that liquor was diminishing his sexual performance, his New Year's resolution as they headed into the last days of 1946 was to get through the next twelve months without a drink. But he was doubtful about his prospects for success.

With Freed, a walk-in guest at the Kelly party on New Year's Eve, Gene's *tête à tête* was much less personal. They talked about the producer's plans for *Easter Parade*, which was having "script trouble." Freed was determined to make it his masterpiece, and Gene was heartened to hear that he had hired Frances Goodrich and her husband, Albert Hackett, a successful team of writers and a bold choice, too, for it was to be their first musical. They were not authors of comedy—their major success was to be the stage play *The Diary of Anne Frank*—but Freed believed, as he told Gene, "They can give substance to the characterizations. The writing of the scenes and the way they are played will take it out of the conventional."

Gene was thrilled. At last, a dream project that could satisfy his passion for excellence. He could only keep his fingers crossed as he and Freed changed the subject to the Department of Justice's edict, out that very day, December 31, 1946. On anti-monopoly grounds, the government had stopped the studio practice of "block-booking," which forced movie theaters across the country (most of which were owned and controlled by the studios) to run Hollywood productions on their screens whether good, bad, or unspeakable. The studios would have to sell off the theaters. Production was to be divorced from distribution.

Gene had studied some law, and Freed, too, was a well-educated man exposed to the financials of the movie industry. They both knew, but did not have the heart to discuss, as the party noisemakers sounded the advent of the New Year, that the prohibition of block-booking marked the beginning of the end for Hollywood.

Fitting, thought Gene: 1946 was that kind of year.

Oh-oh. *The hype-meter's up into the red zone.*

He knows things are getting out of hand when Carl Reiner, a friend and director, says apropos of absolutely nothing, that he's "one of the great stuntmen–actors in the history of the world!" Besides damning with faint praise, Carl's nose should be doing a Pinocchio; it's all more than a tad untrue. Carl, whose idea of a stunt is crossing Broadway against a red light, means it as a compliment. It's a tribute to his courage as an aerialist in Thousands Cheer, *his doing derring-do Doug Fairbanks–style in* The Pirate, *or maybe his much later work with that nutso Evel in* Viva Knievel! *in 1977, when they both were daredevil motorcycle racers. A ramshackle vehicle of a film, if there ever was one. It was his last straight role, no songs, no dances. Then* Xanadu, *in 1980, his last musical: Olivia Newton-John to pull in the MTV generation, GK to draw the parents. A hell of a sad way to go out—the worst musical, positively! The pits! It could have been made in a third of the time at a third of the cost. Showed how depressingly little today's crop of youngsters actually knew about making musicals!*

Back to Carl, up there yakking about his bravery in The Three Musketeers. *Must be a surprise to Joan Collins after what happened only last year—when she was good enough to give a tired old man a break and involve him in a TV flick she was producing and acting in. On the French Riviera! A few days of plush living for a few thou. He was bumped off in the first reel, but they still had to make the shot of him and Joan running away from the bad guys, firing away. TV movies always have somebody running away from the bad guys, firing away. Only the puffs of smoke going off along their path came mighty close in the camera rehearsal. So he had said to her: "These Frenchie special effects aren't so special, Joanie dearest, let's lay on some stunt doubles for this chase, cherie."*

(Truth was, as a single man again after two marriages, and horny as hell, he was coming on to Joan since his arrival in Antibes the night before. As all the running and dodging rendered him breathless, he didn't mind Joan thinking he was a dirty old man, but a decrepit old man—no. The look of astonishment on her lovely face, that the great Gene Kelly wanted a stunt double for this walk in the park!)

In the later years he was always quick to call for a double. Never, never for one of his choreographed pieces, because anyone can tell a dancer's body from a stunt man's when it's hanging in the air. The minute you spot it's somebody else in the middle of the dance, the phoniness ruins it! But stunts—hell, he wouldn't even ride a horse. If there were dialogue scenes, close-ups, in which he had to ride, he would go to the wrangler and say: "Look, I'm a city boy. I worked on a farm but it was with plow horses. Can you get me a horse that will make me look good?"

The wrangler would say: "Shore," and if he thought the critter had a mischievous glint in his eye and was out to upend an old hoofer in a white sombrero, he'd keep turning them down until he got a horse that bounced just right.

There are shots of him in The Three Musketeers *galloping down the sand. But three stunt men—good horsemen, too—broke their backs making the picture. Maybe he should have called in for a stunt double that morning on North Rodeo Drive.*

LOS ANGELES, 1947

* * *

One night at a Kelly open house, pianist Oscar Levant, Gene's frequent guest, made Arthur Freed laugh out loud. Levant was deriding the plots of "those old-fashioned musicals—creaky numbers, a series of catastrophes ending in a floor show." Gene had heard better quips coming from Levant, but Freed thought the *aperçu* was right on the mark.

Gene remembered the veteran producer's reaction as the months went by. Like kids on the sidewalk awaiting a marching band, he and Freed could hardly wait for *Easter Parade* to begin production. The shooting start on it had been delayed several times. Freed seemed determined to bring out something new that combined convincing drama with fresh musical innovation. The story was key. Goodrich and Hackett had done the original script; not completely satisfied, Freed had brought in Sidney Sheldon as script doctor. Sheldon was a popular novelist as well as a recent Academy Award winner for his frothy comedy *The Bachelor and the Bobbysoxer*. Gene had been astounded when he read the "cover"—the summary of the scenario given to executives in lieu of the entire script. For there, on a few pages within a neat blue folder, was the story of Gene and Betsy Kelly.

What the trio of expensive writers, squabbling all the way, had come up with was: A successful professional is suddenly abandoned by his dancing partner. He finds an unknown girl and tries to build her into an exact duplicate of the first. He is older than she, authoritative, always sure he is right. Above all, he wants to make her over into the image he believes a partner should be. Their teaming-up proves to be a mistake; the new act goes badly. But when he finally gives her enough room, physically and psychologically, allowing her to display her natural talent in her own way—here the trio of writers closed on the upbeat note required on such hyped-up summaries beseeching executive support—"their twin-careers take off like a rocket for a new tier of success."

It was, Gene was forced to admit, another version of Levant's "series of catastrophes ending in a floor show." But, for him, the plot of *Easter Parade* had the ring of truth. Simplistic as it seemed, it was a parable of his marriage. And where it was going wrong. More important, it set the course for how he could set it right.

Easter Parade would be the turning point, he vowed. He became more careful about Betsy's feelings. He found he could be easygoing without patronizing her, became less argumentative, and even went so far as to agree with more of her political ideas. She sensed the change, and the atmosphere within the house became more amiable, allowing him to concentrate on preparing for *Easter Parade*. He worked furiously at rehearsals of his solo number "Drum Crazy," working with choreographer Bob Alton. He coached Judy Garland on their song and dance "A Couple of Swells." Things were going well.

He had ideas for everybody, of course, but tried to be more tactful, not coming on to the others with his usual bruising thrust. He now had "suggestions" for the scriptwriters, for Alton, for Freed, on which songs of the Irving Berlin canon should be woven into the film; there were 800 works to be chosen from. He was helpful. He was appreciated. He decided he liked being liked on the set for a change. Sensing that the sessions of sedentary labor mediation in Chicago had softened him, he worked harder than ever to toughen his physique. Since exercising bored him to stone, to shed pounds, strengthen his legs, and "keep the juices flowing" he chose competitive sport. He didn't have far to go for it.

He had never seriously considered building a swimming pool on the North Rodeo Drive property. He considered it to be a status symbol of the elite and, as such, a spoiling influence on his daughter. He wanted Kerry to grow up with the normal, everyday values he himself had as a child. Yet, not at all consistent in his attitude, he spent money lavishly and impulsively on activities he felt would benefit Kerry—books, records, sports, language lessons, trips, holidays. But having a pool for a daily dip was drowning oneself in Beverly Hills posh, as far as he was concerned.

A blue-collar sport prevalent on public beaches and in humble backyards was more to his taste; with a ball and a net stretched between two poles, he had a fun way to work into shape. And he was proud that, despite his height limitation, he was surely the best player in the area, a Gene Kelly requirement for any activity. With *Easter Parade* approaching, he upped the pace and quality of competition.

Van Johnson was one of the participants: "Every Saturday, everybody would meet at Gene Kelly's house for franks, beans, and brown bread and play volleyball." And Bob Fosse, a young choreographer and dancer, also came to play. Intense and ambitious, Fosse was inclined to be resentful of Gene's popularity (he actually did not think highly of his dancing; he considered Gene's repertoire of steps much too limited) but had to admit the volleyball games made for a unique experience:

> It was his backyard and his volleyball, and he wanted to be king. I'd never seen anyone so fierce about a so-called friendly game in my life—before or since. He had a competitive streak in him that was quite frightening. At the same time, he had this tremendous Irish charm and if he saw you were unhappy, he'd flash that smile at you, and all is well.

Still not satisfied with of his athletic conditioning, Gene ratcheted up the level of the game even further. He had been rehearsing his dance numbers in *Easter Parade* for more than a month and shooting was about to begin. He now invited a group of younger men, mostly college athletes from UCLA and USC, honed on the beach competitions at Malibu. These brawny, expert players kept the rallies lengthy and exhausting, which was exactly the idea. As Gene said:

> The volleyball games were famous, I guess, because of the high standards we tried to maintain. We used to invite teams from Santa Monica beach and the YMCA to come to the house. Then we'd get together a team of our own, usually Hollywood actors and we'd fight it out. Some of the games were terrific. They provided me with a most enjoyable way of keeping fit.

Almost inevitably for someone Harriet Kelly had labeled "accident-prone," there came the fateful moment of play: A giant on the opposite side of the net spiked a shot down at a player on Gene's team. The ball caromed off a hapless hand and was arcing up out of reach of everybody, a sure point for the other side. But Gene raced to make a save. He slipped on a patch of wet grass and a foot slid out from under him, simultaneous with a severe twinge in his ankle. The pain was unbearable. He sprawled on the ground, and when he got to his feet it was even worse.

He was driven to the hospital where, after examination, the medical verdict in the emergency room was expressed in a very complicated way, but to Gene the really dismal point of it all was that he had a broken ankle.

Legally and financially, he was in a precarious position. Since the injury was not work-related, MGM could very well dismiss him without salary, under the terms of his contract. Obviously, he could not continue in *Easter Parade*.

L.B. Mayer was furious, but controlled his temper and phoned Betsy to express his sympathies. He then declared—in the sanctimonious way that always enraged her—he would pay a visit. Which he did, almost immediately. It was a incredible for the MGM tycoon to pay such a sympathy visit to their home. Convinced Mayer suspected a plot, a continuation of their long-standing and oft-expressed determination to bring ruin upon the other, Gene decided to do something he never really did: lie.

Mayer was already upset at the way medical problems had affected this major MGM production of the year. Cyd Charisse had notified Arthur Freed she was pregnant and would have to withdraw from *Easter Parade*. Ann Miller replaced her. But who would, who possibly could, take Gene's place? Later, in many interviews, he explained what he did and why:

> I told Mayer I'd been rehearsing a rather complicated dance step. And that I'd damaged my ankle because I didn't think he'd respond too well to the truth. Well, Mayer was beside himself. He didn't have a replacement, and what was he going to do? I said, "Why don't you give Fred Astaire a ring?"

From his ranch in San Diego County, Astaire insisted on phoning Gene before giving an answer to Mayer. In a well-publicized but undoubtedly sincere gesture of mourning, he had announced his retirement at his wife's funeral a few years before. He did not need the money; he was very well paid as a front man for the nationwide chain of Fred Astaire Dance Studios. He was worried the routines conceived and choreographed by Kelly for Kelly would not be suitable for him. Gene did not allow himself to be swayed: "I confirmed that my injury was very serious. I would not be able to dance again for at least six months. I told Astaire the dances could easily be rearranged and not to worry. Fred was a little bit reluctant but finally said okay."

So Astaire was in and Kelly was out, technically unemployed but still on salary. The studios were cutting down. He was worried snooping lawyers would find a way to subvert the contract and let him go, on crutches and unpaid. He felt guilty about his lie to Mayer when the MGM head announced he was taking a twenty-five percent cut in his own salary. When Mayer reduced the staff at the studio by the same percentage, Gene's guilt vanished, replaced by the certainty that even more hard times were ahead for the movie industry.

The outlawing of block-booking by the Department of Justice was now punishing the studios with fierce blows. No longer did Hollywood moguls enjoy cushy arrangements whereby theaters were forced to run a studio's B pictures in order to have hot-ticket draws like Bogart and Bacall—all at inflated prices. No longer did studio-owned theaters contribute vastly to company profits. Reeling, the studios responded in the only logical way, by cutting down on the number of productions.

Yielding to the flood of hostile government interventions, Hollywood's dam burst. In August of 1947, Britain's Chancellor of the Exchequer, Hugh Dalton, proclaimed that henceforth 75 percent of the profits accrued in the United Kingdom by American films were now subject to heavy taxation. Other countries, France and Italy primarily, moved in the same direction. All these nations, appalled by the worshiping of U.S. stars by their citizens, were determined to build up their own film industries. Profits plummeted, and Wall Street took heed. Stock prices of the major film companies sank to new lows. While the once-profitable export market became a thing of the past, dismaying problems on the home front worsened. The war over, Americans no longer felt the need to go to movies three and four times a week. The bloodletting would not stop.

After all, the cost of living was rising. So was unemployment—in every industry, in every part of the nation. People were intent on saving for homes, cars, children's education. Frugality was the spirit of the day. Old folks talked about the 1920s and the Depression, and the young ones heeded and resolved to spend only on necessities. Theater marquees went dark by the thousands. In a period of tense financial uncertainty, Americans seriously believed their country was going under and did not understand why. Where had the good days gone—and so quickly?

The answers were not self-evident; they demanded serious, sustained thought, and above all, calm. The answers, in large part, cast the blame right back on the questioners' life-style, their sloth, their living-for-the-moment passions. Amid the turmoil, only the extreme right wing sailed on with strength. Since the war, powerful ultraconservatives within every major institution had virtually declared another war on not only the Communist Party but on liberalism in general, including the entire tradition of the Roosevelt New-Dealers. They, and the radicals of the left, had led to these troubled times, was it not obvious? Calling enemies Reds and Commie sympathizers became a way of life for flag-wavers across the land—and Hollywood was no exception.

By the summer of 1947, a congressman from New Jersey, a former insurance broker named J. Parnell Thomas, was chairing public hearings on behalf of the House Un-American Activities Committee (HUAC). It was inevitable that Hollywood, with its concentration of left-wing intellectuals and the power they possessed to express their views overtly and covertly through the fantastically effective medium of film, would become the committee's conspicuous target in what became a gigantic Red Scare. Frantic, the prominent members of the Hollywood community turned to their lawyers. What should they do to stay afloat in the threatening, accusatory climate?

Basically, they were advised, they had three choices. In testimony, they could invoke the First Amendment with its guarantee of free speech and association. The risk: going to prison for contempt of Congress. They could invoke the Fifth Amendment with its privilege against self-incrimination. The risk here was being publicized as a Communist sympathizer. After that, a studio employee, at whatever job level, was now an ex-employee and would never work on a studio-produced movie again; there would be no role to perform, rough cut to edit, or dolly to push—even a freelance job was out of the question. A rigidly enforced employer boycott would take over. Once colored Red, once the name came up in a HUAC session or in a deposition by a self-appointed anti-Communist, the unfortunate ex-gaffer or ex-gofer would be—in the chilling parlance of the day—"blacklisted."

The third choice, of course, was to sing along with HUAC.

Gene was recuperating at home now, his ankle still encased in plaster, unable to be physically active. Miserable over the lost opportunity of *Easter Parade*, he and Betsy were watching the situation in Washington with increased tension. They had no illusions. They knew they were vulnerable to the threat of blacklisting, especially Betsy. Along with the many like-minded guests at the Kelly at-homes, they were appalled by the number and prestige of the Hollywood notables who grasped desperately at the third option, the last straw of salvation: to cooperate with the Committee, name names, and continue working.

At a HUAC session in Washington, Robert Taylor complained of being cast in a "wartime pro-Russian movie" and disclaimed any responsibility for choosing the role. Now he vowed to the assembled Congressmen that he would not "work with Communists, and I urge MGM to fire every last one." After his testimony the handsome star strode down Capitol Hill, surrounded by D.C. police, as fans cheered and surged forward for autographs. Gene fumed at such save-your-ass displays, but Taylor had never been a visitor to North Rodeo. They had barely nodded at each other in the MGM commissary, and, said Betsy, "The dumb bastard never dared to play The Game." She added: "He'd be lousy at it!"

As would Gary Cooper, she was convinced, when she read his volunteered testimony in the L.A. *Times*. In his trademark laconic style, Cooper complained grimly that assigned movie scripts "weren't on the level," leaving his HUAC listeners to complete the dire thought. Gene was amused by the choice of Cooper as a missionary for truth-telling, a man who insisted on the clandestine bedding of every one of his leading ladies, despite a longtime and publicly hailed marriage to a socialite wife. "But at least Coop didn't name names," Gene said, with a measure of respect.

He felt disgust at the way even prestigious journalists fanned the flames of the Cold War against the Soviet Union. The tabloids, even worse, turned his stomach; they commonly ran reports fed to them by HUAC operatives with headlines like Hollywood Names Its Reds, or Exposes Red Work in Movies, or Un-Americans Hold Film Jobs. When Katharine Hepburn, resplendent in a coral red dress, attended a political rally for Henry Wallace, an independent candidate for President, she was photographed by an L.A. *Examiner* staffer. The next day's front page carried the actress's picture with the headline At Wallace Hoopla in a Red Gown.

Even the Warner brothers, who, at FDR's specific written and spoken request, had produced propaganda films during the war supporting the Russian allies, notably *Mission to Moscow* and *Action in the North Atlantic*, did a complete turnabout. Gene was one of the first to hear from a secretary at Warner's that cables were going out from Burbank to the booking offices across the country: NO MORE BOOKINGS OF "MISSION TO MOSCOW." Jack Warner's daughter, Barbara Howard, had continued to live in Europe after the war and had "heard about the blacklisting" but only realized the extent of it and its effect on her father later, when she saw newsreel coverage of a HUAC meeting: "Suddenly my father was on the screen, before the House Un-American Activities Committee, saying that he and his brothers would send all the Communists back to Russia and would happily subscribe to a pest-removal fund to get rid of these termites."

The front pages across the country published Walt Disney's claim that "Communists have tried to take over my studio." And finally, the Motion Picture Alliance, the lobbying organization subsidized by the studio heads, saw the anti-Communist issue as a useful tactic to crush the union movement in the film industry once and for all.

It was a trivial piece of testimony at a HUAC session—actually a sequence of questions and answers so comical and absurd that Gene and Betsy didn't know whether to laugh or cry—that finally spurred Gene on to take a leadership role in standing up to the Committee. Leo McCary was a longtime director whose claim to fame was his hit *Going My Way*, the tender story of a priest played by Bing Crosby. After sketching the high points of his career to the HUAC members, McCary discussed the problems faced by a director who was a patriotic American. In the world of Hollywood, McCary said, he had a unique problem. His films were not popular in Russia because of one character always present in his films. And a McCary film without that one character would simply not be a McCary film! At which point he paused for a dramatic flourish.

The Committee was very weary. It had been a long day of declamations, boasts, and *mea culpas,* and the members were fighting off sleep. "Yes, Mr. McCary?" the HUAC counsel edged him forward impatiently.

The director repeated heavily what he wanted to come through loud and clear: "The Commies will have nothing to do with me, and I'll tell you why—he's in every one of my pictures. You know who I mean?"

HUAC had no energy left even to offer a guess. So again the counsel stepped in: "Bing Crosby?"

"No!" responded McCary with an angry passion. "God!"

Surely, Gene felt, when the hysterical laughter sputtered out in the Kelly living room, the situation has gotten out of hand. The bizarre activities of HUAC now shaped up as a monstrous threat to American democracy and justice. He judged Chairman J. Parnell Thomas a fool and an ingrate. (Indeed, only a few years later the New Jersey representative was less a man than a number, serving a sentence for fraud in a federal prison.)

But Gene knew there were other more formidable, quick-witted, and dangerous officials in Washington, appointed and elected, who were interested in gaining power. As a newly transplanted Californian, Gene followed the activities of Congressman Richard M. Nixon very closely. Together with Senator Joseph McCarthy of Wisconsin, Nixon was making often reckless assaults upon the people, values, and institutions of the American Left. And J. Edgar Hoover, director of the FBI, was a wily cynic who tugged into his embrace moguls of the popular media, professional anti-Communist witnesses from the world of academia, and zealots from the American Legion. A fresh new business was prospering: All sorts of con artists and shake-down blackmailers were demanding a price for clearing one's name from lists of alleged subversives. There was money to be made in the blacklisting trade.

In terms of deciding what his personal action should be, Gene was now faced with the dilemma. He could barely contain his contempt for the tactics of such investigative agencies as HUAC and the viciousness of Hoover and McCarthy. But he was honest enough to know the Cold War ran in two directions. There genuinely was, it seemed to Gene, a danger of Soviet aggression, prepared for by American Communist infiltration. On the basis of his labor mediation work in Chicago, trying to end the strike in the film industry, he judged that not *all* the Red Scare victims were innocents. There were 75,000 listed members of the Communist Party in 1947 and, clearly, a sizable number of others who preferred to be, or were ordered to be, covert operatives. He had himself seen the Communist effectiveness in taking control of trade unions.

In the larger picture—and Gene Kelly was one who always tried to work within the larger picture—as the U.S.S.R. became more bellicose, threatened American military security, and gained knowledge of U.S. atom-bomb secrets (as evidence was showing), he concluded that the ultimate danger was Communist aggression. But on a human level he empathized with those being blacklisted. He resolved to focus on bringing the calamity of blacklisting to the attention of the American public.

Once he'd made up his mind to participate fully in the effort, he hobbled on his crutches to the next meeting of the local Committee for the First Amendment (CFA), where he reported later: "We decided to bring this thing out in public, this miasma of fear and oppression!"

Leaving the meeting hall, Gene could see dim figures in the parking lot making note of license plate numbers. These were eerie times. He was concerned that his and Betsy's phones were being tapped.

The CFA was happy to have the active involvement of Gene Kelly. By now his contribution to the Chicago labor-mediation effort was better understood and appreciated. It was known around Hollywood that he was a straight-shooter. Never once had he demanded a "cut," bribe, or commission from a vulnerable young composer for introducing a new song, a grease-the-palm pattern in the movie industry begun years before by luminaries like Al Jolson. Intelligent, articulate and well-educated, Gene would be an effective spokesman.

He immediately threw his support behind the strategy put forth by the three CFA organizers—the writer-directors Philip Dunne, John Huston, and William Wyler—to organize a gigantic national protest against the HUAC reign of terror. The trio decided, along with Gene, to charter a plane, fill it with like-minded prominent figures in the Hollywood community, and fly to Washington. They would insist on presenting the CFA point of view directly to Chairman Thomas and his committee. They were not lacking in confidence. Surely, they were far more skillful in the nuances of persuasion than the members of Congress! Had they not proven themselves as masters of how to shape public feelings and attitudes? Movie fans by the thousands, hundreds of thousands would roar like the MGM lion in defense of those victimized by mindless blacklisting. The dramatic CFA flight to Washington would give credibility and support to those already subpoenaed who were trying to hold firm against HUAC's inflammatory charges.

The departure of the CFA charter flight to Washington was set for Sunday, October 26, 1947, which would enable the celebrities to stop along the way for public rallies of support and still be present for the Monday-morning hearings at the Capitol. CFA put out a press release listing those who would be aboard.

In the hectic few days before the flight, everybody who agreed to participate was inundated by advice from managers, agents, lawyers, accountants, friends, and relatives to the effect that they were committing career suicide. Word was conveyed to Gene of a remark by Louis B. Mayer. During a discussion by MGM top-echelon executives about HUAC charges and countercharges, Mayer said that despite Kelly's leadership and the decision to fly to Washington, which Mayer opposed vehemently, Kelly "couldn't possibly be a Commie because he is a Catholic boy who loves his mother." Almost everything about Mayer continued to enrage Gene—the sanctimoniousness, the conviction that patriotism in America was found only in the ranks of Republicans, the manipulation of actors, the selfish addiction to racehorses while underlings were left with critical decisions, the subsequent unloading of blame on those underlings if the decisions went badly—but in an odd, inexplicable way he was touched by Mayer's testimonial.

Mayer did not give up easily. He sent his right-hand man, L.K. Sidney, to the house on North Rodeo; it was considerate of the MGM head, for Gene, hobbling around as he was, could not easily drive to the studio. Sidney pleaded with Gene not to go on the CFA plane. "You'll only make trouble for yourself," he warned.

Gene wouldn't change his mind. Prior to Sidney's visit he had been contacted by the American Legion and asked bluntly if he was a Communist. If a trifle pedantic, his reply was firm: "I am simply a liberal who believes in the freedom of the artist and therefore cannot stand by while the careers of those I love and admire are being destroyed by a senseless purge. The only line I have ever known how to follow is the American line."

His statement was supported quietly but effectively by Roy Brewer and other labor leaders he had impressed during the IATSE strike against the studios. Gene could be confident he now had an ideological bill of health—at least temporarily.

He knew he was placing his career in jeopardy. After all, MGM—despite Mayer's avuncular support of him—was farthest to the right of all the studios in Hollywood and worked hand-in-hand with J. Edgar Hoover. A worrisome problem was Betsy, seemingly a joiner of every left-wing association in sight: the CFA, the Joint Anti-Fascist Refugee Committee, the Committee to Elect Henry Wallace, the Hollywood Committee for the Arts, Sciences, and Professions—these only headed the parade of activist groups she gave her time and money to. For a lengthy period, until the signing of the Nazi–Soviet pact, she had been a member of the Communist

Party. She had then become prominent in the Campaign for a Second Front to support the Russian defense against Hitler's invading forces. She was still an inveterate signer of petitions, a frequent speaker at rallies.

Mayer himself had even called in Betsy for a chat one day. She had been cast in MGM's *Kind Lady*, playing an important supporting role to Angela Lansbury. There was a rumor around the studio she would lose the part because of her political beliefs. But Betsy surprised Gene by her flexibility. She managed to convince the canny old man she was every bit as patriotic as he. She was allowed to play the role. A realist about the effect of her political outspokenness, Betsy later told Clive Hirschhorn, "When I had this talk with Mayer, most of the studios considered me untouchable and my career definitely suffered. There's no doubt about that."

On Saturday, October 25, Gene and some of the other stars who would be on the CFA flight to Washington appeared on a nationwide ABC network radio show. It was hastily stitched together, but nevertheless it proved effective in exhorting listeners not to go along limply with HUAC's agenda. It was announced that the plane would stop in Kansas City, St. Louis, and Pittsburgh on the way to Washington, ostensibly for refueling. The real purpose of the stop-and-go flight plan was to generate publicity as Humphrey Bogart or Gene Kelly stepped out of the plane to hold interviews with local reporters in the terminals. Indeed, the CFA leaders made Bogart the nominal head of the group; though Gene's speaking talents were impressive, there were concerns about his fiery temperament. The writer-directors who had originated the group—especially John Huston—felt a low-key approach was best, with facts, not frenzy, presenting the CFA case. It was crucial not to frighten the American people that they were a planeload of Hollywood radicals heading for a confrontation with Congress.

On departure day, Gene and Bogart were joined by a crowd of well-known Hollywood liberals: Danny Kaye, Lauren Bacall, John Huston, Paul Henreid, Evelyn Keyes, Jane Wyatt, Marsha Hunt, June Havoc, Richard Conte, Geraldine Brooks, John Garfield, and others—not quite the A list of major players they had hoped for but still an array of notables who could attract attention. Some of the noisiest film-colony leftists stayed away, as expected; at the last minute some of the most prominent so-called liberals were impossible to reach on the phone.

In the air, a party-like atmosphere took over, but with strange, even tense, undertones. To Gene it was like a wrap celebration of a film production, glee and relief tempered by concern for what lay ahead. Underlying everything was a sense of the risk they were running. These were, after all, hardened professionals who had made their way in the pressure-cooker world of Hollywood; they knew one over-heated situation could boil over and a career could go up in smoke. Somebody—nobody quite knew who—had loaded aboard a substantial supply of liquor. There was singing, a barrage of jokes punctuated by giddy laughter. At one point Danny Kaye emerged from the flight deck, following close behind a rumpled young stewardess. Kaye was wearing a pilot's uniform, conspicuously misbuttoned. "Folks, we've kind of lost our way," Kaye said. "Anybody here got a road map?"

The good-natured farce obscured the seriousness of the charter flight, which was as carefully organized as a press tour for a new high-budget movie. Seasoned film-industry publicists had made the necessary phone calls to set up the interviews. They secured radio coverage on the ABC network outlets and affiliates; this newest of the national networks was happy to cooperate because it wanted to prove it could deliver a mass audience.

It all came together on the airport tarmacs, and Gene's morale soared when he saw the large crowds meeting them. He and Bogart wished there had been time to set up a longer tour and visit more cities, but they were pleased with the applause they were receiving. A groundswell of public opinion was what they were going for. In Pittsburgh, the final stop before Washington, Gene did something he was later to regret. He deplaned in order to visit his mother and spend the night at her home. He booked himself on the earliest Monday-morning flight to Washington. Bogart, Huston, and Dunne were concerned by his side-trip. They had found Gene to be the most effective spokesman for the group and warned him to be on time in Washington. "Gene, for God's sake, be sure and arrive before Johnston's presentation," Philip Dunne pleaded.

"Gene, we all have to be there to support Johnston," Bogart added firmly. Eric Johnston, president of the Motion Picture Association of America, the trade and lobbying group, was to open the Monday-morning session of HUAC with a spirited defense of the patriotism in the film industry. A man of many Washington contacts, he would then switch to an attack on the validity of the HUAC charge that the employees within the industry were predominantly Communist sympathizers.

The next morning Gene was playing it close and paid for it. His connection to Washington was late in taking off from Pittsburgh. He fretted throughout the flight, cursing himself for letting down the others who had gone ahead. He was the first off the plane, moving gingerly on crutches. It was one of the few public occasions when he refused autographs, as he lurched through the crowded Washington terminal to the taxi line. It moved slowly. Arriving taxis were few and far between. By the time his cab reached the House Office Building, he was too late to be included in the group shot of "the Hollywood Team." The photograph would be prominently featured in hundreds of newspapers across the country as an important element of the CFA nationwide press campaign. Betsy was upset that Gene "had missed it for mama."

A number of his fellow passengers were furious with him for being away. There were the inevitable suspicions he had lost heart in what they were doing and was in some way protecting his own career. But Bogart was gracious about Gene's late arrival; it turned out that for some reason Chairman Thomas—certainly not to aid the Hollywood group—had already rescheduled Eric Johnston's speech for the afternoon.

The postponement of Johnston's speech turned out to be a crafty move. Already scheduled for the afternoon was the confrontation between HUAC and the "Hollywood Ten," a group of film writers considered "unfriendly witnesses." Though under subpoena, they refused to furnish names of known Communists or to cooperate in any way with HUAC. The Ten were led by John Howard Lawson, an aggressive leader who, Gene learned from Betsy, was a Communist Party member and, indeed, looked on as a guru in Party circles. Lawson was the first witness called by Thomas, and, almost immediately, the two men were red-faced, shouting at each other. Capitol policemen were called into the committee room and dispersed around the perimeter. Gene instantly realized that this was taking the spotlight away from the charter-flight passengers and shining it on the hostile Ten, thereby intermingling and confusing the mission of the groups.

It became worse. Chairman Thomas pounded his gavel and Lawson paid no heed, yelling even louder. Objections, insults, even curses tumbled over each other, distorted by a faulty public-address system. Spectators in the room were divided; they took sides, hissing, booing, clapping. Thomas finally cited the shouting writer for contempt. The effect on the other congressmen was to infuriate them; it was clear they now regarded the CFA delegation and the raucous Hollywood Ten as allies in the threatening array of "Communist fronts."

In that uneasy, suspicious climate, Eric Johnston's speech was a disappointment to Kelly, Bogart, and the others. It was timid and wavering and certainly did not help the situation by stating Johnston's personal position that he, Johnston, would certainly blacklist Lawson if the charge of being a "card-carrying Communist" were true. Johnston's remarks were off-the-point, misleading, and defensive, not at all what Gene felt was needed: a vigorous attack on an out-of-control congressional committee trampling the basic rights of American filmmakers.

Later that afternoon, in a desperate effort to make the charter flight worthwhile despite what had gone so abysmally wrong, the CFA hurriedly set up a press conference in a suite at the Statler Hotel. John Huston and Philip Dunne gave short, punchy speeches to a large gathering of journalists, explaining in a calm and measured way the reasons for the stars' presence in Washington. When the journalists directed their questions at individual actors in the group, Gene was questioned aggressively as to why he had missed the morning session. Asked about his reaction to Lawson's performance, he ad-libbed, unprepared, "A denial of free speech. What if he *is* a Communist?"

Others were also thrown off by the hostile questions. To the Washington press corps, the CFA were outsiders, publicity-hungry, overpaid, lightweight dilettantes, not intellectual enough to participate in the serious national debate. The stars, in turn, had always been cosseted and protected by studio publicists; they were used to smiling flacks fielding the questions for them and printing calculated responses in block letters on index cards. Now, the reporters saw the CFA emissaries as mere handsome mannequins, designed for show, not tell, and completely out of their depth. An unfair judgment, but, ultimately, a correct one, even to Lauren Bacall. "We were so naive, it was ridiculous," she said of the fiasco. "When the press started to ask us questions, they had a field day."

Bogart chain-smoked. Danny Kaye bit his nails. Alluding to his current film, *The Secret Life of Walter Mitty*, Kaye said, "Maybe I should've had another dream scene in it about me being a hot lawyer. Then I'd know how to talk better here." He tittered but nobody else laughed. John Garfield stammered incoherently, "Why doesn't Congress make it illegal to belong to the Communist Party and clear the whole thing up?" Reporters looked at each other.

"It was a sorry performance," was the later verdict of John Huston. "We lost a chance to defend a most important principle." Within a month, the American Legion threatened to boycott films made with the involvement of Communist Party members. Days later, the Screen Actors Guild voted to make their union officers take a non-Communist pledge. In New York, fifty film-industry leaders met behind closed doors at the Waldorf-Astoria Hotel and unanimously adopted a resolution, known as the Waldorf Statement: The studios would no longer knowingly employ Communists. It became the official confirmation of the blacklist.

Feeling the heat on his flight back to California, Humphrey Bogart called a news conference in Chicago, stating he detested Communism and that his trip to Washington had been "ill-advised, even foolish."

Gene Kelly made no comment. He held no press conference. Once again, feeling used and misused, he resolved to concentrate on his film career. He flew back to California, without making a stopover in Pittsburgh.

He's still coming home—that's where his head is—still on those damn crutches, making it slowly up the driveway. Home from the HUAC embarrassment, still warm with the scalding comments of the national press. Up front, at the Beverly Hilton, Shirley MacLaine, still radiant in red—maybe that color is the mnemonic that keeps setting him off—is doing an intro into Singin' in the Rain *which he expected would be saved for the Closer, as usual in these retrospectives.*

He had meant well in Washington, with Bogie and the others. The idea that a few Stalinists and fellow-travelers in the film industry were a threat to the U.S.—what a joke! But the pompous Hollywood Ten and far-leftists like Betsy posing as champions of the Bill of Rights, which a Stalinist regime would have instantly abolished—was that any better?

His mind, almost desperately, calls for a WIPE, *but it is half-hearted, half-screened, as Shirley talks about him and Stanley, some truth, some fiction, like the rest of the evening's spiels. And before one could say* FADE IN, *there on the big screen is "Moses Supposes." He and Donald O'Connor giving the harried speech therapist a hard time. God, the smartass bastards they were in those days; today the guy's craft union would file charges of harassment! And before that notion works its way into him, more mental reprise of the IATSE strike and HUAC and Senator Joe McCarthy, there's the familiar trio, Donald, Debbie, and Gene, tumbling over couches. Then more dancing clips to almost a freeze-frame ogling of Cyd's l-o-n-g legs. But not his number—no umbrella, no lamp post. For sure, no rain yet. They're saving it for tonight's Closer!*

Onstage now are Donald, Debbie, and Cyd, chatting it up until Donald is called upon to speak: "It's not easy working with a genius." A long, almost Jack Benny pause. "That's why Gene was so patient with me."

Which, of course, draws the laugh. The kicker is his reputation around town. Gene Kelly, Mr. Know-All. Unfortunately, life doesn't imitate art. A genius, he ain't! His stumbling, inept performance and his wavering between this side and that on the blacklist issue confirmed that he could be an asshole with the best of them. For almost twenty-five years he'd been wrestling with his conscience. Almost a double-image, as in Cover Girl.

Until one night, in 1970, at a meeting of the Screenwriters Guild. A writer-friend named Dalton Trumbo, a target of HUAC, made a speech that grabbed him. The next morning he called Dalton, got a text of the speech. Read it carefully. Filed it with his own precious archives.

The speech was ashes, of course, along with everything else when his house burned down. But never mind, he had long since committed it to memory—especially Dalton's closing line—what those horrible HUAC days faced him with:

> *Caught in a situation that had passed beyond the control of mere individuals, each person reacted as his nature, his needs, his convictions and his particular circumstances compelled him to. There was bad faith then good, honesty and dishonesty, courage and cowardice, selflessness and opportunism, wisdom and stupidity, good and bad on both sides. When you who are in your forties or younger look back with curiosity on that dark time, as I think occasionally you should, it will do no good to search for villains or heroes or saints or devils because there were none; there were only victims.*

As far as he was concerned, those were the words of a true genius, saying it all. Putting his mind—and conscience—finally at rest.

LOS ANGELES, 1947

* * *

Concerned yet again that the studio might break his contract, and worried about the financial security of his family, Gene turned to radio as a source of income. He was taken on by CBS for a popular running series called *Cresta Blanca's Hollywood Players*, featuring a repertory company of stars: Claudette Colbert, Bette Davis, Joan Fontaine, Paulette Goddard, Joseph Cotten, and Gregory Peck. Hired to augment the celebrity cast from time to time was an unknown young woman with the name of Jeanette Helen Morrison Reames, which she was immediately advised to change. She did, to Janet Leigh. She was paid $500 per performance, much less than what the others received. But it was a big opportunity for her:

> I would have paid Cresta Blanca. I was insecure, sweated through every performance but of all the cast Gene Kelly was always the one to try and help me. I was struck by the dedication he gave to his own role. It was obvious he gave this job—usually, a maudlin little story—the same degree of intensity, the same drive for

perfection as he would one of his dances. I remember at a cast party once wanting so badly to dance with him. But he had an excuse. He was still on crutches because of his broken ankle. Lucky guy! I'd have been so nervous, I would have tripped over my own feet and we'd both go down. All he needed was for me to break his other ankle!

It was a measure of his stature that Gene's responses to the innuendos that he was (at least) a leftist married to (almost certainly) a Communist were believed not only by Roy Brewer of IATSE and Mayer of MGM, but other Hollywood movers and shakers. Only a short while after his return from Washington, with his ankle responding to a severe regime of physical therapy, he was offered a Metro film that he knew at once represented another golden opportunity to restore his fortunes and catapult him into the front ranks. As usual, the chance did not come his way on a silver platter; he had to work for it:

> I thought that MGM would be waiting for me with open arms, with a script, something really solid. . . . I returned the call to Joe Pasternak, a charming man and a good friend of mine. "I've got an idea you'll kill 'em with. You and Frank Sinatra will buy a used aircraft carrier and turn it into a nightclub." I thought, oh, my God, another Navy picture! So I called Arthur Freed and told him I had an idea for a picture, *Take Me Out to the Ball Game*. He said, "Sounds good!"

But Freed had another project he wanted Gene to do first: *The Pirate*, a Cole Porter musical, starring Judy Garland. So for the time being, Gene's idea for a baseball picture was laid aside. He was actually delighted by the change in plans. Here was another, but full-scale, opportunity to do the Douglas Fairbanks–Errol Flynn type of swashbuckler, awash in fast-moving songs and dances no one else could render.

To Lois McClelland, his former Wave assistant working full-time for him, he confided the uncertainties that plague a dancer at age thirty-six. During the first week of shooting on *The Pirate*, he was candid, too, with a reporter from the *Los Angeles Times*:

> Two years in the Navy, three years off the screen, I shall never be the dancer I was. I put on eighteen pounds in the Navy, and I am only just working them off. Besides, I am a lot older now than when I made *Cover Girl* and *Anchors Aweigh*. With Fred Astaire already retiring, I do start to wonder how much longer I've got. Besides, I was a much better dancer when I first got to Broadway than I am now. I was younger, that's why. A dancer is like a prize-fighter. He gets superannuated very early; can't take it nearly so well in his thirties.

It was a gloomy prognosis that, happily, did not apply to Gene Kelly at that point in his life. His greatest films were still ahead of him.

The Pirate led the way. Its origin was a German stage comedy about Macoco, a notorious pirate who becomes the mayor of a Caribbean island. During the 1943 Broadway season, the playwright S.N. Behrman had reworked the story into a hit for Alfred Lunt and Lynn Fontanne. Behrman added the complication of a wandering actor who impersonates the pirate to win the love of the lovely Manuela, Judy Garland's role.

Gene wanted passionately to work with Garland again, especially after his disappointment over *Easter Parade*, a now-completed film that MGM touted as a huge hit. (Already there was the publicity build-up about Fred Astaire's sensational return to the screen and the renewal of the Kelly–Astaire competition.) Gene felt that his own graciousness, easing the way for Astaire's comeback, was ignored. He had not played the Hollywood game, which ruled: *Never to do favors for the competition*. He had freely nominated Astaire to take his place—not Van Johnson, not Dan Dailey. He had not been petty then, nor would he now.

Gene was needed in *The Pirate* for reasons far beyond his part; he simply owed it to Judy to help her through one of the worst periods in an ill-starred life. From the first moment the project reeked of a disaster to come. When shooting started, just after Valentine's Day in 1947, Garland appeared on the set attended by several "therapists," and it was obvious her marriage to director Vincente Minnelli was eroding fast after the recent birth of their daughter, Liza. The star's figure had ballooned during the pregnancy. She had put on a lot of weight, and now studio-mandated diet and drugs were ordered to bring her back into filmable shape. Clearly suffering from a post-partum depression, she had made a few suicide attempts amid a flow of threats to do away with herself. At Mayer's behest, Minnelli had sent her to a private sanitarium for a rest period.

Gene had always felt that Minnelli was part of the problem: an intellectual wrapped up in his work, something of a closed-off aesthete, the director was never available emotionally to Judy. Of course, Gene was sensitive enough to see signs there of his own unsteady relationship with Betsy, but his own wife was far more rugged and psychologically secure; there was no need to panic, and he promised himself to attend to his own marriage once *The Pirate* was completed.

What even Gene did not know was the state of the Minnelli family's finances; they were close to bankruptcy and in serious arrears to the IRS. Judy's income was a necessity to keep the Minnelli household afloat. She had to meet her schedule on *The Pirate* under peril of losing her MGM contract.

As a result she allowed herself to be plied with diet pills and appetite suppressants, some prescribed by legitimate physicians, some from murkier sources. The result was shocking: In an incredibly short time Garland was bone-thin, almost anorexic. For a feature film, which is almost always shot out of sequence, a consistency of appearance from scene to scene is essential. By the end of the first week, the film rushes of her scenes compelled urgent meetings in the executive suites of MGM. What to do about Judy? There was no alternative; *The Pirate* had set sail and Minnelli, with Gene's help, would have to navigate the project safely—and profitably—to port.

True to form, Gene was again into his obsessive working habits, spilling out ideas in every area. Unfortunately, caught up in his own creative ferment, he seemed oblivious to Garland's constant need for personal attention and sympathetic care. Early on, it was clear that she resented the lengthy periods Gene and Minnelli spent together in private, discussing not just the problems of the female lead but every detail of the picture. She found a way to retaliate. The gossip columnist Hedda Hopper found Garland in her dressing room and wrote up her condition in a syndicated column that was distributed to hundreds of newspapers across the country: "She was shaking like an aspen leaf and in a frenzy of hysteria, was claiming that all who loved her had now turned against her and were tapping her telephone calls."

Anita Loos, one of the many writers who worked on *The Pirate*, later wrote:

> I recall an early day at the studio when mild little Vincente Minnelli was waiting to direct Judy in one of the big scenes. As usual she was late for work and everybody, including Kelly and the extras, had been marking time since eight in the morning. Finally, at noon, Vincente was summoned to the phone to learn that Judy required him to get home at once and escort her to an ice-cream parlor for a soda.

Things got worse as Garland's singing talent deserted her. Gene was pained on the day when she came in to pre-record "Love of My Life" and her exultant quality and intensity of delivery were not there. She looked and sounded frail and dispirited. During the following months, the company was more often than not laid off because of her illness. On some days she might come to rehearse for a couple of hours—a bonanza, the cast would cheer among themselves—Judy had turned the corner! The next morning she would arrive and insist on leaving an hour later. By April the entire company was demoralized, unnerved by the uncertainty of the daily schedules and her erratic performances.

Gene now tried to help and, to a measure, was the reason Garland carried on. He was constantly supportive, affectionate, making excuses for her. Once, when he knew Judy was involved in a scene with him and had not yet left her bed, he phoned the unit manager to tell him he was not coming in, and he forced out a joke to the effect that he was hung over, having been out very late the night before. At another time, to spare Judy a visit to the set by Mayer and Freed and protect her from a scolding and, undoubtedly, a severe financial penalty, Gene feigned sickness for a week.

In turn, she cared for him; perhaps she loved him. Or, more accurately, if he had at any time given her the opportunity, she would have loved him.

But Gene was congenitally hesitant to chance an extramarital relationship. Just as he never would give up on a film, he would never stop trying to hold his marriage together. Admitting defeat was an impossibility. For now, Betsy's incipient film career had been stopped in its tracks by blacklisting. With his schedule, they were again in a period when they hardly saw each other. He had to fight off the certainty she was seeing other men. But his priority, relentlessly, had to be *The Pirate*. It was the linchpin of the career he dreamed of, and could be the salvation of Judy's.

He was not present when she came in to pre-record "Voodoo," but as a self-appointed protector of Judy, he went out of his way to be on the set when she came in to shoot the scene. Her assignment was to lip-synch the song near an open fire. When word came that she was *en route*, the fire was lit and Minnelli, Gene, and the entire company were waiting as the star came in, this time close to schedule.

Gene instantly knew there would be trouble: Her eyes widened in fear as she spied the snapping flames. She had been briefed very carefully by Minnelli; a contingent from the studio fire department was right at hand, very visible to all, and the fire was under control. Everything was as Minnelli had promised her. Yet, just after she had taken her position, before Minnelli could call out "Roll, Camera!" she turned away from the fire with a horrified expression on her face. "They want me to burn to death!" she sobbed. "I'm going to burn to death!"

Members of the crew looked at each other in the here-we-go-again way that, all too often, prevailed whenever Judy was on the set. Minnelli tried to calm her. Gene approached and talked to her quietly, but she pulled away from him and ran toward some extras. Addressing each one individually, she asked with a frightening intensity: "Do you have some Benzedrine?" She kept repeating the word as she asked others: "Benzedrine? Benzedrine?" Minnelli had no choice. He had to get her off the set. She was sobbing, then laughing, then bursting into tears again. It was difficult to take hold of her because everybody was tender, did not in any way want to handle her roughly. All of them, Gene realized, had known and loved Judy since her teens. But now she was going public. Her rapidly deteriorating condition could no longer be covered up by studio publicists.

Somehow, once everybody had given up on her, she would suddenly appear and resume shooting as though nothing had gone wrong. Sometimes her performance was thrilling. Sometimes she barely got by, and her scenes had to be shot in separate cuts and then patched together during post-production editing. For weeks at a time she would manage only sporadic appearances of half an hour or so and then leave without having done any work. By June, with the film barely half-finished, Arthur Freed was almost $1 million over-budget.

When they finally reached the production of Gene's pirate ballet, in mid-August, *The Pirate* had taken 135 days to film, for 99 of which Judy Garland had been absent. Despite the mounting costs and the erratic participation of its star, in the judgment of the key creative trio—Freed, Minnelli, and Kelly—*The Pirate* still had hit potential. What would make it work, they decided, was a Douglas Fairbanks bravura, even an exaggerated bravura. Since childhood Gene had worshiped two men whom he regarded as the greatest athletes of his lifetime: Ty Cobb in baseball, Fairbanks in films. Now, strongly supported by Freed, he would not let the chance slip to blend sports with dance into something magical. As he said many times later at revival screenings of *The Pirate*: "I wanted the opportunity to do a different kind of dancing, a popular style with a lot of classic form, acrobatics, and athletics."

Even though Gene believed very strongly in location shooting, *The Pirate*, he felt, was better done on a studio set, and to hell with authenticity of place and atmosphere. Freed gave Jack Smith, the designer, the go-ahead for putting together a conglomeration of styles for San Sebastian, the tropical seaport where the action is set: a smidgeon of South American here, a breath of the Bahamas there, the aura of the West Indies vaguely tingeing everything else. Smith created a palm-fringed enclave for Gene to cavort in and on and above. Smith served him well by following Freed's instruction "to give Gene all the toys he needs," the devices supporting his acrobatics: slippery pillars to slide down, ledges on which to climb up the side of a building, hand-holds, and modeled footholds all over the set.

Gene did not overdo it; not for him the mindless antics of a Tarzan. Rather, his dance creations were modified ballet: confident, seductive, masculine, with a humor that fit Gene's personal style, a zest without pretension. Right from the start, the musical numbers are explosive. "Nina" shows off his athleticism as clearly on a par with Fairbanks's at its most dazzling. To a sensual bolero rhythm, Gene, dressed in black trousers, a trim waistcoat, and a white hat from which thick, black curls of hair dangled (disguising that his hairline had receded during his Navy service), courts every pretty woman in San Sebastian by clambering over rooftops and leaping from drainpipes. Up to now in his films Gene had concentrated on tap numbers. Now, with "Nina," he treated film audiences to a fantastic gymnastic display, breathtaking to watch. The viewer's experience was heightened by the editing of Blanche Sewell, the cinematography of Harry Stradling, and, of course, the Cole Porter music.

A delighted Arthur Freed thought "Nina" was a "knockout" and would edge The Pirate into the profit side of the ledger. But such was not the case. The problem was when the music stopped. When there was no dancing, The Pirate died. Moreover, Gene had regarded his role as a parody of John Barrymore when it wasn't a throwback to Fairbanks, and since Judy Garland's over-the-top emotionalism was handled with kid gloves by her anxious husband who wanted to avoid any more outbursts from her, on the screen there was little moderation in Gene's and Judy's performances. Every word and gesture was punctuated by an exclamation mark, with "all their scenes in capital letters," as a critic has written. With Smith's conglomeration of colors on the set and Irene Sharaff's extrovertive carnival costumes, the production spilled out of control in a way that dizzied—not delighted—the public.

In the years that followed, each of the creators had a different reason as to why The Pirate showed a net loss to MGM of well over $2 million. Vincente Minnelli, in an interview with the French film magazine Cahiers du Cinema, said somewhat self-protectively: "I was very pleased the way the film turned out. Judy gave one of her best performances and the Cole Porter songs were excellent. Unfortunately, the merchandising on the film was bad and it failed to go over when it was released."

Gene, as always, was hardest on himself:

> Vincente and I honestly believed we were being so dazzlingly great and clever that everybody would fall at our feet and swoon away in delight and ecstasy as they kiss each of our toes in appreciation for

this wondrous new musical that we had given them. Boy, were we wrong! About five and a half people seemed get the gist of what we had set out to do and, in retrospect, you really couldn't blame any of the others. . . . whatever I did just looked like fake Barrymore and phony Fairbanks. . . . the sophisticates grasped it, but the film died in the hinterlands. It was done tongue in cheek and I should have realized that never really works.

It was Freed's contention that they had made the film either twenty years too late or twenty years too early. Young people were not sufficiently acquainted with either the elevations of Douglas Fairbanks and the elocutions of John Barrymore to appreciate the intended parody. And the older generation resented having their heroes defiled. It was left to James Agee, the most influential film critic of the late 1940s, to try for the last word on the film: "As an all-out try at artful movie-making, this is among the most interesting pictures of the year. Unhappily, most of the very considerable artistry that Kelly has put into this production collides head-on with artiness or is spoiled by simpler kinds of miscalculation."

The major miscalculation may have been Agee's. Fifty years later, *The Pirate* is constantly being "rediscovered" at film festivals all over the world. Far more than just a cult film, it is considered to be a Gene Kelly masterpiece.

At the time of the initial release of *The Pirate*, the meager box-office results and sulphurous critical comments would normally have commenced another period of self-torture for Gene. But Pandro S. Berman, another MGM producer, alerted him that a new expensive project for the studio, *The Three Musketeers*, was galloping his way at top speed; there would be no period of idleness to strain his workaholic impatience. For this 1948 film version of the classic tale by Alexandre Dumas, the role of D'Artegnan, the trio's leader, was assigned to Gene. For two months he worked closely with Jean Heremens, the Belgian fencing champion, absorbing the rudiments of classical swordsmanship. Heremens was to "double" in the film as various dueling opponents of Gene whose ballet training proved invaluable for those encounters. Gene had never lost his fascination with the relationship of athletics to ballet and now relished its application to fencing; *The Three Musketeers* would be an absorbing immersion into a new sport:

> In both, the feet are always placed outward, making it possible to move quickly from side to side and to use your body to the full. Unless your toes were turned outward, period costumes made it very difficult to move easily in a duel. So when I first started fencing I had no problem in moving around, but the difficulty was to train my reflexes to deflect with speed and then come back at my opponent.

He was impatient for the start of shooting. His only complaint was that the film was not a musical. However, by his lights, all the action moments were extensions of dancing, particularly the sequence when the Musketeers leaped into their saddles and joined forces against Cardinal Richelieu. It would be choreography without music.

He also felt a touch of relief about the assignment. It was an affirmation of the studio's conviction that he was a first-rate actor, a talented presenter of dialogue and emotion *without* the crutch of music and dance. Making the film helped to wipe away some of the critical reaction to his somewhat overblown performance in *The Pirate*. His morale received a further boost when the director Billy Wilder phoned and sent over a first-draft script of *Sunset Boulevard*, inquiring about his interest in the part of the young screenwriter sucked into the orbit of an aging movie queen. His response was resoundingly positive. Unfortunately, MGM would not let him go, citing contractual problems and the starting date of *The Three Musketeers*. Shortly afterward, Gene's agent notified him that William Holden had secured the role, but the idea that so canny a director as Wilder wanted him as a lead actor in a non-dancing, nonsinging role was very comforting.

There had been at least a half-dozen previous American and European film versions of *The Three Musketeers*, but MGM was ready to pour a near-record $3 million into its new production, an awesome investment at the time for a nonmusical. George Sidney would direct. Gene's co-stars were Van Heflin, Lana Turner, June Allyson, Vincent Price, and Angela Lansbury, an uneven cast in terms of acting ability, but it carried sufficient star power to draw in large audiences. The distinction of inheriting the lead from Douglas Fairbanks, the hero of a previous version, gave Gene much pleasure; it was as if his real co-star were his longtime idol.

Vincent Price was cast as the villainous Richelieu. Cautious as ever, L.B. Mayer did not want to offend the sensibilities of millions of Roman Catholics. Accordingly, he set forth only two mandates at the start of pre-production: First, no expensive overtime; and second, Richelieu could never be addressed by his clerical title, Cardinal.

Once more, Gene had to decide whether to use stunt doubles in action scenes. He had never appeared in a cowboy film and to him the project was "like being a kid all over again—playing cowboys and Indians. For what is *The Three Musketeers* if not a Western with plumes?" As a Pittsburgh boy with little tenure in the saddle he had the typical urban skepticism about the intelligence of horses and their commitment to passenger safety. With some trepidation, then, he insisted on doing his own stunts, especially in the closer shots when a face might be recognizable.

His face was actually nicked a few times by one or another of the actor-swordsmen. He was not impressed with the way his cohorts in the cast wielded their weapons like lariats in a rodeo. Unlike him, they had not spent many sweaty practice hours with Heremens. With the passion of someone who was accident-prone, he made sure tiny rubber balls were attached to the sword tips during rehearsals. When cameras rolled the balls were removed but only after careful blunting and dulling of the swords.

Once, during a "go for it" scene with several synchronized cameras rolling, Gene lost part of his false mustache during a clashing, slashing saber exchange with the disguised Heremens. The fight went on and on. It was a magnificent take, and the director let the two men exhaust themselves. Much too late, with Gene wheezing and about to stop the duel, one of the cameramen noticed the shredded half-mustache on the floor and called it to the attention of Sidney, who had no recourse but to call for a second take. "I deserve the Purple Heart for this one," Gene said.

He was not the only one to earn a medal for wounds in combat during the making of *The Three Musketeers*. In the bedchamber scene where D'Artegnan discovers the infidelity of Milady, played by Lana Turner, Gene was so caught up in the action that he flung Turner across her bed with such force that she pitched over the other side onto the floor. Her invaluable face was unmarred, but she suffered a broken elbow and could not appear in front of the cameras for two weeks.

Sword nicks and broken elbows aside, the production of *The Three Musketeers* worked out well, with the tumultuous action taking over the screen. When the action stops, audience interest tends to sag at the predictable plot. Gene Kelly still overacts, but in the Fairbanks world, it fits. The jubilant swordplay, the robust pursuit of Lana Turner, and his swashbuckling demeanor are all of a piece, a consistent performance as Gene has a high old time and his pleasure doing D'Artegnan rolls off the screen to involve and rouse the audience.

Dore Schary, in the first year of his tenure as MGM's production head, was more than satisfied. Schary considered it, as he told Gene, "a rousing hit—and we'll do more of them." Gene was invigorated by Schary's reaction and the implicit promise made. He already had his next project in mind. His creative life was impelled by a torrent of dreams—dance dreams, really, coursing into his mind one after another. Once tested at the barre or on the set, the dream was danced and done; but another was always there, bursting to take shape. Now his ambition was to make the definitive film of *Cyrano de Bergerac*.

Edmund Rostand's play had never before been filmed in English. While he was hoping his pitches to Freed on behalf of *Cyrano* would be fruitful, and waiting for his assignment to a new film, he took to traveling to cinemas in the Los Angeles area where *The Pirate*, and, later, *The Three Musketeers* were featured. Sitting unrecognized in the back row of a dark theater, he tried to judge his performance through the reactions of the ticket buyers fanned out in front of him. Of course, he neither talked to anybody nor asked the audience to fill out response cards. He felt he could measure how the film was working, first, from the audible responses—the laughter, the sibilant suck-in of breaths, the applause, the uncomfortable patches of arid silence—and then the physical responses—his dancer's eye for body language made him confident he could "feel" reactions from the backs of heads, the alert or the lay-back posture of the viewer, the ignoring of the person to the right and left. Such firsthand observations helped him analyze his performances, judge what critics to listen to, and compare Gene with Fairbanks. Reluctantly, Gene conceded that Gene came up short:

> What I most envied about Fairbanks in the silent version was
> the way he would register his satisfaction after completing an

especially dazzling trick without ever being smug about it. There was just something in his expression that acknowledged his own excellence, and he was very engaging. When I tried to acquire the same sort of nonchalance for my D'Artegnan, I was never able to be as ingenuous; with me it always came out taunting. Fairbanks had a combination of naiveté and arrogance which was unrivaled in the cinema. And although there was not a trick in his entire repertoire which I could not duplicate, the "brio" with which he performed them was his and his alone.

Surely, not for the first time, it was brought home to him that he had to do away with the heated overacting that was still his weakness in narrative films. The eyebrow-arching expressions that came out as "taunting" would have to go. To play a great Cyrano he would have to curb his instincts for chewing the scenery; he would have to be natural, lifelike, authentic, underplaying (like Spencer Tracy, like Franchot Tone, the two male actors he knew well and admired most), living by the damn truism about less being more! He resolved that when the Cyrano part came his way, he would do it justice with a sensitive performance that saw into the gallant swordsman's heart and mind, without making a lurid fetish of his famous nose.

Lois McClelland would often see Gene in those brooding, thoughtful periods: "He would just sit there in one of two large red chairs in the living room . . . just thinking and thinking. That's how I remember him." Thanks largely to Lois and her keen-eyed talents as a shopper and manager, dealing with building contractors and renovators—to say nothing of her own dexterity with carpentry tools—the house on North Rodeo was now comfortably and tastefully furnished; if it did not quite measure up to the dreamhouse Betsy had originally envisaged, it now suited the life-style of a major motion-picture star.

Lois arrived early and left late (she herself lived alone in a cottage on nearby Benedict Canyon) after a typical day of typing Gene's many responses to fan letters and the film proposals and outlines he was constantly writing, alone or with a collaborator, and serving as a proxy-mother to Kerry in Betsy's frequent absences, and taking on much of the responsibility for the renewal of that popular Hollywood institution, the Gene open house.

So commenced the era of The Game, Part 2. Nothing had changed. Betsy and Gene were as competitive as ever. Gene could not withhold irritation if his team did not win and pummeled the weak players without mercy. The sandwiches and drinks were still unexceptional, but the guest list grew, the old crowd again gathering around the piano and augmented by newcomers from New York and Europe, eager to participate in the fun.

Celebrated visitors were to arrive in town and be feted in the ornate salons of George Cukor, Jack Warner, or Louis B. Mayer, and then escape to the free-form adventure on North Rodeo Drive. The tide of celebrities always went in one direction. The erudite English critic Kenneth Tynan and his wife, Kathleen, were among those visitors who experienced this two-step introduction to Hollywood nightlife.

Years later, Kathleen published a memoir, looking back longingly at those evenings:

> The company was politically much more convivial than at Cukor's and more dismayingly intellectual. No guest, Ken said, lolled naked here on leopard-skin divans. Instead, the Gene house was animated by the Pittsburgh-Irish host's competitive intelligence and charm and his then-wife Betsy Blair's active support for left causes. Their front door was never locked and through it poured a talent bunch (mostly from New York) who would make their way straight to the bar. There was lively political talk and noisy charades and endless word games. There was usually someone at the piano, Leonard Bernstein or Oscar Levant, who would call out: "What'll it be, kids? A Stabat Mater or a Blues?" Judy Garland and Lena Horne would sing while Marilyn Monroe made hot dogs.

Andre Previn caught the restless atmosphere of those evenings when interviewed, years later, by Clive Hirschhorn:

> I can honestly say I have never met so many extraordinary people in one room, on so many occasions in my life. I met Noël Coward there and Chevalier and Charlie Chaplin. And there was never a fanfare to herald their arrival. The key word was informality but the prerequisite was talent. Gene and Betsy had an unforgivably conceited intolerance of untalented people. If, for example, any one of the bachelors in the group showed up with a girl who was pretty—well, that was okay. But if the girl opened her mouth and turned out to be a dumb broad or tried to play The Game and wasn't particularly good at it, they would be extremely intolerant of her and showed their displeasure. At the time, of course, I couldn't see, where Hollywood and its values were concerned, that we were all on the *Titanic* and the band was playing "Nearer My God to Thee." I was seduced happily and willingly and I learned a great deal from people ranging from the gifted to the merely brilliant.

For Lois McClelland, who did not dare to join in The Game, these were indeed memorable evenings and so was the sight greeting her at 8 A.M. the next day: The rugged survivors of the party furiously involved in volleyball—not that Gene's ankle was healed! Lois watched the King of the Court, determined to prove his accident had not curtailed his athletic prowess, make the most incredible shots, saving a ball flubbed by an exhausted teammate, scrambling to another position, soaring into the air with one gigantic leap, spiking the ball down to an unguarded section of the opposition court. "Winner, and still champion!" she heard Gene crow, his arms thrust upward in victory.

The haggard visitors were not yet released. Challenged by Gene into more games, they went at it until mid-morning, when Lois and a maid served juice and coffee. The vision of sweat-stained guests hobbling toward their expensive cars was still with Lois, many years later, when she described the scene:

> I thought they might be able to sleep off the Gene hospitality, but they would never forget it. Then, more often than not, another group would show up about one o'clock in the afternoon and another volleyball game would soon be in full swing. Gene had invited some new competition over to the house, young college kids from the nearby beach leagues, mostly basketball players. Every one of those kids was taller and much younger—but Gene more than held his own and ran them ragged.

She added: "With all the activity going on night and day at the Gene home, it didn't take me long to realize that the last thing Gene and Betsy wanted was to face each other in an empty house."

For her part, Betsy had developed a full plate of activities to keep herself busy, now that the blacklist was cutting into her chances for film roles. From the women's first meeting in Washington, Lois had marveled at Betsy's quickness and intelligence, but here in California, amid the practical problems of home renovation, Lois found her somewhat disorganized, unpunctual, and even irresponsible, though with a generous spirit that was always captivating. Betsy saw the humor in any situation and, full of surprises and a lover of practical jokes, she would go to fantastic lengths for a good laugh. As when Lois invited Betsy to the cottage she had just bought:

> The Kellys, of course, were the first ones I had over. They loved the place, especially Betsy. I was surprised, though, when she said how much better it would be if some day I could have the wall broken through and have a pass-through window between the kitchen and the dining room. As if I didn't know—and as if I could afford it! It seemed a strange thing to say and it kind of spoiled the mood for me.

But about a week later, Lois left her house early to meet Gene at the studio and help him with some publicity work on *The Three Musketeers*. It was a long working day, and she finally returned home about 7:30 P.M. She opened her front door and nearly fainted at what she saw: a housefull of friends laughing and singing "Home on the Range." Miraculously, there was now a pass-through window between the kitchen to the dining room; cut and fully installed, it showed not a sign of debris or work! The extended kitchen–dining room had even been replenished with additional furnishings, and all partitions and walls were newly painted.

It took a while for Lois to discover how this incredible change had come about. One of Betsy's new friends, a studio production manager, had helped Betsy with the logistics. The operation was planned like a film shooting schedule. Betsy, the ringleader, had gotten the idea and persuaded friends to stash away various items of new furniture in garages until the delivery date. She hired a construction crew to break through the wall, carpenters to build the pass-through window frame, painters to come in for the final task—each specialty operation set with a definite deadline so the entire construction job could be completed prior to the return of Lois from one workday.

Years later, interviewed in her kitchen over coffee served through the pass-through window, Lois told an interviewer:

> How Betsy persuaded those workmen to come under such conditions, I'll never know. You must remember, that was just after the war when it was next to impossible to get a man to come to your house and fix a plumbing leak. I guess Betsy could charm the bark off a tree when she wanted to. And when she didn't want to do something, she just took off! And Gene and I had been foolish enough to keep her away from the renovation job on their North Rodeo house. It would have been done in no time if Betsy had hung around!

Before moving to her own house, Lois had shared the guest quarters at North Rodeo with Jeanne Coyne, Gene's erstwhile dance assistant. The two women became close friends. It took only a few late-night conversations for Lois to realize that Jeanne had been in love with Gene since her dance-lesson days in Pittsburgh, and also that both women were aware that Betsy had certain romantic interests in Hollywood beyond her glamorous husband. In 1948 Lois was thunderstruck when Jeanne eloped with Stanley Donen. Even discounting the build-up of her own personal feelings for her employer, the ex-Wave from upper New York State had found the North Rodeo home too full of intrigue and had made haste to find her own place and ease the emotional pressure on herself.

Years later, in describing his complicated relationship with Donen to his British biographer, Gene showed again how very wrapped up in himself he was; the idea that his wife was looking past him was impossible to contemplate. He described the romantic vibrations within the house on Rodeo Drive in a way that was keenly observed but drastically incomplete:

> Jeannie's marriage to Stanley was doomed from the start. Because every time Stanley looked at Jeannie, he saw Betsy, whom he loved; and every time Jeannie looked at Stanley, I guess she saw me. One way and another it was all pretty incestuous.

After *The Three Musketeers* Gene sensed an uncertainty on the part of MGM. The studio was in no rush to assign him on another feature; he was still waiting on his proposal for the lead in a nonmusical *Cyrano de Bergerac*. The road out of uncertainty, the doldrums of unemployment, was always the same for Gene and always basic:

get to work and do more work. The frenzied schedule of recreational competition—sports by day, partying by night—could not do it. Finally, the suspense ended when Eddie Mannix, Mayer's aide-de-camp, invited himself to Gene's house for breakfast one morning—with a message from his boss. Cyrano and his oversized nose was out of the question; 100 straight minutes of that would compromise Gene's future as a leading man for Metro.

"Then what about a musical version?"

"For an animated cartoon, maybe. But dead in the water for us handsome Irishmen," Mannix grinned. "The old man is looking out for your career."

"I'll bet." There was no arguing; actually that was the point of Mayer's sending Mannix. He had realized by now that Gene was a valuable asset to the company, but the chemistry between them was so volatile that any face-to-face encounter would be too much for an aging executive. Indeed, Mayer was about to retire, and Dore Schary, the vice-president in charge of production, would be running the company in the very near future.

Gene used to joke somewhat bitterly that his employers wanted him less as a movie song-and-dance man than as a winning athlete, for MGM had put pressure on him to play for the Metro Wolves, the Culver City entrant in the studio softball league. Like the competition to present the most glittering USO Canteen shows during the war, the softball league was classically Hollywood in its psychology: a public just-some-fun-for-the-boys attitude, while, burning deep, there was the order from on high to trample and humiliate the opponent the following Saturday afternoon.

Gene was the star shortstop, a fielder of wide range, and a solid batsman. He had wanted to involve younger MGM athletes: muscular grips; quick-handed lighting men; cinematographers with 20-20 vision; chauffeurs who could also drive a long ball. But it was quietly understood the league was for executives and "above the line" employees. Accordingly, the key positions on the team displayed the puffing talents of producer Mervyn LeRoy; Stanley Donen, who contributed youth but no special skills; Buster Keaton, a gaunt relic of the old days who still played a sensational third base; and assorted writers and directors. And joining the Wolves for his first game was the future head of the studio, Dore Schary. Obviously Schary, a former New Jersey high-school player, was sacrificing his free weekend to demonstrate his youth and democratic camaraderie, in contrast with the man he was to replace.

It was Gene's intention to discuss the green-lighting of the *Cyrano* project with Schary as soon as the game was over. On Saturday, as he parked near the baseball diamond, he saw that Schary was already warming up, shagging flies in the outfield. The game started, and Schary, the first batter for the Wolves, hurriedly removed his sneakers and put on a pair of ancient spike shoes.

"Fellow Wolves," Schary announced to his puzzled teammates. "The last time I had these spikes on was a century ago in downtown Newark. When I batted a cool three-thirty-three for my high school team."

Gene had resolved to compete, not to coach, but he couldn't resist warning Schary about his spikes, toward which he pointed a chiding finger: "Uh-uh, Dore."

"What's the matter with my shoes?"

"You haven't worn spikes in ages. Trust me. Dancers and shoemakers are the only experts about shoes. Just wear your sneakers and you won't hurt yourself."

"Don't worry about it," responded Schary as he strode toward the batter's box. The pitcher pitched. Schary's bulky body pivoted with his swing and the ball rocketed off his bat into the outfield for an extra-base hit—or what could have been an extra-base hit. Schary barely left the batter's box. His trailing right foot was mysteriously entangled in the grass, as if a giant grasshopper had bitten and wouldn't let go. Fighting the pain that must have radiated through his leg, Schary tried to run. A few faltering steps and he was writhing on the ground. He never made it to first base.

His brother Wolves escorted him quickly to a doctor, then on to the hospital, where it was reported he had torn a thigh muscle and a calf muscle, twisted an ankle, aggravated a pinched disc, and pulled his back into a state of spasm. He was placed in traction. Doctors estimated it would be at least four weeks before Schary could return to his office. The next day, Lois filed Gene's notes on *Cyrano* in his "Pending" file, the Wolves lost their star shortstop, and the three Kellys left for a ski vacation in Europe. It was the opportunity, Gene decided, for some much-needed bonding-time.

Comes now the homage from Steve Martin, the comedian at the mike. The routine is something he hasn't heard before. And it is, well, cute. Martin's anecdote sets himself up as a sort of kibitzer-observer walking through the MGM lot in the early '50s. It starts to rain. He comes upon a production crew about to wrap because of the weather.

"No, no!" says Martin to the director. "Shoot the scene anyway, rain or not."

The director is persuaded. "Okay. But first let's strike the lamppost off the set."

"No, no!" says Martin. "Keep the lamppost. And give the poor guy an umbrella. Want him to catch cold?"

The dialogue between the all-knowing, all-caring Martin and an acquiescent director draws mounting laughter from the audience. Building the piece nicely, Martin finally intones: "The rest is motion-picture history. The film was On the Town, but the scene was cut from the film. Gene never spoke to me again."

It's a nice tribute, as these things go, but it doesn't compare to what happened only a week before this AFI Salute. He was in New York, filming a promotion spot in Times Square for That's Dancing!, and it started to rain like hell. He waited out the downpour inside a Winnebago, sitting at the window, reviewing his lines. Pedestrians, poor slobs, were sloshing by. He was trying to read, but through the muffled noise, the hiss and clamor of traffic, something made him look out at the sidewalk. A black kid with an umbrella was splashing in the puddles, waving at him, singing. A dignified older man with a huge golf umbrella joined in, waving at him, singing. All at once the sidewalk was crowded with crazy New Yorkers, protected by waving umbrellas or just bravely getting soaked, waving and singing. Exactly what they were singing he couldn't possibly hear, but he damn well knew the lyrics.

In its own very special way it was a moment right up there with what happened in London, at the Coronation of Queen Elizabeth in June of 1953, when he and Betsy and Kerry were on the crowded sidewalk and—but Shirley MacLaine is at the mike again, and he pulls himself back from those moments in Times Square and Trafalgar Square to this one. The show's almost over; no more tuning out. His Closer's coming up soon.

KLOSTERS, SWITZERLAND, 1948

* * *

It was an all-too-short stay that threatened to turn his life around.

Not because he took a few ski lessons and—accident-prone as he was, and to the consternation of Betsy and Kerry—immediately chose to schuss down dangerous trails marked Expert. It was as though the chill air of the Alps buoyed him up from the rut of defeatism that only an abrasive, grinding Hollywood carves away on a daily basis. It made him consider that Europe, not California, could be the place for him and his family. He found himself in tune with the pace of a picturesque Swiss mountainside village, only just becoming a vacation spot for literary and musical artists. Gene became close with Irwin Shaw, the American author of *The Young Lions*, the famed World War II novel. Shaw introduced the Kellys to "the Kloster that counts"—creative people of talent, always a Gene and Betsy requirement in their social life.

He loved speaking French. He saw to it that Kerry's studies in the language had the benefit of local tutors. The close association with Shaw and other hard-working, hard-playing artists firmed up Gene's intention to be treated as a serious filmmaker. Skiing from village to village, enjoying delectable meals enhanced by the local wines, with newfound friends who respected Gene and his career, the holiday was grand—and over in a blink. But he would be back.

At the airport for the return trip, he remembered a fallout of luncheon gossip: Leonard Bernstein, in filling out a visa application, never wrote "conductor" or "pianist" or "teacher" or "composer," but simply "musician." In the same way he resolved hereafter to call himself, starkly, *filmmaker*. It somehow gave heft to his chances of doing *Cyrano* now that Dore Schary had recovered from his athletic misadventures and was back at work.

By this time, however, Schary was under the gun with his new responsibilities. The real leaders of MGM, financial men in the New York office with concerns about balance sheets and cash flow, mandated a renewed emphasis on the bottom line. In the postwar contraction of the moviegoing audience, *Cyrano* did not get the green light—even with a resurgent Gene Kelly as the star, even with *The Three Musketeers* doing famously at the box office, even with *The Pirate* now catching on as an exciting song-and-dance film after its initially mixed critical reception. Gene would have to put on his dancing shoes again.

The Kellys had barely unpacked their ski gear when Gene started on a new Arthur Freed musical, *Words and Music*, based on the life and song catalogs of Richard Rodgers and Lorenz Hart. Gene had been an admirer of Hart, now about five years deceased, and through his *Pal Joey* experience, he had a taste of what Richard Rodgers was made of. He gave out a silent prayer that the screenwriters could somehow put together a scenario bearing some semblance of reality.

It was not to be. Rodgers and his lawyers were known for maintaining a heavy-breathing overview of all the productions, live or filmed, in which Rodgers was involved. With his relentless Broadway activities, Rodgers had not the slightest intention of spending any length of time in Hollywood. He asked Freed to do him the favor of hiring his brother-in-law Ben Feiner, Jr., as his liaison. Aware of the composer's compulsion to control, Freed accepted the shoehorning of Feiner into the production team. Feiner was to be associate producer and credited with the script adaptation. He also affected the bizarre casting. The part of Rodgers was awarded to the handsome, pleasant actor Tom Drake, a straight-arrow, all-American type on a different planet from the composer's sour and finicky personality. Mickey Rooney, a five-times-married Irish-American was signed to be Hart, the gay, alcoholic Jewish lyricist.

Freed realized where the casting was taking the project. As a practical matter, he now decided there was only one way to produce *Words and Music*. He would rely again on a format that had succeeded many times when faced with the challenge of doing a "biopic" about lives that had some edgy aspects. Freed converted the project into an all-star revue. The cinematically transformed Rodgers and Hart served merely to tie together musical numbers that were presented as staged theatrical performances. The camera would be the eye of the audience.

Besides Drake and Rooney, the performers included Judy Garland, Lena Horne, June Allyson, Cyd Charisse, Mel Torme, Ann Sothern, and Perry Como. It was an all-star show, and there is no doubt that Gene stole it, doing an apache dance with Vera-Ellen. It was called "Slaughter on Tenth Avenue." It was and is a classic. Originally staged on Broadway in 1937, by the ballet choreographer George Balanchine, the number wove into the dance the complicated plot of the Rodgers and Hart show that surrounded it. It involved a young dancer who found himself having to hold the body of a dead girl to ward off a gangster's bullet. On its own it would have made no sense in the movie. Moreover, Gene was not comfortable with the gory concept of the original. He simplified the libretto, changing the story completely, and made it a self-contained ballet. Now a gangster and his moll are followed and shot dead in a sleazy Manhattan Hell's Kitchen saloon while doing a passionate Parisian-style Apache dance. Still a bloody ending, true, but bathed in lurid yellow and red lighting and climaxing a performance by Vera-Ellen and Gene, it is so suspenseful and exciting it holds up on the screen for a riveting ten minutes. It proved out what Gene had been arguing: Audiences will accept ballet on film, as long as the story is emotionally involving, not merely a glamorous interruption.

Gene gave the "Slaughter" number extra effort in every direction, which was always his hallmark. His dance with Vera-Ellen ends with the action of her being hit by a bullet. She falls to the bottom of the staircase, very close to the camera setup for the low-angle shot. The talented cinematographer Harry Stradling proposed the use of a 28-millimeter lens that would distort Vera-Ellen's face in a monstrous closeup for a shocking finale. Here again Gene was risking the wrath of Mayer, still on the MGM scene and determined to make the most of it, even with Schary bursting at the seams to take over. Mayer's mandate over the years had always been: "The ladies have to look pretty at all times, no matter what." By this time Freed had so much faith in Gene's constant reaching for moments to spark the film, he gave the special lens choice a go-ahead. "If worse comes to worst," he said, "we can always shoot it again."

They never shot it again. The studio was delighted. *Words and Music* was released on the last day of 1948 and became a welcome cash cow for MGM. Congratulations were passed all around, especially to Gene. Only Rodgers remained grumpy, possibly because Mickey Rooney's surprisingly sensitive characterization of Lorenz Hart made the lyricist more fascinating than Tom Drake's pallid version of himself.

Breaking the Kelly pattern of sporadic employment since coming to Hollywood, Mayer wanted Gene to go directly into his next film. Joe Pasternak was developing a story about two demobilized sailors who buy a surplus aircraft carrier from the Navy and convert it into a nightclub. Gene hated the idea. Again at the fade-in he would be in uniform, and he wanted to dissolve his connection in the public mind with the military once and for all. Even more, he disparaged Pasternak's project as "the sort of thing dreamed up ten years ago for Mickey Rooney and Judy Garland." And he wanted to stay with the more adventurous Arthur Freed unit.

In one of his many attempts to wear a writer's hat and craft an original play or film script, Gene had done an outline based on the life of Al Schacht, the retired baseball player–entertainer who had entertained fans with slapstick routines between innings and was often more popular than the teams. Gene's story was set in the early 1900s and, as usual in his literary attempts, he could not work out a satisfactory ending. He called on Stanley Donen to help him, and out of Gene's idea they cobbled a seven-page synopsis for a film entitled *Take Me Out to the Ball Game*.

Gene and Frank Sinatra would play two baseball players who, off-season, have starred on the vaudeville circuit for a number of years; when one spring arrives, they report as usual to their team's Florida training camp and discover that the owner of the ball club has passed away, willing the club to an heir, one K.C. Higgins. The snapper is that Higgins is a young, beautiful woman (and baseball aficionado) to be played, as stipulated in the Kelly–Donen outline, by Judy Garland. Freed bought the outline for the studio, paying $25,000—a huge amount of money for a sliver of an idea, especially one with an ending still a mystery despite Stanley's energetic efforts. Gene was delighted by the sale, saying: "I'll never forget the look on Stanley Donen's face when he heard about the sale. Though we split the fee, $12,500 for a couple of days' work was money from the gods, and we couldn't believe our luck."

The script collaboration was a long step forward in the tightening relationship between Gene and Stanley. On the surface it was an amiable and fruitful arrangement. But Gene had no real insight into the feelings that stirred his colleague:

a respect for Gene Kelly as a major talent, fractured by a bitter sense of being patronized and insufficiently appreciated for his own contributions. Stanley Donen was twelve years younger; to Gene, he was a drawling boy from the South, sometimes feckless and unambitious, but a periodic source of creative ideas. He was not a particularly proficient dancer, but he could come up with fresh approaches to choreography that Gene could build on. Gene respected Stanley's technical mastery of the motion-picture camera; in time, he thought, Stanley might qualify as a decent film director. Yet he also felt the younger man lacked a true spark, in both his work and personal relationships. He concluded that he—Gene Kelly—provided the passion that led to accomplishment, while Stanley was an intermittent source of problem-solving help.

And had a ga-ga crush on his wife, Betsy. To Gene, Stanley's recent marriage to Jeanne Coyne, the dancer from Pittsburgh whom Gene knew had always adored him, confirmed the younger's emotional immaturity and lack of judgment. It proved something essential if they were to continue to work together: that the boy from South Carolina was not remotely in Gene's class.

Somehow, it seemed important for Gene to register that comparison in a public way from time to time, and hurtfully to Stanley Donen, who could only rage in private. Of course, Gene, forever full of himself, had not the slightest sense of his collaborator's smoldering feelings.

If ever a film project at its inception looked like a sorry candidate for success, it was *Take Me Out to the Ball Game*. Mayer and the New York front office were surprised by Freed's decision to buy the script. In Paris, Milan, and Tokyo, moviegoers did not know a ball from a strike and probably thought a stolen base was something the police should investigate. The subject, baseball, completely ignored the foreign market, which usually made the difference between profit and loss for a released American film. Freed nevertheless pushed on, bringing aboard veteran writers Harry Tugend and George Wells to flesh out a script from the frail outline. The much-admired team of Betty Comden and Adolph Green were called in to prepare some sassy lyrics to the music of Roger Edens.

The conundrum of how to end the story, even as production started, still bothered Gene, not as much as the casting difficulties, which proved to be horrendous and led to temper tantrums and conflicts. Wanted by Freed for the lead role of the new owner of the ball club, Garland continued to be dogged by health problems which defied all sorts of pharmaceuticals. She had barely been able to do her two numbers in *Words and Music*; one of these, "Johnny One Note," had to be shot after the rest of the picture was completed. Once it was clear that Garland could not arrive at a morning call undrugged, Freed engaged Esther Williams, the former Olympic swimmer, as a replacement. Impatient as ever with performers he regarded as talentless, Gene remarked sullenly: "Wet she's a star, dry she ain't." But he was gratified to be paired with Sinatra again, and knowing that Freed was readying the blockbuster *On the Town* for his next project, for once he decided to play the good soldier and not go public with his complaints.

Williams proved no shrinking violet. While Gene's judgment of her acting abilities was on the mark, she was an impressive physical specimen, statuesque in and out of the water and taller than her male co-stars. With the exception of Gene, she was the best athlete on the set. And, with a mean mouth, she was no slacker when it came to passing out insults. She soon made it known around the studio that playing intimate scenes with Kelly or Sinatra gave her a severe case of scoliosis from constantly leaning over to match their diminutive height. Further, she was convinced that Stanley Donen, of all people, "didn't respect her acting." She complained to Freed, who immediately ordered him to make a public denial. But Donen took a deep breath and refused, saying: "I can't do that, Arthur. She's absolutely right."

With so many cross-currents of suspicion and animosity, the production only staggered on. Williams was now constantly bypassing Freed to complain to Mayer directly (she had been a favorite of the MGM head ever since she had been plucked from Billy Rose's "Aquacade," and Gene guessed why: Esther was the name of Mayer's revered mother).

Through the sweltering summer of 1948, Sinatra, too, was a cause for front-office headaches. He continued to fight the need for rehearsals and would simply not attend when the mood struck him. The major problem, however, was the director. Busby Berkeley had been Freed's surprising choice for that all-important responsibility. Five years before, Freed had caught Berkeley tippling on the set of *Girl Crazy* and fired him at once. Now Berkeley had gone through an AA program and the producer, essentially a caring person and eager to salve his own guilt feelings, gave the aging director one last chance.

Unhappily, in the maelstrom of guiding a cast of egotistical malcontents through a scenario potholed with nonsense, Berkeley was not up to the task. When there was no music or dance, he was nowhere. To make matters worse, in contrast to their last experience together in *For Me and My Gal*, Gene was far along in his own conceptions of film choreography and considered Berkeley's work mindless, overblown, and ridiculously out-of-date. He could no longer in good conscience support Berkeley's creative decisions. His temper flared.

Betty Garrett later reported how, on one occasion, Berkeley wanted a panoramic overhead view, a throwback to his style in the golden days of Dick Powell–Ruby Keeler musicals. Not satisfied with the scope of the master shot, he scolded George Folsey, his cameraman: "Back . . . back . . . take the camera back, Folsey!" It was obvious to Gene that the shot would be so long and wide that the action of the two actors within the frame would be lost. "Yeah, back to 1930!" he said, not quite holding it under his breath.

Williams chimed in with her own complaints. She was not a Berkeley admirer, either, and was convinced the director did not pay enough attention to safety factors: "He doesn't believe in using stunt doubles. He expects me to plunge from a ring suspended high over the water into a small circle of kicking swimmers in the water. It's dangerous, and Berkeley doesn't give a damn!"

With the two stars weighing in heavily against him, Berkeley was now finally encouraged by Freed to quit. The excuse was "exhaustion." He was never again to direct a major musical, leaving it to Gene and Donen, at first together and then separately, to fill the gap. This they now did with the direction of *Take Me Out to the Ball Game*. Finally, they had to face the problem that had been there from the beginning: the ending. There were late-night meetings, bull sessions, story conferences galore, but nothing suitable presented itself. The writers, Tugend and Wells, kept swinging and striking out. The moment of truth was approaching fast; the final scene remained to be shot, and then the actors would scatter to other commitments. Freed cajoled, Mayer screamed.

And Gene decided: The way to end the bloody thing is to end it. Accordingly, in one of the most shameless cop-outs in the history of American cinema, the four principals were brought on camera to sing a specially prepared Comden and Green lyric which tidied up the loose ends of a meandering story:

> *The love scene must be played out*
> *Before the final fade-out.*
> *Sinatra gets Garrett,*
> *Kelly gets Williams,*
> *For that's the plot the author wrote.*
> *So we'll turn this duet*
> *Into a quartet*
> *And end it on a happy note.*

Which it did for all concerned, except Busby Berkeley. *Take Me Out to the Ball Game* made a substantial profit, which cemented Freed's standing at MGM. The producer was so appreciative of Gene's dances and Sinatra's songs and their appealing bonhomie that he vowed to have them together again in his next picture, the hoped-for hit *On the Town*. And the Kelly–Donen rescue of Berkeley brought them the assignment as co-directors of *On the Town* (to be credited this time; they had refused any directing credit on the baseball picture, leaving Berkeley to go out in style). Gene, Sinatra, Garrett, and Jules Munshin, the comedian first-baseman in *Take Me Out to the Ball Game* would go before the cameras in March of 1949.

Only Stanley Donen had second thoughts. He was wary about remaining, professionally, a mere satellite in the orbit of the glittering Gene Kelly, a jack-of-all-trades assistant and, in a personal sphere, a young man trying to protect his marriage to Jeanne Coyne. But in the closing days of 1948, he had no other options. For the present, the younger man decided, he would be helpful and await his opportunity to break away from Gene's domination. His balanced judgment was his strongest mental quality.

Gene was no stranger to the strange history of *On the Town* and was, accordingly, surprised that MGM wanted to produce it now. Early in 1944, even before the musical had opened on Broadway, he had seen the notice in *Variety* that MGM had paid $250,000 for the motion-picture rights. It was one of the first preproduction movie sales of a stage property ever to be made. Around Christmas of 1944, when Gene saw the show in New York, at the Adelphi Theater, he was both enchanted and grudgingly impressed with the perspicacity of L.B. Mayer.

Now, however, almost five years had gone by with the studio merely sitting on the property, and instead it had produced *Anchors Aweigh* as the MGM wartime morale-booster. Gene had always been puzzled that Mayer had never insisted on making good his investment in the show. It became another of many irritants peppering his complicated attitude toward his boss, especially when he heard that at the performance Mayer had attended at the Adelphi he was offended by the show's "Communistic and smutty" tinge and racially mixed cast. Now, Gene was certain, the persuasive talents of Freed, who had originally recommended the purchase of the movie rights, had finally won over Mayer. With Sinatra and Gene (or, as he preferred, Gene and Sinatra) paired for the third time, *On the Town* showed every promise of a major hit, and the project was green-lighted. True, after *Anchors Aweigh*, he and Sinatra had sworn never to put on sailor suits again, but this opportunity to be a real triple-threat—star, director, choreographer—was too much to resist.

The story involved three sailors blessed with a twenty-four-hour leave in Manhattan. Their mission: to meet women. Two of them quickly fulfill the mission, while the third spots a photograph of a beauty-contest winner in the subway, then persuades his friends to help him find her. Gene is the determined searcher, Munshin somehow appeals to Ann Miller, a tap-dancing anthropologist he meets at a museum, and Sinatra, again cast emphatically against type, is the innocent with females, especially aggressive ones like the lusting cab driver, Betty Garrett. She has a yen for him and serves literally as the vehicle to take the trio on the town.

What story there is to *On the Town* is slight, even silly, but it's always on the move and saturated with song-and-dance numbers from the moment the three gobs come off their destroyer. The result is a joyous tour of New York City, perfectly catching the can-do optimism of the immediate postwar period. From his first moments on the assignment, Gene was determined to create a film wrenched free of the limitations of the Hollywood studio. He said:

> It was only in *On the Town* that we tried something entirely new
> in the musical film. Live people get off a real ship in the Brooklyn
> Navy Yard [a dock Gene knew well from his own naval service]. . . .
> We did a lot of quick cutting—we'd be on the top of Radio City
> and then on the bottom—we'd cut from Mulberry Street to Third
> Avenue—and so the dissolve went out of style. This was one of the
> things that changed the history of musicals more than anything.

When Gene and Stanley appeared on the set for the first day of shooting, as a joke they both came in dressed in cliché movie-director style, à la Cecil B. DeMille: jaunty caps, dark sunglasses, riding jodhpurs, each carrying old-style megaphones. It drew a laugh. Despite their sporty arrival, they knew that *On the Town* would not be a jolly sidesaddle ride through Griffith Park; ahead loomed an obstacle course with each difficulty topping the last—the essence of any movie-making that tries for something unique and memorable.

To start with, the Breen office, the censoring body for the motion-picture industry, was concerned that the script pushed the propriety envelope a bit too far. When the script and songs were submitted for approval, the directive came back swiftly:

> Regarding the songs:
> (1) "New York, New York": "It's a helluva town" is unacceptable.
> (2) "Prehistoric Man":
>> "Lots of guys are hot for me" is unacceptable.
>> "Libido—I love that libido" is unacceptable.
>> "They sat all the day just beating their tom-toms" is unacceptable.

Actually, headaches about the songs started even before the submissions to the Breen office. Freed never had liked the original score for the stage show composed by the already-famous Leonard Bernstein. He considered Bernstein's style too avant-garde for the cinema audience. Freed assigned Roger Edens to write some replacements. Thirty years later, Bernstein was still seething about the experience:

> Roger Edens, an associate producer who fancied himself a composer, decided to fit six of his own songs into the film, including one called "On the Town." I was young and naive, of course, but the fact remains that there are six songs in that picture which are not good and are not by me, yet people assume I wrote them. I resent that.

Bernstein was so traumatized by the rejection that he was to accept only one composing assignment in Hollywood during his prolific career: the score for *On the Waterfront*.

Anxious to get moving on the project, Gene was quick to sign off on Eden's work, considering it first-rate and entirely in harmony with his own ideas. He felt the same way about the final script by Comden and Green. He was especially pleased with the device they had come up with to show the passing of time—the sailor trio's precious twenty-four-hour furlough: a time bulletin going across the bottom of the screen in the style of the Times Square news "zipper." Culled from the bestselling book *USA*, by John Dos Passos, a manifestation of the Kelly dictum to "steal only from the best."

Freed backed Gene's request for at least a month's rehearsal time before shooting. The entire production went into rehearsal February 21, 1949; the actual shooting began on March 28. Gene argued hard for the opportunity to shoot the entire film in New York City. From the beginning there was executive opposition to the idea of filming sequences involving the cast in Manhattan. Mayer and his immediate group could not visualize the effect Gene and Stanley were after. They thought the audience would find the combination of the real and the unreal confusing. Why not do it on the back lot, like everybody else? As reinforcement for his point of view, Mayer tapped J. J. Cohn, a longtime executive in charge of estimating budgets and ratifying shooting schedules. Cohn was already famous for his declaration: "A rock is a rock. A tree is a tree. Shoot it in Griffith Park!"

Cohn lurched in with his opinion, absolutely true to form. But with Freed running interference for him, Gene was allowed five days of location shooting in New York, sound and picture, including what was to be the opening and closing of the film.

The principal shooting in California proceeded on schedule, thanks largely to the eighteen-hour days put in by Gene and Stanley. They rehearsed the dancers in two adjacent halls, moving back and forth from one to the other as Stanley took Gene's place alongside the cinematographer when Gene had to participate in the number. Betsy hardly saw Gene at home, and weeds grew on the volleyball court. Jeanne Coyne wondered why she had married a man who was always missing and divorced Stanley. Weekends were for working, too. It was as if the two directors—ambitious and driven, though with vastly different ways of showing it—realized that On the Town could be the turning point in their careers.

Sinatra tortured them with his expected lackadaisical attitude toward rehearsals. To Gene, it didn't really matter with Sinatra's songs—which were sublime, he thought—but he was determined to elevate the quality of the crooner's dancing. He practically imprisoned Sinatra to gain time to brush up the simple moves he required and was pleased when Sinatra applied himself, learning the steps with good will and even a mounting enthusiasm. Gene felt his efforts with Sinatra paid off. "Frank improved as a dancer when I took his hands off the mike, so to speak," he said later.

Sinatra's gradual improvement in attitude reflected the cooperation received by the co-directors. They were efficient and creative, gaining the respect of the specialists who were needed. One morning the heads of the special effects and sculpture departments were told by Gene: "I know you guys are busy, but this won't take up much of your time. We need a dinosaur resembling the Tyrannosaurus Rex. Fifteen feet high or so, forty feet long, and twenty-five feet wide."

"A dinosaur . . . okay," said the expressionless pair, taking notes.

"And, of course, the dinosaur must be collapsible so we can do retakes when Jules Munshin kicks the damn thing over by accident."

"No problem."

When Gene was ready to direct the scene, there it was, bulking resplendent on the set, the exhibition room of a museum with the perfect specimen of the dinosaur, circa 6000 B.C. In constructing the skeleton and inventing the mechanism for its collapse, the talented duo with their staffs, famed throughout Culver City for their ingenuity, used corrugated paper in big cubes and carved each vertebra, with buzz saws. To connect 283 pieces, wire was then inserted that would serve both as a "ripcord" for the collapse and for a restoration of the structure, if a retake was needed—as was most likely, given Gene's passion for perfection.

Came the big moment. On Gene's cue, Munshin, ogling the leggy Ann Miller, stumbled against the dinosaur as called for by the script. Down it came in a tumbled, incoherent mass. Everybody looked at Gene, especially the crew prepared to raise the huge contraption for the second take.

"Wonderful!" exclaimed Gene. "Cut and print!"

A memorandum was received then from Arthur Freed:

> Dear Gene & Stanley:
>
> I just ran the cut numbers of On the Town and they were the greatest and most inspiring works I have seen since I have been making moving pictures. Pressburger and Powell did pretty well with Red Shoes, their ballet film. But that pair can't shine your shoes—red, white or blue.
>
> Much love from your proud producer.
>
> Arthur

The last nonmusical production sequence of the California shooting involved Jules Munshin hanging from a ledge of the Empire State Building. It was a creation on a par with Tyrannosaurus Rex. Given the five-day limit on the location shooting in New York, Gene and Stanley decided that what was needed was a mock-up of the skyscraper's roof deck in the center of Esther Williams's swimming pool on Stage 30. There was another urgent reason for the mock-up: Munshin had a fear of heights so bad he actually had a history of fainting in upward-moving elevators. Contract or no contract, he could not possibly cavort on the actual windswept observation deck of the Empire State Building. But by putting the fabricated roof into the 10-foot-deep pool, a set was created which rose 45 feet into the air. Surrounding it on three sides was a 250-foot-wide by 60-foot-high background, with the skyline of New York (facing north) painted on it: Manhattan with Central Park, the East River and the Hudson, and beyond, stretching into the distance, was the George Washington Bridge. Craftsmen had cut out tiny windows with lights behind them, and miniature neon signs flashed on the streets. Putting the observation deck into the pool enabled the camera to shoot upward for the required shot of Munshin—panicked, legs threshing wildly—against the sky.

Buoyed by Freed's constant support, on May 5, when the principal photography, with the exception of Gene's and Vera-Ellen's ballet, was "in the can," all six stars and the crew left for New York.

From the moment Gene, Sinatra, and Munshin came off the destroyer in the Brooklyn Navy Yard, it was a joyous tour of the city. "The Bronx is up and the Battery's down" went the Comden and Green lyric, and so did the ebullient coverage of the three sailors tasting their first experience of the metropolis: from the subway to a double-decker bus to the roofs of skyscrapers (hanging on to the quivering Munshin); the Statue of Liberty; Central Park; Rockefeller Center; Greenwich Village . . . it was the first musical to be shot on the streets of New York in the actual places named in the plot—the sights tourists yearn to see. The camera crew was incredibly productive, even though on two of the five days the weather was cloudy and unsettled, making filming continuity impossible; no work could be done and Gene feared a phone call from Mayer's office breaking off "the experiment" and ordering everybody back to California.

The difficulties were monumental, as Gene told his English biographer:

"We had to 'steal' and 'cheat' every shot and somehow keep our cameras hidden from the passersby who would only delay us further and crowd around if they knew a picture was being made."

Especially in areas with substantial Italian-American populations, such as lower Greenwich Village, the word had spread that "Sinatra's here!" Crowds surged past police lines to touch the idol of the bobby-soxers and beg him for autographs, spoiling many shots by encroaching on the camera's view. For a retrospective interview in *American Film* magazine, in 1979, Gene recalled vividly the whirlwind effort to make every New York moment count:

> The first stumbling block was Frank Sinatra. Those were his famous days, and he was as hard to hide as the Statue of Liberty. He was always being mobbed. To get around that problem, we decided not to hire any limousines. Now that was unheard of. The studios always gave the stars and the directors limousines when they were on location. Instead we hired Yellow taxis. We would push Sinatra on the floor of the taxi, and I'd get on top of him and Jules Munshin would get on top of me so that the taxi would seem empty. Munshin and I were stronger than Sinatra and so we always made him the low man in the taxi. No, he didn't like that.

On the preceding night, Stanley and Gene would always line up the shot. They hid the camera in a station wagon. Hal Rossen, the cinematographer, and his assistant would lie down inside on their bellies. They would rehearse the coverage until the camera move was satisfactory for the next morning.

> When I jumped out of the taxi I'd give a loud whistle, the station wagon would start moving and we'd follow. I had a stopwatch in my pocket. I'd say, "And-a-one, and-a-two, and-a-three, and-a-four . . ." then we'd sing, "New York, New York . . ." and that's the way we shot all that stuff. We never had any protection and we did the whole thing in five days."

Not quite true. To Gene's frustration they never did shoot the closing fade-out as he'd planned it. It began with a repeat of the film's opening, a dockworker, barely awake as he reports for his shift, singing "I feel like I'm not out of bed yet." A Navy destroyer moored at the dock disgorges a horde of eager sailors as they start their furlough with the song "New York, New York." Donen was set up with the cinematographer on a giant crane for the master shot of the action, both for the opening and the final fade-out. Since destroyers are not easy to come by, the plan was for the same destroyer to immediately ready itself for departure.

For the film's ending, the six principals arrived. The three girls kiss the three gobs goodbye, and all the sailors board ship. Donen's camera pulls back for a wide master shot of the destroyer pulling away. Final fade-out.

However, the weather was foggy and drizzling when they first tried to shoot the scene. Gene had to use all his contacts with the Navy to have the destroyer for another day and another try.

But good luck still eluded the co-directors. Sinatra, staying at an apartment in Manhattan, did not receive his wake-up call and failed to arrive on time. The departure of the destroyer from the pier took much longer than the filming landlubbers had anticipated; Gene was given the wrong information and his walkie-talkie connection with his men on the towering crane crackled, popped, and cut off before he could inform Stanley. Then dark clouds rolled in for a differently emphasized THE END than the one they were going for. The ending to be in the release prints of On the Town was reconstituted jumpily on a sound stage after the film crew returned to the West Coast on May 23. Gene and Stanley both hated it.

The working styles of the co-directors meshed well enough, but Stanley, whose placid exterior hid a fragile sensitivity, continued to be bothered by Gene's takeover attitude. Early on, when he had complained about it to his former wife, Jeanne Coyne, he had been disturbed by the almost frantic way she rallied to Gene's defense. He knew she idolized Gene; he assumed they were having an affair. But he had the internal strength to "compartmentalize" his personal problems. He gave his best to On the Town and the final result reflected his many contributions. Gene told Clive Hirschhorn: "If it hadn't been for Stanley, who was still considered by the studio to be my whipping-boy, I don't know how I would have managed. He alone knew what I was after in those opening scenes of On the Town and what I wanted to achieve in the picture as a whole."

Still to do was Gene's ballet with Vera-Ellen, titled "A Day in New York," a rendition of a sailor's chase after the elusive Miss Subways. In essence it was a balletic repeat of the overall story of the film, and he and Stanley argued about its inclusion. His colleague felt that Gene went on too long with his ballet material, slowing the film's pace. But Gene called the shots and Stanley gave way.

Neither the lackluster ending nor Gene's overshadowing of Stanley affected the ultimate success of On the Town. On its first national release the box-office returns reached $4,500,000, more than three times the film's budget. In New York, where it was booked at Radio City Music Hall, the Herald Tribune reported a crowd estimated by police at 10,000 ticket-buyers. They lined up to see the movie, forming two files stretching for seven city blocks. It was an all-time record for the famous theater. Gene summed up the picture's impact at the time:

> It was only in On the Town that we tried something entirely new in the musical film. Live people get off a real ship in the Brooklyn Navy Yard and sing and dance down New York City. . . . this was one of the things that changed the history of musicals more than anything.

The audience proved it would follow Gene Kelly anywhere. Especially down familiar streets and into a dance:

To make a musical in which people don't just say "I love you" and burst into song was real hard work. But we did it. And once I had broken the ice and *On the Town* had become a hit, Metro let me do pretty much what I liked.

For the next three years or so, he was right. He could do nothing wrong. His touch was golden—on the screen. His personal life was something else again.

A clip from An American in Paris *is on the screen now, the "I Got Rhythm" number, best thing he has ever done with kids. The song itself was used goods. It had already appeared in two films—*Girl Crazy *and* Rhapsody in Blue—*and the challenge was, as always, to do the damn thing in a fresh way. Watching it now for the millionth time, he still feels he filled the bill, teaching those Paris boys and girls (okay, from Central Casting) some easy moves like the time-step, the shim-sham, and the Charleston.*

The air seems to ripple with the pleasure of the audience, which has to be thinking: This Gene guy, he has a way with the kids, all right. (But not with the ladies, some of the Gene-haters here tonight might respond.)

The number ends with his "C'est tout," that's all, and the lights of the ballroom come up to find Shirley at the mike. He's not looking at the stage, but at where his three kids are sitting. There's Kerry (whom Betsy didn't want to name Bridget), and Bridget (whose mother okayed the name he still wanted), and Tim (who saved his life in the fire that destroyed everything). Three class acts. But if he could do it over again, he'd give his off-screen kids the energy and care he gave to those on-screen. At least take the time to do the shim-sham with them once in a while! Easier said than done. Those were eighteen-hour days in the coils of Culver City.

Dance is a butterfly profession. A tiny window of time to attain perfection. When On the Town *was released, he was thirty-eight, close to forty. Was there—is there—any alternative, except to hurry, hurry?*

LOS ANGELES, 1950

* * *

With the completion of *On the Town* Gene had counted on spending some time with Betsy and Kerry, perhaps a return to Europe for an extended stay. But a vacation was not in the scheme of things for him. MGM was determined to keep its contract players busy, especially those at a salary level of $2,500 a week. When his next project was announced, his first reaction was one of irritation, stemming from his ever-present competitive instincts: It was a role first offered to Robert Taylor, who had turned it down. Bad enough a bruised ego as a second choice; what made it worse was picking up something discarded by somebody he detested.

The rancor went both ways. The two actors were very cool to each other when they crossed paths at the studio. In the commissary they never took seats at the same table. Indeed, knowing the other was already there was reason to go elsewhere for lunch. Gene's contempt for Taylor's behavior during the HUAC Washington hearings had not diminished. What made him finally decide to take the role was his conviction that Taylor lacked the acting skills to handle it and had backed off for that reason.

The offered film project was a low-budget Mafia thriller titled *The Black Hand*, which centered on the shady activities of Johnny Columbo, a tough gangleader working his way up in the Mob's hierarchy. It was intended as a down-and-dirty programmer with a shooting schedule of a mere three weeks. Gene knew he was in good hands with Richard Thorpe, the director, and the script by Luther Davis offered some spirited scenes.

Gene was determined to relax and had fun working with Jack Dawn, head of the makeup department. The challenge was to make him look more convincingly Italian and, in the end, just curling his hair, sporting a bow-tie and a fedora, and snarling a few guttural Italian insults did the trick. Luther Davis remembers that he fit in very well with a cast that was entirely ethnically Italian. He was careful to moderate his transformation and fought the temptation to color the role excessively, especially during his menacing moments, which were plentiful. He avoided carica-ture and came through as tough and confident. Thorpe was happy with his work.

Gene always kept close track of the box-office records of his films. Over the years *The Black Hand* took in much more money than had been anticipated. Gene was given the credit and always believed he deserved it. The experience sparked his desire once again to try for dramatic, nonmusical roles. Producer Joe Pasternak had the misfortune of approaching Gene at this time and proposing a musical project. Based on an original screenplay that Gene felt was not very original, *Summer Stock* was at least ten years late, in his view. It would have been perfect for Mickey Rooney and Judy Garland in their old "Hey, let's put on a show" days.

Gene was upset by the thought of retreating to tired, overused material after the trail-blazing *On the Town*. Pasternak was living up to his Hollywood reputation, which plastered him with the professional credo "If at first you succeed, try again." Gene had no wish to make waves with a powerful producer at Metro who was close to Mayer, but he resolved now to be firm—like Robert Taylor, only for more valid reasons—and decline the role. He tried to talk Pasternak away from choosing him for *Summer Stock* but, for the producer, casting Gene made good sense. Mickey Rooney was no longer a suitable box-office attraction. "And Judy—well, you know," Pasternak shrugged.

No response was needed from Gene. Everybody knew about Garland's health problems. Her last two film experiences had been expensive fiascos for the studio. Set to play opposite Fred Astaire in *The Barkleys of Broadway* she took sick just before the start of production. Ginger Rogers had to replace her. The specialist sent by the studio to Garland's home to verify her condition, for legal reasons, had declared the problem "purely mental." When she recovered, the studio was happy to cast her in the lead of *Annie Get Your Gun*. Shooting started. So did the pattern of last-minute cancellations, excuses, crying jags. The repeated absenteeism forced the studio to fire her after three weeks. She was placed under suspension, and Betty Hutton was brought in to replace her.

Hollywood wrote Judy Garland off. No one would cast her now until she proved she could function through an entire grueling shooting schedule. The last time she had come to a Kelly party she appeared puffy and overweight. When coaxed to sing, she went at it so disjointedly, her vibrato out of control, that—always the best judge of her own performance—she broke off and started to cry, then fled the house. That night Gene had told Betsy that Judy's career was history.

Apparently everybody thought so except Louis B. Mayer. In reviewing Pasternak's tentative casting for *Summer Stock*, the Metro head surprised the producer by questioning why Garland had been bypassed. He was not satisfied with his underling's doomsday catalog of her recent disasters, which had cost Metro hundreds of thousands of dollars in reshooting costs. "I know all that," snapped Mayer. "Judy Garland has made this studio a fortune in the good days. And the least we can do is give her one more chance. If you stop production now, it'll finish her."

It was incredible that MGM would take a chance on the troubled star again. Mayer's decision rattled Gene's long-held conviction the studio head was the devil incarnate. He knew Mayer felt some responsibility for Garland's condition, and *Summer Stock* was, at least in part, a well-meant bid to help her onto her feet again. In his fatherly, sentimental, almost tearful way, Mayer must have felt guilty for the careless way MGM had inflicted a torrent of drugs on the pliant young star in the old days, to keep her working and the crowds lined up at the box offices. By a long shot, Garland was not the only misused actress in Hollywood, and Mayer's concern for her, late but essential, was exceptional. And if Mayer was doing the decent thing, how could Gene do anything less?

Gene telephoned Pasternak, impelled by the twin stabs of recollection, like movie flashbacks, that always bonded him to Judy: riding in a carriage through Central Park at night talking about films they could make together, and hearing her buoyant laughter, which eased the mood on the set, as he missed his marks and stumbled through the first shooting days of *For Me and My Gal*. He actually talked himself into the part of Joe Ross, head of an off-Broadway troupe which finds its way to a New England farm owned by Jane (Garland's role) and, of course, they "put on a show."

Even though Gene had told Charles Walters, the director, that the script was "a piece of crap," he would go all-out. The last thing she needed (the same for him, for that matter) was a flop. But with his participation perhaps the project could be lifted—and her with it—to a level that was at least satisfactory and she could continue her career. After all, she was a genuine talent, and so was he; perhaps a certain synergy would propel *Summer Stock* out of the ranks of the ordinary. Here was a challenge that was like being in a volleyball game with the score against you—but the ball is in your hands.

Gene and Walters were immediately put to the test by Judy's problems. When shooting started, her psychiatrist was at the studio every day. After every take, the two of them would disappear into her dressing trailer. It was the trauma of *The Pirate* set reincarnated; *Summer Stock* quickly fell behind schedule. During the line rehearsals with Judy, Gene would hold her left arm and Walters would take her right arm, and between them they would maintain her on her feet. Years later, when the revelations could do no more harm to the actress's reputation, Walters described their difficulties:

> Emotionally she was at her lowest ebb. Physically she was pretty unsure of herself as well. There were even times when we had to nail the scenery down and provide her with supports so she wouldn't fall over. Once, I remember, she had to walk up a few steps and she couldn't do it. . . . She'd call us around two or three o'clock in the morning to tell us she didn't think she was going to be able to come in for work the next day, and would I please try to shoot around her. She had always been a neurotic and insecure performer, but never as bad as this.

Pasternak, normally a jovial sort, was horrified at the way *Summer Stock* was falling deeper and deeper behind schedule. Several times he went to Mayer pleading for the production to be shut down and started anew with a replacement for Garland. Mayer would have none of it.

The production lurched on in spasms of progress. Several of the dancers had to leave the film, committed to other jobs. Astonishingly, Garland would insist on a farewell party, and, despite all her absences, she would always appear and find her way to the piano. She delighted the parting dancers and singers with a performance that could go on for many hours. For the first time, Gene realized her appeal with the homosexuals among the chorus; somehow she provided a secret language of emotion that reached gay men. Unfailingly, when the camera wasn't turning, she was magnificent.

Gene faced the challenge of shepherding her through the dances they were to do as a team, the first being "A Portland Fancy." Gene thought, overweight as she was, she came through appealingly. In spite of his difficulties, he was cheered by his own inner certainty that the tenderness and feeling of their relationship was flowing on to the film. He felt the fit of their balanced talents, much as did the *New Yorker*'s Pauline Kael when the film was unveiled to the public: "She joined her odd and undervalued cakewalker's prance to his large-spirited hoofing, and he joined his odd, light, high voice to her sweet deep one. . . . They could really sing together. There was a vulnerability both Gene and Judy brought out in each other and which neither had with anyone else."

But the best numbers in *Summer Stock* are not when the two dance together. It might have been due to the strange difficulty Gene encountered when working closely with his co-star. There was a peculiar odor coming from her that really bothered him. It smelled like formaldehyde. At first, he resolved not to say anything about it. But when the condition persisted he became concerned that she was addicted to drugs and was hiding a health problem. He was about to approach her psychiatrist on the set when, one night at a Kelly party, Dore Schary took him aside:

"It's not a very gentlemanly thing to talk about, Gene—but have you noticed . . . when you're dancing with Judy . . . sort of a . . ." And Schary hesitated, embarrassed about going on.

"Yeah, the smell, Dore. Something . . . well, like formaldehyde."

"There've been complaints. Makeup, a couple of the female dancers, others in the cast. You've been a gentleman, Gene."

"To hell with that! What is it, anyway?"

Schary had called Garland into his office and talked to her "in a fatherly way" about this and that, all the time finding reasons to get close enough to sniff. It was admiring an earring that finally made it possible. "I got a whiff of the stuff," he told Gene, "and immediately checked with her specialists in Boston." (More than once, Mayer had financed medical checkups, as well as stays in a sanitarium in New England for his ailing actress.) "It's actually paraldehyde, a drug used to bring drunkards out of their deep comas or delirium tremens. Gene, can you cope with it?"

"Jesus. If that poor kid can, I can."

Summer Stock reflected the weakness of the story and the tensions of the production. Toward the last shooting days Gene knew the finished film would not be at the level of his best work. It was a thought that pained him. He decided to choreograph and perform a highly original solo number before Pasternak consigned the footage to the editing department.

Gene approached the creative challenge as he always did, with a writer's perspective. Since the story's location is Jane's farm, is it not plausible for Jane to drift away from the hubbub of show performers, seeking the solitude of the barn which will serve as their theater only a few nights later? Joe finds her there and it is apparent to both of them that each is attracted to the other. What starts as small talk becomes warm talk as he explains how the show's music and dance will create magical moments onstage. What better demonstration than to sing "You Wonderful You," which draws them even closer and into a kiss? All at once, stunned by her disloyalty to her own fiancé and to her sister, Joe's girlfriend, she breaks away, leaving him alone.

The camera pulls back as he remains pensive. As though to hold onto the moment with Jane, he starts to quietly hum a reprise of "You Wonderful You," which eases him into a solitary dance. There is no instrumental music, only his soft voice—and the tap and slide of his quicksilver feet finding a creaky floorboard and a sheet of newspaper on the floor. The setting may be forlorn, but the glow and promise of Jane fill his heart as his whispery song ends. Now love is the music, his dance intensifies, and the loose floorboard resonates again and again, like a heartbeat, and the tearing of the news sheet punctuates the gathering emotion.

In this way Gene Kelly creates a libretto for dance out of the valid sights and sounds of his immediate surroundings. Buoyed now by a soaring musical score, he jumps onto a riser where the remainder of the newspaper rests, tears off another sheet, plays with it, skates on it, suddenly as a toreador challenges a bull with it, and then lets it flutter to the floor for his feet to bisect, *rripp* . . ., this way and that way. Then, as a printed item catches his eye, he picks up what is left of the paper and exits while reading-the floorboard wailing out a final goodbye, until showtime.

The dance turned out to be one of the breakthrough numbers of Gene's career. And what pleased him most was that in no way could it be duplicated as well in a stage performance. It was made uniquely for movies, and that was exactly what he wanted.

The summer of 1950 came hard upon the completion of *Summer Stock*. It was a torrid July day in the MGM commissary. If no culinary paradise, at least the place was a welcome refuge from the heat. Famous faces here were as common as ketchup bottles, so it was considered gauche and unprofessional to make a fuss about the celebrity status of anyone. But with the entrance of Arthur Freed and Vincente Minnelli, producer and director, respectively, of the current production of *An American in Paris*, there was a stir of recognition caused by their guest for lunch, a small, older gentleman in an un-Californian dark suit. He was Irving Berlin.

The waitress had barely turned away with their order when Freed removed a set of drawings from a portfolio. These were renditions by art director Irene Sharaff of the sets and costumes for the Gene Kelly ballet that was to conclude Freed's new picture. Freed and Minnelli were quite tense and, of course, made every effort to appear casual with Berlin. They knew the noted songwriter had access to the top echelon of MGM executives, Mayer and Schary in California, and Joseph Schenk in New York. A few words of praise from the taciturn Berlin would go a long way in easing the pressures on them. It was no secret that, at the highest level of the company, there were worries about *An American in Paris*, its concept and, primarily, its cost. And what was ballooning the dollar amount to an unprecedented level was the ballet.

Berlin did not appear very interested in the sketches. The frown across his face was unsettling. "Am I to understand," he asked, "that you fellows are going to end this picture with a seventeen-minute ballet and that's it? No dialogue? No singing? Nothing?"

Both his listeners nodded, wary of what was coming next.

"Well, I hope you know what you're doing."

Gloom settled over his hosts at the table. If only Gene had never mentioned to Freed his idea for a story about an ex-GI, an aspiring painter who decides to remain in Paris after the war! Freed had taken to the concept because one night in the late 1940s he had been at a concert featuring the music of the late George Gershwin. The composer's *An American in Paris* had evoked romantic memories of that city for him. At the intermission of the concert he ran into George's brother, Ira, the well-known lyricist who was a trustee of the Gershwin estate. Without further ado he asked Ira if MGM could buy the title of the Gershwin tone-poem he had so much enjoyed. Ira agreed, provided that if any film with that title were actually produced, all the music in it would have to be by George and Ira Gershwin. To Freed, that was certainly no hardship; that was a coup, one of those rare opportunities to produce a musical of distinction.

The prominent writer-lyricist Alan Jay Lerner was brought in to work up the scenario while Gene, Minnelli, and music director Saul Chaplin pored over the extensive Gershwin catalogue, deciding what songs to include in the picture. Their choices passed on to Lerner, who had the difficult task of threading them into his script with appropriate lead-ins. He prepared a serviceable screenplay fleshing out Gene's ideas. The expatriate artist, Jerry Mulligan, pursues both art and romance simultaneously. He is being pursued by a wealthy American woman, a patron of the arts, who helps him financially and serves as his agent. The essential complication is provided by a pretty French girl, a clerk in a Paris parfumerie, with whom Jerry falls in love. She has no money and no connections beyond the older man she lives with, a famous song-and-dance performer who has finally decided to marry her.

It was surely not a script that taxed Lerner's imagination, but it was what Gene wanted: a framework that allowed him room for his creative input. He turned immediately to the challenge of casting.

In later years Gene took the credit for finding and signing Leslie Caron. He claimed that two years prior to his involvement with *An American in Paris* he had enjoyed the performance of a young ballet dancer with the Roland Petit company. During their discussions about the casting, he told Freed about that stirring performance and insisted on flying to Paris to find her again. Freed's version of the tale, sourced in his archives, is that the producer was flipping through a copy of the French magazine *Paris Match* one weekend afternoon and came upon a photograph

An American in Paris (1951)— *an ode to Gene's favorite city and his discovery, Leslie Caron. (Culver Pictures)*

of an unusually attractive and *sympathique* dancer, Leslie Caron. He phoned Gene in New York and asked him to fly to Paris and test two possibilities for the role: Caron, and Odile Versois, a well-regarded French actress-dancer, who had the advantage of being fluent in English. Caron's English was very primitive.

Whichever version is correct, Gene did fly to Paris, screen-test Caron, and air-express the film to the studio. Minnelli and Freed came out of their screening certain that Gene's recommendation was on the mark: Caron was perfect for the role.

For the part of Jerry Mulligan's rival, the aging music-hall entertainer intent on marrying his sweetheart, Gene wanted Maurice Chevalier. Despite outrageously high sums of money offered by Freed, Chevalier turned down the offer. Gene believed it was because Lerner's script called for the older man to lose the girl. Unduly proud of his reputation as a womanizer, Chevalier would say only that the script did not appeal to him. It was fortunate for MGM, which avoided a possible public-relations disaster, for a short time later investigative reporters for a Paris newspaper put out front-page articles about Chevalier entertaining German troops during the war. The role was given to George Guetary, a French singer-dancer whom Lerner spotted in the Broadway musical *Arms and the Girl*. Guetary was somewhat young for the role, but a touch of gray to the hair added the necessary years to make him a formidable rival to Gene's Jerry.

Shortly afterward, Caron arrived in Hollywood accompanied by her mother, who once had been in a Gershwin musical. When the young dancer was presented to Freed, he was immediately sorry he had not chosen Odile Versois. Shy, and dressed untidily like a lycée delinquent, Caron displayed no trace of French chic, and her English was deplorable. How Gene had gotten her through the test was a tribute to his directing talents (as well as, Freed thought mischievously with Betsy in mind, Gene's rapport with seventeen-year-olds!). But Gene himself remained happy with his choice and emphasized Caron's intelligence and quick-study talents. He turned out to be right. By the end of the first week of rehearsal, her shyness was gone and she was becoming popular on the set as her language skills flourished.

From the very beginning Gene had the dream of taking the *On the Town* approach to *An American in Paris*: doing the production on location in the fabled City of Light. And from the very beginning Freed, usually very accommodating to Gene's wishes, had misgivings about this one. Just the thought of maintaining crowd control among testy Parisians, the difficulties of liaison with the home office in California, the Kafkaesque torment of dealing with the Parisian bureaucracy for permissions to close off the Place de la Concorde and other revered locations, made Freed come down hard in favor of making Culver City serve as Paris. Which, Freed told Gene, the astonishingly artistic and variegated talent pool at MGM was well prepared to do. "Let's not repeat ourselves, Gene," Freed said, referring to their *On the Town* experience. "Do it here, at the studio, in the Paris of the impressionists."

Gene had fought the good fight and was not inclined to sulk with such a supporter as Freed. But with the passage of time there was always a tinge of embarrassment that he had done an ode to his favorite place on earth on the back lot of MGM. For years, in interviews, some grumbling and grudging adjustment to the facts showed through:

> . . . After all the arguments the [Paris] city council wouldn't allow it. Metro, who never liked to admit they'd been thwarted, simply put it out that they preferred to shoot it on a back lot because Kelly couldn't dance on cobblestones! Believe me, I've danced on a lot worse!

So it was that *An American in Paris* had only two establishing shots actually done on location by a second unit dispatched to Paris for the assignment. One was an opening aerial view, and the other covered the arrival of Jerry and his wealthy admirer (played by screen doubles for the long shot) arriving at the Ritz in a vintage roadster.

Preproduction work on the settings and rehearsals of the scenes and dances went fast, energized by Gene, who was back to his regime of eighteen-hour days. Caron found it hard to keep up the pace; having suffered from malnutrition during the war, she turned out to be quite fragile, and Gene had to make allowances for her lack of stamina by careful scheduling. But while Caron was consistently cooperative and all-out in her effort, Gene had to simply drive past the negative attitudes of some others among the cast and production staff. The pianist Oscar Levant, cast as Jerry's sidekick in the film, was a concert virtuoso of some distinction who had known George Gershwin and wanted to have a sequence covering his performance of Gershwin's *Concerto in F*. Gene managed to switch the idea to a dream-sequence for Levant in which he imagines himself as a soloist and conductor as well as every member of the orchestra and even the audience during the performance of the concerto. While not a high point of the film, at least it offered a pace, vitality, and sense of surprise that Levant's original idea lacked.

In order for Jerry to be presented as a talented painter, Freed had engaged Saul Steinberg, well-known for his cartoons in *The New Yorker* and his serious *trompe l'oeil* art. A studio was set up for Steinberg at the back of a soundstage where the artist busied himself by painting through the day, interrupted by visits from his many admirers. A man of force and temperament, Steinberg asked to see the script and had some acerbic comments about it. He demanded a voice in how his paintings would be regarded and promoted in the film and requested to be present during the final editing sessions. Gene responded by having Freed pay Steinberg a "kill fee" and happily said goodbye to the artist, who returned to New York.

Rehearsals began on June 5, 1950, and shooting commenced on August 1. Gene danced with Caron on the mock quay near Notre Dame, singing "Our Love Is Here to Stay." He choreographed his young protégé for her introductory solo vignettes that illustrated six facets of her life—student, party girl, refined young lady of good family, and so on—all done to "Embraceable You." Each of the vignettes enjoyed different color schemes and styles of dance. He showed children how to cavort American-style to "I Got Rhythm." He paired with Guetary in an exuberant "S'Wonderful." He designed a lavish production number for the French entertainer with "I'll Build a Stairway to Paradise."

Dialogue sequences were filmed, and the establishing shots, exterior and interior, and all at once it seemed, on November 1, that everything was done—with the exception of the all-important ballet. But as far as the "money men" in New York were concerned, the picture was complete and could be released in its current state! A seventeen-minute ballet coming at the end of the film was extra baggage to them. So far, the picture had cost close to $2 million. The first budget estimate for the ballet alone was $500,000, exclusive of the significant cost of costumes. The word from New York horrified Gene. By phone and letter he protested, not bothering to be polite. Freed backed him up. Earlier in his career, he'd carried the rough cut of the just-made *The Wizard of Oz* to New York for a screening. The judgment of the top executives then was that the film was too long; their unanimous verdict was that the song "Over the Rainbow" should be eliminated. Freed had been adamant about retaining the song then. He would be just as adamant about retaining the ballet now.

Once more, it was L.B. Mayer who surprised Gene. Shortly before the executive's retirement, Mayer supported Freed in the increasingly angry dispute. Moreover, he put pressure on his successor, Dore Schary, until the younger executive issued a firm statement that turned the tide: "I feel so strongly about Gene, a brilliant talent, and Minnelli, so gifted . . . and Freed has impeccable taste. So I'm telling New York this picture is going to be great because of the ballet— or it'll be nothing. Without the ballet it's just a cute and nice musical. So that's what we're gambling on."

On November 2, the go-ahead came through. Gene was given six weeks to rehearse the ballet. Enormously supportive to him with their talent, spirit, and ideas were his assistant choreographers Carol Haney and Jeanne Coyne. Production closed on the film January 8, 1951, and soon, heading for cinemas all over the world was—in the enthusiastic words of Bosley Crowther, critic of the *New York Times*— "a grandly pictorial ballet which placed the mark of distinction on this lush, Technicolor escapade."

Gene's ballet is more than a poem to Paris; it stays within the framework of the life and loves of Jerry Mulligan, now bereft of the woman he adores, as he leaves the Beaux Arts Ball and steps out on a terrace overlooking the city. We share Jerry's ever-changing emotional state on his imagined dance-panorama across Paris—from Montmartre to Montparnasse, from the Ritz to the banks of the Seine and from a popular cave to the Rue de la Paix. In one scene, the legendary work by Toulouse-Lautrec, "Chocolat dansant au Bar Achille" comes to life with Gene as Chocolat, participating in a cancan. In another scene, the pastel colors of Utrillo evoke a delicate dance, while Renoir's "Marche aux Fleurs" is the setting for a contrasting performance. Finally, there is the grand finale, played against a setting suggested by Dufy's "La Place de la Concorde": Gene and Caron lead a swirling company of dancers—soldiers, the fire department, lovely midinettes, mustachioed gendarmes, available ladies of the town, and costumed students from the Latin Quarter.

And so it goes, a music-and-dance revelation of the excitement of Paris, birthed by the best ideas of the best in the profession of producing film musicals. Officially, the director was Vincente Minnelli, but so strong was Gene's control over the film that Minnelli was able to take leaves of absence to direct another picture and sort out the legal complexities of his divorce from Judy Garland. The heart and soul of the film was Gene. *An American in Paris* still stays with us as an affirmation of the longest lasting love of the kid from Pittsburgh.

An American in Paris was barely in distribution and he was looking forward to a vacation when the studio cast him closer to home in *It's a Big Country*. The new film was a veritable unleashing of patriotic fervor as the Cold War was heating up,

American men were boarding troop ships headed for Korea, and right-wing zealots were again seeing Red in everything and everybody coming out of Hollywood. MGM thought it politically apt to produce an all-star tribute to the United States, a bouquet of eight shorts emphasizing the melting-pot democracy of America. Still nervous about the resilient HUAC hearings and the perils of blacklisting, Gene felt he could not refuse. It took only a few shooting days for him to play the part of an all's-right-with-the-world Greek soda jerk named Icarus Xenophon, who falls in love with the daughter of a Hungarian-American shopkeeper. For Gene, it had its laughable moments—but not enough.

On a most unamusing note, Gene's domestic life was in a shambles since coming off An American in Paris. He hardly saw Betsy, and he heard it from certain sources that she was having an affair with her friend, the director Anatole Litvak. Yet, at the same time something inspiring loomed on the horizon once again: the third in the stunning sequence that had begun with On the Town two years earlier—and the last truly great film he would ever make.

Back in 1921, Arthur Freed had worked as a lyricist with a song composer named Nacio Herb Brown on a number of popular songs. They did relatively well in the bustling music business of New York's Tin Pan Alley, and then recognized a greater opportunity when motion pictures began to talk and sing. They relocated to Hollywood and did even better. In 1929 their songs were featured in The Broadway Melody, advertised as "the first all-talking, all-singing, all-dancing" musical. Their studio contract called for a salary of $250 a week from MGM. They made $500,000 in outside performance royalties for the year.

The same year their catchy number "Singin' in the Rain" was featured in Hollywood Revue of 1929, the first of many renditions in a series of MGM pictures. Twenty years later, by the time Freed had his own production unit at MGM, the studio bought out his and Brown's songs under copyright, known in the music trade as their backlist, or catalogue. With An American in Paris, Freed had produced forty musicals since 1939 and, like many occupants of high positions in the film industry, he desired recognition. Now powerful, rich, and the owner of a vast estate where he raised his orchids, Freed still felt insufficiently appreciated in the creative sphere; he had been a distinguished lyricist (he classed "AA" in ASCAP, having had at one time five of the ten best-selling songs in America to his credit), but his subsequent producing career had overshadowed that accomplishment. And he was getting on. The time had come, he decided, to celebrate his own work. He would tap into the trove of his and Brown's songs, much as he and Gene had mined Gershwin treasures for An American in Paris.

Freed decided a new film would carry the title of the first best-selling song he and his partner had done in 1929. But what would this Singin' in the Rain be about? He didn't have a clue. Gene hated the idea of jumping in with a song that had, as yet, no context-and the blatant cheerfulness of the title set his teeth on edge. Still, he was confident of the solution: The story structure would be the task of On the Town's team, Betty Comden and Adolph Green. When Gene had a few story conferences with Comden and Green, they were not very far along, but they thought that this film, too, should embrace an original ballet. That was fine with Gene, but he was definite on one point: He didn't want to end the picture with it.

When Gene and Stanley Donen next saw Freed, the producer was anxious to know if Gene had any ideas on how Gene was going to choreograph the title number. "Well, Arthur," Gene responded, "I think I've got a fantastic idea for the way I'm gonna do the number."

"What's that?"

"I'm gonna be singin' and dancin', and it'll be rainin'." With that response Gene looked at his co-director and they broke out laughing. Freed did not think the encounter was very funny.

After several false starts Comden and Green were making progress. They spent many days listening to the Freed–Brown repertoire, hoping that a particular song might ignite at least a promising direction. It is difficult to pinpoint the provenance of an idea, but certain factors and happenings tilted Comden and Green to the coming-of-sound period in the film industry. Certainly the atmosphere and sense of period evoked by the songs, pushed them in the direction of setting the story when the songs were written, when movies were making the transition from silent pictures. While Gene was finishing his work on the ballet in *An American in Paris,* he and Stanley Donen watched a stream of old movies such as *Platinum Blonde* and *Bombshell.*

Around this time Billy Wilder's *Sunset Boulevard* was released, the story of a silent-film star, played by Gloria Swanson, whose career was terminated by the coming of sound. Comden and Green found it a riveting film. Gene told them he had once been considered for the William Holden role of the young writer caught in the spell of the strange household. By coincidence, Comden and Green—who were each happily married to another partner—shared in the rental of a house during their stint in Hollywood. The real-estate agent revealed it was the home of Marie Prevost, an actress who had suffered through the transition to talkies. Artifacts and pictures of the era were around the house. Years before, in Westport, Connecticut, when they had first met Gene doing summer theater, Comden and Green had written and performed a sketch concerning a silent-screen star trying to cope with the coming of sound. Now the influences they were experiencing resonated; they felt confident they were on to something. They would definitely set *Singin' in the Rain* between 1927 and 1931, using Hollywood as the main locale and the awkward transition from silent pictures to sound as the basis for their scenario.

Gene finally managed to tuck in a short vacation and came back refreshed and ready to go at the project with his usual ferocity. On his own, he plunged into a study of the period. He screened *Hollywood Revue of 1929,* Buster Keaton's first talkie, with an all-star cast. He was friendly with Keaton, a teammate on the Metro Wolves baseball team, and he intended to interview Keaton in depth. Keaton had plenty of time.

He would hang around the area circumscribed by the commissary, the shoeshine parlor, and the barber shop. I used to see him every day for a chat. At a time when MGM was reducing its production output from fifty-two pictures a year to half that number, there was no work for Keaton. He would pass the day socializing with friends, eager for the next game on the Metro Wolves schedule.

Keaton was another great talent victimized by progress, Gene thought, in much in the same way as his own father. He watched *Hollywood Revue* carefully, studying the factors dealing with sound or recording. Joan Crawford was featured and sang dreadfully off-key; he wasn't sure whether it was her fault or the primitive equipment. He paid particular attention to John Gilbert's high, fluttering voice. In one sequence, Gilbert improvised some lines, forgetting where he was, and almost manically repeating "I love you . . . I love you . . ." in the romantic scenes, as though it were still the old days and he was protected by a curtain of silence. In the finale, Keaton joined the chorus to do "Singin' in the Rain," and the sound quality was dismal and choppy.

When he had his next chat with Keaton, he was impressed by the old actor's husky baritone and wondered why he had been a casualty of the movement into sound. Then he realized it was because Keaton's voice failed to match his screen persona. It was a whiskey and cigarette-scarred voice, perfect for a cowboy star but not for Keaton's hapless victims; a light voice, insecure and shaky, might have served him better. Keaton described to a fascinated Gene the stress of being in one of the first talkies. The studio had insisted he first submit to a test. He and Norma Shearer were the first MGM actors to take the hour-long examination. They had to enter a specially constructed boxlike contraption, small and claustrophobic, and read some lines to each other. Both were visibly nervous. Finally the door was pulled open and they heard the welcome decision by one of the technicians: "Shearer and Keaton talk!"

The fallout for those whose voices didn't meet the standards needed in the new sound movies was devastating. Chaplin's voice would not be heard till 1936. Clara Bow simply told *Photoplay* magazine she was planning to take a year's trip abroad. It was believed Greta Garbo's Swedish accent would kill her chances for stardom—as it did with John Gilbert. Norma Talmadge completed two sound movies that received poor reviews and she announced her retirement. The experience made her sister Constance Talmadge, a prominent stage star, so skittish about appearing in the new-fangled talkies that she refused to try and eloped with a wealthy Chicago department-store owner instead. The impact of these and other true-life experiences of actors during the invasion of sound fired Gene's enthusiasm for the scenario that Comden and Green turned in.

It fastened on the life of a matinee idol of the period, Don Lockwood (Gene's role) and a struggling young movie extra, Kathy Selden. They meet by accident when Don, escaping from some overactive fans, jumps into her convertible jalopy from the top of a moving trolley. After the usual misunderstandings and some unusual complications, a romance develops between them, much to the irritation of Don's screechy-voiced co-star, Lina Lamont. But Lamont is forced to accept Kathy because the young actress has a lovely voice and can dub Lamont's dialogue and songs. The age of sound has come to Monumental Pictures, their employer, and it drastically affects the lives of all three film performers.

Gene was his usual independent self; he called the shots as he saw them. Freed, as the songwriter as well as the producer, saw the film as centered on singing. Gene saw dancing as the element providing the emotional thrust of the plot. The role of his sidekick Cosmo Brown was given not to the pianist Oscar Levant, as Freed wanted, but to the ex-vaudeville hoofer Donald O'Connor. Gene must have known his choice might force the audience to compare his and O'Connor's dancing skills to his disadvantage—but he never wavered in his decision. Despite his magnificent physical condition, Gene was nearing his fortieth birthday, and he knew he was past his prime as a dancer. And the focus of his interest in dance was changing, as he said at the time: "I never was crazy about performing even as a dancer. I liked to create the stuff. I liked directing but I never really worked at the dancing."

O'Connor was capable of doing any kind of move Gene might make up on the spot. He was a remarkably quick study; one look and he could do the most unusual step combinations. When they met, Gene was all business, insisting on a complete understanding of the character O'Connor would portray. Gene would expand on the lives of Don and Cosmo, how they had grown up together, how they would dance together—and here Gene would jump up and demonstrate the required moves and leaps, the position of the hands, the step routines. After one exhausting day of briefing and rapid-fire demonstration, O'Connor started to drive home when he was assailed by a worry that made him sweat. As he later described it: "Everything sounded wonderful, we would get along fine. But as I was driving I suddenly thought: Oh my God! Which way does he turn? I only turned to the left."

O'Connor scarcely slept all night, and the next day he wanted to pose the question during the first moment of their session, but he couldn't quite get it out. It seemed so unprofessional.

> I was just about to ask Gene which way he turned, and he looks at me sheepishly and he asks: "Say, Donald. Which way do you turn?"
>
> "To the left," I said, worried stiff. And he says: "Thank God. So do I."
>
> And we got to work. And, you know? It wasn't till I worked with Gene Kelly that I started to dance as a total dancer."

When the selection of songs was made it was obvious there was no suitable song for O'Connor in the Brown–Freed catalogue. Donen went to Freed's office. "We need another song, Arthur."

"What kind of song do you want?"

"Well, it should be 'Be a Clown'-type number kind of like Cole Porter did in *The Pirate*."

It made for a complicated situation because, as Donen described it:

Arthur came back with "Make 'em Laugh," which, in my opinion, is 100-percent plagiarism of the Porter song. And partly we were to blame. None of us had the courage to say to him, "For chrissake, it obviously works for the number but it's a stolen song, Arthur."

Only a wealthy gentlemen of Porter's tact and forbearance would have chosen to ignore the existence of "Make 'em Laugh," which turned out to be a rollicking performance by O'Connor using, in his own words, "a compendium of gags and shtick" he had done for years on the vaudeville circuit.

The starring female role of Kathy Selden went to Debbie Reynolds, a provocative casting choice by Freed. She was a young dancer not remotely up to Gene's standards and, consequently, terrified by him. In a 1998 interview she showed that the passage of many years had not eroded the memory of torture suffered in the rehearsal rooms: "Gene Kelly made me work so hard that I'd almost pass out trying to keep up. He taught me how to work beyond all reason."

Many afternoons her feet were bleeding but she still would not be excused.

> Gene would put me in a rehearsal studio with either Carol Haney
> or Jeanne Coyne, his assistants . . . and he wouldn't let me leave
> until I was letter-perfect. Sometimes I danced for eight to ten
> hours a day and, perfectionist that he is, he'd come in and say,
> "Okay, show me what you've learned."

She felt he was a short-tempered, inconsiderate egotist, prone to rage. But in her own spunky way she had a will to match his. She lived far away from the studio, with her parents, in the San Fernando Valley. Six days a week her alarm clock would go off at 4 A.M. She had to board a succession of three buses to arrive at the studio on time for makeup. Some nights, unknown to anyone else, she would linger in the dressing room, scarf down a sandwich and go to sleep there, rather than undergo the exhausting rides home. But she hung in and took Gene's bruising lessons with grace.

In the key scene when the female lead, Lina Lamont, is revealed to have an atrocious voice and swears vengeance on Kathy, who runs out of the theater, Don Lockwood calls her back with "You Are My Lucky Star." Gene wanted to cut to a closeup showing tears streaming down Kathy's cheeks.

But Reynolds was not one to cry. She just couldn't bring forth tears. "Dammit," snapped Gene. "Think of something sad!"

Still no tears. "Nothing bad had happened to me," she explained later. "My dog hadn't even died."

Brusquely, Gene ordered a gofer to buy an onion from a nearby greengrocer. He thrust it under her nose. "Do the shot. Your eyes'll put out more water than Niagara!"

An athlete—she had planned to teach gymnastics before she was discovered at a beauty contest in Burbank—Reynolds was "strong as an ox," according to Gene—who, she always felt, treated her accordingly.

Rehearsals started on April 12, 1951, and went well. By mid-June, *Singin' in the Rain* was in production on a schedule which ended on November 21. As on all of Arthur Freed's pictures, the closing day was celebrated with a party which the set-decorator Randall Duell arranged on Stage 28, in the standing set of a luxurious house. Duell described the arrangements for the festive event: "We brought the guests into the stage door and . . . I rigged up several pipes of rain. So the only way you could get to the party was by taking an umbrella, which we handed out at the door, and everybody walked through the rain."

Everybody understood what it meant. The celebrating cast and production staff had come a long way since the morning Comden and Green handed in the finished screenplay, a spirited satire on a Hollywood gone forever. The new film memorialized a cornucopia of songs: "Should I?" . . . "Beautiful Girl," . . . "All I Do Is Dream of You," . . . "You Are My Lucky Star," . . . "Moses Supposes," . . . "I Got a Feeling You're Fooling," . . . a joyride of music and dance that, years later, luminaries like Mikhail Baryshnikov and Twyla Tharp would study avidly on their VCRs.

Especially two of the Kelly creations. His "Broadway Melody," another complete ballet-on-film—the saga of a young hoofer in pursuit of stage stardom—breaking away for a dazzling turn, in a pink, mystical desert, by Cyd Charisse, wrapped in a 25-foot-long piece of white China silk which magically, and in harmony with her pirouettes, billows up, a graceful swirl in the sky.

Spectacular. And yet the single most memorable dance number on film—not just in this production, but in any film since the dawn of motion pictures—has to be when Gene Kelly steps out into a pelting downpour. He kicks and stamps at a gutter full of water. He swings his umbrella around to tell us all's right with his world. He climbs up a lamppost. He extends his arms, his face gleaming wet. He turns toward the sky and the rosy future awaiting him. All the while . . . singin' in the rain.

He comes off the lamppost as a chiding cop approaches and he strolls off jauntily through the night. Surely with no idea of the metaphor of that moment: coming down from on high.

Downhill from here on in.

He *had worked so hard on the sound effects—the hiss of the rain, just the right splats when his feet pummeled the puddles, the sliding crunch of his tapshoes on the wet pavement—that the perfection of the applause at the end of the film clip—bursting, jump-for-joy, supportive—is of a piece with his own work, seemingly a product of the same dubbing room.*

But this is live. It's appreciated. A signal to rev himself up, get ready to say a little something.

After decades and decades and decades of Gene Kelly retrospectives and homages in every language and a roomful of plaques and cups and awards burned away in the big fire two years ago, after at least ten-thousand interviews—who's counting?—what is there left to say?

The curtains have joined to close off the screen (get ready!) and there is George Stevens, Jr., the founder and head of the American Film Institute, talking about the hardscrabble background in Pittsburgh (he wiggles toes), the dance-studio days (stretches hamstrings), Broadway and Pal Joey (a sip of water), the Hollywood hits (couple of deep breaths), and the final encapsulation of the intro that some poor slave of a writer has sweated over: ". . . created a musical signature that will live forever—Gene Kelly!" (Up on his feet, like the juice is still there, like a real danseur-noble, for chrissake!)

On the stage, approaching George as bouncily as his knees can stand, he accepts the trophy. Again, the perfect sound effect from the audience. It fades down.

So many times through all this, it is as though a teleprompter's in his head, cueing him through it:

> MA . . . how his "sainted mother" must be looking on gratefully.
>
> SS . . . how he never wanted to be a dancer but a shortstop for the Pittsburgh Pirates.
>
> GIRLS . . . how, for his generation, dancing was a form of courtship.
>
> JERRY . . . how a mouse was his favorite dance partner (LAUGHTER).
>
> TEAM . . . how there are no auteurs in musical movies. Collaboration's the ticket. The pleasure of working with Minnelli, Freed, and (DON'T FORGET!) Donen.
>
> CLOSING . . . how (POINT TO SCREEN) that's what you do up there. You dance love and you dance joy and you dance dreams.
>
> RAISE TROPHY . . . how I won't worry any more that the Pittsburgh Pirates lost a hell of a shortstop!

And, as he says to the kids when he finishes the sidewalk dance lesson in An American in Paris: C'est tout.

He's not sure it was planned or not, but all at once they're singing "When Irish Eyes Are Smiling," which is what his are doing now with, yes, a teary sincerity, as he waves goodbye and is . . . outta there!

Having laid a hefty tip on the valet parkers, his car'll be right up front. He'll be home on North Rodeo Drive, letting it all hang out in the sanctuary of his quiet, empty house, in time for the 11 o'clock news.

FAST FORWARD, 1951–1996
* * *

Over the next forty-five years of Gene Kelly's life, he received many honors. The American Film Institute's tribute, when Gene was seventy-two years old, was one of the finest: a Life Achievement Award for his many contributions to the art of motion pictures, presented in a CBS telecast in 1985. In the Beverly Hilton ballroom and throughout the world audiences saw and reminisced about the Kelly legacy: the alter-ego dance in *Cover Girl*; the duet with an animated mouse in *Anchors Aweigh*; the exuberant *An American in Paris* ballet; the pivotal production of his career (and, consequently, his own favorite) *On the Town*.

Beyond these universally acclaimed highlights there were other gems, personal, even quirky favorites—a smorgasbord of entertainment delights provided by an important and unique talent.

Whatever he created during his lengthy career, in the eyes of the public one filmgoing (and video-renting) experience truly represented the Life Achievement of Gene Kelly: the 103 minutes of the finest musical ever made, *Singin' in the Rain*. Whether he would agree or not, it was his masterpiece.

It was 1951. Gene Kelly was closing in on a feisty forty, still eager and energetic. He had every intention of applying his innovative talents to more cinema break-throughs. As performer, choreographer, and director, his passion was to experiment and explore. He was a man who lived by the admonition "to keep going."

After *Singin' in the Rain*, it would not be easy. Even as it was hailed as a triumph, the film posed its own very special dilemma to Gene: where to go from there? The question was not a theoretical weighing of "this way or that?" or of one tempting role over another. In a not-very-funny way this very funny film about the end of one movie era coincided with the imminent end of another—his own.

There was the distinct possibility his time was up.

Gene was an intelligent, logical man, when he was calm, and he sensed he would have to move quickly, make some changes—anything to ward off a dismal retreat back into the obscurity from which he had emerged barely a dozen years before. In late 1951 he analyzed the overall situation dispassionately before making a crucial personal and career decision: to pull up stakes in Hollywood and take his family to Europe.

Moreover, in those same last days of the year, just before abandoning a snowy Washington for their cheerier home districts, the members of Congress had pushed through a bill that would turn Gene's career on its head. The new legislation stipulated that any U.S. citizen who spent seventeen out of eighteen months away from home would be exempt from paying income tax for that period. For Gene it appeared to be a once-in-a-lifetime opportunity to improve his financial position. For several years now, he had earned a substantial salary, but he had never invested adroitly. Budgeting expenses was never a priority in the Kelly home. What with Betsy's impulsive expenditures and his own inconsistencies about money—obsessively tight-fisted one moment, extravagant the next—he had not put much aside, to the distress of his accountant, who constantly implored Gene to build up his net worth. The windfall offered by Congress was a way to do it.

And Gene had no illusions that song-and-dance films would hold their own in the foreseeable future. Indeed, Metro was in financial trouble. Not only was the affluence of Louis B. Mayer's reign a thing of the past, there were even rumors the studio was headed for bankruptcy. Dore Schary, now in charge, was becoming, as the cynics in Hollywood maliciously put it, "Mayer while Rome burned." Schary's approach was to green-light low-budget message pictures "made for spit," with the emphasis on story, not spectacle.

As far as musicals were concerned, Gene put Schary down as tone-deaf. But Schary was also a liberal who, years before in his playwriting days, had crafted *Sunrise at Campobello*, a sentimental and successful Broadway play about Franklin D. Roosevelt's courageous fight against polio. Gene, always passionately pro-FDR, was accordingly inclined to give Schary's strategy for saving the studio the benefit of his doubt:

> Schary was trying to save MGM from ruin and doing it in the only way he knew how. Unlike Louis B. Mayer, who spent the last ten years of his tenure at MGM breeding race horses, Schary was really concerned about what was going on in the studio and in the industry . . . and he had integrity. He had a job of work—trimming the fat—and that's what he tried to do.

In more than one interview about the decline of the "got ta dance" film genre, Gene—true to his Depression roots—would stick with humble mealtime metaphors, falling in with Schary's reading of what was needed: "When a large family must cut down on expenses at the table, the desserts are the first to go. Musicals are considered the desserts, the costlier taste thrills of the production table."

And so he was the first of numerous Hollywood film stars to take advantage of the newly instituted tax law. He and Betsy would rent out their home on North Rodeo and spend the next eighteen months in Europe. It was no sacrifice, of course; they loved the European life-style. They saw many educational advantages for Kerry.

Betsy was optimistic; her good friend, Anatole Litvak, had relocated to Paris and set up a production company, she told Gene enthusiastically; he would find gainful employment for her there, if only as an English-dialog director on film sets. It would be a breath of fresh air, film work at last, a breakout from the shackles of the blacklist. There was a boom in the casting of self-declared bilingual French actors in the flood of American movies now being shot in Europe. But distressingly often, it turned out—once the cameras rolled—that the *lycée* graduates could barely make their way through their speeches. Betsy would be useful to Litvak.

Of that Gene was certain—but what else? What more? From the first, even before the catty Hollywood rumors reached him of sightings of Betsy and Litvak together *à deux*, far from cameras and lights, his pride had made it impossible to confront her with accusations of an affair. Marital rupture was just not in the Kelly canon; his Catholic background aside, if only for Kerry's sake the link with Betsy had to be sustained. His hope was for their marriage to revive in the more relaxed European atmosphere, half a world away from the serpentine tensions of the American film capital.

Best of all, Gene could continue to work and be sumptuously paid. MGM would now use its "frozen currency"—cash receipts from films that could not legally be withdrawn from overseas—and spend the pounds, francs, and marks on new productions shot in Europe. Not musicals, of course, but these programmers could then be shown worldwide, including in America, to enormous profit. What the studios needed were stars like Gene to be the box-office draws.

It's a win-win situation, the Kellys chortled, explaining their imminent departure from Hollywood to friends. But they were not entirely candid. There was yet another factor underlying their decision to live abroad—quite possibly the most important. It also had its genesis in what was happening in Washington.

Earlier in that year, in March, at 10:35 A.M., in Room 226 of the Old House Office Building on Capitol Hill, Chairman John S. Wood of Georgia had called to order, yet again, the House Committee on Un-American Activities for another determined investigation of "subversive activities in the entertainment industry." The first surge of HUAC had ended with a weakened Hollywood, but at least there had been a face-saving happenstance when the HUAC chairman, the Honorable J. Parnell Thomas, was carted off to jail for taking kickbacks from his staff. Hollywood had breathed easier for a while, although the blacklist of leftist talent was still in force (making Betsy, without doubt, unemployable). Now HUAC, fairly inactive since Gene's first brush with it in 1947, was again a threat, reflecting a violent swing to the right in Washington and fears of Soviet world domination throughout the country. The Korean War, waged against Communism, was an inferno of bombing and killing. The elaborate espionage apparatus of the Soviet Union had been identified, sometimes exaggerated, in the nation's media, stirring up paranoia about American military secrets passing to Moscow. Headlines blazoned the latest reports on trials involving the Rosenbergs, Alger Hiss, Whittaker Chambers, and others, the Cold War accusers and accused. It was as if Americans were panting for the arrival of a twentieth-century Paul Revere to sound the alarm that the Russians were coming, the Russians were coming!

The role of the man on horseback was now seized by Senator Joe McCarthy in his rise to power, feeding a rabid energy and passion to the network of anti-Communists all across the country. In California, the notorious Tenney Committee, a clone of HUAC chaired by the headline-seeking State Senator Jack Tenney, had already put out two successive reports criticizing Gene Kelly for membership in "Communist Party fronts." Despite his friendship with his "rabbi" Roy Brewer, the conservative union leader, Gene feared being blacklisted—not so much because of his prominence in the liberal-left political movement within the film industry, but because of Betsy's history as a Party member.

His concerns became acute in that same December of 1951, when the veteran anti-Communist journalist "Doc" Matthews, now featured as a columnist for *American Legion* magazine, named *Singin' in the Rain* in his cover story entitled "Did the Movies Really Clean House?" Pointing out what he decried as Communist propaganda within the movie—the rain as perhaps a symbol of a capitalist-induced Depression; the implication that the rich studio heads were incompetent buffoons— Matthews challenged the Hollywood leadership to invigorate the purge of the left and adopt the Legion's terms for blacklist and clearance procedures.

So, Gene felt, McCarthyism meant it was the time to get away. He left for

Europe several months ahead of Betsy, who would join him later. Early in January of 1952, he checked into the Bayerischer Hof Hotel, in Munich, for location work on his next film, a low-budget thriller called *The Devil Makes Three*. His European sojourn immediately took a bad turn. Just before shooting began he was rushed to the hospital for an emergency appendix operation. By the time he recovered, production on the film had started. The script was inadequate; true to form, Gene spoke up to try to get it extensively rewritten. He was overruled. Metro was only interested in grinding out titles for the sole purpose of unfreezing company earnings abroad. The director, Andrew Marton, known for his brilliant staging of the chariot race in *Ben Hur*, instinctively gave priority to action over acting. Gene worked hard to give the film some distinction, but it was impossible. His constant advice and suggestions were not appreciated and were reported back to Culver City as "vintage Kelly."

Feeling mired in mediocrity, he managed to get away from Munich for a weekend of solitary drinking and soul-searching in Paris. At a bar he bumped into the columnist Art Buchwald, then reporting on Americans abroad for the *International Herald-Tribune*. Buchwald made a try at interviewing him about *The Devil Makes Three*; Gene cut him short. "Please, don't ask me. Don't even ask me what the title means. I haven't got the slightest idea."

His sour mood did not improve with the news he received of the just-announced Academy Awards via a crackling overseas telephone call. *An American in Paris* had swept the Hollywood evening with seven Oscars, including the award for Best Picture, against such formidable competition as *A Streetcar Named Desire*, *A Place in the Sun*, and *Quo Vadis?* Also among the Academy Awards for 1951, the Arthur Freed production won for Best Picture, Best Cinematography, Best Screenplay, Best Art Direction, Best Musical Direction, and Best Costumes.

For himself Gene had hoped for Best Actor or, at the very least, for sharing the Best Director designation with Vincente Minnelli. It was never to be.

Incredibly, Gene Kelly was not even mentioned in connection with his film. He did receive, *in absentia*, a "special Oscar" praising him for "extreme versatility as an actor, singer, director, and dancer, but specifically for his brilliant achievement in the art of choreography on film." Perhaps, he was to brood for a very long time, the Academy had no hesitation about showering honors on everybody connected with a masterpiece—except the creator at its core.

Gene would place his "special Oscar" of that year on the mantel at North Rodeo Drive. After it melted away along with everything else in the Christmas fire that destroyed his home in 1983, he never really missed it. It didn't say "Best," which was the only word he ever wanted to hear.

Once he'd settled down in Europe and his irritation about the Academy Awards started to fade, Gene realized for the first time he would be missing out on important promotional opportunities by being so far away. Out of sight, out of mind: Rearing a shaking head again was the no-no of Johnny Darrow. Gene had made the decision to move to Europe without consulting his agent and friend.

His second European picture was no improvement. It was *Crest of the Wave*, a farce about the British Navy. He was the only American in the cast. The cockney accents were so strong, the film could as well have been recorded in Urdu. When the footage arrived in Hollywood for post-production editing, serious consideration was given to adding subtitles. But the decisive question was: Why throw good money after bad? Gene agreed with the negative decision. *Crest of the Wave*, in Gene's dispirited postmortem, "was torpedoed and sank with all hands."

In March of 1952, Betsy, Kerry, Lois McClelland, and Jeanne Coyne left New York harbor on the *Ile de France* and arrived in Le Havre five days later. It was no surprise to Gene that the family adored living in Europe from the start. With Anatole Litvak opening up contacts for her, Betsy was soon busy as a dialogue coach on the American films that were taking advantage of Washington-mandated tax breaks. Gene rented a villa outside Paris. The Kellys promptly had an open house and invited the Mayor and the local townspeople. No charades were played to liven up the evening, though; there were songs and the local *vin* did nicely.

After a while, however, Gene took a permanent suite at the Savoy Hotel, in London. He enrolled Kerry, now an alert and attractive eleven-year-old, at the Royal Ballet School. On free days, he took the family "on paid holidays" to enchanting corners of Europe in Austria and Bavaria, as well as in France and England.

But Gene's workaholic side jarred the easygoing atmosphere. He felt the constant need "to keep going"—to really involve himself in what he hoped to be the most meaningful film of his lifetime.

On the basis of a somewhat grudging okay from Schary, Gene started to develop *Invitation to the Dance*. For a number of years now, Gene had nurtured a dream for a full-length ballet film. Now, thanks to Metro's ample frozen currency sequestered in British banks, the project seemed possible, despite the lack of a penchant at MGM for making cinematic confections of that kind. His concept for the film was to bundle together four totally different ballets, each featuring the finest performers in Europe and America: "Circus" would be about a lovesick clown falling to his death from the trapeze highwire while trying to impress the girl he loves. "Ring Around the Rosy" would follow a bracelet passing through a dozen different hands, affecting each owner's life before it was given as a mark of love to the next recipient. The third ballet would be "Sinbad the Sailor," using a mixture of live-action and animation in a rendering using the Rimsky-Korsakov score, *Scheherazade*. And the fourth ballet would feature Gene himself—a concession to the reality that a film star with box-office potential was needed—as he and a supporting troupe interpreted a dozen American songs popular throughout the world.

It was a staggering task Gene had cut out for himself. The mystery back in Culver City was how a professional of his caliber and experience could possibly believe *Invitation* was something he could bring off so far from the support infrastructure of the home studio. But it now became his passion—his mission—to introduce the world's most brilliant performers of ballet to a worldwide audience of believers that only Astaire and Kelly were the great dancers. He was later to say to his biographer Clive Hirschhorn:

Of course, this wasn't news to people in the more sophisticated cities. But what about audiences in the provinces of Vietnam? Or Senegal? Or Indonesia? Or Central Africa—who'd never seen a ballet company in their lives? Or even people nearer home— in Dubuque or Hackensack? It was to them I wanted *Invitation to the Dance* to appeal.

It was, of course, an idea so visionary as to be breathtaking. It was also over-ambitious. The home office of MGM was informed by Gene that the "Sinbad the Sailor" ballet, blending live-action and animation, à la Jerry the Mouse in *Anchors Aweigh*, would require the preparation of 250,000 preliminary drawings and 57,000 painted film frames. Metro's animation department, headed by the esteemed team of Hanna and Barbera, estimated that the project would tie up more than forty artists for more than a year.

Recognizing that he himself was past his prime and did not remotely belong in the ranks of the ballet talents he recruited, Gene wanted to restrict his participation to just one dance but to create the librettos, direct, and produce all four ballets at the MGM studios in Boreham Wood, Elstree, where the technical support and staff no way measured up to that of Culver City.

No! came the dismayingly curt response from Schary. Frozen currency or not, he was on again, off again about the project from the start, and insisted Gene cast himself in all four segments. Since the ballet stars Gene intended to feature were unknown to the general public, the only way for the studio to recoup its investment was by promoting *Invitation to the Dance* as a musical starring Gene Kelly.

It turned out to be an *Invitation to the Disaster*. Though not in artistic terms, for there are moments in the completed film when the dancing is of a uniquely high level, tastefully and ingeniously committed to the film medium, and offering much pleasure. But the production was plagued by difficulties unexpected by Gene. Everything that could go wrong, did—almost with a vengeance.

Right from the beginning, Arthur Freed—a loyal admirer and supporter to the end—sensed that not even one of the ballet sequences for the film was clear in Gene's mind. There were countless transatlantic calls, a blizzard of promissory and ebullient memoranda, but still Freed waited for more clarification, specifics, facts. Could he have a more detailed synopsis? Did Gene have a composer in mind? A set designer—not to speak of four of them? A union settlement, special effects, cast negotiations, preliminary budgets, revised budgets, music releases, liability insurance, a tangled thicket of unresolved problems—it became clear to Freed as the weeks flew by that Gene's picture was in a state of nervous flux, a runaway production, operating completely (and wildly) on its own, unresponsive to directions from Culver City.

Ironically, Gene's foremost problem—perhaps the root of the whole mess—was the issue that had drawn him to Europe in the first place: avoidance of taxes. The Boreham Wood studios were subject to the edicts of the British Home Office in regard to the importation of foreigners, notably Gene and his growing contingent of French and American dancers. Under English tax law, a non-British subject was permitted to remain in Great Britain for only a limited time without paying the high British income tax. Gene decided to commute from his rented country estate in France, an hour's drive from Paris. It was a rhapsodically scenic place for creative inspiration, but the commuting was an exhausting horror-show of last-minute arrivals and departures that sapped his energy. Travel problems aside, the lead dancers often were not available to Gene because of prior commitments to their own ballet companies; Gene twisted himself into knots adhering to the various schedules, often changed at the last minute. The film crew at Boreham Wood proved to be inexperienced. Gene was rattled by the British come-what-may insistence on "tea breaks." The camera cranes essential for dance coverage were not up to par. Audio facilities were primitive. Gene proved to be excessively demanding of stage performers with little experience in motion-picture technique. He over-rehearsed the company, and the concrete floors of the Boreham studio laid low knees, right and left.

*For the "Sinbad the Sailor"
segment of* Invitation to
the Dance, *Gene—
with Jeanne Coyne looking
on—rehearsed with
Carol Haney (center),
the stand-in for his eventual
partner, an animated
cartoon character.
(Courtesy of Photofest)*

Not a day went by without him raging against the slowness of the shooting, the excessive tea breaks, the British resistance to going past the closing bell even at overtime rates of pay. After three weeks of camera-work Gene had eleven minutes and twenty seconds on film. During that period, two full studio days passed without Gene's thumbs-up signal and relieved yell: "That's a print!"

A contemporaneous cablegram in the MGM archives from Arthur Freed to an underling at Boreham perhaps says it best:

> IS THIS REPORT CORRECT THAT ON THE TWENTY-FIRST THERE
> WAS ONLY THIRTY SECONDS NET, ALSO ON THE TWENTY-
> SECOND ONLY FORTY-FIVE SECONDS NET WITH EIGHT SET UPS?
> CABLE ME AND KEEP CONFIDENTIAL."

At least Freed kept his aplomb, and even joked in a letter to his Boreham informant: "Thanks for your comprehensive reports. After reading them, I immediately stopped to have some tea. Tell Gene that if we do a fifth ballet it seems we should call it 'Tea Party'." In fact, Freed canceled the fourth ballet, the American song medley segment. Gene, relieved and actually rescued, rationalized that with *Invitation* now in three parts the film would correspond better to an evening of ballet such as one sees in the theater.

As hard as Gene worked in the time available, it was difficult to edit the film. It came through as a surrealist hodge-podge. (He must have thought despairingly from time to time: Where, oh where is Stanley Donen?) Back in California MGM arranged some sneak previews of what took shape as a work in progress. The reaction was dismal. Gene's sequence as the tragic clown was regarded as pretentious. Unsure of their capacity to render a critical judgment on so esoteric an activity as ballet, Schary and other Metro executives were quick to accept the judgment of Igor Youskevitch, the noted dancer recruited by Gene for his film. Still irritated by Gene's incredibly demanding schedule, Youskevitch allowed that Gene "could be" an excellent creative choreographer but was dismayingly blunt in rating him as an authentic ballet performer: "Kelly is not an ideal classical dancer. He does not have the proper training. His technique is not good enough."

Schary had soon had enough of Gene's grandiose venture and suspended the production. From then on, when facilities and talent were available, work resumed, often in Gene's absence. Two years went by in stuttering fashion. *Invitation to the Dance* became an embarrassment, a punchline for jokes, as it was cut and recut, dubbed and redubbed. In 1955, Gene and Jeanne Coyne recorded a new tap-soundtrack to render Gene's dances more dynamically. Each burst of activity was preceded and followed by executive screenings and meetings and memoranda— but no firm decision came to start distribution.

And so it went, until *Invitation to the Dance* was finally taken off the shelf and premiered at the Plaza, an art theater in Manhattan, on March 1, 1957. It was a last gasp, a throwaway. Gene took it as an insult. He felt it was the delay that had been disastrous. By that time, television sets were in most American homes, and a number of prestigious network programs had featured great ballet soloists and troupes on shows beamed coast-to-coast—available for home viewing at no cost. Result: There was no novelty perceived in *Invitation to the Dance.*

By the date of the premiere, the film's accumulated cost was $1,419,105. In spotty distribution, the box-office returns were paltry: Worldwide, it grossed $625,000, and the domestic portion of that was a mere $200,000. *Invitation to the Dance* undoubtedly had a lot to do with the dismissal of Dore Schary as MGM head, at the end of 1956.

A grim MGM swallowed its losses on a motion picture that derailed Gene Kelly's career and probably broke his heart. Yet, later on, even Gene agreed, with surprising equanimity:

> There were some things in it that didn't come off as well as I had hoped, and in the end I found myself agreeing with those who found the whole thing a bit much. Each ballet is enjoyable by itself but three in a row was probably more than most people could take at one cinema sitting.

After the triumphant trio of *On the Town*, *An American in Paris*, and *Singin' in the Rain*, the life of Gene Kelly, starting with the move to Europe in 1952, can be viewed as bedeviled by frustration. But at least his tax-free sojourn compensated him with many delightful hours, especially in Paris and London. With his typical bounce-back quality, he determined to make the best of his stay, bonding more closely with his daughter, who hadn't been able to see much of him in Beverly Hills. Once he rented a boat and took Kerry on a ten-day trip up the Thames to Oxford. They cooked meals on a small portable stove, walked amid the students on the ancient campus, then went on to stay overnight at picturesque riverside inns. Several times during the trip, they were joined by Betsy at the end of the day. Betsy was never one for the confinement of a small boat, but she would enjoy a relaxed supper with her family and drive back to London the following morning.

Every Sunday in London, he and Betsy and some friends would shrug off their hangovers and motor to his favorite exurban restaurant for several rounds of Bloody Marys, a platter of smoked salmon, and a splendid lunch that gave the lie to the repeated canard that only squalid food is available in England. Or they might stroll across Hyde Park Corner to a pub frequented on Sunday mornings by theater people. After closing time, at two o'clock, they would go on to an illegal watering hole, where they would relax the rest of the afternoon, drinking and gossiping. Later there were cocktails and highballs at Les Ambassadeurs, or "Les A," as everyone called it, where they met every night when they were in London.

Betsy couldn't help thinking the conversation was a great deal less intense than at Louie Bergen's on New York's West Side. The hours passed effortlessly, especially with friends from California like Humphrey Bogart, Lauren Bacall, and Errol Flynn. Even Robert Taylor's Communist baiting during the 1947 HUAC hearings in Washington was water under the dam as far as Gene was concerned, and the two stars buried the hatchet, though Betsy still retained her grudge against Taylor.

Betsy was still commuting to Paris often because of her connection with Anatole Litvak. Battered as he was by his three-strikes-and-out movie record in England, in June of 1953, shortly before their return to California, Gene's spirits were raised by an unexpected psychological boost during the Coronation ceremonies for Queen Elizabeth II. Jules Stein, the wealthy American agent, invited the Kelly family to watch the elaborate royal procession from Stein's balcony window, which overlooked the route. Gene, Betsy, and Kerry awoke to a morning of dreadful London weather—rain, gray skies, unseasonable cold. The sidewalks were packed with bystanders waiting to see the young queen pass by, and a cordon of bobbies prevented access to the streets. To go to Stein's by taxi or even by foot was impossible. Gene tried to lead his small group by squirming through the crowd. No progress. The rain rewarded their efforts by coming down even harder. Nobody was going anywhere. Suddenly, Gene heard:

> Over the loudspeaker system a man who had been keeping every-
> one informed about what was happening, said: "Now, ladies and
> gentlemen, I'd like you all to join Gene Kelly in 'Singin' in the

Rain,' and on came my record. A few seconds later, thousands of lovely, cold, wet, shivering English men and women started to sing. It was the biggest thrill of my life . . . and I felt if I never achieved another thing—which was the way things seemed to be going—I'd have justified my existence.

What was left of Gene's euphoria faded on his return to California in August of 1953. By then, Congress had adjusted the law allowing the tax windfall. The exodus of movie stars during the past eighteen months had propelled union lobbyists to Washington in full force, complaining that American jobs were being lost. All that Gene was able to keep was the first $35,000 of his earnings, which, as an American living abroad, he would have been able to retain anyway. But with a shrug he brushed mercenary considerations aside. He was eager to rejoin the top-notch MGM professionals in Culver City. As always for Gene Kelly, the prospect of work, to keep going, was the best sweetener.

His return to Hollywood contrasted starkly with his first arrival fourteen years earlier. The competition of television had ground down MGM's annual output of films to a new low. With two European flops and *Invitation to the Dance* still bogged down in expensive post-production, auguring little or no eventual profit, Gene was not exactly king of the hill, as he found out at his first meeting with Dore Schary on the subject of his next musical, *Brigadoon*. Vincente Minnelli would direct, Schary explained. After the nightmarish experience of *Invitation*, it would be cruel and insensitive to plunge Gene into another problem-racked project. It would be best if Gene got back into the swim of things gradually. Gene didn't believe a word of what he was hearing. He was being shunted aside as director and as a participant in the crucial production decisions on *Brigadoon*. While in Europe he had broken away for a location survey in Scotland and had worked out a plan for shooting exterior locations in the highlands there, interiors at the Boreham Wood Studios near London and, finally, the songs and dances in Culver City. He had spoken to the legendary English ballerina Moira Shearer about the lead female role opposite himself and had planned to engage the Sadler's Wells Ballet Company for the ensemble numbers.

Schary cut him short. The MGM head would have no more pie-in-the-sky thinking. No location shooting; painted backdrops will be fine, thank you. Forget Shearer and Sadler's Wells. Cyd Charisse, under contract, would do nicely. And to beat the competition of television, *Brigadoon* would be shot in CinemaScope.

The new wide-screen technology was Hollywood's not-so-secret weapon, which studio heads were gambling would shatter the surging postwar popularity of home TV. Through the use of an anamorphic lens, the CinemaScope camera could "squeeze" a wide image onto regular-width film, and the projector lens would "unsqueeze" the picture, or spread it back out, onto a wide theater screen. In the commissary, in the screening room, and on the studio lots, movie executives who fancied themselves technically sophisticated chatted about the width-to-height ratio in the CinemaScope process, an incredible 2.35 to 1, almost double the standard screen rectangle, which was 1.33 to 1. The viewer would enter a fantastic other-world experience, leaving the tiny, blurry screen of TV as a miserable eye-straining option. Earlier in 1953, Darryl Zanuck had introduced CinemaScope with his production of *The Robe*. The box-office returns were spectacular. Schary had similar hopes for the wide-screen version of *Brigadoon*.

While there were cynics about CinemaScope as the miracle drug for the sagging motion-picture industry (the screenwriter Nunnally Johnson, content-oriented and acerbic, reacted: "What do you want us to do, Darryl? Put the paper in the typewriter sideways?"), Gene was always open to new processes and techniques. He saw potential in rendering *Brigadoon* in CinemaScope, a road to repair his ailing career that would restore him as a leading lion at MGM. What concerned him more was that he did not see eye to eye with Minnelli on many aspects of the production.

Brigadoon was a story about two sophisticated Manhattanites who come to Scotland for grouse shooting. One day they stumble across the fairy-tale village of Brigadoon, which emerges mysteriously from the highland mists once every hundred years and is allowed only one day of reality before disappearing again. The American visitor, to be played by Gene, is enamored of a beautiful village girl. He wants to stay behind in Brigadoon and forsake Manhattan for whatever fate awaits him and his beloved. As a stage production, *Brigadoon* had run for more than 600 performances on Broadway and a further 700 in London. When Gene started work on the movie version, there was an immediate tension between him and Minnelli, the director. Later, explaining the debacle, Gene explained: "Vincente and I were never in synch, I must confess. I remember him telling me that he hadn't liked the Broadway show at all, and I loved it."

Gene envisioned *Brigadoon* almost as a Scottish Western, an outdoor picture radiant with vistas of heather on which he and the company would dance. He was aware, nervously so, that the stage play had been hailed for the brilliant choreography of Agnes de Mille, linking classical ballet to traditional Scottish dancing in a way that moved the story along—an approach entirely consistent with Kelly principles. But he had no intention of collaborating with her; at this point it would do his fading career no good merely to serve as a conduit for de Mille, ushering her well-received dance concepts into the film version. Just the thought of being elbow-to-elbow with a strong-minded woman choreographer (whom he personally abhorred for her conservative politics and homophobic prejudices) set him firmly on the path of sweeping aside de Mille's work. He rationalized that he and only he could best marry the enchantment of Scottish dancing to the CinemaScope medium. He knew he would be crucified for the decision—unless his own work was sensational.

Minnelli saw another *Brigadoon*. To him it was more a singing show than a dancing one. His key priority was to retain its mysterious flavor as a whimsical love story spun out against the suspenseful deadline. Jostling against each other, Minnelli and Gene had no recourse but to move ahead, each constantly revamping ideas to fill up the huge screen for the moments of visual spectacle and somehow handle the intimate sequences of two lovers in closeup, dwarfed in each direction by lengthy strips of distracting pseudo-Scottish panorama.

They had to overcome a tremendous handicap: Production of an outdoor motion picture on an MGM sound stage. Pressured by the front office with an unrealistic schedule, the construction department was soon running up overtime charges, much to Schary's dismay, as hills and valleys took shape, surrounding a village with a clutch of cottages set against a background of purple heather, a bridge spanning a brook, the watering spot for appropriately living livestock. The visual illusion was so realistic that even local crows were attracted and flew caw-cawing through the open stage doors straight into the backdrops, causing havoc to the shooting and more headaches for the camera crews, who were in trouble enough with the cumbersome CinemaScope cameras. After all the exhausting effort, there was only disappointment when the daily rushes were screened the next morning. The huge backdrops still dripped of artificiality, more Culver City than Scottish moor.

Several times Gene barged into Schary's office, demanding at the very least a shift of the outdoor shooting to Northern California's scenic Carmel area. Schary, fighting for his corporate survival, turned him down—with no points scored for Gene, who was fast reinstating himself as the "always-bitching" MGM firebrand. Minnelli, knowing well they were fighting a losing battle, sympathized with Gene's reaction to the front-office hostility:

> Gene seemed to have lost all faith in the project. He seemed curiously remote and slightly down. He had come back from Europe to find the musical genre at MGM in a steep descent. I had many talks with him, trying to impress on him the need to show exuberance in the part. If the film was to work, he had to light up the sky with his amazement of the Miracle of Brigadoon.

Emphatically, neither *Brigadoon* nor CinemaScope was the miracle that MGM desperately needed. In the end, the wide-screen panacea was the nail in the coffin for the movie, as Gene was to complain bitterly in interviews throughout the years:

> The studio betrayed us. It promised that all its picture houses were changing to CinemaScope, so we filled in the whole screen. Then we found that most movie houses were still showing in the old dimensions and most of the choreography was really messed up.

The creative dissension between Gene and Minnelli, the brouhaha over shooting locations, the technical lapses (especially the poor color and sound-dubbing) and spiritless contributions from those in front of and behind the cameras all took their toll. The reviews were devastating, along the line of *Newsweek's*: "Hollywood can still put its worst foot forward and does so in *Brigadoon*." Rather than Minnelli, the onus fell on Gene because he had dispensed with Agnes de Mille's choreography. His substitutions, even his own solos, lacked energy and appeal and today are considered derivative of his earlier work. At the end of the picture when he finally joins Cyd Charisse, his Scottish lassie, the fade-out is bizarrely and harshly quick.

It is as though both of them want to avoid further embarrassment and just get the hell out of *Brigadoon*.

It was now 1954, and in the transient "what's-for-today?" atmosphere of Hollywood, Gene Kelly was being written off as history, and he knew it. All he could do, again, was work. He snared a cameo role for himself and his brother Fred in *Deep in My Heart*, a musical biography of Sigmund Romberg co-starring José Ferrer and Merle Oberon. Gene and Fred did a vaudeville routine straight out of their nights in the "cloops" called "I Love to Go Swimmin' with Wimmen." In a sense, it was a comedown from Gene's once-lordly status as a famous filmmaker, but for a long time he had wanted to appear with his brother in a movie. He felt he had to—at least once—do a film number with Fred. For his mother's sake. What it had to do with Romberg is still not clear, but the Kelly duet is surely the most entertaining bit in *Deep in My Heart*.

It rankled Gene, however, that MGM had assigned Stanley Donen, very much on his own, to direct *Deep in My Heart*. His competitive instincts bristled on seeing that the professional relationship was changing between them; no longer would the younger man play second fiddle. His "boy Stanley" had grown into manhood.

Gene's spirits were at a low ebb as he went back to Switzerland for a solitary, reflective stay. He needed time and isolation to think through the options for his career. And he had to do some hard evaluations of his marriage, which had resumed its faltering way upon the return to North Rodeo Drive. Betsy, however, had just received good news: She was to play a leading role, opposite Ernest Borgnine, in the film version of Paddy Chayefsky's television drama, *Marty*. Now the separation of thousands of miles between the Kellys seemed appropriate. They had seen each other only occasionally at home anyway. Gene knew she was considering divorce. He wasn't sure what to do about it.

Once more he buried his concerns about Betsy in obsession with his own work problems. The heyday of the Arthur Freed unit at MGM was over. So it was with movie musicals. Comden and Green were joking that their films once premiered at Radio City Music Hall; now "they open at drive-ins." It was all due to—was there any longer even a question?—the change in popular musical taste. Elvis Presley and Company had swamped romantic ballads with rock 'n' roll, where the Kelly choreography could find no foothold. Simple as that. George Balanchine had once put it memorably: "Music is the floor that dancers dance on."

Similarly, in a London newspaper Gene told how musicals—and his own film choreography—must have a type of romantic music that was being supplanted:

> Dance follows music. If you ask me if there's romance in musicals, of course there is. I think that's why [the musical] has died as a movie form. Since the revolution of the Beatles that music has got louder and a bit more frightening for dancers. It's very hard to say "I love you" to modern pop music. To the music of our generation it was easy and the dances became an extension of that.

Still the fighter, he thought about changing directions, abandoning musicals for acting straight roles. Broadway was a possibility. Had not Elia Kazan once come close to offering him the role of Biff in the original cast of Arthur Miller's *Death of a Salesman*? Then Kazan came back again with a definite role in *Camino Real*, by Tennessee Williams, but he couldn't fit it in.

For films, he was often on the short list for key parts. The producer of the movie version of *Teahouse of the August Moon* had initially wanted him for the lead role of Sakini. Then Marlon Brando had conveyed his interest and that was that.

A greater disappointment came with Samuel Goldwyn's 1955 movie version of the stage hit *Guys and Dolls*. If ever there was a role for the original Pal Joey, it was his brother-in-spirit Sky Masterson, the gaudy street gambler in love with the prettiest girl in the Salvation Army. Gene thought he was "born to play Sky the way Gable was born to play Rhett Butler." MGM would not release him. Again, Brando gobbled up his role.

Alone in Klosters, Gene brooded about the cavalier, offhand way the studio was always treating him when a fantastic role was within reach. No to *Pal Joey*. No to *Cyrano*. Procrastination on *Invitation to the Dance*, the ongoing, diabolical refusal to green-light its release date. It was too damn much! He had no choice, he finally decided, except to quit the studio where he had worked for the past sixteen years. He was packing his bag for the flight back to the U.S. when the overseas call came from Arthur Freed: MGM was ready to go with him on yet another musical. Perhaps he—with Stanley Donen, the studio head made clear in his pumped-up style—could bring back the old magic!

The third musical directed by Gene and Stanley was written by Comden and Green. Titled *It's Always Fair Weather*, it could have been called *On the Town II*. The story begins as three just-discharged GI pals, facing the prospect of never seeing each other again, vow to have a tenth-anniversary reunion at their favorite bar. Ten years pass. Each one comes to the bar doubting the possible arrival of any other. When they all do show up, the passage of time and their pursuit of civilian livelihoods have changed them profoundly, and their get-together turns out badly. The all-for-one, one-for-all spirit of their Army days is long gone. Competitive, almost hostile with each other, they stick it out for the rest of the 24-hour time-frame of the musical. It all ends on an improbable note of reconciliation.

In making the film there were technical difficulties encountered in the still-novel use of CinemaScope, notably in the color resolution and split-screen sequences. The score by André Previn was not up to the Freed standard. MGM's emphasis on economizing showed itself in some tacky interiors. But Comden and Green's script, for the most part, was bright and original, with a satiric spin that scored points. Gene joined Michael Kidd and Dan Dailey just ahead of the garbage collector in the clanging "dustbin dance" that is still celebrated, and he did an engaging solo song-and-dance on roller skates that proved he was still a Mozart of the rink.

It's Always Fair Weather opened the following year, in early 1956. The reviews were surprisingly sour—perhaps matching the mood of the co-directors. For the first time their creative disagreements had exploded on the set. No longer did Stanley give way all the time; he considered himself an equal, not an assistant. When interviewed for the book *Hollywood's Greatest Musicals*, he candidly told author Hugh Fordin:

> I didn't want to co-direct another picture with Gene at that point. We didn't get on very well and, for that matter, Gene didn't get on well with anybody. It was the only picture during which the atmosphere was really horrendous. We had to struggle from beginning to end. I can only say it was an absolute one hundred percent nightmare."

The younger man's fury had to stem from causes that were not only professional but personal. He wanted to move forward, continue to direct movies on his own, but there was the longtime affection of his ex-wife, Jeanne Coyne, for Gene. (No slouch at discerning the wants of the opposite sex, Donen was to be married five times; there was also a much-publicized year-long affair with Elizabeth Taylor.) Jeanne Coyne's desire for Gene had survived being Mrs. Donen—and undoubtedly had been acted upon when she was still Mrs. Donen. That stinging rebuff had given Stanley Donen a further motivation to separate himself from the Gene Kelly entourage for good.

It is ironic that *It's Always Fair Weather*, a film about the difficulty of maintaining long relationships, signaled the end of the Kelly–Donen partnership. The film was released at the same time as *Love Me Tender*, the breakthrough rock 'n' roller, starring Elvis Presley that marked the close of the Gene Kelly era of movie musicals.

Gene was now forty-three. For the rest of his life, he was like a prizefighter pinned against the ropes by misfortunes and disappointments, rallying with periodic surges of counter-punching. In the midst of his professional upheavals, Betsy finally asked him for a divorce. Aided by therapy, she had come to the conclusion she and Gene could no longer stay together. It was as if he sucked up all the oxygen in their home. His constantly paternal attitude toward her, which she may have needed as a seventeen-year-old, impelled her as an independent adult to behavior and relationships that became heartaches for both of them. She admitted:

> For quite some time I felt I should leave Gene. But somehow I couldn't . . . I remember seeing *Singin' in the Rain* a couple of years after it was released, at a point when our marriage was becoming pretty shaky, and at the end of the Broadway ballet there was this enormous closeup of a smiling Gene which came sailing out of the screen, and I realized I was never going to escape him . . . he would always be larger than life. So when the situation became intolerable, I decided to go to an analyst and see if he could help me. He did. He made me face the reality that the only way out was divorce.

When Betsy was offered the *Marty* role, her first part in years, the studio ordered her to write a letter to the American Legion explaining her past left-wing politics and saying she had been "misled." They even told her to "name names." She refused, and called Gene instead. She reached him on the set of *It's Always Fair Weather*. Gene, on hearing that his estranged wife might lose the role if she refused to write the letter, once again stormed into Dore Schary's office. He demanded that the MGM head call the Legion and vouch for her Americanism. He shouted, slammed a stiffened palm down on Schary's desk. He threatened to walk away from his own film. Schary did as Gene wanted. Betsy held on to the part.

Gene would no longer stay at Metro and forced his release from the studio— only to do a string of undistinguished pictures, including the 1957 films *The Happy Road* and *Les Girls* (his final MGM musical, co-starring a charming Kay Kendall); in 1958 Gene directed *The Tunnel of Love*, starring Doris Day and Richard Widmark, to fulfill the end of his MGM contract. As the first nonmusical he directed, that film opened a door for his future. In the same year he also co-starred with Natalie Wood in *Marjorie Morningstar*.

His morale was not helped in early 1957 when his marriage of fifteen years officially ended and Betsy received an uncontested divorce, a settlement of $180,000 in lieu of alimony and joint custody of Kerry. Soon afterwards Betsy moved to London and to her second marriage, to the director Karel Reisz.

It was a low point, but he fought off depression, helped enormously by Jeanne Coyne, who now moved into his home on North Rodeo Drive. She was almost the same age as Betsy but of very different temperament. Uninterested in politics, she focused on making Gene happy. They were married in August of 1960, in the County Court House in Towapah, Nevada.

Theirs had been and always would be a steady and steadfast relationship. They had come a long way together ever since Jeanne, a wiry and knock-kneed child in Pittsburgh, had first been spotted at his dance studio. She showed talent and so— such was Gene's value-judgment—she was worth his attention. She, in turn, had idolized her glamorous teacher from the first tap. She had followed him to New York as soon as she could, working as a dance captain and then, in California and Europe, as his assistant choreographer. Whatever the number, solo or ensemble, he would develop it on his own, and she was the only one allowed to see his creation at that unfinished stage. With very little indication—perhaps a hint of a gesture from him, a guiding grasp of her hand, a quick rat-tat-tat riff of demonstration, a light touch on her elbow—she was astonishingly quick to learn any routine. Then in a flurry of moves, taps, and slides she was ready to assume his role, while he watched and took in and critiqued the number's overall impact. If it was an ensemble number she would teach it to the dancers. For the first time he could really see his own creation in Jeanne's; more than anyone else, she was his dance-dream come true.

Impelled by the surges of their back-and-forth collaboration drawing them ever closer, physically and emotionally, a love took hold that deepened and went both ways. Once Betsy had left the scene, Jeanne became the avowed lady of Gene's life who could be counted on as a wife and mother. Over the years, they were to raise two more children, Tim and Bridget—until Jeanne became seriously ill. He, in his turn, was determined to give their children more time than he had provided Betsy and Kerry.

That was easier to do now that his life-style had calmed down with the advent of the new Mrs. Kelly, who was never one for late-night parties, volleyball tournaments, and, least of all, bitterly competitive charades. She was a devoted hands-on parent and expected Gene to be one. To the very end, he never let her down despite the still-churning demands of work, the calls to action that he could never bring himself to refuse.

Into the middle years and into a fended-off senior-citizenship Gene Kelly worked steadily, acting or directing or both. He decided that TV was not the enemy; indeed, it was easy money, and he made dozens of appearances. On *Person to Person*, with Edward R. Murrow, both host and guest seemed quietly conscious of their fall from the heights. Had not one helped topple Joe McCarthy as the other had tapped out a reassuring vote of confidence along a rainswept pavement? Later there were the brassily hard-sell (the Gene Kelly Pontiac Specials); the affectionately retrospective (the 1970 *Gene Kelly and 50 Girls 50* and the 1978 *An American in Pasadena*); the ridiculous and even demeaning (serenading Miss Piggy and teaching Kermit the Frog to dance); and, of course, the insipid, in the form of countless interviews calling for celebrity banter.

Gene did leave his mark on serious-minded television, notably with the 1958 documentary program he wrote and directed for the prestigious *Omnibus* series on NBC, entitled "Dancing: A Man's Game." The show linked athletics and ballet, demonstrating that each dance step had its physical counterpart in sport (Gene had done it years before with the reluctant bar-mitzvah boys of Pittsburgh's Beth Shalom Synagogue). Gene directed stop-motion vignettes featuring such stadium heroes as Mickey Mantle slugging a home-run, Johnny Unitas fading back to rifle a quick pass, Sugar Ray Robinson ducking and countering with a wicked jab, and other luminaries of the sports page to underscore his theme: athletics is competitive and dance is creative, but both are rooted in the same balletic movements.

"Dancing: A Man's Game" was Gene's outstanding contribution to television's so-called Golden Age, when fine arts programming on the major networks was not uncommon. (Courtesy of Photofest)

The show was reviewed enthusiastically by the press, but Gene was even more pleased by his brother Fred's exuberant post-show phone call: "It's the best damn dance documentary ever made!" Gene was invited to do two specials sponsored by Pontiac, a company now interested in being represented with a higher level of program. For one show, Gene commissioned the poet Carl Sandburg to write and recite an original poem along with a dance accompaniment by three European ballerinas. The same program introduced the thirteen-year-old Liza Minnelli in a debut song performance. A proud and elated mother, Judy Garland, telephoned her dear friend and screen partner immediately after the show to congratulate him for his discernment as a producer and, especially, as a casting director. They laughed and talked about old times and, of course, he urged her "to keep going."

He wanted very much to do more television of a serious nature, but apparently specials did nothing to improve Pontiac sales, and so his work fell back under a barrage of sentimental look-back gigs ("The Movie Palaces") and guest appearances (Dean Martin "Celebrity Roasts"). He was pleased enough to be slotted for lucrative TV appearances, but with the demise of *Omnibus* Gene gave up on television as an asset for intellectual development. Many years later, more as a concerned parent of three children than as a showman, he voiced criticisms of the medium whenever he had the chance:

> Educationally, television has been proved to be bad. My younger daughter sees some television every night. But she also does her homework and she's bright. But I know a lot of her peers who watch too much television and they can't read. They look at television all the time and don't have enough time for homework.

Always striving for a comeback, in 1962 Gene attempted a weekly situation-comedy series, *Going My Way*, based on the 1944 Academy Award-winning film starring Bing Crosby. Gene played the lead role of Father O'Malley, a New York priest, but it was no godsend; the shooting schedule was extremely tight, "down and dirty," with each show shot in four frantic days—not exactly in accord with the Kelly perfectionism. Nor did he appreciate the competition between ABC, the ever-accommodating network, and the Church as to which could insist on more censorship and script restrictions.

On the plus side, in addition to a weekly salary of almost obscene dimensions, the series was shot at Universal Studios, only a short drive from home, where Jeanne was pregnant with their first baby. (For a while Gene was setting up a film production in Paris, and Jeanne sent him a birthday card from Beverly Hills that casually said: "Your present is inside me."). A boy, whom they named Timothy, came into the world. *Going My Way* left it. Pitted against the vastly more popular *The Beverly Hillbillies*, the show's Nielsen ratings did not go Father O'Malley's way heavenward, and the series was cancelled.

Television may have helped to fill the Kelly coffers, but ultimately it did little to satisfy his passion for innovative work. After *Marjorie Morningstar*, with no beguiling offers on the film horizon, he took his entourage to Zermatt for a skiing holiday. Intent on being the best on the slope and accident-prone as ever, he promptly fell on a patch of ice. He ripped the cartilage in one of his knees. "The end of serious dancing for me," he said—and so it was.

Jeanne and Gene posed for the press photographers in a proud display of their month-old son Timothy, in 1962. (Courtesy of Photofest)

That same winter, still hobbling about with a bandaged knee and a cane, he received a call from Oscar Hammerstein II about a new show the Rodgers and Hammerstein team was preparing for Broadway, *Flower Drum Song*.

"It's sort of a Chinese *Life With Father*" was the flippant way the famous lyricist described it. "Gene, we want you to direct it."

It would be Gene's first theater activity since *Pal Joey*, eighteen years earlier. He had never directed a Broadway show, and *Flower Drum Song* immediately reverberated with problems, starting with the casting. The story was set in San Francisco's Chinatown and dealt with two Chinese fathers and the problems they faced controlling their increasingly Americanized children. Heavily plotted by book-writer Joe Fields, the show was embellished by a florid Rodgers and Hammerstein score, and if the performers were not professionally on the mark it could all tip over easily into an emotional chop-suey.

Carol Haney had been engaged to do the choreography, which was fine with Gene; she had assisted him on a number of film productions. But for the musical numbers, they could not use the usual cadre of "dance gypsies" whose professional journey had begun in childhood somewhere in America with lessons at studios like Gene Kelly's, then onto a career path through television commercials, summer stock, and even shows on cruise ships, to the final station, the snap and strut of a Broadway chorus line. They were good. But they were white, and fresh Asian faces were needed. Remembering the catastrophic Cockney incoherence of the English-made *Crest of the Wave*, the most ill-fated and ill-spoken of his "frozen-currency" films, Gene needed Asians who could sing and act in understandable English.

It was a task that required far more than theatrical know-how and had much to do with why, surprisingly, Gene had been chosen over directors with many more credits listed in Broadway playbills. In the memorable musical *South Pacific*, Hammerstein's song "You've Got to Be Carefully Taught" had been an emotional appeal for racial harmony. Gene's relaxed attitude about people of color and couldn't-care-less feelings about ethnicity were well-known to Rodgers and Hammerstein. He was one of the very few who could direct a story about the clash of a gentle, ancient Asian culture against the bruisingly modern American way without patronizing or insulting.

He met the expectations of Rodgers and Hammerstein. He and Jeanne worked hard at casting interviews and auditions in San Francisco and Hawaii, returning there several times before signing the leads and several supporting actors. Despite the show-business inexperience of many in this cast, they were guided by Gene to successful Broadway debuts. The curtain went up on *Flower Drum Song* on December 1, 1958. As Gene recalled to his English biographer, Clive Hirschhorn:

> The show was nowhere near *South Pacific* or *Oklahoma!* but it had warmth and a sweet sentimentality about it. I knew that as long as I crammed the production brimful of every joke and gimmick in the book I could make it work, but this was always an audience show rather than anything for the critics.

He was right. The reviews ranged from poor to lukewarm, but the ticket lines were long and gratifying to Rodgers and Hammerstein. The show went on for more than 600 performances, and since Gene's arrangement called for a percentage of the gross, 1959 looked to be a banner year financially. He had returned to Broadway in style. His success in dealing with a hit stage property, augmenting his vaunted (even if considered slightly old-fashioned) filmmaking skills, would be responsible for his choice, a decade later, as the director of the much-awaited blockbuster film version of *Hello Dolly!*

That would turn out to be a totally different experience. But at the dawn of the New Year, 1959, Gene could only assume he had come through the last bad patch; he was in step again, the buoyant rhythm was right. The upward thrust of his comeback would continue stronger than ever.

On a winter night only a few months later, his optimism was tested. He was a passenger on a Pan American Jet Clipper high over the dark North Atlantic, en route from Paris to New York. He wasn't even supposed to be on the flight. Originally booked on a conventional piston-engine plane, at Orly airport in Paris Gene had encountered his good friend Harry Kurnitz, the screenwriter, who was also returning to New York but on the faster, just-inaugurated jet flight. Kurnitz was interested in involving Gene in some film projects and persuaded Gene to join him at the last minute. Gene secured a still-available seat and was soon relaxing on the aisle in first-class Seat 1D, just behind the forward lounge. The giant airliner was the grandest of the newest Boeing 707 jets and, enlivened by the champagne, scarfing down the canapes on his tray, he "kicked around" some story ideas with Kurnitz. The realization had just sunk in that he was probably flying higher than he had ever been in his life—a thought prompting him to notice the dangling seat belt he had carelessly unclipped—when it happened.

Inconceivably, he was heading straight down, as though not on a luxurious plane but a rickety elevator whose cables had snapped. He was pinned back in his seat, unable to move. A long hot needle of pain slashed into one ear, then both were inflamed. He thought he was screaming—at least his mouth was open—but he couldn't hear his own voice, or any sound. He saw a stewardess writhing on the floor, broken bottles and glasses scattered, the gray rug darkened with wet. A crewman tried to help her and went sprawling. The pain was maddening. Gene wanted to tug his ears off, or at least lift his hands to hold his nose and somehow pop his ears clear. At the same time—he cursed himself for drinking, he couldn't seem to think straight—he knew he had to clip on his seat belt. He felt the chair was slipping away beneath him. It was like coming off a ski lift. The tray with his drinks and food had vanished. The stewardess had just done a refill, and there had been a tall flute of glistening champagne. Gone now—he had missed out—and then he realized he was behaving like an ass; he was going to die with all the others:

> The plane was spinning as it plunged. . . . I felt as if all the blood was being drained out of my body and my lungs were tearing to shreds . . . my first thought was, should I pray or not, and I decided I wouldn't because I hadn't been in a church or prayed for several years and the last thing I wanted to be was a death-bed Catholic and a coward.

He did, however (as he later told *Family Weekly*, the Sunday supplement distributed in newspapers across the country, for its front-page feature story "Gene Kelly's Brush with Death"), thank the Lord that his life insurance was paid and his family—and "sainted mother" still in Pittsburgh—would not be left in poverty. The thought consoled him, and then he saw the floored crewman stumbling toward the pilot's deck, and he realized the plane had leveled off. An announcement was coming over the loudspeaker. He could not make sense of it through the buzzing in his ears. A stewardess leaned over him and shouted that an emergency landing would be made at Gander, Newfoundland. The tension remained. The plane still rattled and shook. Gene looked over at Kurnitz. The writer's face was pale, strangely contorted. Passengers were instructed to take out life jackets. Gene helped Kurnitz put his on. Rafts were made ready by Pan Am crewmen. Nobody spoke. It was a long descent into Gander.

There was the delicious jounce against the airport tarmac, and the plane rolled on. Cheers broke out, a salvo of whistles and applause. Here and there some of the 124 passengers were crying. They were safe on the ground. Gene would have joined in the applause, but he was busy getting medical attention for Kurnitz, whose hand pawed at his chest; the writer had suffered a mild heart attack.

A few hours later, the passengers were picked up by another Boeing 707 for the flight to New York. Minutes before landing, catastrophe came close again: The

Boeing just avoided collision with a small private Cessna during the descent over the East River. Gene heard later from Jeanne, who had rushed to the airport and flung her arms around him, that there had actually been a collision of two planes earlier that day.

"Oh, Gene, I thought one was your plane," she said tearfully, "I thought you'd been killed."

"Easy, easy," he said, hugging her. "I may be accident-prone, but this is crazy."

Harrowing as the plane trip had been, there was to be no cutback on Gene's air travel. Although he was relaxed and happier than ever in Beverly Hills with Jeanne, eager to raise their new family, he could not bear sitting at home waiting for the phone to ring. His passport always close at hand, the slightest possibility of a new film project would have him packing quickly—he still traveled light with one carry-on suitcase—and have Lois McClelland drive him to the Los Angeles airport. He would think nothing of flying to London or Paris, New York or Las Vegas, anywhere, so long as there might be a significant assignment in theater or film—anything not cursed with the quickie "do it by Tuesday" standards of television. He was regularly being called for TV appearances, inevitably his film retrospectives, and the fees were still welcome ("TV's like going to the bank and drawing out money," he would repeat to Jeanne), but he was tired of being forced to trundle out the set-piece anecdotes about the making of *Singin' in the Rain*. He had long since run out of things to say on the inevitable comparisons with Fred Astaire. He resented television's focusing his fans on the past while he had plenty of future left to ignite their interest.

And so the phone would ring with a long-distance call, and a possibility would shape up somewhere, and he would be off with high hopes. He preferred to go one-on-one right away with the decision-making principals, giving his energy, thrust, and creativity to the original idea that had attracted him. Wanting and needing to get to work, he drove hard to bring closure to preliminary discussions. He despised intermediaries, the second-tier executives in dark suits whom he regarded as negative influences, deal-killers, their expensive haircuts automatically shaking side to side, grounding any original notion before it took flight. His was a brusque pattern of behavior that made enemies of some younger men on the road to influence. They would pay him back in the years to come with hostility or neglect. He knew of this, but did not care. *Flower Drum Song* had broken his string of commercial failures. He needed a successful follow-up now!

Strain though he did, it seemed that every discussed deal curdled along the way. Something always surfaced to upend the project—a Something that was never fully explained. In London, he discussed the Rank Organization's offer to direct and star in a musical called *Gentleman's Gentleman*, set in Edwardian England. The elusive ballerina Moira Shearer was to be his co-star. Financing fell through. Or Something. There was an ambitious plan to join the Frank Sinatra "Rat Pack" on a three-picture contract; he would immediately produce the first, a musical called *Robin and the Seven Hoods*, but the Sinatra group couldn't set up a starting date that was appropriate for Gene's schedule. Or Something. There was the possibility of a screen adaptation of the Broadway comedy *Send Me No Flowers*, for which he would direct

Warren Beatty. The star became unavailable. Or Something. He was called in for a series of meetings to direct a remake of *Beau Geste*. Again, there was always Something stopping the project from going forward, and he never found out what the Something was.

When Lois McClelland would meet his return flight at the airport, he would flash his smile at her. "But I always knew things had not gone right. He would be thoughtful and depressed all the way home. He wasn't nearly as resilient as in the old days."

The Somethings were wearing him down. So in the summer of 1959, when he was invited to be on the jury of the Cannes Film Festival, he accepted. It gave him a chance to visit with Kerry, still a student in Europe. A wealthy ship-owning family they had met in Klosters then invited Gene and his daughter to an island retreat off the Greek mainland. It was there that Gene received a call from the director-producer Stanley Kramer. He wanted Gene for a key supporting role in his forthcoming film *Inherit the Wind*.

Kramer had given Fred Astaire a serious nondancing role in his previous movie, *On the Beach*. En route from Greece, Gene joked to Kerry that the director was making sure, by casting against conventional thinking, that no dancers were left unemployed. But he was dead serious about the assignment and flattered that he was to be in the distinguished company of Frederic March and Spencer Tracy, his friend and acting idol.

In New York, *Inherit the Wind* had been a successful stage play based on the famous prosecution of a young school teacher in Tennessee, John Scopes, who had been charged with illegally teaching Darwin's theory of evolution—the so-called "monkey trial" of 1925. The opposing attorneys, though called by different names, were clearly meant to be Clarence Darrow, played by Tracy, and William Jennings Bryan, performed by March. Gene's role was based on H.L. Mencken, one of America's best journalists of the time who had been an observer at the actual trial. Gene saw it as his last opportunity to force-feed a career as an important film actor. It would be a learning experience, he felt, to work with such revered professionals as March and Tracy.

He would be disabused of this idea the first day on the set. Far from running an acting school, the stars did not set a good example. As was his habit, Tracy tended to intimidate a director right from the start, though he and Katharine Hepburn had a liking for Kramer. Determined to show who was boss, on the first day of shooting Tracy did not speak sufficiently clearly for Kramer, who politely requested a second take. Tracy looked at the director for a glowering moment, as the crew waited, then said: "Mr. Kramer. It has taken me thirty years to learn how to speak lines. If you or a theater arts major from UCLA want to do this speech, I am quite willing to step aside." Then Tracy added quietly: "All right, we ought to try it again."

Worse, March and Tracy hammed it up at every opportunity, trying to top each other. When Tracy had a lengthy monologue, March fluttered a large straw fan as he listened. In the same situation Tracy did not need props; he would simply pick his nose throughout March's flamboyant summation. "I just couldn't keep up with this pair," Gene said in later interviews, putting the most generous light he could on the situation.

> It was impossible to learn anything from either of them because whatever they did came deep down from some inner part of themselves, which, for an outsider like me, anxious to learn, was totally inaccessible . . . all you could do was watch the magic and be amazed, and I really learned from them that no matter what I did, I would never be as good as they were.

Gene was much too hard on himself. Undoubtedly the most recent tide of disappointments and debacles, despite the driblet of success with *Flower Drum Song*, had scoured away what was left of his self-confidence as an actor. He actually did very well in the role. His Mencken came across as a caustic, complicated, and vital character. But the performance could not get past the haze created by the two leading men, who sucked up all the critical attention. In any event, what mattered even more, *Inherit the Wind* did not prove to be a financial success. It was now finally accepted as holy writ in Hollywood that Gene was no box-office asset. He was never called on for a serious role again.

Back to television he retreated. Now described often by younger and unsympathetic film-industry leaders as "the King of Retrospectives," he did more Specials that were in no way very special. Surprisingly to the Hollywood community, he took it well. He held his temper in check. He seemed more relaxed, less abrasive, content to be spending more time at home with Jeanne and his new family. The following year, though, Gene's *la belle France* lured him back with an offer he couldn't refuse.

The ballet company of the Paris Opera, as eager to stay *à la mode* as they thought Gene was, invited him to choreograph a modern ballet. As he had done years before in *An American in Paris*, Gene turned to the music of Gershwin and chose the *Concerto in F* for a bedroom-farce scenario about the goddess Aphrodite descending to earth for one last fling. Mischievously playing off the central *pas de deux*, Gene titled the work *Pas de Dieux*—a double-entendre, of course, but the project needed more than the grace of the gods to be ready by opening night.

For three arduous months he exposed the *corps de ballet* to the Kelly treatment: rehearsing to the point of exhaustion. He had not lost his passion for the prodigious effect and placed incredible demands on the Opera's stage design team. He wanted war chariots to descend from the heavens. He called for beds to float through the air. He required large traffic lights flashing red, yellow, and green as signals of Aphrodite's moves. It was avant-garde, probably too avant, and Gene ran out of pre-curtain time. When the ballet opened, on July 6, 1960, it simply wasn't ready.

The critic for the influential *Le Monde* newspaper complained about "dreadful noises behind the curtain" during scene changes and "vociferous shouts and hammer blows" obliging the conductor "to interrupt the third movement of Gershwin's *Concerto* and wait with arms crossed as the din swelled." The ending of his review did not mince words: "The only person responsible for the scenic chaos is Monsieur

Gene Kelly himself. He had three months to rehearse his ballet. If he did not have the time to try out the stage and costumes more than once, then it is his fault."

Thankfully, the *New York Times* rescued Gene's reputation by ignoring the clatter of scene changes: "The American dancer Gene Kelly invaded the musty confines of the Paris Opera with a leggy, sexy modern ballet that shook the crystal chandeliers. Nothing like it had ever been seen on the stage where ballet is treated with fragile care."

What he now enjoyed most of all about Paris was that he was being talked about, in delight or dismay—it did not matter to him. He was not ignored as he was at home. The French still considered his musicals the greatest of all time, and to them Monsieur Kelly was still a productive, creative artist. They paid him the supreme compliment of being attentive to his work and reacting with passion.

Later in the run, as the scene changes went more fluidly and noiselessly, *Pas de Dieux* invariably received a long series of curtain calls from intrigued Parisians with cries of *auteur, auteur!* They peered around for Gene, who, with Jeanne, had settled in for a spell in a luxurious apartment on the Avenue Foch. The staggering rent absorbed every franc he earned that spring, but the expense proved well worth it. *Pas de Dieux* caught on with the ballet-going public. The Kellys were at a performance when Gene was led up to the stage for twenty-seven curtain calls.

Here in his beloved Paris, Gene was receiving the kinds of current honors and recognition denied him at home. He was not a Buster Keaton, an unappreciated icon from the past, wandering around the MGM lot looking for someone to talk to. At a special ceremony in the Opera building, he was made a Knight of the Legion of Honor.

Nor was he a one-night stand in France. The following year, as the climax to a glittering evening, he was presented by Jean Cocteau with a Lifetime Achievement Award from the Cinémathèque Française, an honor doled out sparingly to foreigners; only Alfred Hitchcock and Fred Zinnemann, director of *From Here to Eternity*, had been previous non-French recipients.

Gene's French connection was not abandoned when he finally returned to Hollywood and the film medium for his next two movie involvements. The first, a cameo role, was not very important to him; it was more an act of good will to support the American debut of his friend Yves Montand who, though still not fluent in English, was the co-star of Marilyn Monroe in the 1960 trifle *Let's Make Love*. Gene's French came in handy as he clowned through a sequence, presumably teaching Montand (who was actually an accomplished French music-hall performer) how to dance. The assignment took only a day to shoot, and the following morning Gene was Paris-bound to direct Jackie Gleason in the television superstar's assault on the feature-film world, *Gigot*.

Bored with his role in the long-running TV sitcom *The Honeymooners*, Gleason had dreamed up a scenario about a deaf-mute who lives in a filthy basement near Montmartre, his only life companion an alley cat. Treated as the Paris slum version of the village idiot, he is constantly tormented by neighbors, and his only pleasure is to attend funerals, whether or not he knows the deceased, and to cry over the harshness of fate. He befriends a child, the sickly daughter of a prostitute whom he puts up in his hovel. And there is not much more to the patchy plot, except in the end when Gigot, after an improbable chain of circumstances, attends his own funeral and is discovered. He is last seen running away from the angry neighborhood riffraff as the credits roll.

Like most of the stories and characters Gleason favored, it was at once cynical and pessimistic, with cruelty unpunished and kindness unrewarded in a crass world. A fleshy mountain of a man who gained and lost poundage on a wholesale basis, Gleason—referred to as The Great One by his TV associates—made it plain he expected to win an Academy Award by playing Gigot. It immediately became apparent to Gene that Gleason was a performer with a mountainous ego. He saw himself as another Charlie Chaplin and Gigot as Chaplin's little tramp writ large. To bring off the TV star's dream on film would be an incredible challenge— and unknown to Gene, it had already been turned down by many directors who knew Gleason's work habits. Though Gene was far from Gleason's first choice, the comedian made the best of it with his usual ebullient spin for public consumption. "A dancer is the best director for a comedian," he would say to the press. "The timing is the same."

But Kelly and Gleason danced to different drummers. Gene's workaholic ways were beyond the capacity of Gleason, who had no lines to memorize but still arrived unprepared. The comedian constantly invited American celebrities coming through Paris to "drop by the set," where he made sure the atmosphere was congenial, a non-stop cocktail party. Each saw a different city, too. The director saw the dream world of *An American in Paris*, the star a stinking neighborhood of petty merchants and sadistic bullies on the dole. Gene had checked in with his one suitcase, used the metro, and joked with cab drivers. Gleason's sacred belief was that one did not have to be a millionaire to live like one: From his penthouse in the priciest hotel, he would be driven to and from the studio in a burgundy and opal Rolls Royce and had no interest in mingling with the locals. The only French he bothered to learn was how to order another round of drinks—"*encore du vin!*" His pronunciation was perfect. The comedian constantly put down the City of Light ("There ain't a pizza joint in Paree or a poolroom within five miles"), and offended the local press.

The Great One stopped looking for pizza when he discovered French cuisine. His weight went off the scales, and there was soon a problem with the visual continuity of the film; sequences, as always, were shot out of order. Once scene showed Gigot as a somewhat tattered Stan Laurel, the next cut displayed a decidedly fatter Oliver Hardy.

In the constant arguments between director and star, Gene did not back down. He felt he carried the sole responsibility for bringing in a film that at least made some sense. He insisted on a diet for Gleason, exercise routines, even had The Great One running up and down flights of stairs. He was relentless. At one point Gleason hung up a sarcastic sign in his dressing room: GENE KELLY IS ALWAYS RIGHT!

Somehow they made it through the months of shooting. But Gene, for the first time in his directing career, chose to escape the project and would have no part in the post-production editing. When *Gigot* was selected for exhibition at Radio City Music Hall, he came out of the theater and complained crankily to the movie critic of the *New York Times*:

> It doesn't bear much resemblance to the film I directed. Last December I finished in Paris. The picture then went into the hands of its owners, Seven Arts Productions. They made some forty-odd cuts and changes. I don't like the result. However, I recommend that you go and see it to watch the phenomenal Gleason at work. He's a joy!

Gene's criticism was on the mark; the editing (dominated by Gleason) had simply removed most of the scenes in which The Great One did not appear. Thus the released production had Gleason following Gleason in scene after scene, with tedium smothering any attempts at Chaplinesque poignance. Unrelieved Gleason proved to be unwatchable Gleason, and *Gigot* lay like a leg of mutton (its meaning in French) at the box office. Gene's departure before the editing and his unusually deft diplomacy regarding Gleason allowed him to get through the fiasco with his reputation reasonably intact.

But now more than three years had gone by since *Inherit the Wind*, the first in a disconnected series of bequests of bumpy professional opportunities. With each he had exhausted himself by giving his all, and all for . . . rampaging film stars Tracy and March grossly upstaging him . . . tired TV retrospectives . . . a fleeting cameo role obscured by the dazzle of Marilyn Monroe . . . theatrical successes made dubious by their one-shot discontinuity . . . the maneuvering of a comic Leviathan into the tiny harbor of film stardom . . . all of it bridging him to little work besides that of filling out his idle mornings by pushing on with his memoirs . . . and on and on, until he felt his career had lurched out of control like a run-on sentence without a conclusion. And Gene's pride was not declining with advancing age. Waiting for the phone to ring was no easier than it had ever been.

At that point, late 1963, an interesting offer came through from an unusual source, appealing to his patriotic instincts: The State Department asked him to undertake a six-week propaganda tour of Central Africa. The Cold War was showing no boundary limits. The Russians were sending elaborate entertainment units to the newly independent French colonies in order to draw them into the orbit of Soviet influence. In response, the United States Information Agency (USIA), underfunded for this purpose, would send him on an expense-paid tour throughout Central Africa with a film projectionist and a half-hour compilation of his most famous dance numbers.

He did not want to be away from Jeanne for a lengthy period because she was showing signs of some worrisome health problems. She insisted he go "to prove his patriotism to those right-wing nut cases once and for all." So he went—and was astonished at the widespread demonstration of interest in him and his movies. The USIA was delighted and wanted to set up even more visits, but Gene would not stay away from Jeanne any longer. The trip served to bolster his morale. He returned to Hollywood, feeling better about the work he had done, freshly resolved "to keep going."

In a way, that was what he didn't do in his next film role, a fairly outrageous comedy called *What a Way to Go!*, starring Shirley MacLaine, Paul Newman, Dean Martin, Dick Van Dyke, Robert Mitchum, and Gene. MacLaine played a simple country girl who marries, in orderly sequence, six millionaires, none of whom—for the needs of the plot—can keep going. Gene had the brief role of a celebrated nightclub hoofer trampled to death by his own fans after one dance duet with MacLaine that showed up well enough, despite Gene's arthritic knee.

Then it was back to the salt mines of TV—until 1965, when the French director Jacques Demy had the insane notion of doing a postwar French musical homage to *On the Town*, and wanted Gene to star in it. Again Jeanne insisted he accept the foreign assignment. He was no help to her when he was moodily unemployed, so he decided to accept Demy's offer.

The film, *The Young Girls of Rochefort*, centered on two sisters played by the two French stars Catherine Deneuve and Françoise Dorleac, sisters in real life, neither of whom could sing or dance. In the completed film, Gene's musical skills showed signs of erosion, too. For the first and only time his voice had to be dubbed. But it actually did not matter much; Demy had engaged Gene not for himself but for his image. As good as it was to see Gene Kelly in a musical again, this time as an American in Rochefort, the various strands of the story and minglings of French and foreign atmospheres did not meld. An artificial hybrid of a movie, it felt cobbled together uncertainly, what *The New Yorker* later put down as "less art than Cuisinart."

Yet the film has held on in popularity. More than thirty years later, it was the leading attraction of a French film festival of distinguished revivals held in New York. Invited as a special celebrity guest was Catherine Deneuve, still a leading lady, who had especially good remembrances of one of Gene's final film appearances: "What I remember most is the joy of making *The Young Girls of Rochefort*. Gene Kelly was in this film and we were so amazed that on the set he was like he was on the screen: white pants, charming, seeming to work without any effort."

She was referring to a man who had most certainly mellowed as a person and as a professional who had finally come to terms with the reality that the original screen musical was a thing of the past.

While accepting TV gigs and cameo movie roles, Gene's career would aim at directing studio productions where he would be able to stay home with Jeanne. He had missed her steadying presence during the *Rochefort* shoot, and he was bewildered, almost panicked, by her failing health. He realized when he returned home from France and was greeted by his two young children at North Rodeo Drive that he was not being fair to her; he'd left the burden of raising them squarely on her shoulders. Not for the first time, he resolved to change the situation:

> My kids looked as though they were twenty years older. In six weeks they had changed enough for me to feel resentful that I had missed out on some vital part of their development, and I made up

my mind never to spend any time away from home unless I could take them with me.

Fortunately at this time, Frank McCarthy, a producer at 20th Century–Fox invited him to direct a comedy called *A Guide for the Married Man*. Blessedly, it would be filmed at the Hollywood studio complex. So far, so good, but there was one sticky point which made Gene hesitate. Ironically, at a time when he felt closer to his wife than he had ever felt with any woman, the proposed film was largely a series of vignettes setting out the various ways a Mister could cheat on his Missus. Further— outrageously reflecting the softening code of sexual conduct of the late 1960s—*A Guide*'s thesis was that it was perfectly possible to be a good husband and have affairs on the side. McCarthy, a personal friend of the Kellys, was aware of their intense relationship and, even more to the point, Gene's regard for the sanctity of marriage. As far as Gene was concerned, the original script by Frank Tarloff was almost a graduate-school course in advanced adultery, and at this point in his life he had no stomach for a leering sex-mania film. But he found Tarloff reasonable and concluded that they could change the script, keep it funny, and not bring on a stroke to his mother—Harriet Kelly was now an aging widow still in Pittsburgh— who rushed to every one of his films. He agreed to direct the movie.

What Gene did was prompt Tarloff to turn the basic idea 180 degrees, so that the philandering husband, rather than the unknowing wife, was now the figure of ridicule. At once, the comedy lost its cruel, anti-feminine edge; it became almost wholesome, good-natured, and acceptable to a mass audience. Gene then persuaded his friend Walter Matthau to take the lead role, supported by an all-star cast of comedians and beauties persuaded to participate only because of Gene's reputation: Jack Benny, Sid Caesar, Jayne Mansfield, Art Carney, Carl Reiner, Phil Silvers, and others. More than all the TV retrospectives, Gene Kelly festivals, and *Singin' in the Rain* revivals, Gene felt bolstered by the vote of confidence from his acting peers.

After all these years the bitterness and anger were starting to slide away, and it showed in his approach to directing. Later on, in his patented brash, unrestricted me-included way, Matthau summed up the result of Gene's decision to direct *A Guide for the Married Man*:

> I'm happy to say it was a most pleasant experience. He's an easy person to work with, comfortable and relaxed, with a definite flair for comedy and directing comedy. The film was full of pretty girls whose breasts and bums bounced pertly and a lot of Jew comics. An impeccable formula for success.

Matthau was kidding himself and his fellow jokesters, of course, but his appraisal of the film's box-office record was accurate. *A Guide for the Married Man* was one of the big money-makers for 20th Century–Fox in 1967. Once again, Gene's faith in himself was restored. He was even able to keep pace with the free-flowing '60s.

Bankable once again, and acceptable to Darryl Zanuck, Gene was now tapped by the 20th Century–Fox studio head to take on another project, the Barbra Streisand blockbuster *Hello Dolly!* Buoyed by the recent success of *The Sound of Music*, Fox had bought the film rights to the hit Broadway show for $2.5 million, plus a percentage of the gross—and the company was on its way to producing the most expensive movie musical ever made.

Set in Yonkers and New York in the 1880s, *Hello Dolly!* is about matchmaker Dolly Levi, a middle-aged widow who suddenly realizes the time has come to find a second husband for herself, before it is too late. Unlike her first mate, the chosen man will be wealthy. She sets her sights on a rich feed-and-grain merchant, a part awarded by the producer, Ernest Lehman, to the ubiquitous Walter Matthau.

From the beginning Lehman had assumed that Carol Channing would play the title role she had originated on Broadway. By then, she had done the hit show for eighteen months in New York and had taken it on the road, with sellouts everywhere. Shortly before he engaged Gene as director, Lehman had viewed a rough cut of another film, *Thoroughly Modern Millie* in which Channing, supporting Julie Andrews, played an heiress. The producer was bowled over—with the appalling certainty that Channing was the wrong choice! The ultimate stage actress, she simply wasn't made for movies. He was shocked by the outsize, almost grotesque and cartoonish way she appeared; it was as though her features seemed to explode from the screen. Lehman felt the camera could not contain her look or personality, and he prevailed on Zanuck to withdraw the offer to Channing.

With the clock ticking and the studio anxious to put its investment to work, Lehman considered and rejected other female leads, notably Elizabeth Taylor (couldn't sing) and Julie Andrews (too ladylike). He signed Barbra Streisand, who was destined (it was being prophesied) to be a dazzling success in her first movie, *Funny Girl*; she had just come off shooting it and would later win an Oscar for her performance.

It was at this point that Gene entered the picture. Immediately he knew that Streisand was both the hope and the handicap of *Hello Dolly!* Streisand's talent was undeniable. It was her age that did not add up. The key scene of the movie was the return of Dolly to New York's opulent Harmonia Gardens dining room. In she struts, down the staircase, as everybody in the place, including Louis Armstrong, sings the title song, welcoming her back after a long widowhood absence of fourteen years—meaning that, since Streisand was visibly in her mid-twenties, Dolly had barely been out of grade-school when she'd last dined there! Streisand herself realized the situation was ridiculous, and worry over this caused her sleepless nights. She would telephone Lehman in the middle of the night and insist he find a way to alleviate this impossible position. Lehman then pressured Gene to help her find some nuances of character and personality that would make her believable beyond her years. Years later Gene admitted he wasn't very helpful:

> If only there'd been more time, I'd have tried to help her work out
> a clear-cut characterization, but we had a tight schedule and I left
> it up to her. With the result that she was being Mae West one
> minute, Fanny Brice the other, and Barbra Streisand the next. Her

accent varied as much as her mannerisms. She kept experimenting with new things out of sheer desperation, none of which really worked to her satisfaction. And as she's such a perfectionist, she became terribly neurotic and insecure.

Perhaps Gene had expected the young star to regard him with a respect that acknowledged who he was and what he had accomplished, but instead she placed demands on him for a special handling that was impossible to satisfy. While unsure of herself in the role, she did have an overbearing confidence in her mental acuity and aesthetic taste and began to second-guess Gene's decisions. Because Gene was unable to help her find an appealing and logical interpretation of Dolly Levi, Streisand lost confidence in him by the time shooting began in Hollywood, and she disagreed with him publicly about the script, about line readings, most of all about the need for retakes. She always saw something wrong, and she wanted more, more, more.

The explosion came amid the sweltering heat of Garrison, New York, the location for the exterior shooting, where a more photogenic late nineteenth-century Yonkers had been simulated at huge expense. In April and May, during the Hollywood on-camera work, tempers had already been on edge. Then, on June 5, 1968, Senator Robert F. Kennedy was assassinated. It was the day before the major scene at Garrison was to be filmed. The tragedy cast a pall over the company, especially Walter Matthau, a Kennedy friend and supporter who admitted later: "I took it hard."

It was difficult for the cast and crew to concentrate. Augmented by giant, bright lights of tremendous wattage, the temperature hovered at 100 degrees. Streisand, wearing a topaz gown weighing over twenty pounds, tried to keep cool and to protect her makeup by pointing a small portable electric fan at her face as they did the dialogue run-through of a rather complicated scene. She had already called for a number of retakes, and though the cast was tense and irritable, Gene had chosen not to dispute her wishes. Now as he explained what he wanted everybody to do, the star broke in with an idea for a script change, a humorous quip. Most of the crew, she recalled later, laughed appreciatively at her suggestion. But not Matthau.

"Who does she think she is?" he bellowed. "I've been in thirty movies and this is only her second—the first one hasn't even come out yet—and she thinks she's directing!" Gene clutched at Matthau's arm and tried to pull him away but the actor persisted: "Why don't you let Gene direct this picture?"

"Why don't you learn your lines?" Streisand shot back at him.

Aware that Matthau had come through two heart attacks (the production had to take out special insurance coverage) Gene was desperate to move on past the moment without something terrible happening.

"You might be the singer in this picture," was Matthau's out-of-control response. "But I'm the actor. You haven't got the talent of a butterfly's fart."

Streisand turned and ran to her dressing room and called Lehman, complaining through her sobs about both Matthau and Kelly. The producer raced to the set and attempted to soothe the devastated star. In all this, Gene got left on the sidelines. He had watched these verbal brawls with irritation and amazement and could do little else but cut the lights and, once Streisand had settled down, persuade her and Matthau to continue the sequence. He finally got what he wanted, yelled "Cut and print!" and gave them the sought-for thumbs-up signal. But enormously expensive hours had drifted by and he felt that, professionally, he was being misused.

He managed to contain his temper when he read a newspaper interview Streisand gave just a few days later. She was quoted as saying that "while Gene was satisfactory at the geography of pictures," he had "no idea at all about characterization." Gene never remotely went so far as Matthau, who loudly described the star as "a freak attraction," but her immaturity and insecurity, manifesting itself in aggression and manipulation, threw him. It was enough to poison the pleasure of directing what was potentially a first-rate movie musical.

Directing Streisand in Hello Dolly!, *Gene sometimes wished for* Goodbye Dolly! *(Courtesy of Photofest)*

His sense of humor held on, though. He was amused one morning when Streisand, as tough in her own way as Matthau was in his, ceremoniously presented her glowering co-star with a bar of soap. "For your old sewer mouth," she said, and then proceeded, in *yenta* fashion, to remind him the film was not in fact to be called *Hello, Walter!*

Deep down, Gene respected the standards Streisand held herself and others to. He had been handed an established Broadway hit to shepherd onto the screen, and, as always, he proved an immensely creative problem-solver. Though not creating a breakthrough Metro musical of the glory days, still he kept *Hello Dolly!* on course to the end of the shooting schedule. Which couldn't come too soon, as far as he was concerned—he had been away from Jeanne and his kids long enough.

The world premiere of *Hello Dolly!* took place on December 16, 1968, at the Rivoli Theater, on Broadway. More than a thousand fans waited for hours in freezing temperatures to catch a glimpse of Barbra Streisand. Hundreds broke through police barricades and surrounded her royal-blue limousine as it pulled up in front of the theater. In her Arnold Scaasi–designed leather coat edged with white fur and a white-and-orange pillbox hat, she had to wait for the police to clear her way into the theater. Emerging finally onto the red carpet, she heard her name screamed out: "Barbra . . . Barbra!" It took a wedge of cops and private security guards to advance her slowly, in surges of forward progress, toward the lobby. She looked radiantly serene, as if this overflowing reception were the culmination of what had been a wonderful, even joyous adventure.

Gene had been invited to the premiere but wanted to remain at home with his ailing wife. They were watching TV when a news clip came on covering the event in New York. When it was over, Gene's eyes shifted across to the gift-memento Barbra had given him at the wrap party for *Hello Dolly!* It was one of the large World War I recruiting posters by the artist James Montgomery Flagg, the familiar image of Uncle Sam pointing his finger directly at the viewer above the words "I want you!" Across the bottom of the poster Streisand had written: "To Gene. Thumbs up . . . and thanks for everything. Love, Barbra."

He turned from the poster to find his wife looking at him. Jeanne let out a sigh. A small smile, something of a shrug, and then she said: "That's show biz." He could do nothing but smile also and nod in agreement.

They understood each other, did not have to spell it out. Only his dear Jeanne knew the hell he had gone through with *Hello Dolly!* Yet somehow, amid the fury of the arguments, the sullen weather, and the dark clouds of a tragic assassination that leached away the spirit of the cast and crew, and burdened by the inevitable snafus of a complicated production and the poor chemistry between him and the leading lady, he had held things together, allowing Streisand's talent to shine in full splendor. What could have been a mess had somehow emerged as a work of distinction, at this moment reaping a storm of cheers and applause in New York, making him and Streisand and all the rest forget the pain and the insults and the anger—that was yesterday. Today was for the warm exchange of kisses and gifts. Of course, it made no sense. But that was the crazy world of show business—passionate, volcanic, make-or-break—which was his life.

Effectively, *Hello Dolly!* became Eugene Curran Kelly's goodbye to a life of dance and dreams. The Fox studio was convinced that Gene had brought forth a winner. But the box-office returns were instructive. In the era of the Vietnam War and the hippie counterculture, a sea change was taking place. Despite the youthful admirers who had mobbed Streisand at the New York premiere, the under-thirty mass audience that year had gravitated even more to gritty and realistic films such as United Artists' *Midnight Cowboy*, a portrait of a bisexual hustler, and Columbia's *Easy Rider*, the archetypal protest film of the 1960s. Soon *Dolly!*, though it was a top-grosser along with those films, was incapable of making a profit and was accordingly explained away as fluff, a mindless throwback to the past.

Gene's reputation, briefly sparked by *A Guide for the Married Man*, now fluttered into a slow spiral of decline and loss almost too painful to recount. Still, he managed to keep going. There were still projects that came his way: *The Cheyenne Social Club*

(1970), the only western he ever directed, starring his graybeard friends Fonda and Stewart. He did a comic turn in the glistening comedy *Forty Carats* (1973).

MGM came to the rescue with *That's Entertainment!* (1974) and *That's Entertainment! Part II* (1976), the incredibly successful film compilations (they eventually spawned *That's Entertainment! Part III* in 1994). Along the way Gene was persuaded to do a role in the absurd *Viva Knievel!* (1977). He reached bottom with pop star Olivia Newton-John in *Xanadu* (1980). Another compilation on a theme close to Gene's heart succeeded like the others, *That's Dancing!* (1985). The world responded: You bet it is! The audiences came in droves.

He wouldn't quit. Still intent on creating the new, the different, Gene continued to put time and energy into speculative projects. There was a Broadway show about Louis Armstrong. A mammoth film for Darryl Zanuck based on the children's book *Tom Swift and the Wizard Air Ship*. A traveling spectacle to play in arenas and stadiums called *Clownaround*.

Disappointment after disappointment. He turned down an offer to direct the 1972 film *Cabaret* because it meant a long shooting schedule in Munich. The rest of the time there was always the perennial Something to stop the show.

On a day when he was in the Midwest casting some specialty acts for *Clownaround,* Jeanne went for one of her regular medical checkups and heard the grim, shattering news, corroborating what she suspected. She had leukemia.

She would live for another fifteen months, in and out of the City of Hope Hospital in Duarte, a noted cancer-research center, making sure with an unbelievable serenity that Gene and the children could carry on well when she was gone. Jeanne died in May of 1973.

Harriet Kelly passed away the same year. The two women closest to Gene had left him. He took on the raising of the children alone, though, thankfully, Lois McClelland was always on call.

It was in his blood to keep going. He joined with Francis Ford Coppola in an ill-fated effort to bring back the big movie musical. For a time he worked with Sony as a consultant on programming for the company's VCRs and television sets. Somehow he enjoyed the family feeling of coming full circle, sharing a tradition. After all, his dear father, long deceased, had once sold records and phonographs.

He turned seventy on August 23, 1982. The days and nights hurtled by. His own health was beginning to decline. He found he needed more rest.

On December 22, 1983, a malfunction in the lighting on a Christmas tree caused the nighttime fire that destroyed his North Rodeo home. Watching television, half-dozing, Gene was unknowing as the flames reached the bedroom door. His son Tim charged up the stairs to pull his father from bed and lead him through blinding smoke to safety. Valuable art, furniture, cherished mementoes, collected papers for the autobiography he had started—all lost. Said Dale Olson, his publicist at the time: "All Gene Kelly has left is the pajamas he was wearing."

The next morning Gene told his family and Lois that he wanted to rebuild the same house in the same place. No lousy fire was going to remove this Gene Kelly from his place in Beverly Hills!

His life-force did not ebb. In 1985, Gene narrated a documentary for the Smithsonian Museum, in Washington, D.C. The scriptwriter was a talented, statuesque, and self-assured young woman named Patricia Ward. Gene was about fifty years older than she. When the assignment was over, in what seemed a curious repetition of his invitation to Wave Lois McClelland at the close of his wartime naval service, he invited Ward to come back to California with him. But the circumstances now were to be very different.

Pat moved into the new house on North Rodeo. Gene was developing health problems. He suffered one mild stroke, then another, and he needed practical help—someone to be at his side, attractively, at the parade of industry banquets, public screenings, and fundraisers, and to manage his home. Pat took over the driving. He grew more and more dependent on her. His children were now scattered.

Never one to be concerned with discrepancy in age, he proposed. She accepted.

Gene and Pat were married in a private ceremony at Santa Barbara, in July of 1990. None of his children attended the wedding. Contrary to the usual Hollywood practice, the press release of his publicist added a few years to Pat's age, which was reported as thirty-six (she had been in the Class of 1980 at Colorado University).

A quiet elopement to Santa Barbara united Gene with Patricia Ward—his third marriage. (Coutesy of Photofest)

His young wife decisively took over the reins of the household. Lois McClelland was dismissed, and the domestic staff replaced. Friends noticed with some concern that Gene, always considered by cronies such as Phil Silvers as "very gentle with a buck"—even tight-fisted—purchased an expensive car for Pat, and, it was rumored, a separate condominium for her own use. There was the usual unsympathetic, smirking speculation about the intimate side of their May–December relationship, and the tabloids were especially unkind in Hollywood and elsewhere. Even the London *Sunday Times* put out a lead feature headlined "Is Three Always a Crowd?" stating boldly that Pat was having a romantic affair with the Kelly attorney, a handsome and garrulous fellow in his thirties who now rented the North Rodeo guest cottage.

Gene and his wife tried to ignore the gossip and did their best to carry on despite his declining energy. One by one, his contemporaries were fading and dying—the closest being two longtime friends, Richard Brooks, the writer-director, and Irving "Swifty" Lazar, the colorful talent agent. Pat, despite the disparaging rumors, turned out to be a sturdy support for him and his declining cronies. She wrote a sensitive magazine account of Lazar's life and death that reads almost like a tender dress rehearsal for her husband's approaching end.

At the world premiere of *That's Entertainment! Part III*, Gene showed up at the National Theater, in Westwood, using a cane and supported by his wife. He was interviewed by reporters, as was Ginger Rogers, who came in a wheelchair. There were yet more banquets, fund-raisers, and film retrospectives until the last of the energy ran out. In July of 1994, a television audience of millions in America and abroad saw him manage to react with the familiar endearing grin at a packed Dodger Stadium when the renowned Three Tenors—Domingo, Carreras, and Pavarotti—closed out their concert with "Singin' in the Rain." Shaking off Pat's helping hand, he struggled to his feet and gave what had to be a wave of farewell to the trio—and the watching world.

Shortly afterwards, Gene's condition weakened even more. No longer could he make public appearances. On February 2, 1996, he had a massive stroke.

With Pat at his bedside, Gene Kelly died in his sleep.

Television channels the world over ran his movies. Tributes were quoted from those who simply loved him, like Sinatra and MacLaine, and from those with more complex feelings, like Donen and Streisand. But the mourning was universal.

The funeral was private. Shortly afterward, the rift was apparent between Gene's third wife and his three children over the terms of his will. The legal squabble was settled out-of-court, and the results are sealed by court order. As is frequent with deceased movie stars, whose graves may become grotesque attractions for overzealous fans prone to carry off a memento or souvenir, Gene's place of burial has not been made public.

It does not matter. Only one thing matters: Rain or shine, one will never forget Gene Kelly and his life of dance and dreams.

BIBLIOGRAPHY

A Note on Sources   Many books and publications offered me incidents or perspectives on Kelly's life and career and the changes he brought to the movie musical. But until now there has not been available a full-length biography following the arc of his career and life to the end, casting light on some previously shadowed, unpublicized areas of his personal relationships as well as his surprisingly vigorous and committed political activism, for which his career paid dearly.

I have elsewhere singled out Lois McClelland, Gene's personal secretary for more than forty years who maintained a diary reflecting the activities of her employer. Space precludes any details of the inputs and contributions of others, whose names follow.

George Abbott	Michael Crawford	Van Johnson	Donald O'Connor
Mikhail Baryshnikov	Luther Davis	Fred Kelly	Ruth Portnoy
	Catherine Deneuve	Pauline Kael	John Springer
Saul Chaplin	Henry Fonda	Bebe Kline	James Stewart
Cyd Charisse	Peter Filichia	Alan Jay Lerner	Ben Vereen
Joan Collins	Betsy Garrett	Walter Matthau	Theresa Wright

Many books provided me with an understanding of what Gene Kelly had to contend with, socially and professionally, as he made his way. It would be remiss not to mention the 1974 work *Gene Kelly*, by the English journalist Clive Hirschhorn, who, by virtue of the early publication date, 1974, had the advantage of interviewing Kelly during his lifetime, leaving a seminal record. More recently, Hirschhorn's fellow Britons, Sheridan Morley and Ruth Leon, put out *Gene Kelly: A Celebration* (1996), an attractive pictorial book which carries some thought-provoking commentary on highlights of the Kelly phenomenon.

Other works I consulted are:

George Abbott, *Mister Abbott*.
Fred Astaire, *Steps in Time*.
Scott Berg, *Samuel Goldwyn*.
Walter Bernstein, *Inside Out*.
Daniel J. Boorstin, *The Americans*.
Humphrey Burton, *Leonard Bernstein*.
Saul Chaplin, *The Golden Age of Movie Musicals and Me*.
John Cogley, *Report on Blacklisting Movies*.
Betty Comden, *Off-Stage*.

Communist Infiltration of Hollywood Motion-Picture, Industry Part I, U.S. Government Printing Office
Arlene Croce, *Sight Lines*.
Edwin Denby, *Dance Writings*.
Anne Edwards, *Streisand: A Biography*.
Gary Fishgall, *Pieces of Time: The Life of James Stewart*.
Hugh Fordin, *The World of Entertainment*.
Rusty E. Frank, *Tap!*

John Fricke, *Judy Garland, World's Greatest Entertainer*.

Philip Furia, *Irving Berlin: A Life in Song*.

Max Gordon, *Live at the Village Vanguard*.

Martin Gottfried, *All His Jazz: The Life and Death of Bob Fosse*.

Richard Griffith, *The Cinema of Gene Kelly*.

Peter Hay, *MGM: When the Lion Roars*.

William A. Henry III, *The Great One: The Life and Legend of Jackie Gleason*.

Charles Higham and Roy Moseley, *Cary Grant: The Lonely Heart*.

David A. Jasen, *Tin Pan Alley*.

Pauline Kael, *500 Nights at the Movies*.

Elia Kazan, *My Life*.

Arthur Knight, *The Liveliest Art*.

Donald Knox, *The Magic Factory: How MGM Made An American in Paris*.

Clayton R. Koppes and Gregory D. Black, *Hollywood Goes to War*.

Janet Leigh, *There Really Was a Hollywood*.

Alan Jay Lerner, *The Street Where I Live*.

John McCabe, *Cagney*.

Patrick McGilligan, *Tender Comrades: A Backstory of the Blacklist*.

David Martin, *The Films of Busby Berkeley*.

Gerald Mast, *Can't Help Singin'*.

Marion Meade, *Buster Keaton: Cut to the Chase*.

Victor Navasky, *Naming Names*.

John O'Hara, *Pal Joey*.

André Previn, *No Minor Chords: My Days in Hollywood*.

Debbie Reynolds, *My Life*.

Richard Rodgers, *Musical Stages*.

Ginger Rogers, *Ginger: My Story*.

Martin Rubin, *Showstoppers: Busby Berkeley and the Tradition of Spectacle*.

William Saroyan, *The Time of Your Life*.

Dore Schary, *Heyday*.

Ellen Schrecker, *Many Are the Crimes: McCarthyism in America*.

Ted Sennett, *The Art of Hanna and Barbera*.

Stephen Silverman, *Dancing on the Ceiling: Stanley Donen and his Movies*.

Phil Silvers, *The Laugh Is on Me*.

Nancy Sinatra, *Frank Sinatra, My Father*.

A.M. Sperber and Eric Lax, *Bogart*.

John Springer, *They Sang! They Danced! They Romanced! A Pictorial History of the Movie Musical*.

Tony Thomas, *The Films of Gene Kelly*.

Harry Warren, *The Golden Age of the Hollywood Musical*.

Peter Wollen, *Singin' in the Rain, a Monograph*.

INDEX

Printed in the United States
203976BV00002B/4/A

9 780823 088195